Software Engineering: Concepts, Analysis and Applications

Software Engineering: Concepts, Analysis and Applications

Edited by Cheryl Jollymore

CLANRYE
INTERNATIONAL
www.clanryeinternational.com

Clanrye International,
750 Third Avenue, 9th Floor,
New York, NY 10017, USA

ISBN: 978-1-63240-599-9

Cataloging-in-Publication Data

Software engineering : concepts, analysis and applications / edited by Cheryl Jollymore.
    p. cm.
Includes bibliographical references and index.
ISBN 978-1-63240-599-9
1. Software engineering. 2. Computer software--Development. I. Jollymore, Cheryl.
QA76.758 .S64 2017
005.1--dc23

For information on all Clanrye International publications
visit our website at www.clanryeinternational.com

Printed in the United States of America.

Contents

Preface

Software engineering is the study of the conceptualization, design, development and maintenance of software. It covers sub-discipline like software testing, configuration management, quality, etc. This book on software engineering deals with the analysis, specification and development of software. It presents some of the vital pieces of work being conducted across the world, on various topics related to software engineering. This book covers the theoretical and practical approaches of software engineering. Students, researchers, experts and all associated with this field will benefit alike from this book. For all readers who are interested in software engineering, the case studies included in this book will serve as excellent guide to develop a comprehensive understanding.

This book is a result of research of several months to collate the most relevant data in the field.

When I was approached with the idea of this book and the proposal to edit it, I was overwhelmed. It gave me an opportunity to reach out to all those who share a common interest with me in this field. I had 3 main parameters for editing this text:

1. Accuracy – The data and information provided in this book should be up-to-date and valuable to the readers.

2. Structure – The data must be presented in a structured format for easy understanding and better grasping of the readers.

3. Universal Approach – This book not only targets students but also experts and innovators in the field, thus my aim was to present topics which are of use to all.

Thus, it took me a couple of months to finish the editing of this book.

I would like to make a special mention of my publisher who considered me worthy of this opportunity and also supported me throughout the editing process. I would also like to thank the editing team at the back-end who extended their help whenever required.

Editor

Context-based web service discovery model

Hamid Mcheick[1], Amel Hannech[1], Mehdi Adda[2]

[1]Computer science department, University of Québec at Chicoutimi, Chicoutimi (Québec) Canada
[2]Computer science and Engineering department, University of Quebec at Rimouski, Rimouski (Quebec) Canada

Email address:
Hamid_Mcheick@uqac.ca (H. Mcheick), Amel.Hannech1@uqac.ca (A. Hannech), Mehdi_adda@uqar.ca (M. Adda)

Abstract: Web services offer a vast number of interoperable programs using a basic (syntax) method to discover services. The problem of web services is how to develop mechanisms to locate automatically the correct Web service in order to meet the user's requirements, that is appointed by the discovery of web services. Indeed, it is beyond the human's capability to manually analyze web services functionalities. This paper proposes an architectural model to assist the user by taking into account its constantly changing context. This model uses the ontologies and RFD language to describe semantically and formally the resources and their meta-data. Therefore, this model selects services based on the query semantics, which consist of preferences and context. These preferences may be digital, for example the price of a ticket when booking a flight or QoS desired.

Keywords: Component, Semantic Web Service, Ontologies, Indexation, Context, QoS

1. Introduction

A service-oriented architecture (SOA) is the underlying structure supporting communication between services. SOA defines how two entities (programs) interact to enable one entity to perform a unit of work on behalf of another entity. Service interactions are defined using a description language. Each interaction is self-contained and loosely coupled, so that each interaction is independent of any other interaction [1].

The technology most commonly used and based on this architecture is that of Web Services [3]. According to [2] a Web Service can be defined as software designed to support interoperable machine interaction over a network. This interoperability is possible with the description language WSDL [4] and the communication protocol SAOP [5].

Architecture-based services meet the needs to satisfy flexibility and adaptability; it is flexible since a failed service can be replaced by another without changing the entire application. It is adaptable due to the fact that the selected service is chosen as the best in a given context.

Web 2.0 is a combination of technologies and tendencies where service-based architectures are widely used. This infrastructure allows naming new applications and appearances of Web such as Mashups (application whose content comes from a combination of sources), mobile applications, etc.

The concept of Web 2.0 can be enriched by the semantics of the domain [7, 8], the so-called Web 3.0 which aims to define and relate semantically resources and web services to simplify their use, discovery, integration and reuse in many applications [9]. This concept thus facilitates the search and selection of services in the SOA-based applications.

1.1. General Problem

The main objective of the Service Oriented Architecture (SOA) is to reuse of offered services based on the fact that services are accessible on the web and may be used by a large number of users through a standard protocol. In order to be used, a service has to be previously described by its provider [10]. This is the second stage of web service life cycle, it is necessary for the service publication by its provider in a register and its subsequent selection by customers via this register. The general problem is how to develop mechanisms to automatically locate the correct Web service in order to meet user requirements, especially since it is beyond the capacity of humans to manually analyze Web services features; it is named by the Web services discovery.

Semantic web services and ontologies allow the sharing of web services to the context and use the concepts useful for search, communication and composition; we propose to base our architecture on the Semantic Web. But there is no established method for the acquisition of semantic Web service descriptions. The main topic of this paper is to explore the problem of acquiring a web service that best meets the user's request.

In the proposed approach we rely on the idea and assumption that one has to supplement web services with semantic description of the domain of interest and use context associated with our services using ontologies to facilitate their discovery and integration; we propose an architectural model to ease the selection of web services based on the query semantics that comprise use preferences and use context.

1.2. Contribution

The present study summarizes our proposition to represent the domain of interest and the context of use of a web service in the form of ontologies. Then, design these last ones as well as the system which is going to exploit them to answer the users' requests by taking into account their semantics. Thus, our work consists in representing in a first place the domain of interest and the context of use using the descriptive language OWL. This is done after choosing a construction method among the existing methods, then we shall pass to the design of the ontology-based Services Search System. This paper proposes Web services classification that meets user needs according to a degree of satisfaction of the user.

1.3. Organization of the Article

This paper is organized as follows. We discuss related work in section 2. We describe the proposed approach in section 3. A conclusion and future works are given in section 4.

2. Related Works

Web service discovery is a dynamic search field where various discovery mechanisms have been recently proposed in the literature. In [6], the authors defined discovery mechanism as "the act of locating a web service description treatable by machine, not known before, and describing some functional criteria".

Initially web service discovery was primarily syntactic. With the development of semantic Web technologies, the proposed techniques for web service discovery became essentially semantic (level of semantic similarity between query terms and semantic web service description).

The general principle of syntactic approach is to compare between the query syntax based on user's keywords and the syntactic Web Services description (WSDL).

In the approach proposed in [11], UDDI is used a central repository for publishing and discovering web services based on keywords. In the search phase, user or search program sends a query that consists of keywords; this query is compared with registry keywords. The search result is a set of web services descriptions; the user selects the web service that best meets its requirements.

The disadvantage of this method is that it may return a large number of results or, conversely, too few results. Another syntactic approach for discovering web services was proposed in [12] and is called AASDU. The AASDU (Agent Approach for Service Discovery and Utilization) is a multi-agent approach containing four components: a graphical user interface (GUI), an agent query analyzer (QAA), a system used to reference agents according to their expertise, where each agent has only knowledge of services related to their field of expertise, and the last component is the service module that offers to providers the capability to publish web services' descriptions. In this system, to answer a query Q, the user enters his search query as a string through the user interface. This request is sent to the QAA agent that extracts from this request relevant keywords. Agent QAA selects a set of expert agents. The selected agents transmit parameters of the services to which they are linked to the composition agent. This later invokes a service according to user's choice.

Recent work has focused on semantic description web services and ontologies are mainly used to model the semantic service representation. It helps to establish semantic relations between concepts of the domain under consideration. We also have to mention that the OWL-S [13] approach that uses the ontology OWL-S to extend UDDI with semantic description of Web services.

It describes a web service using three classes; Service Profile is the class that provides the functional parameters for discovery such as enter expected, results produced, precondition and effects.

In this method, the discovery is based on a Matchmaking algorithm, which allows to find web services descriptions that have a semantic correspondence between functional parameters defined in the descriptions and those introduced in the search query.

Semantic correspondence between two concepts is based on the relationship between these ones in their respective OWL ontologies. The algorithm identifies four levels of semantic correspondence between two concepts, namely: Exact, Plug in, Subsume, and Disjoint.

At the last, web services are classified by semantic correspondence level between their output parameters and those cited in the query.

If two services have the same correspondence level with the request, a comparison on semantic correspondence level relative to the input parameters is performed. Another work adds the context parameter in the web services discovery process. In [14], the search for context-aware services is defined as the ability to use context information to find the most relevant services to the user.

The adaptation process is directly implemented in the mechanism of search services. This mechanism is based on the reference architecture of the service-based systems; the provider publishes its services on a server that is used by the user to send service requests. We summarize the steps of this work in the following steps: The provider must publish in the context manager the context in which the service can meet and conditions of use according to a description of the user and his/her environment. The web service description can be published on two levels: basic description expressed in a low-level language such as XML, or WSDL for Web services and semantic description (Semantic Service Description) expressed in OWL-S. The provider must publish in the register the two descriptions and the semantic service conditions of the use of the service, and the reference of its context. This information is stored in a server module called Service Provider – SP. The user must save its context (User Context) in the context manager (Context Manager) before he/she can make a request.

This request may be a basic query expressed in low-level search language (such as Service Location Protocol or UPnP62 - Universal Plug and Play) or query semantic: expressed as a semantic language query of high level (such as OWL-QL and RDQL). Then the user sends to the server a request and a pointer to his/her context. This information is stored in a server module named User. Once the user request is received, the search service enables the filtering engine service based on three filters: i) the filter base for selecting the category of service, ii) the semantic filter that returns a list of services that meet the exact specifications desired by the user, without the context information, and iii) context filter that refers to the list of services that match the context.

Semantic Annotation for WSDL (SAWSDL) [19] is a semantic language of Web service description. It is scalable and compatible with the existing Web services standards, and more specifically with WSDL. SAWSDL increases the expressiveness of WSDL with semantics using concepts similar to those used in OWL-S. On the one hand SAWSDL provides a mechanism to semantically annotate data types, operations, inputs and outputs of WSDL and secondly, it adds elements to specify preconditions, effects and classes Web services. Aspects related to the quality and service orchestration are not treated in SAWSDL. in summary, this semantic language is incremental and used on top of Web service standards.

3. Proposed Approach

After giving an overview of some work around the problematic, we now may present the proposed architecture to perform a service discovery, in agreement with constraints given by the user in the form of requests. These constraints can be for example non-numeric values placed on the choice of departure and arrival cities when booking a plane ticket, or digital as constraints placed on the price ticket or the QoS desired (response time, security, etc.). It is also based on the use context and its changes. For constraints treatment, we have relied on the benefits of the web semantic (ontologies) and fuzzy logic.

This proposed architecture takes into account the user context and his/her preferences and offers him/her the ability to classify results. We start by presenting the domain of

interest in the form of an OWL ontology. Then we present how this ontology is conceived from web services use context. To illustrate our architecture, we use a trip and tourism example.

3.1. Approach Presentation

The goal through this example is to develop a service web discovery system based on domain ontology and use context. This system allows to index web services by calculating the satisfaction degree with regard to the various concepts that belongs to our ontology. To meet non numeric request constraints, the present proposal is based on the similarity degree calculation between two concepts in an ontology.

As for the digital constraints we are using fuzzy logic to its calculation. This part will be much detailed later. To better understand the topic we will present an example that consists on planning a trip. The first task consists at representing the domain of interest using an OWL ontology. To do so, we need to:
• Determine domain knowledge element and represent use context elements, to conceive and build so that the corresponding ontologies represented under OWL language.
• Exploiting ontologies developed to index web services and thus be able later to locate relevant information in the list of web services related to interest domain
• Propose a classification of results according to user needs (preferences and use context).

3.2. User Context Definition and Modeling

We propose to store the context before its dissemination to the application to keep track of the historic data captured.

This created a new need, the context modeling to find a rich and reliable representation of the captured data.

A widely accepted definition of context in the field of context-aware computing (context awareness) is: "context is any information that can be used to characterize the situation of an entity (person, place or object), considered relevant in the interaction of a user and an application" [15]. In the work presented in this paper, we are interesting in the use context as a characterization of the user himself and his access device to the system.

Class diagram representing use context is illustrated by the above figure:

Use Context is associated with a session; a session is the act of connection by user to the system. Use Context is associated with a session while in a session can be associated with multiple use context. It is defined by a set of characteristics that are related to either user or device used for a session (class device characteristic). A feature is represented by a pair attribute / value. The attribute specifies the name of the feature and its value is given by the facet of the same name. The user characteristics are: Static, dynamic or preference.

User static characteristics are recorded during the first session and remain unchanged for the following. For example, static characteristic representing the user's first name is identical to each session. For example the welcome message to the system, taking into account user's first name remains unchanged for all sessions.

Dynamic characteristics and user preferences are stored in the first session, but may change from one session to another or during the same session, if we place ourselves in an e-business system, if a user is under 25 years (dynamic characteristic representing user age) the system can offer preferential prices. The same user logs later, he has now over 25 years; the system does not propose him anymore,

preferential prices.

From this example we show that user context may change from one session to another. Another example of dynamic use context is user location. This dynamic feature may vary during a single session if user has for access terminal a mobile device. Use context may change over time in the same session. The representation which we make of use context provides that its definition is dynamic and scalable since it is composed of one or more characteristics.

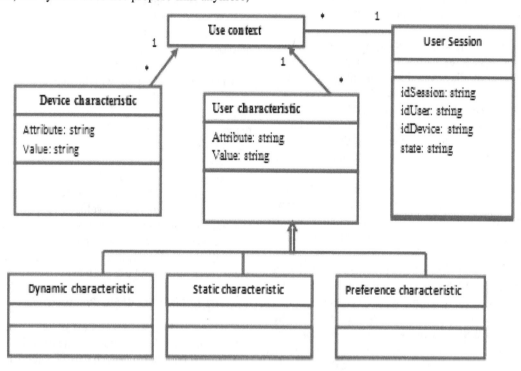

Figure 1. Context Model.

These characteristics are not fixed in advance and are defined by the system designer as needed.

Modeling pairs (attribute / value) is very low without any resistance to conflict. So a domain ontology for modeling context is necessary, to consider the relationship of concepts with other concepts. It has an expressiveness and richness semantic.

Table 1. Strengths and weaknesses of context modeling.

Model features	Semantic richness	Resistance to conflict	Ease ton im plementation
Pairs(attribute/value)	Low	Low	Strong
Ontology	Strong	Strong	Average

3.3. System design

The proposed system consists of:

1) Four modules: indexing module, search module, enrichment ontologies module, and the satisfaction degrees computation and service classification module.

2) A set of domain ontologies {01, 02,...,0n} that

represent different categories of service businesses.

3) To each domain ontology is associated a use context ontology.

4) Each of these ontologies a meta-database is assigned. The later contains synonyms or other words that car be used by the user.

5) RDF data representing all classes instances of our ontologies.

6) Ontologies and metadata base are possibly enriched by a domain expert.

7) A set semantic web service descriptions (OWL-S) stored in different registers and classified by domain of (business service categories). This classification takes advantage of a direct access to the services.

8) Database indexing services with different ontological concepts.

3.3.1. Indexing Module

Ontologies improve considerably the relevance of the results in the search process; it is the reason why we opted for an indexing method by means of ontologies. The improvements one may expect are related to the fact that the indexing process takes into account the different concepts and relations between them supplied by the ontology. Consequently, contrary to methods based on the use of simple and static keywords matching when looking for services, the ontology-based indexing method takes into account the semantic relationships among query terms.

Since one side each concept is linked to other concepts in the ontology and on the other hand we have a basis of metadata that enriched our ontology with a set of synonyms and different interpretations of each concept can give the same meaning to the concept sought.

3.3.2. Concepts search and Satisfaction Degree Computation

In this step we need the list of different concepts of our ontology of use context and interest domain corresponding to the domain of services to be processed. For this, we used a search engine called cores that can query an OWL ontology type and return a list of existing concepts. For every concept belonging to both ontologies we calculate its resemblance degree with service concepts to be indexed. This one is based on semantic similarity between two concepts. Services indexing process is presented in Figure 2.

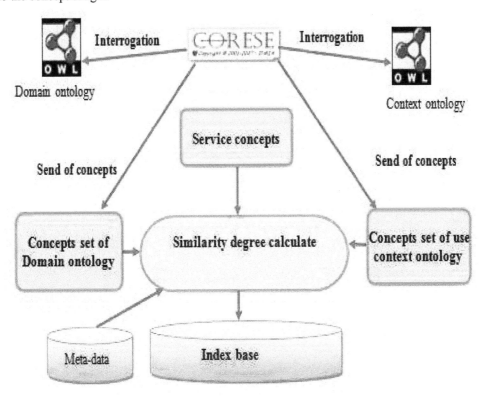

Figure 2. Indexing process.

Given an ontology O and two concepts c1 and c2, the semantic similarity between c1 and c2 is given by:

$$Sim\ (C1, C2) = \begin{cases} 1 & if\ C1 = C2 \\ 1 - \frac{dist(C1,C2)}{21+\max TCx}, & else \end{cases} \quad (18)$$

TCx is the weight associated to the type of the edge x which is the relationship between C1 and C2, for further explanation of this equation read [18].

3.3.3. Updating Index

In this phase, the index is implemented in a relational database for a more explicit data, the conceptual model formalism "entity association» is given by the following scheme:

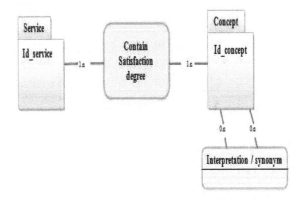

Figure 3.Index conceptual data model.

Each service is related to various concepts of our ontologies. Every concept is connected with all various interpretations in the meta-database. This information is later used when searching and selecting services. It is also used to calculate service satisfaction degree with regard to user complex requests. It is noteworthy that we designate by the *atomic request* a request that is composed of a single preference, and the term *complex request* is used to designate requests containing several preferences.

3.3.4. Search Process

It represents the system interface with the user. Indeed, it is through the search process that the user expresses his needs by formulating requests and entering his/her preferences. A request is represented by a string. The display of results should be in a form that allows the user to easily exploit search results. Hence, the search process is completed by a service classification process. The search process is represented in the Figure 4.

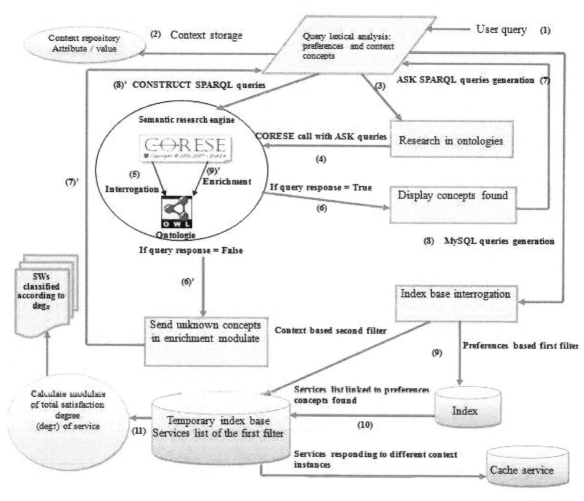

Figure 4. *Research process.*

This process consists of following stages:

Request lexical analysis: a graphical interface is available and is used to enter string queries. An entered query is lexically analyzed, This stage is necessary because a term in the query may have several forms in a text but its sense remains the same, thus it is enough to only use one of them to represent the concepts extracted from the query.

Use context identification: user session allows the identification of concepts related to the user context. These concepts are stored in the registry "context repository" and will be followed by the service "context manager" which is based on context comparison algorithm (current / predecessor) for detecting the change in state.

Generation of SPARQL query system: concepts extracted from resulting query in the previous stage are used to generate ASK SPARQL queries. The later allow the examination of the data sources to check the existence of the concepts.

Concepts search: search in our ontologies and metadata concepts related to query preference and context, this is done by calling semantic search engine CORESE [17] that executes queries system generated in previous step.

Concepts display and classification: all concepts found are stored; a concept can be of type "class" or "instance". If a concept is of type instance is found, we add the associated class to the list of our list of found class concepts.

Sending unknown concepts to the enrichment module: concepts not found will be sent to the enrichment module for possible addition by the domain expert; it is done by calling CORESE system that executes a CONSTRUCT

SPARQL query.

Querying data sources: the first step consists at building SQL queries to query our index database using concepts of type "class" found earlier. Then, a list of services related to these concepts is returned. In the second stage, SPARQL queries are generated using the concepts of "instance" to select from the list returned by the first stage, services meeting these instances. This is done by querying our RDF data using two filters: user preferences and use context concepts.

Calculating the query satisfaction degree: based on user request, we compute the degree of satisfaction of each service that is obtained from the filtering phase.

Processing the digital preferences: a user request may contain a numerical value of type:

Between (concept, v1, v2), max (concept, v1) or min (concept, v1).

And to calculate service satisfaction degree towards a digital concept Ci, we need concept value (x) in the service process. Based on this this value, a satisfaction function g(x) is calculated. This function takes into account the value vi required by the user.

Unlike Boolean logic, fuzzy logic allows a condition of being in a state other than true or false. There are degrees in the verification of condition. In our case it is used to calculate the value of g(x) that evaluates the degree to which a service web value (x) satisfies value (v) desired by user. G(x) is thus calculated according to its type (around, max, min) and the value wished by the user. Inspired by the example given in Wikipedia [16] that explain how to consider the speed of cars, we give the following formulas:

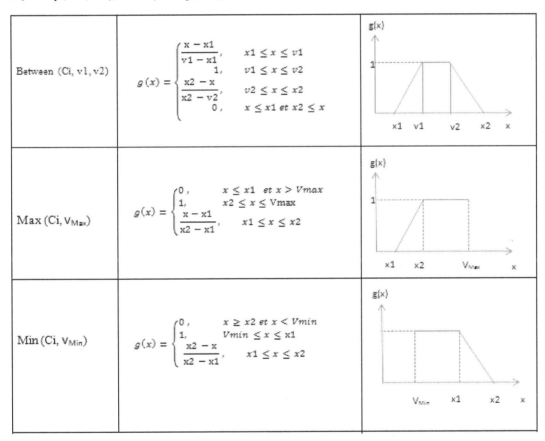

So in order to compute service satisfaction degree with regard to the user request, the user has to provide an ordered list of his/her preferences. An interest degree will be assigned to each element belonging to the list.

Given Ci a set of concepts extracted from the user request :

$Ci = \{C1.....Ci\}$, interest degree is assigned to each concept: $Di = \{D1 .... Dn\}$.

To calculate concept interest degree, we ask the user to gather concepts that have the same level of importance and rank them. This is done using the two interpretations Pareto preference and Prioritized preference from preferences SQL language. Using Pareto preference we will have n subsets of concepts that have the same level of importance. These subsets will be ranked together with Prioritized preference. We get the ordered set:

Ci': $Ci' = \{e1, e2, e3,......, en\}$ when $e1 = \{ (C1 ,C2)\}$, $e2 = \{ (C3)\}$, $e3 = \{ (C4 ,C5 ,C6)\}$, $en = \{ (Ci,....Ci)\}$.

The subset belonging level is equal to its ranking in Ci and is noted by Lev(ei). The number nb represents the number of subsets ei belonging to Ci'. Interest level of each subset ei belonging to Ci is equal to the division of its level of ownership in Ci on the total number of subsets belonging to Ci'.

Concepts representing query preferences will therefore be classified by interest level, we obtain a graph of several levels in ascending order.

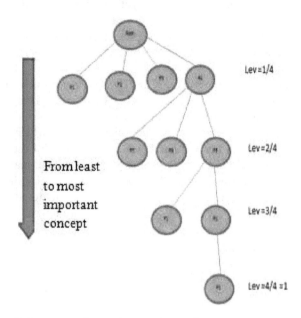

f(x): request degree interest in service.

$$Interest\ degree\ of\ concept = \frac{Lev(ei)}{nb}$$

$f(x) = \Sigma\ (\ \text{satisfaction degree concept i} * \text{interest degree i}\ )$

Result classification: if the request is atomic (contains a single concept), the classification of services related to this concept is based on the recorded level of satisfaction of those services with regard to the single concept contained in the request. In the case where the query is a complex, the classification is done according to the satisfaction degree obtained from Equation (3).

3.3.5. Ontology Enrichment Module

The presented system needs the richest possible ontologies to have a better indexation and consequently make a better search. To that end, we propose a simple way to help domain experts enrich ontologies in addition to his own expertise on his/her field. Concepts not found in ontologies during search process are stored in a list and when domain expert connects for the enrichment he will find a list of these concepts and choose among them those suitable to the domain of interest. The effective enrichment of our ontologies is done using the SPARQL CONSTRUCT query system and the semantic search engine CORESE (figure 5).

Figure 5. *Enrichment module.*

4. Conclusion and Future Works

In this work, we presented the detailed steps we followed to model specific domain ontologies. Then, we showed how they may be integrated in a web service retrieval system. We opted for a modular architecture to build the system that consists of five main modules. The main idea was to solve the problem of web service discovery and be able to locate automatically the "correct" web service in order to meet user requirements.

To that end, we proposed an architecture for a service selection system in accordance with user constraints and context by means of web semantic technologies. As of our perspectives, we are planning to evaluate the effectiveness of our approach using a real use case and real data. Also,

we are planning to study how it may be generalized and extend its scope.

References

[1] Papazoglou, M. P. Service-Oriented Computing: Concepts, Characteristics and Directions. In: Procs of the 4th International Conference on Web Information Systems Engineering (WISE 03), Dec. 2003, Washington, DC, USA, 2003. IEEE Computer Society, 2003, pp.3-12.

[2] Steve, J. Toward an Acceptable Definition of Service. IEEE Software, 2005,vol.22, n°3, pp.87-93.

[3] Erl, T. Service-Oriented Architecture: Concepts, Technology, and Design.Prentice Hall PTR, 2005, 760p.

[4]   Chinnici, R., Moreau, J.-J., Ryman, A., Weerawarana, S. Web Services Description Language (WSDL) Version 2.0 Part 1: Core Language. W3C Recommendation [en ligne], 2007.

[5]   Mitra, N., Lafon, Y. SOAP Version 1.2 Part 0: Primer (Second Edition). W3C Recommendation [en ligne], 2007.

[6]   F.NewcomerE.ChampionM.FerrisC.Orchard   :   Booth, D.Haas. Web services architecture.

[7]   Wahlster, W., Dengel, A. Web 3.0: Convergence of Web 2.0 and the Semantic Web. Technology Radar Feature Paper, Edition II/2006, Deutsche Telekom Laboratories, pp.1-23.

[8]   Hendler, J.Web 3.0: Chicken Farms on the Semantic Web. Computer, 2008,vol. 41, n°1, pp.106-108.

[9]   Berners-Lee, T., Hendler, J., Lassila, O. The Semantic Web. In: Scientific Americain, 2001.

[10]   KaarthikSivashanmugam, KunalVerma, Amit P. Sheth, and John A. Miller. Adding semantics to web services standards. 2003, In ICWS, pages 395–401.

[11]   Eric Newcomer. Understanding Web Services- XML, WSDL, SOAP and UDDI, chapter 5, Finding Web Services : UDDI Registry. Addison Wesley Professional, May.

[12]   Paul Palathingal and Sandeep Chandra.Agent approach for service discovery and utilization.In HICSS, 2004.

[13]   David Martin and al. Owl-s : Semantic markup for web services. Technical report, W3C, 2004.

[14]   Vincenzo Suraci1, SilvanoMignanti, Anna Aiuto, University of Rome "Sapienza", Department of computer and system sciences, Context-aware SemanticService Discovery

[15]   A. K. Dey, G. D. Abowd, and D. Salber. A Conceptual Framework and a Toolkit for Supporting the Rapid Prototyping of Context-Aware Applications. Human-Computer Interaction Journal, 16(1), 2001.

[16]   http://fr.wikipedia.org/wiki/Logique_floue.

[17]   http://www sop.inria.fr/edelweiss/software/corese/v2_4_0/manual/index .php.

[18]   RESNIK P. (1995). Using information content to evaluate semantic similarity in a taxonomy.In IJCAI, p. 448–453.

[19]   Large Scale Distributed Information Systems. SAWSDL: Semantic   Annotations   for   WSDL. http://lsdis.cs.uga.edu/projects/meteor-s/SAWSDL/   (Avril 2011).

2

An approach to virtual laboratory design and testing

A. Hovakimyan, S. Sargsyan, N. Ispiryan, L. Khachoyan, K. Darbinyan

Department of Programming and Information Technologies, Yerevan State University (YSU), Yerevan, Armenia

Email address:

ahovakimyan@ysu.am (A. Hovakimyan), siranushs@ysu.am (S. Sargsyan), nispiryan@ysu.am (N. Ispiryan),
lkhachoyan@gmail.com (L. Khachoyan), kdarbinyan@ysu.am (K. Darbinyan)

Abstract: Laboratory experiments and research are important parts in natural science education. They supplement the theoretical learning material and contribute to deeper learn of a subject. The realization of such activities requires an appropriate laboratory equipment and reagents that are often either inaccessible or incomplete. Virtual labs solve this problem and provide the performing of the same experiment repeatedly without any restriction. An interactive laboratory environment engages pupils in active learning to enhance their understanding of processes and practical skills and promotes a successful e-learning strategy. Virtual Lab includes a lot of embedded experiments that the student must perform via certain scenarios. In the paper an approach to design of laboratory experiments for virtual lab environment and their scenarios implementation testing is suggested. Experiments design patterns are based on finite-state automaton model. The object-oriented approach for virtual experiment implementation is provided. For testing pattern a methodology of class testing is used. The suggested approaches are realized in the presented virtual laboratory environments for Chemistry and Biology that have been developed to support laboratory study in Armenian schools, colleges, and universities. These methods will be used in long-term research activity in the field of creation of virtual laboratories on different disciplines: organic and inorganic chemistry, physics, and biology as well as during developing others virtual laboratories.

Keywords: Virtual Experiment, Virtual Laboratory, Experiment Modeling, Implementation and Testing, Class Algebraic Definition, Class Testing, Test Case

1. Introduction

In the modern society e-learning is an inherent part of education and gives the students and pupils a proper possibility to get knowledge independently of time and place.

Laboratory experiments and research in different natural subjects essentially supplement the theoretical learning course and provide deeper acquirement of the learning discipline [1, 2]. The realization of laboratory experiments and research needs an appropriate laboratory equipment and reagents that are often either inaccessible or incomplete. On the other hand, even the laboratory equipment is complete, it is necessary and desirable to make the same experiment repeatedly with different substances with their various proportions and by different sequence of actions. Undoubtedly during the laboratory experiments' realization it is necessary to keep the precautionary measures whereas in virtual conditions the student is being given some free hand. The pedagogical agent can prevent the attempts of the dangerous actions making outline of warnings and undesired reactions and effects [3, 4]. At the same time it is desired to

organize the laboratory study whenever and wherever without any equipments and reagents. So it is very important and actual to develop virtual environment for laboratory research.

The problems considered in the paper are related to definition of general templates for the virtual environment for laboratory studies in different subjects, creation patterns in order to design and test virtual laboratories supporting software, realization virtual laboratories according to these patterns. The problems include the identification of basic concepts, elements, operations for different laboratory experiments, relations between them as well as the main concepts of execution of virtual experiments.

The essential part of a virtual laboratory is a set of embedded experiments that the student must perform via certain scenario.

To develop virtual experiments and to provide the performance of experiments scenarios some design and testing patterns are described in the paper. Virtual environments for Chemistry and Biology laboratory research that have been developed to support laboratory study in Armenian schools, colleges, and universities, are presented.

It is intended that the suggested approach will be embedded in long-term research activity in the field of creation of virtual laboratories on different disciplines: organic and inorganic chemistry, physics, and biology as well as during developing others virtual laboratories. It can be used by subject-specialist for adding the new experiments in developed virtual laboratories. The software developer can use the created patterns for developing and testing of others virtual laboratories.

2. Virtual Laboratory Experiment Modeling, Implementation and Testing

As a pattern for design of a virtual laboratory experiment a finite-state automaton model is suggested [5]. The experiment is presented as an automaton, and the automaton's states correspondent to those states in which the experiment can appear during the experiment implementation. The automaton's states are classified as following:

initial state – the state from which the experiment begins,

state without any effect - the state in which any effect doesn't occur,

state with an intermediate effect- the state in which some effect can occur but it is not a final effect of the experiment,

state with the final effect - the state corresponded to the experiment's final result.

Automaton's transitions correspond to activities performed by concrete substances and tools that can lead to changing of the experiment common state. An experiment performance scenario is presented as a path from the initial state to any other state. On these paths a state may be repeated only if some transition in the automaton is done under an edge which doesn't change a state of the automaton. If there was a change of the automaton state then returning to any of previous states isn't possible.

For the implementation of the automaton modeled experiments the object-oriented approach is suggested. For this aim appropriate data types are needed.

Let us specify some of them for chemical research. Data type Substances={S1, S2,,...} describes the chemical reagents used in an experiment, for example, acids, alcohols, data type Tools={T1, T2,,...} defines all the tools used for experiment performance, for example, glass, tube, spirit lamp, data type SubstanceEffect describes chemical reagents' set received by some effect achieved etc.

Each experiment is presented by a separate class. Class data-members' values represent a current state of the experiment, and class methods represent activities carried out with tools and substances during the experiment. A method can change the experiment state.

So a class for an chemical experiment should be declared via the following pattern.

```
enum Substances={S1, S2,...};
enum Tools={T1, T2,...};
enum SensitizableEffects={T1, T2,...};
typedef set<Substance> SubstanceEffect;
typedef pair< SensitizableEffects, SubstanceEffect> Effect;
class ExperimentName
{
private:
set<Substance> sSubstance, sSubstanceEx dended;
set< Tools > sTools, sTubes;
map< Tools, set<Substance> > ExpState;
map< Tools, Effect > ExpEffect;
public:
Method1(...);
Method2(...);
Method3(...);
...};
```

The variable sSubstance holds the set of the substances explored in this experiment while the variable sSubstanceExdended holds the set of auxiliary substances used in this experiment. The variables sTools and sTubes are reserved for tools and tubes. The variable ExpState represents a current state of the experiment, i.e. it is a pair where a mapping of toolset into set of substances is presented. The variable ExpEffect holds a chemical effect occurred in some state of experiment.All the listed variables are initialized by class constructor.

The class for the experiment creating an ether (E) from two types of organic acids (AC1, AC2) and two types of alcohol (AL1, AL2) is outlined below.

```
enum Substances={AC1,AC2,AL1,AL2,E};
enum Tools={Measure,Glass, Tube, Bath, Tunnel, Stopper, Fire};
enum SensitizableEffects={no_effect, odour, colouration, dimming};
typedef set<Substance> SubstanceEffect;
typedef pair< SensitizableEffects, SubstancEffect> Effect;
class EtherFromAcidsAndAlcohols
{
private:
set<Substance> sSubstance, sSubstanceExdended;
set< Tools > sTools, sTubes;
map< Tools, set<Substance> > ExpState;
map< Tools, Effect > ExpEffect;
public:
EtherFromAcidsAndAlcohols (...);
void fillInMeasure(Substances);
void putMeasureInBath(Tools);
void fillMeasureInGlass(Tools);
void fillGlassInTunnel(Tools);
void showEffect();
};
```

For a virtual laboratory testing we use the TACCLE (Testing An Class and Claster LEvel) methodology where an algebraic definition of classes is provided [6]. Such a definition of class has two parts: syntactic declaration and semantic specification. Syntactic declaration is a set of class interfaces as given above, and semantic specification is a set of axioms that describe class methods behavior. The semantic specification of the class is based on the finite-state automaton model described the experiment and may be presented in XML format [7]. A part of the XML description of semantic specification is outlined below. For each method both initial and next states are indicated.

-<experiment name=" EtherFromAcidsAndAlcohols">
-<states>
-<state name="S0" state ="init">
-<transitions>
<transition name=" fillInMeasure(AC1)" priority="1" nextstate="S1"/>
<transition name=" fillInMeasure(AC2)" priority="2" nextstate ="S2"/>
<transition name=" fillGlassInTunnel()" priority="4" nextstate ="S3"/>
</transitions>
</state>
+<state name="S1" state ="no effect">
+<state name="S2" state ="mid effect">
+<state name="S3" state ="fin effect">
</states>
</experiment>

Test cases for experiment implementation testing are terms. A term is a sequence of a class methods' calls that represents the sequence of actions performed in the experiment.

Let _exp.Method(c1, c2,...,cn): ExpState*C1*C2*...*Cn → ExpState is an elementary term, where ExpState is a type for experiment's states, and $C1,C2,...,Cn$ are types for method's parameters. An elementary term provides an experiment transition from a state to another.

We define the applicability operation on terms. Let u=f0f1...fi and v=g1g2...gj are terms. It is said that the term v is applicable to the term u if and only if the output state of the term fi is an input state for the term g1. In this case w=u.v is a new term.

For a class C we distinguish four type of methods: observers that return the values of the attributes of the experiment object, creators that initialize the experiment object, and constructors and transformers that transform the states of the experiment object. For example, the method showEffect() is a observer for the class EtherFromAcidsAndAlcohols while fillInMeasure(C1) and putMeasureInBath() are transformers. The current state of an experiment is the combination of current values of all attributes of the object presented the experiment.

An observable context on a class C is a sequence of constructors and transformers of C followed by an observer of C. For example, the term fillInMeasure(C1). putMeasureInBath().showEffect() is an observable context on the class EtherFromAcidsAndAlcohols.

An observable context sequence on a class C is a term $oc=oc_1.oc_2....oc_n$, where oc_i (i=1,2,...,n) is an observable context, and oc_j(j=2,...,n) is applicable to oc_j-1.

A term applied to the experiment object transforms it to some state.

On the set of terms and objects it can be defined different types of equivalence. Terms that lead the experiment to the same state are called equivalent. Two objects O1 and O2 are said to be observationally equivalent if and only if the following condition is satisfied: if no observable context oc on class C, is applicable to O1 and O2, then O1 and O2 are identical objects. Otherwise, for any such oc on C O1. oc and O2. oc are observationally equivalent objects.

Note that if class implementation satisfies with class specification then for two equivalent terms u1 and u2 the objects O.u1 and O.u2 are equivalent, and for two nonequivalent terms u1 and u2 the objects O.u1 and O.u2 are nonequivalent.

For terms transforming we define the loops exclusion operation on terms. If $u=f_0f_1...f_n$ is a term and there are i, j (i<j, $f_i=f_j$) and such observable contexts oc1 and oc2, that

O.oc1 and O.oc2 are equivalent,
f_i is applicable to oc1,
f_j is applicable to oc2,
$O.oc1.f_i$, and $O.oc2.f_j$ are the same,
then fi is deleted from the term u.

Any term on experiment class can be used as a test case for experiment implementation testing. For example, the term fillInMeasure(C1).putMeasureInBath() is a test case for the experiment E if it is applied to the object E.

For the complete testing the class must be tested on the pairs of both equivalent and nonequivalent terms. These terms are constructed via XML description of semantic specification of the class.

The infinite set of terms is reduced to an finite set of terms with loops exclusion operation. This set can be embedded into the test driver to test the laboratory automatically.

3. Case Study

Virtual environments VirtChemLab and VirtBioLab for Chemistry and Biology laboratory research based on described approach are developed by authors [8, 9]. About 50 traditional laboratory experiments of Inorganic and Organic Chemistry and Biology are modeled, realized and embedded into these systems.

The created environments allow to carry out the conventional chemical and biological experiments interactively with various collection of substances and objects which are typical for that experiment, to understand chemical reactions in experiment between substances. Working in the virtual laboratory helps the student to recognize the properties of suggested substances in frame of that experiment, as well as to organize practical laboratory research wherever and whenever, to study the experiment's correct scenario by attempts and mistakes method, to observe experiments results by different visual effects, chemical formulas and animated molecules (Fig. 1).

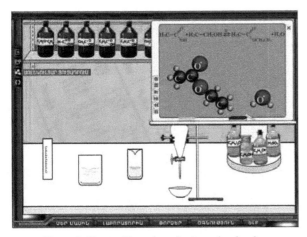

Figure 1. Chemical formula and animated molecules.

The same experiment can be done many times with different substances with different proportions to receive deeper knowledge about investigated chemical and biological reagents. The colorful didactic materials, illustrations and different multimedia animations for chemical and biological experiments make learning more interesting and easy to understand. Laboratory study is accompanied with recommendations, advice and remarks. In virtual laboratories there are also the information making the theoretical base of the experiment and textual description of experiment's scenario with sound.

The virtual environments provide also experiments' demonstration in real chemical and biological laboratories taken by a video camera as well as a gallery that obtains necessary laboratory equipments, glassware, tools and reagents and so on. In the gallery there is a brief information about each substance and its chemical and biological properties.

The lab equipment and reagents availabled to learners are placed in virtual laboratory depending on the experiment to be made. All actions in virtual laboratory are made by mouse. The correct selection of experiment's substances and tools leads to simulation of real effects and actions by activating the corresponding animations (e.g. pouring the solution into the glassware, mixture color changing etc.). There is a blackboard on which the comments and recommendations of pedagogical agent and experiment's reactions formulas are placed.

4. Conclusion

To develop the suggested approach for virtual laboratories design and testing the main following problems are explored:
- identifying of a uniform approach on the problem of interactive experiments designing.
- establishing and identifying main concepts of execution of virtual laboratory studies.
- identifying of experiment's basic elements, operations and relations between them.
- identifying of basic methods to do experiments inte-

ractively.
- identifying of means and ways for experiment's reagents' characteristics presentation.
- developing of the formal model for laboratory experiment's scenario and it's adaptation to appropriate mathematical computing model.
- developing of virtual laboratories design patterns.
- identifying of object oriented approach on laboratory experiments' scenarios programming.
- identifying of the role of virtual teacher during laboratory research.
- simulating of 2-3 classic experiments on different subjects.
- defining of virtual laboratories testing methodology and testing patterns used the testing theory of object oriented software on class level.
- elaborating of methods for constructing the test cases complete system.
- the suggested approaches implementing for some real-life examples.

5. Further Work

We continue works in direction of developing Virtual Laboratories to cover the other natural subjects, expand their functional abilities, provide much more experiments and increase the flexibility of these systems. The modifications of the systems are planned to implement in following directions:
- increasing the interactivity in virtual environments;
- design and testing template toolset extension;
- user interface improvement;
- creation of new services to support connection between laboratories and practicing classes;
- feedback system developing;
- translation into English and Russian.

According to W3C consortium standards regarding Web Ontology and Learning Objects we assume to continue our works by using OWL to describe basic elements of laboratory research as well as semantic relationship and dependency between different components and parts of a laboratory experiment. We suppose to create mechanisms and tools to analyze the quality of such laboratories to provide the quality of e-education.

References

[1] D.Carnevale, The Virtual Lab Experiment.Chronicle of Higher Ed, January 31, 2003, p.A30.

[2] J. Robinson, Virtual Laboratories as a teaching environment: A tangible solution or a passing novelty?,// Proceedings of the 3rd Annual CM316 Conference on Multimedia Systems, based at Southampton University, http:/mns.ecs. soton.ac. uk/ papers/5.pdf.

[3] Y.J.Dori, M. Barak, Virtual and Physical Molecular Modeling: Fostering Model Perception and Spatial Understanding.

Educational Technology and Society, 4(1), 2001, pp. 61-74.

[4] M.Morozov, A.Tanakov, A.Gerasimov. Virtual Chemistry Laboratory for School Education. // Proceedings of the IEEE International Conference ICALT2004, 30 August-1, September, 2004, Joensuu, Finland.

[5] B.A. Trachtetbrot, J.M.Barzdin. Finite automata. Behavior and synthesis. (in Russian). - M.: Nauka, 1970, p.400.

[6] H. Y. Chen, T.H. Tse, H. Y. Chen. TACCLE: a methodology for object-oriented software Testing At the Class and Cluster LEvels. // ACM Transactions on Software Engineering and Methodology, 10, 2001, pp.56-107.

[7] S.G. Sargsyan, A.S. Hovakimyan, S.V. Barkhudaryan, Using Template Processing Technique in the Pervasive e-Learning Supporting Systems.//Proceedings of the International Conference: Information Technologies in Education in the 21st Century, May 21-23, 2007, Yerevan, Armenia, pp.24-34.

[8] S.G. Sargsyan, A.S. Hovakimyan, K.S. Darbinyan, N. Ispiryan, Modeling and Implementation of Virtual Chemistry Laboratory. // Proceedings of the International Conference: Computer Sciene and Information Technologies (CSIT2005), Yerevan, Armenia, 2005.

[9] S.G. Sargsyan, A.S. Hovakimyan, K.S. Darbinyan, N. Ispiryan, Basic Concepts of Creation of Virtual Chemical Laboratory. Learning Technology Newsletter, Vol. 7, Issue 4, October 2005,Publication of IEEE Computer Society ISSN 1438-0625, pp. 43-45.

3

Supporting engineering design modeling by domain specific modeling language

Japheth Bunakiye. Richard.[1], Ogheneovo Edward. Erhieyovwe.[2]

[1]Department of Mathematics/Computer Science, Niger Delta University, Yenagoa, Nigeria
[2]Department of Computer Science, University of Port Harcourt, Port Harcourt, Nigeria

Email address:
jbunakiye@yahoo.com(B. R. Japheth), edward_ogheneovo@yahoo.com(E. E. Ogheneovo)

Abstract: Domain specific modeling methodology employed in this solution provides abstractions in the problem domain that expresses designs in terms of concepts in the application domain. Presented in this paper therefore is a metamodelling tool, an integrated platform which offers layered collections of reusable software primitives whose semantics are familiar only to engineering design mechanisms. It is intended to eliminate the complexities associated with the domain of computing technologies such as CAD systems where the focus is solely on engineering designs expertise in the software systems logic. This tool which was built on the DSL processor engine that compiles the DSL Builder files at the core will enable non design experts to be able to evolve designs specific to their domains of operations and reflecting their view points. At the Development Interface, the templates are created for every transformation added to our model that can be applicable in the physical design of objects in the engineering industry. It will in line remove hassles and complexities of expertise centric design platforms to produce artifacts that will help engineers manage very complex design concepts.

Keywords: Domain-Specific modeling, Primitives, Models, Platform Complexity, Domain Classes

1. Introduction

Computer graphics often referred to as graphics models are representations on a computer screen of physical entities [1]. Graphics [21], models usually are created interactively from graphics primitives (primitives are stored libraries of shapes from common interactive CAD Systems) and can be assembled to more complex forms known as graphics assemblies. A graphics model could also be a final product of the aggregation of graphics primitives, graphics assemblies and subassemblies. The entire process of creating a final graphics model is termed graphics design and the result is termed graphics model [9, 12]. This graphics models can then reflect human conceptions in different domains. In the domain of engineering, it invariably becomes the engineering design.

1.1. Engineering Designs

Design is the creation of a set of drawings for the production of an object or a system of objects. Engineering designs are examples of such objects created from design activities. They are usually graphics [12], models created interactively from graphics primitives withspecificationsthat describe the function the designed piece is to achieve [8].

These models representsalient characteristicsof target domains of technological advancement and can also be expanded into concepts that explain simplifications of systems at certain circumstances that can be built upon abstractions [11].

As much as Common interactive CAD systems (e.g. AutoCAD) are utilized by designers for graphics design modeling, they lack the power of expression to specify the engineering design in formal notations [13]. A language which could capture concepts of a specific application domain as formally specified and reflected in the engineering design and can link these concepts to appropriate abstraction levels within the problem domain [17, 11].

What is required to overcome the stated inability of CADs to express domainconcepts effectively is domain specific representation.Domain specific representation is made possible through domain specific modeling (DSM). It requires the construction of a domain specific modeling language that can provide a means for expressing domain concepts in a model [17]. This leads to increase in productivity, and provides non-designers and domain experts the resource to operate on very familiar notations without being burdened by expertise on design [18].

The focus of this paper therefore is utilizing this DSM technology as the background methodology to develop a metamodelling framework in order to tackle the associated complexities of design software. Interactive CADs design platforms usually requires specific expertise in design practice to be able to develop a design solution. But with a modelling tool that offers familiar notations, non-designers and stakeholders of target domains will find it easy for likely design and related activities [20].

The rest of this paper is organised as follows: Section 2 provides related work and review of engineering designs; section 3 discusses the methodology and materials; and section 4 describes the framework in more details. First, we show the modelling framework where concepts are captured from a possible engineering design to form the grammar metamodel. Second, we gave the interpretation and the benefits of the framework. Third, we show the relationships between model elements and the subsequent XML tree representations. Section 5 concludes the paper.

2. Related Work

Quite a number of research works have dealt with efforts geared towards using domain specific modeling in the creation of technologies that addresses platform complexities. Domain specific modeling further addresses the inability of general purpose computing systems such as interactive Computer-Aided Design systems to alleviate these complexities by expressing domain concepts effectively. Douglas C. Schmidt [13] gave a lot of fruitful notes for the development of a domain-specific layer as part of the Model-Driven Engineering (MDE) technologies that can expressing concepts as a necessary step in tackling platform complexities. In the scope of engineering designs, the work by Melgoza, E. L., Rosell, A [5], has a considerable relationship with our focus, and in addition Selic B, [3] gave much insight on determining ways to enable the extraction of concepts from a model as the core entity throughout development in the application of DSM. In this context Marcus Volter [20] did showcase some results in implementing the DSM approach where some useful guidelines were translated into the processes that made our framework feasible [18, 16, 11].

2.1. Solid Modeling

Engineering designs [1] are simply solid models. They are modeled by building them up from primitives found in the libraries of interactive CAD systems such as AutoCAD. Two basic data structures employed in solid modeling are constructive solid geometry (CSG) and boundary representation (B-rep) respectively [2]. CSG as shown in figure 1 uses primitives such as cylinder, sphere, and prism with combined Boolean operations to produce the solid [8].

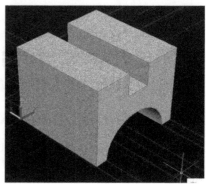
Figure 1: A CSG Solid Model

B-rep solid models as shown in figure 2 are usually constructed using surfaces, curves and points in a 3D space.

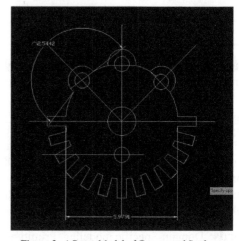
Figure 2: A B-rep Model of Curves and Surfaces

The users often times find it difficult to change the geometry of these solids especially because of the static nature of their dimensions [1]. But parametric modeling capabilities, recently associated with common interactive CAD systems such as AutoCAD however [10] addresses all of the shortcomings of static dimensions. With parametric modeling they can be used for detailed engineering of 3D models of physical components [5]. This possibility however is seen in conventional modeling where objects are clearly labeled [9].

The resultant effect is that quite a lot of modifications have to be made to reflect the intentions of the designer whenever one aspect of the model is changed. The expertise of the designer is greatly depended upon in all circumstances of the application of the rules of the software during design because the software itself lacks the ability to automatically keep track of the changes. The use of common interactive CADs such as AutoCAD for creating conventional engineering designs however, hampers non AutoCAD experts and other domain stakeholders from bringing up engineering designs that could possibly reflect the perspectives of their domains [12]. This means current CAD systems coupled with the third generation programming APIs inherent in them still lack sufficient linguistic power to handle domain and platform complexities. These systems hasn't moved speedily with domain technologies i.e. software engineering methodologies that can be used to foster model interaction in order to create new objects that encapsulate and relate the details pertinent to the viewpoint of domain experts.

The believe is that such software development efforts will enable stakeholders to cope with platform complexities, it will also be cost effective, save time, and raise productivity levels [8].

Major efforts in tackling these problems are putting the model at the core of development and ignoring any detail not relevant to the application domain perspectives that these models represent. Concepts associated with the domain's technical content are specified and appropriate reductions are made by raising the abstractions and expressions of the characteristics of the models as they relate to engineering designs [2]. Critical in the process is identifying the problem domain (i.e., the problem space), the exact needs these raised levels of abstractions are to be met and the task of how these different domains can be integrated to form a whole modeling platform. A capable software engineering practice to addressing the mapping of these abstractions from the problem domain that expresses design in terms of the concepts to the application domain is the Model-Driven Engineering technology (MDE).

Model-Driven Engineering technology is powered by the Model-Driven Development software paradigm. There are two approaches to Model-Driven Development; the Model Driven Architecture (MDA) and Domain-Specific Modeling (DSM) [14].While the Model-Driven Architecture (MDA)[20] as part of the object management group (OMG) standards is focused more on the concepts of the problem domain and not on the technical contents of the application domain [2, 14], the Domain-specific modelling approach focused on semantic mappings of the concepts in the application domain to the problem domain and then enabling the system to process the models via the semantic relationships to produce desired artefacts as well as automating transformations and code generation [10, 18].

MDE with the DSML approach is declarative, usually expresses what the program should accomplish without presenting the complexities of how to solve a problem in terms of sequences of actions to be taken. Policies are specified at a higher level of abstraction using models and are separated from the mechanisms used to enforce the policies. DSMLs help overcome the semantic gap between the design intent and the expression of such design intent, and help users from difficulties of how the policies are mapped onto the underlying mechanisms implementing them, thereby, allowing system reuse easily [5, 6].

3. Method and Materials

3.1. Method

The initiative is a modelling tool that could aid domain experts develop and produce designs directly related to their view points. Applying the DSML approach, the complexities of CAD engineering designs were incorporated as design concepts and the platform complexities of constructing codes from programming languages were encapsulated as abstractions. These concepts were then mapped to the abstractions via semantic relationships [2, 5]. The application domain was taken to be pipelines design domain where design issues pertaining to pipelines can be tackled.

The problem domain was then considered i.e. the concise information about stakeholders needs in this language, the needs that when met, pipeline design issues can be solved by the pipelines design engineers and related experts. The information in this direction led the gathering of a component library framework in order to identify the concepts and associated rules targeted at this methodology to be created utilizing a Microsoft DSL tool (Visual Studio Visualization and Modeling SDK) [2].

In addition to the experts viewpoints we looked at the existing system descriptions, component devices and services, and standards to form the concepts. From the components frameworks relevant vocabulary was created in terms of physical products structures in pipelines design e.g. valves, joints, loops, angles etc., the attributes such as size of pipe, shape, direction of loops etc. were sorted, rules on how a valve may relate to angle etc., and taking note of several levels of abstractions possible only with pipelines design industry. We continued to adding the grammar to the vocabulary and on into the language construct.

In the language construct, the abstraction rules were followed, and the semantics specified. The abstract syntax representing the structure and appearance of our sentences is being generated resulting directly from language definitions and the concrete syntax in form of notations about the key words describing concepts mapped to the design symbols.

3.2. Materials

The solution was built employing the Microsoft Visualization and Modeling SDK in Visual Studio 2012. The System structure was a refinement of the semantic base of the .Net framework built on the DSL processor engine that compiles the DSL Builder files at the core. This possibility created a layer of reusable software, an integrated environment for seamless operations.

4. Solution Framework

The framework as shown in figure 3 is a modelling tool specific to the engineering field in the domain of engineering design. The domain model, which invariably is the engineering design, depicts the domain concepts and then these concepts are mapped to the abstractions via semantic relationships.

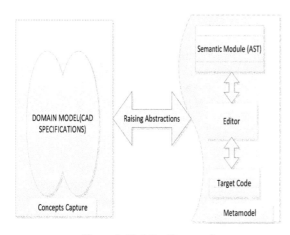

Figure 3: *Modeling Framework*

The result will be a metamodel, a language definition covering all of the application and problem domains into one development environment capable of processing these models via the editor to produce desired products and automatic code generation [2] [5].

4.1. Solution Interpretation

A primary purpose is the generation of efficient implementation code for the target engineering design domain by enabling domain experts to express their view points through the interface. At the heart of the solution framework is the definition of the model created to represent concepts in the application domain. The chosen example as shown in figure 4 isthe pipeline design domain. It is the graphical editor component of the framework in which users can view the model definitions. It is an example of the expression of the models in the DSL core with concrete notations.

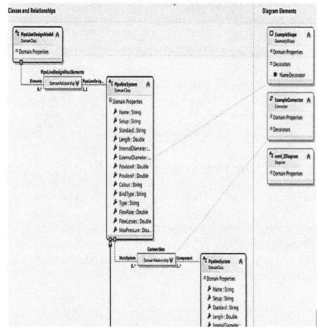

Figure4: *Graphical Component of Solution Framework*

These notations represent the language concepts captured from peculiar domain terminologies embodied in the model and are expressed as the concrete syntax through abstraction rules. The model definition therefore signifies the specification of the actual abstract syntax of the language that renders processing feasible by enabling users to be able to read and write through this graphical interface with the familiar notations. In the internal structure, the grammar which was created out of the concepts generates the abstract syntax trees as readable XML as shown in figure 5. The essence is for the ability to generate code and other artifacts.

```
<?xml version="1.0" encoding="utf-8"?>
<xsd:schema id="eeml_2Schema"
targetNamespace="http://schemas.microsoft.com/dsltools/eeml_2"
elementFormDefault="qualified" xmlns="http://schemas.microsoft.com/dsltools/eeml_2"
xmlns:core="http://schemas.microsoft.com/VisualStudio/2008/DslTools/Core"
xmlns:xsd="http://www.w3.org/2001/XMLSchema">
  <xsd:import id="CoreSchema"
namespace="http://schemas.microsoft.com/VisualStudio/2008/DslTools/Core" />
  <!-- PipeLineDesignModel -->
  <xsd:element name="pipeLineDesignModel" type="PipeLineDesignModel"
substitutionGroup="core:modelElement" />
  <xsd:complexType name="PipeLineDesignModel">
    <xsd:annotation>
      <xsd:documentation>The root in which all other elements are embedded. Appears
a diagram.</xsd:documentation>
    </xsd:annotation>
    <xsd:complexContent>
      <xsd:extension base="core:ModelElement">
        <xsd:sequence minOccurs="0" maxOccurs="1">
        <!-- Relationship: PipeLineDesignModelHasElements -->
        <xsd:element name="elements" minOccurs="0" maxOccurs="1">
          <xsd:annotation>
            <xsd:documentation>Instances of
PipeLineDesignModelHasElements</xsd:documentation>
          </xsd:annotation>
          <xsd:complexType>
            <xsd:sequence>
              <xsd:choice minOccurs="0" maxOccurs="unbounded" >
                <xsd:element ref="pipeLineDesignModelHasElements">
```

Figure5: *Readable XML nodes*

The names in each of the XML nodes havethe same name as it is in the domain class name. For example, *PipelineDesignModels* and *PipelineDesignSystem*properties such as Name, diameter, position etc. are serialized as attributes in the XML nodes.

The relationships between the core model elements are at the same time embedded and serialized as XML nodes inside the core of the framework. For example, in the XML, this is represented by the node named *PipelineDesignModeHasElements* andin the DSL Definition, this part can befound at the *DomainRelationship* class. The result of the relationship is a serialized content of the target code at the code generation level and then a reusable editor platform showcasing different parts of the model and diagram files.

4.2. Discussion of Results

The Code Generator drives the solution created with model to the possible layer of reusable software with interconnected interface of domain notations. These notations which are familiar with users and representing the domain model, i.e. the engineering design are carefully scripted in the interfaces for ease of use. Having applied C# *SerializableAttribute Moniker*class which creates a strong name for the components, single assemblies were formed basically to link the logically related code into independent layers that also makes it easy to capture specific pieces of inputsinto the core domain model as shown in figure 6.

The salient technical characteristics of the domain prevalent in the domain model clarify the identity of the concepts and associated rules. These are relational abstraction rules from which the relevant vocabulary is created in terms of the physical products structures and attributes in the model such as the Domain Classes, Connectors and Elements and the concrete syntax in form of notations about the key words describing concepts mapped to design symbols.

The Code Generator actually generates all the codes that will drive the solution created with the MS VMSDK modeling tool. The models drives the template files (.tt) which drive the resultant compile (.cs) files which are the actual compiler files working the resultant language model. To build the solution model, all templates were transformed to ensure that the model items are captured and updated in the code generator; and then build and debugged to see the user experience as shown in figure 4 above.

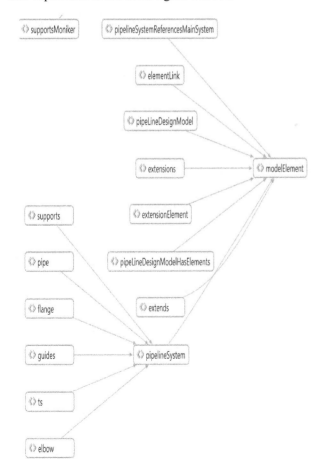

Figure6: *Core Domain Model XML Schema*

5. Conclusion and Future Work

This framework is applicable in the physical design of objects in the engineering industry. It will produce artifacts that will help engineers manage very complex design concepts. The core part of it is built on the DSL processor engine that compiles the DSL Builder files at the core. At the Development Interface, the templates are created for every change or line added to our model. The abstractions would offer benefits such as removing the difficulties in creating engineering designs currently experienced bynon-professional CAD users.It will in line, remove hassles and complexities of expertise centric design platforms.

As work progresses with accompanying requirements elicitation in the pipelines design domain, we will extend the proposed approach for more concrete language specifications that can enable editing actions that directly modify the abstract syntax tree. In such away, the consideration will be directed along framework extensions involvingtransformation of the DSL models and implementation results that justify stakeholder's perspectives. As much asUML profiles provide powerful mechanismsfor modelling, in the future,use-cases will be avoided as much as possible to drive home our focus on both the concepts of the problem domain as well as the technical contents of the application domains as opposed to code centric diagram definition standard to resolving deficiencies prevalent with the object management group (OMG). The aim would be to provide engineers with hands on modeling tool with which they can readily develop designs and related systems.

References

[1] Autodesk Inc. (2013) AutoCAD Release 2013 Programmers Reference Manual.

[2] Alessandro NADDEO (2010), Cad Active Models: AnInnovative Method in Assembly Environment, Journalof Industrial Design and Engineering Graphics Volume5 Issue No. 1

[3] Selić, B. (2011), the Theory and Practice of ModellingLanguage Design (for Model-Based Software Engineering), MODELLS 2011 Wellington New Zealand

[4] Seifert, D., Dahlweid, M. and Santen, T. (2011), AFORMULA for Abstractions and AutomatedAnalysis, Wellington New Zealand MODELS 2011

[5] Melgoza, E. L., Rosell, A. (2012), An integrated parameterized tool for designing a customized tracheal stentComputer-Aided Design, Vol. 44, Issue 12, pp.1173-1181

[6] Giachetti, G., Marín, B. and Pastor, O. (2009), Integration of domain- specific modelling languages andUML through UML profile extension mechanism, Int'lJournal of Computer Science and Applications, Vol. 6,No. 5, pp. 145-174.

[7] Vangheluwe, H. (2010), Domain-Specific ModellingLanguage Engineering, Lisboa, Portugal

[8] Deng, J., Hormann, K. and Kazhdan, M. (2012), Geometric Modeling and Processing, Computer Aided Geometric Design, Volume 29, Issue 7, October 2012, 421.

[9] Leake, J. (2012), Engineering Design Graphics:Sketching, Modeling, and Visualization. John Wiley &Sons, Inc. USA.

[10] Stavric, M. and Marina, O. (2011), Parametric Modeling for Advanced Architecture, International Journalof Applied Mathematics and Informatics, UniversityPress 9 16.

[11] John Charlery, Chris D. Smith, An approach tomodeling domain-wide information,based on limited points' data – part I, American Journal ofSoftware Engineering and Applications 2013, 2(2):pp32-39www.sciencepublishinggroup.com/j/ajsea)

[12] Lockhart, S. and Johnson, C. (2012), Engineering Design Communications: Conveying Design throughGraphics (2nd Edition), Prentice Hall, USA.

[13] Douglas C. Schmidt (2006) Model-Driven EngineeringVanderbilt University, the IEEE ComputerSociety

[14] Nicola CAPPETTI (2010), Parametric Model ofLumbar Vertebra, Journal of IndustrialDesign andEngineering Graphics Vol. 5, Issue No. 2.

[15] Mernik, M, Heering, J., Sloane, A. M. (2005) Whenand how to Develop Domain-Specific Languages,ACM Computing Surveys Vol. 37, No. 4, pp. 316-34.

[16] Baker, S. D. and Slaby, J. M. (2006), Domain-SpecificModeling Languages for EnterpriseDRE SystemJournal of Computers, IEEE Computer Society 2006

[17] Kelly, S. (2007), Domain-Specific Modeling Languages: Moving from Writing Code to Generating It,[DSM Forum, 2007] "DSM Tools."

[18] SannaSivonen (2008), Domain-specific modellinglanguage and code generator for developing repository-based Eclipse plug-ins, VTT Technical ResearchCentre of Finland

[19] Gustavo C. M. Sousa Fábio M. Costa Goiânia-GOPeter J. Clarke Andrew A. Allen (2012),Model-Driven Development of DSML Execution Engines, Proceedings of ACM Conference,eduMRT '12, Innsbruck, Austria

[20] Markus Völter (2008) Domain Specific LanguagesImplementation Techniques voelter@acm.orghttp://se.radio.net

[21] Petru DUMITRACHE (2011), Parametric Modeling of Rops/Fops Protective StructuresGeometryInOrder To Study Of Their Behaviour Using FiniteElement Method, Journal of Industrial Design andEngineering Graphics Vol. 6, Issue No.

4

Contributions to the adoption of a service-oriented architecture in an autarchy

Paul Andre da Fonseca Moreira Coelho, Rui Manuel da Silva Gomes

Escola Superior de Tecnologia e Gestão, Instituto Politécnico de Viana do Castelo, 4900-348, Viana do Castelo, Portugal

Email address

padfmc@gmail.com (P. A. d. F. Moreira Coelho), rgomes@estg.ipvc.pt (R. M. d. S. Gomes)

Abstract: The implementation of e-Government in public administration allows the development of more service channels with its suppliers and relationships with its citizens, promoting a safe service and securing the confidentiality of information. Service-oriented architecture (SOA) is a new way of developing systems that promotes a shift from writing software to assembling and integrating services. By adopting an SOA approach and implementing it using supporting technologies, companies can build flexible systems that implement changing business processes quickly, and make extensive use of reusable components. In this paper we describe the approach we followed in adopting an SOA in an autarchy with regard to the implementation of a process of public procurement integrated with the existing systems. We present the steps followed, the difficulties and the advantages of this integration, pointing out the facilitator role of Web services in the design and implementation of the Service.

Keywords: SOA, Integration, Services, Business Processes, Public Administration

1. Introduction

The service-oriented architecture (SOA) approach is the latest in a long series of attempts in software engineering that try to foster the reuse of software components [1]. The SOA is a new way of developing systems that promotes a shift from writing software to assembling and integrating services [2].

As reported by [3], SOA can be viewed from three different perspectives:

- The business perspective: Set of provided services by an organization to its stakeholders;
- The architecture perspective: An architectural view which consists of a service provider, a requester, and a service discovery;
- The implementation perspective: Set of standards, tools, and technologies, such as Web services.

SOA usually refers to an organizational ICT architecture whose unifying or coherent form serves the purpose of organizing and designing the construction, selection and interconnection of hardware, software and communications assets of the enterprise. With [1], we wish to stress the fact that as an enabler of application integration, it brings an undisputable strategic value. Technically, the main components of SOA are:

- The service directory, where all information about all available services is maintained;
- The service provider, which aims to offer services by putting appropriate entries into the service directory;
- The service requester, which uses the service directory to find an appropriate service, i.e. a service that matches its requirements. Some of the most important standards are:
- SOAP (Simple Object Access Protocol) defines a mechanism for communicating with the Web services over the Internet. It deals with the format of the messages exchanged between the service requester, the service provider and the service directory.
- WSDL (Web Services Description Language) defines the structure and the contents of the service directory. Two related pieces of this standard are: 1) service types which are typically standardized by standards; and 2) actual business information.
- UDDI (Universal Description, Discovery, and Integration) provides the capability to describe a Web

service, without the need to have it formally standardized. A WSDL description of a Web service provides all information needed to actually invoke it [4].

SOA simplifies the development of enterprise applications as modular, reusable business services that align existing information technology infrastructure and systems to achieve end-to-end enterprise integration by removing redundancies, generating collaboration tools, and streamlining information technology processes. By adopting an SOA approach and implementing it using supporting technologies, companies can build flexible systems that implement changing business processes quickly, and make extensive use of reusable components [5]. SOA supports an information environment built upon loosely coupled, reusable, standards-based services. Increased interoperability, increased business and technology domain alignment, increased return on investment, and increased organizational agility are all benefits of an SOA approach [6].

Although many organizations are considering adopting SOA, some are doing this from a purely IT perspective, while others are really looking for a new way to do business. ITs make up a part of the main budget of many businesses, especially those that offer financial services. They affect all aspects of these organizations, including the costs of daily transaction, but they give very good results in terms of efficiency. They allow interdisciplinary collaboration through the company's business, and this leads to better inter-departmental cooperation, better information sharing, and greater capacity for internal union in order to compete in the market. They improve many business processes, they increase productivity throughout the organization, and they lead to more productive and more efficient processes, whether internal or related to commercial partners and customers. An SOA is difficult to implement, manage and control, not because of the technology but due to the organizational, cultural and behavioral aspects that guarantee the SOA's success. Despite the huge progress that has been made with the standards, tools for support and development, and run-time platforms, some issues are still to be solved. These include support for transactions, delays in execution times, safety concerns, and many others.

Organizations have to establish an approach to SOA architecture in which their processes and the control of their business architecture adjusts to the requirements of the SOA. The application of an SOA in businesses depends on their level of maturity regarding the existing architecture and applications. The adoption of an SOA in a given project can be an integration or a partial or full migration, depending on the costs, relevance and life-span of the original applications [7], [8], [9], [10], [11].

The SOA is fundamental for the modernization and optimization of any business. The orientation of an SOA for a business aims to define its services with the business context always in mind. The business defines the policy for the development of new SOA projects, it establishes priorities with regard to business needs and the strategy for orienting services, either by integration or full or partial migration, which is a key factor in the evaluation of the benefits that an SOA brings to the organization [12].

The SOA is an architecture that establishes a new paradigm for information systems, one which is closer to the real business needs of a company, allowing its business processes to be independent from technology, based on the concept of service.

2. Case Study

In an ideal system, the ITs should be the means by which these services are supported, not factors that condition the modelling of procedures. Taking into account the advantages of SOAs and the need to speed up the processes related to the providers of public administration, here we present the following approach for the integration of a platform for public procurement with the existing systems in an autarchy, adopting an SOA.

2.1. Research Method

Olesen and Myers' research [13], which investigates the relationship between the introduction of groupware into an organization and the consequent changes in individuals' work habits and the structure of the organization, was supported by action-research method. The authors argued that the method "enables a researcher to intervene in the organization while at the same time generate knowledge about the process." (p. 321). They approached research in an interpretive manner, which allowed them to focus their research on how individuals attempted to make sense of the specific situation. Like Olesen and Meyers [13], we employed a five-stage action research cycle. The stages are as follows:

- Diagnosing: identifying the research question.
- Action Planning: determining the actions to be undertaken to address the research question.
- Action Taking: conducting and monitoring the planned actions.
- Evaluating: determining if the actions have addressed the research question.
- Specifying Learning: documenting the knowledge obtained by conducting the project.

2.1.1. Diagnosing

The challenges of a society that is intended to be modern and competitive in the global market are directly related with the degree of evolution of each public administration. Faced with the challenges generated by today's knowledge society, it becomes necessary to incorporate and to implement, in a continuous way, technological development and modernization at all levels of activity, from education to culture, also including the business activities. However, by cross- articulation with all of the agents of this society, it is in public administration that this modernization and technological development will be most necessary in terms of the income and efficiency, and transparency and productivity that it will bring to their services.

Considering the advantages of SOAs and the importance of adapting information systems to the real needs of a business, the aim is to carry out a study of the implementation of the architecture that is oriented towards services. The objective is to improve and optimize the procedures and services of the internal workings of an autarchy, as well as those provided to its suppliers and citizens.

PECP is a web platform that controls and manages the processes involved in public procurement through their various stages. Use of the platform is obligatory and acquired from external bodies certified by CEGER (Centre for the Management of the Information Network of the Portuguese Government), and is in accordance with the code of public procurements. The direct stakeholders of the platform are defined as the adjudicating body, in this case the autarchy, which opens to tender the public acquisition procedure (PPA) and manages the platform from the applications point of view; the suppliers, which compete in the PPA; and the jury, which evaluates the proposals submitted and gives its adjudication.

It is necessary to note that this process is not integrated with the autarchy's existing information system as our aim is to adopt an SOA, setting out a new approach and identifying its advantages for the autarchy.

2.1.2. Action Planning

After identifying the objective of the project, the next step was to plan a study and survey of the workings of the autarchy, according to the concept of value chain, proposed by Michael Porter [14], [15].

The process and procedure of public contracts was analyzed, as well as the respective support platform and its sectional and functional interdependencies. An analysis of the existing information system was also planned – applications, data bases and support technologies. The approach to the development of the SOA was selected, with the proposal made by Erl [16] being chosen. This begins with a Top-Down approach, followed by a Bottom-Up approach. The tools needed for the integration of the process of public procurement were identified, mainly with regard to the creation of diagrams that represent the architecture of the information systems and ontology of the organization, IDE[1] of programming, Business Process Modelling [2] with a BPEL[3] extension to describe the interaction between the different applications, and to allow the generation of WSDL and XML to create the web services.

The chosen tools were: Dia [17]; Protégé [18]; Intalio [19] and JDeveloper [20]. The Dia application is an open

source tool which allows the creation of diagrams, flowcharts and organigrams Protégé is an open source platform for editing the ontology of organizations and knowledge data bases. For the representation of the processes, Intalio Designer, an open source framework for BPMN modelling was used. Jdeveloper was selected for the development of the web services, being an IDE in Java of Oracle. This allows the web services to be represented in BPEL through the creation of a project of the JAVA Web Service type. These will be generated later and installed in the application server of the Oracle architecture. The applicational server is managed by the Oracle Enterprise Manager 10g.

2.1.3. Taking

The next stage was to develop the applicational integration following the Top-Down and Bottom-Up approach.

2.1.3.1 Top-Down Analysis

The development stages were as follows:

1st. Define the most relevant elements of the ontology of the Autarchy

In this stage, the ontology of the institution was surveyed in the Protégé framework. The most relevant elements of the organization were considered to be human resources management; management in terms of education, bodies, technologies and information systems (TSI); and management of documents, services and infrastructures. The element 'bodies' includes the executive board, collaborators, citizens and suppliers. The TSI are a key element for the evolution of an organization as they are made up of the active and passive infrastructures, and the Information System software. Documentation management is relevant because all the information regarding processes in the organization is managed through this element.

Services are a major part of the ontological elements since, by definition, they are the organization's reason for existing. This element covers the movements that can be fiscal or counter-orders; work related to infrastructures; complaints; citizens' web area; financial area composed of treasury, accounts and provision elements; cultural promotion; communication service; requests related to sanitation and water supply, library services, availability of cultural and sport venues, licensing, museum, renting, weather services, archive services and transport services. The provisioning element covers the elaboration of the public procurement process which is divided into purchases and payments. The final element is infrastructures, which can be cultural or sport related.

2nd. Align the most relevant business models, according to the analysis made in the first point

In the analysis of the most relevant business models, taking into account the services to be offered to the citizens and the procedures that are important for the institution to function, following the ontology of the institution, the following business processes were identified: licensing request; reception; service request; public procurements;

---

[1]Integrated Development Environment
[2]BPM
[3]Business Process Execution Language

meeting payment; complaints; information.

Licensing requests are defined as the process of requesting the approval and issue of licenses in different areas, such as private building work, business establishments, and advertising, among others. The process of reception consists of procedures for the payment to the institution of services, taxes, licenses, sales or fines on the part of citizens. Service requests are the process of citizens' acquisition of a service from the autarchy. Public procurements are the acquisition of goods and services following the public procurement rules. This is analyzed in detail as it was chosen for the development of an SOA, integrating the PECP platform with the existing systems. Meetings payments make up the process of paying amounts to politicians for their attendance at meetings. Complaints is a process that is covered by law and all citizens can make a complaint if they are not satisfied with the autarchy's services. The information procedure can be a request for or a submission of Information in order to establish communication between the institution and the citizen about any issue.

3rd. Carrying out an analysis regarding services

Based on the processes identified and carrying out an analysis regarding services, bearing in mind the simplification and speeding-up of the processes and business model, the following services were obtained: licensing; treasury; public procurements; service requests; and communication. In the next stage, only the public procurement system is analyzed, following the proposal for this project.

4th. Proceeding to the design regarding services

For the design of the SOA in the top down approach, the process of public procurement was described, presenting all the tasks from the initial acquisition request to the payment for the acquisition of services or goods. For each task, the description, actions carried out, and departments involved were all defined.

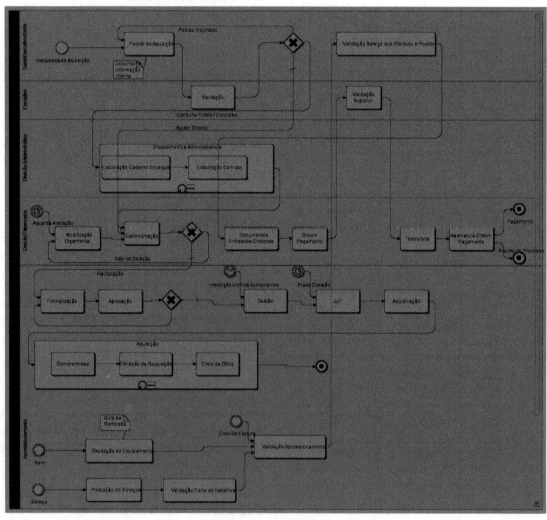

Figure 1. PECP Modelling.

1ˢᵗ Task – Acquisition Request

Description – The acquisition request is made according to the needs of the department and whether it is a direct adjustment, previous consultation, or tender.

Actions – Drawing up of the type of request; appending the technical characteristics.

Department – Any

2nd Task - Validation

Description – The acquisition request is authorized or not.

Actions- Dispatch about the request

Department – Mayor's Office

3rd Task - Administrative Procedures

Description – All the necessary documentation is drawn up for the type of procedure.

Actions - Preparation of the administrative documentation

Department - Administrative

4rd Task - Financial Procedures

Description – The request is validated financially according to the budget and rubric corresponding to the official accounts plan (POCAL).

Actions – The appropriate part for the expenditure is selected.

Department - Financial

5th Task - Formalization

Description – Opening of the PPA (Public Acquisition Procedure)

Actions- A new process is opened; all the documents pertaining to the process are introduced (book of charges)

Department –Supplies

6th Task - Approval

Description – Validates the PPA data

Actions – The approver checks that the PPA is correct; validates the PPA to make it available to the market

Department - Appointments

7th Task - Management

Description – Charged with putting the PPA on the market.

Actions – Communication between candidates and the institution, dealing with doubts and possible changes.

Department - Appointments

8th Task - Jury

Description – Decision about the proposals

Actions – Validate the proposals; Analyze the proposals for the PPA according to the rules of the tender; Chose the winning proposal

Department - Appointments

9th Task - Adjudication

Description – Responsible for registering the intention of adjudication of the system.

Actions – Final validation of the Jury's decision

Department – Executive Board

10thTask - Acquisition

Description – the goods or service are received

Actions – The data related to the management of stocks and register/patrimony are updated; the acquisition is validated by the requesting supplies section

Department – Supplies/Requester

11th Task - Payment

Description – Payment of the acquisition.

Actions - Verification of the documents of the creditor bodies; Elaboration of the payment order; Payment.

Department – Financial and Executive Board

An initial modelling process of the public procurement

process was developed using the application Intalio Designer, Figure 1.

The diagram shows the tasks and respective work flowcharts. The public procurement process is defined as the main pool and the sub-processes are defined as lanes of the departments involved, these being: requesting sector; executive board; administrative division; financial division; supplies.

2.1.3.2 Bottom-Up Analysis

The stages developed were:

1st. Definition of the model for service applications

Give that the information system of the institution possesses different applications and data bases with different architectures, an analysis is made of the interactions between the different technologies in which it makes sense to adopt the bottom up approach. The diagram in Figure 2 shows the various existing architectures and their interconnections.

Regarding the public procurement process this is under study, it became clear that it depends on the document management system - GSP/GSE, of the ERP and on the public procurement platform (PECP) that can be found online. These systems have different architectures that require integration, thus necessitating the creation of web services.

2nd. Proceed to the design of the applications of services defined in the model

In the bottom up approach, the public procurement process encompasses more tasks then the top down approach. This is due to the fact that establishing the integration requires the introduction of stages of interconnection with the different systems. The new tasks were: putting the request in the document management system; putting the request in the ERP; putting in the PECP; updating the acquisition in the ERP; registering the acquisition in the ERP.

1st Task - Putting the request in the document management system

Description – Send through the document management system

Actions- Putting the request in the document management system; appending technical documentation

Department - Any

2nd Task - Putting the request in the ERP

Description – The request is introduced in the financial management application

Actions – Putting in the ERP

Department - Financial

3rd Task - Putting in the PECP

Description – The request is introduced in the PECP

Actions – Putting the process in the PECP

Department - Supplies

4th Task - Updating the acquisition in the ERP

Description – The request is introduced in the ERP

Actions - The ERP is updated with the winning proposal; the winning body is attributed to the tender in the ERP.

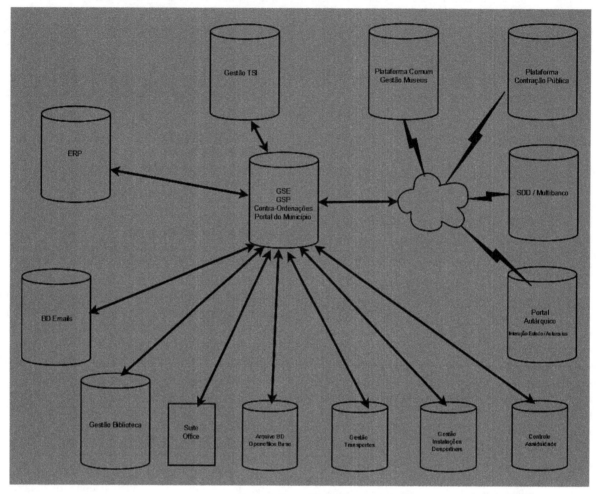

Figure 2. *Bottom Up Analysis.*

Department – Supplies

5th Task - Registering the acquisition in the ERP

Description – Registering the acquisition in the ERP. The data relating to the management of stocks and register/patrimony are updated.

Actions – Registering in the ERP management of stocks module; Registering in the ERP register/patrimony module.

Department - Supplies

The modelling in the Intalio Designer shows the introduction of new tasks in the BPMN diagram with regard to the respective lanes of the stakeholder departments, Figure 3.

The diagram becomes more complex but it is the only way to take advantage of the existing systems, establishing the interconnection and the orientation to the business model based on the SOA.

2.1.3.3. Implementation

The final phase is the implementation, where the project's web services were developed. The development of the services is carried out based on the new tasks found in the modelling for the integration of the different existing architectures. The need arises to create the following web services: GspGseWS; ErpWS; PecpWS.

The GspWS web service includes methods which allow the integration with the document and process management system (GSP/GSE), the ErpWS web service includes methods which allow the integration with the ERP system, and the PecpWS web service has methods for the PECP.

The IDE JDeveloper allows the diagram and generation of the BPEL code for the creation of the web services.

a) Web service GspGseWS

The GspGseWS web service is composed of the following methods:

- public Vector GspGse_ws(),
- public Vector GspGse_ConfereFatura_ws(Vector res_ParaConferencia).

The GspGse_ws method makes the request in the document management system (GSP/GSE) for the acquisition resulting in a vector composed of the requisition sector, the internal information number, the products required, the units, the values, the justification for the acquisition, date of the request and a Boolean according to whether the acquisition is approved or not.

The GspGse_ConfereFatura_ws method verifies the invoice taking as parameter a vector with the sector of the acquisition request, the external information number, the winning supplier, the products to be supplied, the units and the values. A vector is returned with the sector of the acquisition request, internal information number, the observations about the verification of the invoice and the Boolean result of the confirmation.

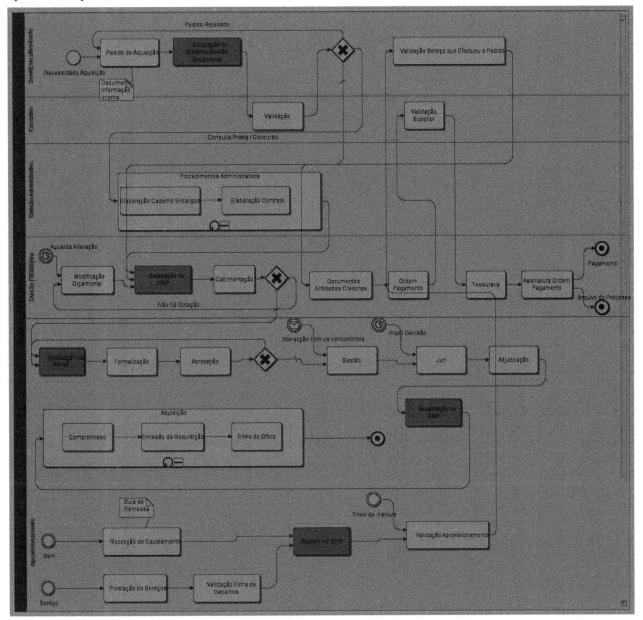

Figure 3. *Bottom Up Modelling PEC.*

What follows is part of the GspGseWS web service code.

....

```
<element name="GspGse_ConfereFatura_wsElement">
    <complexType>
        <sequence>
            <element name="n_inf_int" type="int"/>
            <element name="resultadoPecp"
type="ns1:vector" nillable="true"/>
            <element name="res" type="boolean"/>
        </sequence>
    </complexType>
</element>

    <element
name="GspGse_ConfereFatura_wsResponseElement">
    <complexType>
        <sequence>
            <element name="result" type="ns1:vector"
nillable="true"/>
        </sequence>
    </complexType>
</element>
<element name="GspGse_wsElement">
    <complexType>
        <sequence>
            <element name="setor" type="string"
nillable="true"/>
            <element name="n_inf_int" type="int"/>
            <element name="produtos" type="string"
nillable="true"/>
```

```
                    <element name="unidades" type="int"/>
                    <element name="valores" type="double"/>
                    <element name="justific" type="string"
nillable="true"/>
                    <element name="data" type="dateTime"
nillable="true"/>
                    <element name="res" type="boolean"/>
                </sequence>
            </complexType>
        </element>
        <element name="GspGse_wsResponseElement">
            <complexType>
                <sequence>
                    <element name="result" type="boolean"/>
                </sequence>
            </complexType>
        </element>
    </schema>
```

b) ErpWS Web service

The ErpWS web service is made up of the following methods:

- public Vector Erp_ws(Vector res_erp)
- public Vector Erp_ParaConferencia_ws(Vector resPecp)
- public void Erp_RecebeConferencia_ws(Vector res_Conferencia)

The Erp_ws method makes the register of the acquisition in the ERP, taking as a parameter a vector composed by the requisition sector, the internal information number, the products required, the units, the values, the justification for the acquisition, date of the request and a Boolean according to whether the acquisition is approved or not. It returns as a result a vector with the external information number, the products required, the units and the values.

The Erp_ParaConferencia_ws method receives the information on the adjudication taking as parameters the external information number, the invoice number, the winning supplier, the products to be supplied, the units and the values. It returns a vector with a Boolean that indicates that it was already received for verification, the sector of the acquisition request, and the internal information number.

The Erp_RecebeConferencia_ws method receives as a parameter a vector with the sector of the acquisition request, the internal information number, the observations about the verification of the invoice and the Boolean result of the confirmation.

c) PecpWS Web service

The PecpWS web service is made up of the following methods:

- public void Pecp_ws(Vector Res_erp)
- public Vector PecpResult_ws()

The Pecp_ws method carries out the collocation of the acquisition request in the PECP taking as a parameter a vector composed of the external information number, the products required, the units and the values.

The PecpResult_ws method results in a vector composed of the external information number, the invoice number, the winning supplier, the products to be supplied, the units and the values.

d) BPEL Description of the Process

The public procurement process, in the modelling in BPEL, based on a bottom up approach from the web services, can be described in the following way:

1. The request is made in the GSP which makes the GspGse_ws web service available with the content of the acquisition request;
2. With the result of the web service of point 1, the Erp_ws web service is performed to introduce the acquisition request in the ERP;
3. After validation by the financial area, the result of the information of point 2 is introduced as a parameter in the PECP from the Pecp_ws web service ;
4. From the PecpResult_ws web service, the result of the adjudication of the acquisition of the public procurement platform is made available;
5. After reception of the invoice, the data of the adjudication are put in the Erp_ParaConferencia_ws as parameters. The function returns the document and the results of the adjudication.
6. From the GspGse_ConfereFatura_ws web service it is sent for verification for the GSP/GSE application based on the parameters of the requesting sector and the result of the information of point 5, which in turn returns the result of the validation;
7. Finally the ERP receives the result of the verification from the RecebeConferencia_ws web service in order to proceed to payment of the invoice.

2.1.4. Evaluation

The aim of this project was to contribute to the adoption of an SOA in an autarchy. However, although this is only one step in this process, it seems to us that the use of both top down and bottom up approaches made it possible to analyse the advantages and disadvantages in the decision-making process, having carried out the actions that satisfied the aim.

With the implementation of the adoption of the SOA, in the majority of cases, it is possible to take advantage of the existing applications based on the integration of standard technological mechanisms, thus reducing costs with the evolution in this kind of architecture. The evolution to the SOA allows the dependency of the architecture of the technological layer to be reduced so that it favours the services of the institution's business model. The progressive transition to the SOA also leads to the optimization of human resources and an improvement in the functioning of the processes in the organization, resulting in greater efficiency and speed in the responses to citizens' requests and needs.

The integration of the public procurement system based on an SOA seems to be the solution, as it has the following advantages:

- greater speed in the public procurement processes;
- it avoids the reintroduction of the information in the various systems of applications;
- simplification of the public procurement process;
- greater financial control of the public procurement process;
- more efficient control of the duration of the tenders and their better management;
- dematerialization of the processes. Elimination of paper documentation, allowing the connection between the various systems of applications ;
- speed in the preparation of payments for the acquisition of goods and services;
- future SOA projects, adaptability in incorporating necessary changes and integrations.

2.1.5. Specifying Learning

With the development of this project, we realized the importance of the initial study of the ontology, workings and culture of the organization as it allows detailed knowledge to be acquired, as well as its particular features. It is important to assimilate the existing processes in the organization and identify the interactions that take place with their actors. This kind of survey must be carried out and supported in communication with the different elements of the departments and their functional units. The creation of work teams across the projects facilitates and speeds up the resolution of problems. It is only possible to find a correct and true approach in the organization in this active and participative way, as it becomes crucial in the elaboration of IT projects.

Projects must also begin on a small scale, and then the SOA model can be applied gradually. This form of implementation makes sense given the quantity and complexity the processes and the different application that already exist in organizations. All activity in an organization is defined in processes that establish patterns of response and routine that are appropriately structured and optimized.

In information systems, the applications that are inherited and the various architectures should be analyzed to decide whether there is to be integration or substitution in the new projects. The evaluation needs to be done bearing in mind the question of finances and the impact with regard to the needs of the business. This change should have as little impact as possible but it must always depend on the speed of change in the market.

The implementation of an SOA requires constant supervision, in that it is dynamic and is constantly iteration; for this reason, the governance of the SOA must be an ongoing concern for organizations.

3. Conclusion

In this paper we described an approach followed in the adoption of an SOA in an autarchy with regard to the implementation of the integration of the public procurement process (PECP) with the existing information system in the organization. We presented the activities developed in the diagnosis, action planning, action taking, evaluation, and specifying learning phases.

We reached the conclusion that the adoption of an SOA in an organization must always be oriented by the business itself, even though it is technological; that the methodology has to begin with a Top-Down approach, followed by a Bottom-Up approach, given that the organization has a high number of systems. We also noted that the results achieved were as advantageous with regard to the functioning of the public procurement process, integrated with the existing IS, as in the future development of the SOA in the autarchy.

References

[1] F. Leymann, D. Roller, and M. T.Schmidt, "Web services and business process management," IBM Systems Journal, Vol.41, No.2, 2002.

[2] Z. Mahmood,"Service Oriented Architecture: Potential Benefits and Challenges," Proceedings of the 11th WSEAS International Conference on COMPUTERS, Agios Nikolaos, Crete Island, Greece, July 26-28, 2007.

[3] M. Ibrahim, and G. Long, "Service Oriented Architecture and Enterprise Architecture" IBM developer Works, IBM Corporation, May 2007.

[4] B. Baskerville, M. Cavallari, K. Hjort-Madsen, J. Pries-Heje, M. Sorrentino, and F. Virili, "Extensible Architectures: The Strategic Value of Service Oriented Architecture in Banking," proceeding of European Conference on Information Systems (ECIS), 2005.

[5] IBM, "The Solution Designer's Guide to IBM on Demand Business Solutions," IBM 2005.

[6] N. Bieberstein, S. Bose, M. Fiammante, K. Jones, and R. Shah, *Service Oriented Architecture (SOA) Compass – Business Value, Planning, and Enterprise Roadmap*: IBM Press, published by Pearson plc, 2006.

[7] Chen, F. et al., 2005. Feature analysis for service-oriented reengineering. Software Engineering Conference, 2005.APSEC'05. 12th Asia-Pacific, 15-17, 8 p.

[8] Chung, Davalos, 2007. Service-Oriented Software Reengineering: SoSR. 40th Annual Hawaii International Conference on System Sciences (HICSS'07). p. 172c.

[9] Kontogiannis, K., Lewis, G. and Smith, D., "The Landscape of Service-Oriented systems: A Research Perspective for Maintenance and Reengineering", Site: http://www.cs.vu.nl/csmr2007/workshops/1-%20PositonPaper-SOAM-v2-4.pdf.

[10] Zhang, Z., Lui, R., Yang, H., Service Identification and packaging in service-oriented reengineering. In: Proceedings of Seventeenth International Conference on Software.

[11] Umar, A., Zordan, A., 2008. Reengineering for Service Oriented Architectures: A Strategic Decision Model for Integration Versus Migration. DICS. Fordham University.

[12] Bell, M., 2008. Service-Oriented Modeling - Service Analysis, Design, and Architecture. New Jersey. Wiley.

[13] K. Olesen and M.D. Myers, Trying to improve communication and collaboration with information technology: An action research project which failed. Information Technology and People, 12(4),1999, pp. 317–328.

[14] Michael Porter, Competitive Advantage, Free Press, New York, 1985.

[15] Michael Porter, Strategy and the Internet, Harvard Business Review, March 2001.

[16] Erl, T., 2008. SOA Principles of Service Design. Boston. Prentice Hall.

[17] Dia, <http://projects.gnome.org/dia/>.

[18] Protégé, <http://protege.stanford.edu/>.

[19] Intalio, BPM <http://www.intalio.com/bpms/designer

[20] JDeveloper, Java SOA <http://www.oracle.com>.

5

Generic object recognition using graph embedding into a vector space

Takahiro Hori, Tetsuya Takiguchi, Yasuo Ariki

Graduate School of System Informatics, Kobe University, Japan

Email address:

horitaka@me.cs.scitec.kobe-u.ac.jp (T. Hori), takigu@kobe-u.ac.jp (T. Takiguchi), ariki@kobe-u.ac.jp (Y. Ariki)

Abstract: This paper describes a method for generic object recognition using graph structural expression. In recent years, generic object recognition by computer is finding extensive use in a variety of fields, including robotic vision and image retrieval. Conventional methods use a bag-of-features (BoF) approach, which expresses the image as an appearance frequency histogram of visual words by quantizing SIFT (Scale-Invariant Feature Transform) features. However, there is a problem associated with this approach, namely that the location information and the relationship between keypoints (both of which are important as structural information) are lost. To deal with this problem, in the proposed method, the graph is constructed by connecting SIFT keypoints with lines. As a result, the keypoints maintain their relationship, and then structural representation with location information is achieved. Since graph representation is not suitable for statistical work, the graph is embedded into a vector space according to the graph edit distance. The experiment results on two image datasets of multi-class showed that the proposed method improved the recognition rate.

Keywords: Generic Object Recognition, Graph Edit Distance, SIFT

1. Introduction

Generic object recognition means that the computer recognizes objects real world images by their general name (see Fig. 1). It is one of most challenging tasks in the field of computer vision. Regarding the achieving of near-human vision by a computer, it is expected that any such technology will be applied to robotic vision. Moreover, due to the spread of digital cameras and the development of high-capacity hard disk drives in recent years, it is getting difficult to classify and to retrieve large-volume videos and images manually. Therefore, computers are being looked at to assist in automatically classifying and retrieving videos and images. In particular, generic object recognition is becoming more and more important.

There have been two typical approaches in the past concerning general object recognition. One is a method based on image segmentation. This is a technique for automatic annotation to the segmented image area, word-image-translation model by Barnard [1, 2, 3]. However, when the image has occlusion and the image segmentation fails, it becomes difficult for this technique to work correctly.

On the other hand, to solve this problem, a method based on the local pattern is proposed. This is a technique for collating the image by combining local features of the image. The technique for characterizing the entire image is often used for the appearance frequency histogram of the localizing features (known as Bag of Features, as shown in Fig. 2 [4]). However, there is a problem with this approach because the location information and the relationships between keypoints are lost.

Figure 1. Generic object recognition.

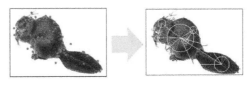

Figure 2. Bag of features.

To deal with this problem, we propose a method in this paper to connect keypoints with lines, as shown in Fig. 4, and to express the sets of the local features as a graph. Moreover, we propose a technique with high recognition performance that integrates the object structure and the local features by embedding the graph into a vector space using the graph edit distance (GED). Thus, the objects are expressed by a simple vector of the statistical work, and trained and classified by Support Vector Machine (SVM). The results of our object recognition experiments show the effectiveness of our method.

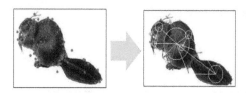

Figure 4. *Graph construction.*

This paper is organized as follows. In Sections 2, 3, 4, and 5, the proposed method is described. In Section 6, the performance of the proposed method is evaluated for a 10-class image dataset. Section 7 provides a summary and discusses future work.

2. Overview of the Proposed Method

Fig. 3 shows the system overview. First, the SIFT keypoints and features [5] of all images are extracted. The extracted keypoints are connected and a graph of each image is constructed. The graphs constructed from the training images are called training graphs and those of the test images test graphs. Next, n prototype graphs are selected from the training graphs, and GED is calculated n times between the prototype graphs and each graph (training graphs and test graphs). Thus, the graphs are embedded into an n-dimensional vector space. The classifier is trained by the n-dimensional vectors of the training images. Finally, the test data is classified by the trained classifier and the recognition result is output. In the following sections, each process in the proposed method is described in detail.

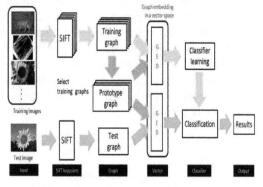

Figure 3. *System overview.*

3. Graph Structural Expression

In this paper, we use the notation and structural representation of the graph proposed in [6]. In the formalization, the graph is noted as G = (V, E, X) where E represents the set of edges, V is the set of vertices and X the set of their associated unary measurements (in our case, a SIFT descriptor). The node is a keypoint detected by SIFT, and the associated unary measurements represent the 128-dimension SIFT descriptor of the corresponding keypoints. Hence, prototype graphs Gp and other graphs (called scene graph Gs) are distinguished. Similarly, we denote the set of nodes of the prototype graph by

$$V^p = \{u_1, u_2, ..., u_\alpha, ...\} \qquad (1)$$

whereas the nodes of the scene graph are written with

$$V^s = \{v_1, v_2, ..., v_i, ...\} \qquad (2)$$

Note that the subscript variables associated to the nodes also differ: we have used a Latin subscript for the scene nodes and a Greek subscript for prototype nodes. The associated unary measurements $x_\alpha \in X^p$ and $x_i \in X^s$ are treated the same way. Also, an edge between two nodes u_α and u_β is denoted as $e_{\alpha\beta}$ (e_{ij} for an edge of the scene graph). Finally, the assignment of a scene node v_i to a prototype node u_α during the matching process is represented with the notation $v_i \rightarrow u_\alpha$.

3.1. Proximity Graph

It is a complete graph if all the keypoints extracted from the image are connected mutually by the edges. However, it is not usually suitable for the calculation. Additionally, because the relationships between keypoints over a long distance are weak, it is preferable to connect them only within their "neighborhood." Thus, we simply define the proximity graph as a graph in which distant keypoints are not connected. Formally, we restrain the set of edges to:

$$E = \left\{ e_{ij} \middle| \forall i, j \ \frac{\|\mathbf{p}_i - \mathbf{p}_j\|}{\sqrt{\sigma_i \sigma_j}} \right\} < \chi \qquad (3)$$

where $\mathbf{p} = (p_x, p_y)$ denotes a keypoint position, σ its scale, and χ is a constant. By this definition, the larger scale keypoints connect to the more distant keypoints. The edge is not drawn in case where the value is longer than constant χ. Because an extra edge is not drawn by this constraint, the constructed proximity graph reduces the computation load considerably, and improves the detection performance at the same time. Both the prototype graphs and the scene graphs are constructed as proximity graphs.

3.2. Pseudo-Hierarchical Graph

In general, when the scale is large, the SIFT features show high reliability. Therefore, the proximity graph is divided into the hierarchy by the size of the scale of the keypoints. This is defined as a pseudo-hierarchical graph. The improvement in recognition and computation performance is achieved by starting the graph matching from a hierarchical level that has high reliability, and going down the hierarchy gradually. We decompose the graph into a set of subgraphs $\{G_l\}_{l=1}^L$ based on the scale of the keypoints. For each level l, only the features whose scale is superior to a threshold s_l are retained.

$$s_l = \sigma_{min}\left(\frac{\sigma_{max}-\sigma_{min}}{\sigma_{min}}\right)^{\frac{L-l}{L-1}} \quad (4)$$

where σ_{max} and σ_{min} are the maximum and minimum scale of the keypoints in each graph. Fig. 5 shows an example of subgraph $\{G_l\}_{l=1}^3$ divided into three hierarchical levels. Note that only the prototype graphs are decomposed to the pseudo-hierarchical graphs.

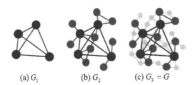

(a) G_1 (b) G_2 (c) $G_3 = G$

Figure 5. Pseudo-Hierarchical Graph.

4. Graph Edit Distance

The process of evaluating the structural similarity of two graphs is generally referred to as graph matching. This issue has been addressed by a large number of studies [7]. We use the graph edit distance [8, 9], one of the most widely used methods, to compute the difference between two graphs [10, 11, 12]. A pseudo-hierarchical graph is employed in order to improve the computational complexity of graph edit distance.

The basic idea of the graph edit distance is to define the difference of two graphs as the minimum amount of edit operations required to transform one graph into the other. Namely, it is computed using the number of edit operations composed of insertion, deletion, and substitution of nodes and edges. Two graphs G_1 and G_2 have the edit path $h(G_1, G_2) = (e_{d1}, ..., e_{dk})$ (each e_{di} indicates the edit operation) to convert G_1 into G_2 using specific editing. Fig. 6 shows the example of an edit path between two graphs G_1 and G_2. Each edit cost c is defined as the amount of the distortion in the transformation. The graph edit distance between graphs G_1 and G_2 is computed as

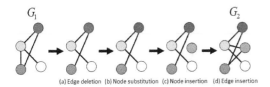

(a) Edge deletion (b) Node substitution (c) Node insertion (d) Edge insertion

Figure 6. An edit path between two graphs.

$$d(G_1, G_2) = \min_{(e_{d1}, ..., e_{dk})\in h(G_1,G_2)} \sum_{i=1}^k c(e_{di}) \quad (5)$$

where $c(e_d)$ denotes the penalty cost of the edit operation e_d. The final complete matching procedure is summarized in Fig. 7.

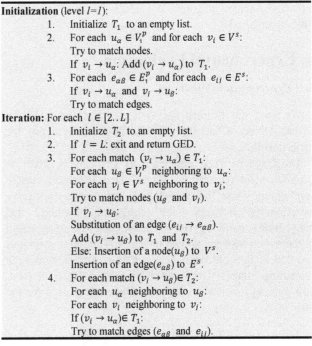

Initialization (level *l=1*):
1. Initialize T_1 to an empty list.
2. For each $u_\alpha \in V_1^p$ and for each $v_i \in V^s$:
   Try to match nodes.
   If $v_i \to u_\alpha$: Add $(v_i \to u_\alpha)$ to T_1.
3. For each $e_{\alpha\beta} \in E_1^p$ and for each $e_{ij} \in E^s$:
   If $v_i \to u_\alpha$ and $v_j \to u_\beta$:
   Try to match edges.

Iteration: For each $l \in [2..L]$
1. Initialize T_2 to an empty list.
2. If $l = L$: exit and return GED.
3. For each match $(v_i \to u_\alpha) \in T_1$:
   For each $u_\beta \in V_l^p$ neighboring to u_α:
   For each $v_j \in V^s$ neighboring to v_i;
   Try to match nodes (u_β and v_j).
   If $v_j \to u_\beta$:
   Substitution of an edge ($e_{ij} \to e_{\alpha\beta}$).
   Add $(v_j \to u_\beta)$ to T_1 and T_2.
   Else: Insertion of a node(u_β) to V^s.
   Insertion of an edge($e_{\alpha\beta}$) to E^s.
4. For each match $(v_j \to u_\beta) \in T_2$:
   For each u_α neighboring to u_β:
   For each v_i neighboring to v_j:
   If $(v_i \to u_\alpha) \in T_1$:
   Try to match edges ($e_{\alpha\beta}$ and e_{ij}).

Figure 7. Graph edit distance algorithm.

5. Graph Embedding in a Vector Space

The embedding method used in this paper follows the procedure proposed by [13]. This technique is used for the computation of the median graph etc., and the effectiveness is shown in [14, 15]. The approach is described as follows, and the outline is shown in Fig. 8. We prepare a set of the training graphs $T = \{G_1, G_2, ..., G_n\}$, and compute the graph edit distance $d(G_i, G_j)$ $(i, j = 1, ..., n; G_1, G_2 \in T)$. First, the set of the m prototype graphs $P = \{G_1^p, G_2^p, ..., G_m^p\}$ is selected from $T(m \le n)$. Next, the graph edit distance between scene graph G^s and prototype graphs $G^p \in P$ is calculated. As a result, the m graph edit distances $d_1, ..., d_m$ $(d_k = d(G^s, G_k^p))$ to the scene graph are obtained and assumed to form the m dimensional vector D. Thus, all scene graphs G^s can be embedded into the m dimensional vector space by using prototype graph set P. It can be described as follows:

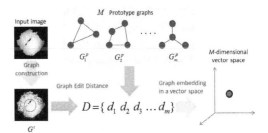

Figure 8. Graph embedding in a vector space.

$$\psi: G^s \to \mathrm{R}^m \quad (6)$$

$$\psi \to (d(G^s, G_1^p), d(G^s, G_2^p), ..., d(G^s, G_m^p)) \quad (7)$$

where $d(G^s, G_i^p)$ is a graph edit distance. In this paper, a set of the prototype graphs P is selected from a set of the training graphs T.

6. Experimental Evaluation

6.1. Experimental Conditions

We used the Caltech-101 Database and the PASCAL Visual Object Challenge (VOC) 2007 dataset for the experiment.

The Caltech-101 is composed of 101 classes, used for generic object recognition. We selected 10 object classes from among these 101 classes, and carried out comparative experiments between the proposed method and conventional methods (BoF). The examples of images used in the experiment are shown in Fig. 9. The training images were 30 images randomly selected from each class and the remaining images were used as the test images. In total, 300 training images and 541 test images were used for the 10 classes.

Figure 9. *Caltech-101 dataset.*

The PASCAL VOC dataset consists of 9,963 images containing at least one instance of each 20 object categories. It is a benchmark for the general object recognition. These images range between indoor and outdoor scenes, close-ups and landscapes, and strange viewpoints. The dataset is more difficult than Caltech-101 because all the images where the size, viewing angle, illumination, etc. appearances of objects and their poses vary significantly, with frequent occlusions. In the experiment, we used the images cut out from the original one by its bounding boxes. We randomly selected 10 object classes, and carried out comparative experiments using 4,986 training images and 4,963 test images. The examples of images of PASCAL are shown in Fig. 10.

Figure 10. *PASCAL Visual Object Challenge (VOC) 2007 dataset.*

The threshold χ, hierarchical level L of pseudo-hierarchical graphs, and edit cost c of the graph edit distance were used as the best value in the experiment. As a set of the prototype graphs, a set of the training graphs employed for the Caltech tasks. Because the number of training images was 300, all the images were embedded into the 300 dimension vector spaces. For the PASCAL tasks, the 50 prototype graphs are randomly selected from the training images of each class. On the other hand, the codebook size of the BoF method was 1,000, the best value in the experiment. We used as the classifiers k-Nearest Neighbor algorithm (k=10) and multi-class SVM (linear and radial basis function (RBF)) [16] to classify the vector formed by each method.

6.2. Experimental Results and Discussion

Fig. 11 and Fig. 12 show the recognition results for all classes. As shown these figures, it can be confirmed that the proposed method improved the accuracy. The recognition rate has improved with SVM (RBF) by 13.38%, SVM (linear) by 14.08%, and k-NN by 8.02% in the Caltech tasks, and SVM (RBF) by 4.42%, SVM (linear) by 3.62%, and k-NN by 9.32% in the Pascal tasks, compared to the conventional method BoF.

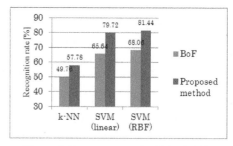

Figure 11. *Recognition results (Caltech-101).*

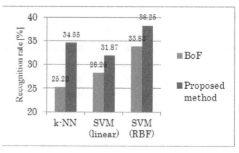

Figure 12. *Recognition results (PASCAL).*

Fig. 14, Fig. 15 and Fig. 16 show the recognition results for each class. As shown in these figures, the recognition rates of leopards, soccer ball, stop sign, and umbrella were greatly improved.

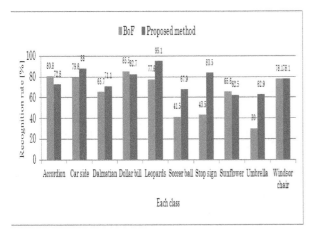

Figure 14. Recognition results of each class using SVM (RBF).

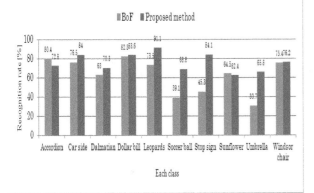

Figure 15. Recognition results of each class using SVM (linear).

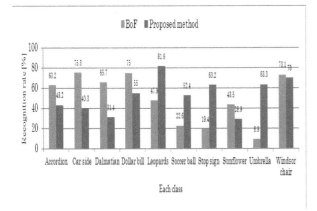

Figure 16. Recognition results of each class using k-NN.

This is because the conventional method uses only SIFT features, so it is strongly influenced by the accuracy of these features. The SIFT features respond strongly to the corners and intensity gradients, so it is not appropriate when they are scarce. In contrast, the proposed method can represents the shape and structure of the object using the graph. Fig. 13 shows the images that was recognized by the proposed method and was not recognized by the conventional method.

Figure 13. Examples of images which were recognized using the proposed method and were not recognized using the conventional method.

In Fig. 16, the recognition rates of accordion, car side, dalmatian, and dollar bill were decreased compared with BoF. However, this decrease is improved in Fig. 14 and Fig. 15. Therefore, the proposed method with SVM can demonstrate the better performance.

Figure 13. Examples of images which were recognized using the proposed method and were not recognized using the conventional method.

7. Conclusion

In this paper, we proposed a new method to recognize generic objects by incorporating graph structural expression by embedding a graph into the vector spaces. By employing the graph structure of the object, the class recognition became robust to the SIFT features variance. As a result, the recognition accuracy was improved considerably compared to the conventional method in the experiments of two datasets. In the future, we will study the selection method of more effective prototype graphs and the method of reducing calculation cost for graph edit distance. Moreover, we are planning to extend this proposed method to three-dimensional graphs and general object recognition using three-dimensional information.

References

[1]   K. Barnard and D. A. Forsyth, "Learning the semantics of words and pictures," Proc. of IEEE International Conf. on Computer Vision, pp. 408–415, 2001.

[2]   K. Barnard, P. Duygulu, N. de Freitas, and D. Forsyth, "Matching words and pictures," Journal of Machine Learning Research, vol. 3, pp. 1107–1135, 2003.

[3]   P. Duygulu, K. Barnard, N. de Freitas, and D. Forsyth, "Visual categorization with bags of keypoints," Proc. of European Conference on Computer Vision, pp. 97–112, 2002.

[4]   G. Csurka, C.R. Dance, L. Fan, J. Willamowski, and C. Bray, "Object Recognition as Machine Translation: Learning Lexicons for a Fixed Image Vocabulary," Proc. of ECCV workshop on Statistical Learning in Computer Vision, pp. 1–22, 2004.

[5]   D. G. Low, "Distinctive image features from scale invariant keypoints," Journal of Computer Vision, vol. 60, pp. 91–110, 2004.

[6]   J. Revaud, Y. Ariki, and A. Baskurt, "Scale-Invariant Proximity Graph for Fast Probabilistic Object Recognition,"

Proc. of Conference on Image and Video Retrieval, pp. 414–421, 2010.

[7] D. Conte, P. Foggia, C. Sansone, and M. Vento, "Thirty years of graph matching in pattern recognition," International Journal of Pattern Recognition and Artificial Intelligence, vol. 8, pp. 265–298, 2004.

[8] H. Bunke and G. Allerman, "Inexact graph matching for structural pattern recognition," Pattern Recognition Letters, vol. 1, pp. 245–253, 1983.

[9] A. Sanfeliu and K. Fu, "A distance measure between attributed relational graphs for pattern recognition," IEEE Transactions on Systems, Man, and Cybernetics, vol. 13, pp. 353–362, 1983.

[10] D. Justice and A. Hero, "A Binary Linear Programming Formulation of the Graph Edit Distance," IEEE Transactions on Pattern Analysis and Machine Intelligence, vol. 28, pp. 1200–1214, 2006.

[11] M. Neuhaus, K. Riesen, and H. Bunke, "Fast suboptimal algorithms for the computation of graph edit distance," Joint IAPR International Workshops, SSPR and SPR 2006, Lecture Notes in Computer Science, vol. 4109, pp. 163–172, 2006.

[12] K. Riesen and H. Bunke, "Approximate graph edit distance computation by means of bipartite graph matching," Image and Vision Computing, vol. 27, pp. 950–959, 2009.

[13] K. Riesen, M. Neuhaus, and H. Bunke, "Graph Embedding in Vector Spaces by Means of Prototype Selection," Graph-based representations in pattern recognition (GbRPR), F. Escolano et al, Ed., Springer-Verlag Berlin, Heidelberg, pp. 383–393, 2007.

[14] E. Valveny and M. Ferrer, "Application of Graph Embedding to solve Graph Matching Problems," Proc. of CIFED, pp. 13–18, 2008.

[15] M. Ferrer, E. Valveny, F. Serratosa, K. Riesen, and H.Bunke, "Generalized median graph computation by means of graph embedding in vector spaces," Pattern Recognition, vol. 43, pp. 1642–1655, 2010.

[16] C. Cortes and V. Vapnik, "Support-Vector Networks," Machine Learning, vol. 20, pp. 273–297, 1995.

6

A Modified fingerprint image thinning algorithm

Davit Kocharyan

Digital Signal and Image Processing Laboratory
Institute for Informatics and Automation Problems of NAS RA, Yerevan, Armenia

Email address:
david.kocharyan@gmail.com (D. Kocharyan)

Abstract: Most fingerprint recognition applications rely heavily on efficient and fast image enhancement algorithms. Image thinning is a very important stage of image enhancement. A good thinning algorithm preserves the structure of the original fingerprint image, reduces the amount of data needed to process and helps improve the feature extraction accuracy and efficiency. In this paper we describe and compare some of the most used fingerprint thinning algorithms. Results show that faster algorithms have difficulty preserving connectivity. Zhang and Suen's algorithm gives the least processing time, while Guo and Hall's algorithm produces the best skeleton quality. A modified Zhang and Suen's algorithm is proposed, that is efficient and fast, and better preserves structure and connectivity.

Keywords: Image Thinning; Fingerprint Recognition; Minutiae; Image Enhancement

1.Introduction

Fingerprint image thinning is a very important step in fingerprint recognition algorithms. In this step the ridge lines of the fingerprint image are transformed to a one-pixel thickness. This process is fundamental for fingerprint recognition algorithms [1], as thinned images are easier to process, and reduce operations processing time. As thinning does not change the structure of the fingerprint image and preserves the locations of the fingerprint ridge and valley features, it makes easier to identify the global and local features of the fingerprint image (such as Core, Delta, Minutiae points) that are used for fingerprint classification, recognition and matching [2].

An example of thinned fingerprint image is shown in Figure 1 below:

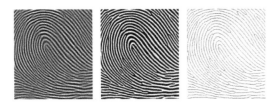

Fig. 1. From left to right: original fingerprint image, binarized image and corresponding thinned image.

An effective and accurate thinning algorithm directly affects the fingerprint feature extraction and matching accuracy and results.

Most known thinning algorithms fall into the following two categories [3]:

- Iterative
- Non-iterative

Iterative algorithms delete pixels on the boundary of a pattern repeatedly until only unit pixel-width thinned image remains. Non-iterative distance transformation algorithms are not appropriate for general applications since they are not robust, especially for patterns with highly variable stroke directions and thicknesses. Thinning based on iterative boundary removal can be divided into sequential and parallel algorithms.

Thinning is mostly done on the binarized image of the fingerprint. The mostly discussed and described thinning algorithms are based on parallel thinning, as they are fast and efficient. In this paper we intend to describe and compare the most used iterative fingerprint thinning algorithms: Zhang-Suen (T. Zhang and C. Suen, "A fast parallel algorithm for thinning digital patterns" *Communications of the ACM*, vol. 27, pp. 236–239, Mar 198),Guo-Hall(Z. Guo and R. Hall, "Parallel thinning with two-subiteration algorithms"*Communications of the ACM*, vol. 32, pp. 359–373, Mar 1989.), Abdulla et al(W. Abdulla, A. Saleh, and A. Morad, "A preprocessing algorithm for hand-written character recognition," *Pattern Recognition Letters 7*, pp. 13–18, 1988.), R. W. Hall(R. Hall, "Fast parallel thinning algorithms: Parallel speed and connectivity preservation,", *Communications of the ACM*, vol. 32, pp. 124–129, Jan 1989.), understand their strengths and weaknesses and propose a modified and more efficient algorithm.

2. Concepts

The binary image I is described as a matrix MxN, where x(i, j) represents the binary value of the pixel (i, j), equal to 1, if the pixel is black, or 0, if the pixel is white.

Any pixel which is at distance of 1 from the pixel (i, j) is considered a neighbor for that pixel.

Connectivity is defined as the number of neighbors to which the pixel is connected:

* 4-connectivity: The pixel is connected to every horizontal and vertical neighbor (Fig. 2).

	1	
1	P1	1
	1	

Fig. 2. 4-connectivity: P1 is is connected to every horizontal and vertical neighbor.

* 8-connectivity: The pixel is connected to every horizontal, vertical and diagonal neighbor (Fig. 3).

1	1	1
1	P1	1
1	1	1

Fig. 3. 8-connectivity:P1 is connected to every horizontal, vertical and diagonal neighbor.

3. Known Thinning Algorithms

In this chapter some known fingerprint thinning algorithms are described.

3.1. Zhang-Suen's Algorithm

The algorithm works using a 3x3 sized block. It is an iterative algorithm and it removes all the contour points of the image except those that belong to the skeleton. The algorithm is divides into two sub-iterations [4].

The algorithm is describes below:
1. While points are deleted, do
2. for all p(i, j) pixels, do

3. if(a)

$$2 \leq B(P_1) \leq 6$$

(b) A(P1) = 1
(c) One of the following is true:
1. P2 x P4 x P6 = 0 in odd iteration,
2. P2 x P4 x P8 = 0 in even iteration,
(d) One of the following is true:
1. P4 x P6 x P8 = 0 in odd iteration,
2. P2 x P6 x P8 = 0 in even iteration,
then
4. Delete pixel p(i, j).

where A(P1) is the number of 0 to 1 transitions in the clockwise direction from P9, B(P1) is the number of non-zero neighbors of P1:

$$B(P_1) = \sum_{i=2}^{9} P_i$$

P1is not deleted, if any of the above conditions are not met.

The algorithm is fast, but fails to preserve such patterns that have been reduced to 2x2 squares. They are completely removed. It also has problems preserving connectivity with diagonal lines and identifying line endings.

3.2. Guo-Hall's Algorithm

The algorithm works using a 2x2 sized block. C(P1) is defined as the number of distinct 8-connected components of P1. [2]B(P1)is defined as the number of non-zero neighbors of P1. , □ and □ symbols are defined as logical completing, AND and OR, respectively. N(P1) is defined as:

$$N(P_1) = MIN[N_1(P_1), N_2(P_1)]$$

where:

$$N_1(P_1) = (P_9 P_2) + (P_3 P_4) + (P_5 P_6) + (P_7 P_8)$$

$$N_2(P_1) = (P_2 P_3) + (P_4 P_5) + (P_6 P_7) + (P_8 P_9)$$

$N_1(P_1)$ and $N_2(P_1)$ divideneighbors of P_1 into four pairs and calculated the number of pairs that contain one or two non-zero elements.

The algorithm is describes below:
1. While points are deleted, do
2. for all p(i, j) pixels, do
3. if(a) C(P1) = 1
(b)

$$2 \leq N(P_1) \leq 3$$

(c) One of the following is true:
1.

$$(P_2 P_3 \bar{P}_5)P_4 = 0$$

in odd iteration,

2.

$$(P_6 P_7 \bar{P}_9) P_8 = 0$$

in even iteration,

then

4. Delete pixelp(i, j).

WhenB(P_1) = 1, P_1 is an ending point and N(P_1) = 1. But whenB(P_1) = 2, P_1 could also be a non-ending point. The definition ofN(P_1) preserves the ending points and remove redundant pixel in the middle of the curve.

Guo-Hall [5]algorithm is more precise than Zhang-Suen's [4] algorithm, but needs more computational time to execute .

3.3. Abdulla et al's Algorithm

The algorithm uses a 3x3 sized block and consists of two sub-iterations [5]. The first sub-iteration scans the image horizontally using a 3x4 sized block (Fig. 4). Any two points which are horizontally adjacent to each other and horizontally isolated from other pixels are deleted. The second sub-iteration scans the image vertically using a 4x3 sized block (Fig. 5). Any two points which are vertically adjacent to each other and vertically isolated from other points are deleted.

P_9	P_2	P_3	P_{10}
P_8	P_1	P_4	P_{11}
P_7	P_6	P_5	P_{12}

Fig. 4. 3x4 sized block.

P_9	P_2	P_3
P_8	P_1	P_4
P_7	P_6	P_5
P_{12}	P_{11}	P_{10}

Fig. 5. 4x3 sized block.

The algorithm is describes below:

1. While points are deleted, do

2. for all pixels p(i, j) do

3. First iteration:

4.if(a)

$$\overline{SP_{1.1}} \ P_6 = 1$$

or

(b)

$$\overline{SP_{1.2}} \ P_2 = 1$$

or

(c)

$$[(P_2 \ \bar{P}_3) \ (P_3) \ \bar{P}_2 \ \bar{P}_9]$$

$$[(\bar{P}_5 \ P_6) \ (P_5 \bar{P}_6 P_7)] = 1$$

then

5.Deletepixel P1.

6.where

$$SP_{1.1} = P_3 P_2 P_9, \ SP_{1.2} = P_6 P_5 P_7$$

$^{-}$, $\Box$ and $\Box$ are defined as logical completing, AND and OR, respectively.

7. ifP1 is not deleted

then

8.if

$$(\bar{P}_3 \ P_{10}) \ (\bar{P}_5 \ P_{12}) = 1$$

then

9. Deletepixel P_4.

10. Second iteration:

11. if(a)

$$\overline{SP_{2.1}} \ P_4 = 1$$

or

(b)

$$\overline{SP_{2.2}} \ P_8 = 1$$

or

(q) $[(P_8 \ \bar{P}_7) \ (P_7) \ \bar{P}_8 \ \bar{P}_9]$

$$[(\bar{P}_4 \ P_5) \ (P_5 \bar{P}_4 P_3)] = 1$$

then

12. Delete pixel P_1.

13.where

$$SP_{2.1} = P_9 P_8 P_7, \ SP_{2.2} = P_3 P_4 P_5$$

$^{-}$, $\Box$ and $\Box$ are defined as logical completing, AND and OR, respectively:

14. ifP1 is not deleted

then

15.if

$$(\bar{P}_7 \ P_{12}) \ (\bar{P}_5 \ P_{10}) = 1$$

then

16. Delete pixel P_6.

3.4. R. W. Hall's Algorithm

The algorithm [6] consists of two parallel sub-iterations, functions by first identifying in parallel all deletable pixels and then in parallel deleting all of those deletable pixels except certain pixels which must be maintained to preserve connectivity in an image.

The algorithm is describes below:

1. While pixels are deleted, do

2. for all pixels p(i, j) do
3. Determine whether p(i, j) should be deleted
4. if (a)

$$1 < B(P_1) < 7$$

(b) P_1 's 8-neighborhood contains exactly one 4-connected component of 1s.
then
5. p(i, j) should be deleted
6. for all p(i, j) pixels, do
7.if(a)

$$P_2 = P_6 = 1$$

and P_4 is deletable,
(b)

$$P_4 = P_8 = 1$$

and P_6 is deletable,
(c)
P_4, P_5, P_6 are deletable,
then
8. Do not delete pixel p(i, j).
The above mentioned conditions preserve local connectivity, end-points and 2x2 sized patterns.

4. Comparison

During the comparison the evaluation is based on the following criteria: connectivity, spurious branches, convergence to unit width and data reduction efficiency/computational cost.

Connectivity preservation of a fingerprint pattern is crucial fingerprint recognition, as disconnected patterns may produce false minutiae points.

Spurious branches also produce false minutiae points. Some post processing operations may be applied to re-

move spurious branches, but it will cost extra processing operations and execution time.

A perfect skeleton must be unitary, meaning that it does not contain any of the patterns given in Figure 6:

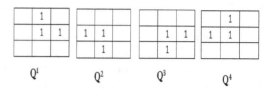

$$Q^1 \qquad Q^2 \qquad Q^3 \qquad Q^4$$

Fig. 6. *Patterns of non-unitary skeletons.*

Jang and Chin [7] introduced a measure m_t to compute the width of the thinned S_m skeleton:

$$m_t = 1 - \frac{Area[\cup_{1 \leq k \leq 4} S_m Q_k]}{Area[S_m]}$$

where Area[] is the operation that counts the number of pixels with the value of 1. If $m_t = 1$, then S_m is a perfect unitary skeleton [7].

An effective thinning algorithm must be also **fast**. A measure to evaluate both the data reduction efficiency and the computational cost was defined by Jang and Chin [7] as:

$$m_d = min[1, \frac{Area[S] - Area[S_m]}{n \; x \; Area[S]}]$$

where n is the number of parallel operations required to converge, and S is the original input image. This measure has a value between 0 and 1. The larger the value, the higher the efficiency [7].

To compare the above described algorithms, they have been applied to thin five different images, shown in Figure 7.

Fig. 7. *Five different fingerprint images used for comparing the thinning algorithms.*

1) 276x408 pixels

2) 408x480 pixels

3) 264x264 pixels

4) 336x336 pixels

5) 420x600 pixels

The results of the values m_t and m_d are given in the table below:

Table 1. *Results of the tests.*

Image	Algorithm	Results	
		m_t	m_d
1	• Abdulla et.al	0.996	0.117
	• Guo-Hall	0.998	0.062
	• Hall	0.991	0.083
	• Zhang-Suen	0.698	0.129
2	• Abdulla et.al	0.974	0.120
	• Guo-Hall	0.997	0.065
	• Hall	0.988	0.085
	• Zhang-Suen	0.790	0.137
3	• Abdulla et.al	0.997	0.122
	• Guo-Hall	0.998	0.061
	• Hall	0.999	0.084
	• Zhang-Suen	0.864	0.130
4	• Abdulla et.al	0.978	0.105
	• Guo-Hall	0.993	0.056
	• Hall	0.993	0.079
	• Zhang-Suen	0.747	0.115
5	• Abdulla et.al	0.985	0.118
	• Guo-Hall	0.997	0.064
	• Hall	0.993	0.085
	• Zhang-Suen	0.695	0.134

The results show that Guo-Hall's algorithm best preserves the structure of the image, but the efficiency and speed is low, giving the result of $m_d = 0.062$, a comparatively low value.

Zhang-Suen's algorithm is the most used in literature and shows an average $m_d = 0.129$.

But in some cases it does not preserve the structure of the image and even removes some ridges and end-points [8].

5. Proposed Modification

We propose a slight modification to the Zhang-Suen's algorithm to improve and preserve structure of the image and stop unwanted removal of lines and end-points.

End-points are detected by the $A(P_1) = 1$, but it does not apply to diagonal ridges that have 2 pixel thickness, as in that case $A(P_1) = 2$. The following conditions can be added to Zhang-Suen's algorithm to eliminate those problems:

In odd iterations: when $A(P_1) = 2$, the following conditions are checked:
1. P4 x P6 = 1 and P9 = 0 or
2. P4 x P2 = 1 and $\bar{P}_3 \, x \, \bar{P}_7 \, x \, \bar{P}_8 = 1$

In even iterations: when $A(P_1) = 2$, the following conditions are checked:
1. P2 x P8 = 1 and P5 = 0 or
2. P6 x P8 = 1 and $\bar{P}_3 \, x \, \bar{P}_4 \, x \, \bar{P}_7 = 1$

These conditions are added to avoid deleting diagonal lines and preserve connectivity.

The modified algorithm is described below:
1. While points are deleted, do

2. for all p(i, j) pixels, do
3. if $2 \leq B(P_1) \leq 6$
4. if $A(P_1) = 1$ and
(a) One of the following is true:

    1. $P_2 \, x \, P_4 \, x \, P_6 = 0$ in odd iteration,

    2. $P_2 \, x \, P_4 \, x \, P_8 = 0$ in even iteration,

(b) One of the following is true:

    1. $P_4 \, x \, P_6 \, x \, P_8 = 0$ in odd iteration,

    2. $P_2 \, x \, P_6 \, x \, P_8 = 0$ in even iteration,

then
5. Delete pixel p(i, j).
6. else if $A(P_1) = 2$ and
(a) One of the following is true:

    1. $P_4 \, x \, P_6 = 1$ and $P_9 = 0$, in odd iteration,

    2. $P_2 \, x \, P_8 = 1$ and $P_5 = 0$, in even iteration,

(b) One of the following is true:

1. P4 x P2 = 1 and $\bar{P}_3 \, x \, \bar{P}_7 \, x \, \bar{P}_8 = 1$ in odd iteration,

2. P6 x P8 = 1 and $\bar{P}_3 \, x \, \bar{P}_4 \, x \, \bar{P}_7 = 1$, in even iteration,

then
5. Delete pixel p(i, j).
where $A(P_1)$ is the number of 0 to 1 transitions in the clockwise direction from P_9, $B(P_1)$ is the number of non-zero neighbors of P_1:

$$B(P_1) = \sum_{i=2}^{9} P_i$$

P_1 is not deleted, if any of the above conditions are not met.

After adding the above mentioned conditions, Zhang Suen's algorithm preserved structure and fairly maintains connectivity. A comparison of skeletons produces by the original algorithm and the modified version is shown in Figure 8, where the corresponding minutiae points are also shown:

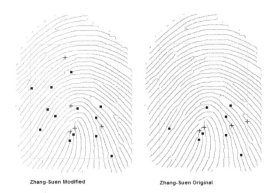

Zhang-Suen Modified   Zhang-Suen Original

Fig. 8. *Left to right: Modified and original versions of Zhang Suen's algorithm.*

A noticeable improvement in maintaining structure and connectivity can be seen.

The modified algorithm has been applied to thin five different images, shown in Figure 7.

The results of the values m_t and m_d are given in the table below:

Table 2. *Results of the tests.*

Image	Results	
	m_t	m_d
1	0.897	0.130
2	0.943	0.132
3	0.976	0.143
4	0.935	0.113
5	0.896	0.136

The modified algorithm shows a noticeable improvement, with average mt= 0.929 and an average $m_d =$ 0.130.

6. Conclusion and Future Work

In this paper we discussed the most used fingerprint thinning algorithms and showed their comparisons. Zhang Suen's [4]. algorithm proves to be the most efficient and with the proposed modification shows the best result among all with regards to the comparison criteria.

As the next step, creation of a fingerprint recognition software solution based on minutiae matching and the proposed thinning algorithm is planned.

Fingerprint recognition is the most widely used biometric authentication and identification technology[10], and heavily relies on efficient image processing algorithms and techniques[11]. It has many applications, from consumer to commercial sectors.

References

[1] Davide Maltoni, Dario Maio, Handbook of Fingerprint Recognition, Springer, 2009.

[2] Z. Guo and R. Hall, "Parallel thinning with two-subiteration algorithms,"Communications of the ACM, vol. 32, pp. 359–373, Mar 1989.

[3] R. Gupta and R. Kaur, "Skeletonization algorithm for numerical patterns", International Jornal of Signal Processing, Image Processing andPattern Recognition, vol. 01, pp. 63–72, Dec 2008.

[4] T. Zhang and C. Suen, "A fast parallel algorithm for thinning digital patterns," Communications of the ACM, vol. 27, pp. 236–239, Mar 1984.

[5] W. Abdulla, A. Saleh, and A. Morad, "A preprocessing algorithm for hand-written character recognition",Pattern Recognition Letters 7, pp. 13–18, 1988.

[6] R. Hall, "Fast parallel thinning algorithms: Parallel speed and connectivity preservation," Communications of the ACM, vol. 32, pp. 124–129, Jan 1989.

[7] B. Jang and T. Chin, "One-pass parallel thinning: Analysis, properties, and quantitative evaluation," IEEE Transactions on Pattern Analysis andMechine Intelligence, pp. 1129–1140, 1992.

[8] G. Raju and Y. Xu, "Study of parallel thinning algorithms," IEEE International Conference on Systems, Man, and Cybernetics, vol. 01,pp. 661–666, Dec 1991.

[9] S. Prabhakar, A. K. Jain and S. Pankanti, "Learning fingerprint minutiae location and type", Pattern Recognition, 36(8): 1847–1857, 2003.

[10] Kalyani Mali, Samayita Bhattacharya, Fingerprint Recognition Using Global and Local Structures, International Journal on Computer Science and Engineering, Vol. 3 No. 1 Jan 2011.Ratha, Nalini; Bolle, Ruud, "Automatic Fingerprint Recognition Systems", Springer, XVII, 458 p. 135.

[11] James L. Wayman (Editor), Anil K. Jain, "Biometric Systems", Springer, 2004.

[12] Bir Bhanu,Xuejun Tan, "Computational Algorithms for Fingerprint Recognition", Springer, 2004.

7

Intelligent assessment and prediction of software characteristics at the design stage

Oksana Pomorova, Tetyana Hovorushchenko

Department of System Programming, Khmelnitskiy National University, Khmelnitskiy, Ukraine

Email address:
o.pomorova@gmail.com (O. Pomorova), tat_yana@ukr.net (T. Hovorushchenko)

Abstract: This article is dedicated to intelligent method and system of design results evaluation and software characteristics prediction on the basis of processing of software metrics sets.

Keywords: Software Complexity, Software Quality, Software Metrics, Artificial Neural Network (Ann), Neural Method For Design Results Evaluating And Software Characteristics Prediction, Intelligent System Of Assessment And Prediction Of Software Characteristics

1. Introduction

The development of software is the knowledge-based activity that requires a detailed study of the subject area and a full understanding of the developed product goals. The characteristics of software include: software cost, software protection, completeness of requirements realization, the size of software files, requirements to system software and hardware, the size of required RAM and disk storage. But the most important characteristics of the software are its complexity from the developer's perspective and its quality from a user perspective.

The crisis in the software quality providing was noticeable more than 50 years ago. Since then, many methods, techniques and tools have been developed, the best specialists were involved in the development of technologies and standards to ensure the software systems quality. But the quality of software is still dependent on the knowledge and experience of developers.

According to approximate estimates the cost of software development is about 275 billion dollars, but only 72% of projects reach the implementation stage and only 26% of projects are completed successfully [1]. According to The Wall Street Journal, more than 50% of corporate software projects fall short of expectations and over 42% of projects are terminated long before their logical completion [2].

One of the criteria for the success of software projects is their complexity, and hence cost. Research of Standish Group showed that projects costing less than 750 thousand dollars are successful in 55% cases, projects costing from 1 to 2 million dollars are successful in 18% cases, projects costing from 5 to 10 million doolars are successful only in 7% cases [2]. The permanent growing of software functions complexity inevitably leads to increasing of their size and creation complexity. Modern software with millions of lines of code in principle can not be infallible, faultless and accurate, so the problem of achieving the required level of quality is actual.

1.1. Results of Manifestation of Software Quality Level in Complicated Hardware-Software Complexes

Thus incidents caused by software failures continue to appear. The most known incidents for the severity of its consequences are:

1) Six patients received overdoses of radiation during sessions of radiation therapy with radiation therapy machine Therac-25 in 1985-1987. Catastrophic consequences of programming bugs and defects in the project development and formulation manifestated repeatedly and for a long time [3];

2) The subject of European Community pride, rocket Ariane 5 self-destructing 37 seconds after launch because of a malfunction in the control software (1996). This explosion led to huge losses - only scientific equipment on it was worth half a billion dollars plus astronomical "profits" from not occurred commercial launches [4];

3) The Space Shuttle Columbia disaster occurred in 2003, resulting in the death of all seven crew members. The fire was happened because the report on plating damage was incorrectly prepared in the program MS PowerPoint [5];

4) While attempting its first overseas deployment to the Kadena Air Base in Okinawa, Japan, in 2007, twelve fighter stealth aircrafts F-22s flying from Hickam AFB, Hawaii experienced multiple computer failures while crossing the International Date Line (or 180th meridian of longitude dependent on software programming) [6];

5) The triple satellites, critical for the Russian navigation system Glonass (rival American GPS), fell into the Pacific Ocean in 2010. Loss of satellites caused by the programming bug is estimated 1387 million dollars [7];

6) On 1 February 2013, during the launch of Intelsat-27, a Russian rocket Zenit-3SL launch vehicle suffered a premature engine shutdown, as the rocket strayed from its lift-off trajectory, plunging into the Pacifc Ocean shortly after launch. Falling of rocket caused by failures in the control system [8].

In December 2011, NASA specialists successfully fix a bug in the software of onboard computer complex of spacecraft, which moved to Mars with rover "Curiosity" on board. But this example of software troubleshoot at the operation stage is very rare. Typically, these incidents lead to significant human and economic losses.

Therefore, the software quality requirements are necessary to formulate and test at the the early stages of software life cycle, preferably already at the design stage. The dependence of the cost of bugs correcting from the stage of the life cycle is shown on Fig.1 [9].

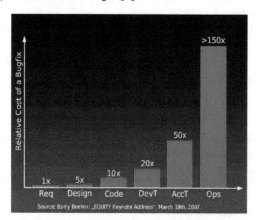

Figure 1. *Cost of a Bug Within a Software Lifecycle.*

Generally, according to known scientist in the software engineering Barry Boehm, software industry is nearing to technogenic catastrophe, which is caused by defective software that penetrates into all spheres of human activity.

While the complexity of some software development today already exceeds the complexity of many engineering and infrastructure projects, and the consequences of errors are catastrophic and disastrous, software engineering is not ensured with the fundamental theory and methodology.

If the software development industry will not radically changes, the world will inevitably not be able to avoid disasters caused by errors in the code or failures in the management of complex software systems.

1.2. Problems of Using of Software Characteristics As-

sessment Tools and Means

The series of software testing methodologies are developed to improve the software quality. They are based on the code reveiw. Review of the entire code is not possible due to the high laboriousness, so different methods of reducing the tested code size are used. For this purpose static code analyzers (PVS Studio [10], CAST Application Intelligence Platform [11], IBM Rational AppScan Source Edition [12], SofCheck Inspector [13], Visual Studio Team System [14]) are used. They on the basis of specialized rules and metrics allocate the code with low quality.

Software acquires high quality not so much a result of comprehensive testing of the final product, but in the during of its development. If bugs trapping at all project stages is the basis of methodology of creating software, the project will be almost infallible. IBM Corporation provides the methodology to creation of complex software systems - Cleanroom Software Engineering [15]. It provides teams of developers to plan, to measure, to specify, to design, to code, to test and to certify the software products. The tool for automated testing and software reliability evaluation in this methodology is environment Cleanroom Certification Assistant [15], which uses statistical test results to calculation of software reliability metrics by mathematical methods. The global market proposes many products for automation of metrics calculation: IBM Rational Logiscope [16], Test-Center [17], Rational Purify [18], IBM Rational Software Group [19].

The common lacks of these quality assessment tools are: 1) subjective dependence of choice of metrics that tool calculate; 2) subjective interpretation of metrics values, because exact (etalons) values of metrics are available; 3) tools of automation of metric information calculation are oriented on testing and metrology of finished source code and not oriented on prediction and calculation of software metrics at the design stage. At the design stage the finished product is missing, only informational, functional and behavioral model of requirements analysis for the software are. Consequently, the existing tools of software quality evaluation are ineffective at the design stage.

Software metrics can be useful for the evaluating of the project quality and complexity and the prediction of quality and complexity of the developed software by the project. The modern software industry has accumulated a large number of metrics that assess individual software features. However, the desire of their versatility, ignoring the type and scope of the developed software, ignoring the stages of the software life cycle and ungrounded their using significantly undermined the confidence of developers and users to software metrics. These circumstances require: the careful selection of metrics for a particular type and scope of the developed software, the considering their limitations at various stages of the life cycle, the establishing of possibilities and order of metrics sharing, the accumulation and integration of metrics to make timely production decisions.

Several unresolved issues is in the assessment and prediction of software characteristics at the design stage: 1) quality measurement technology has not yet reached maturity - only 1,5% software companies are trying to evaluate the quality of processes and ready product using metrics, and only 0,5% software companies are trying to improve their work on the basis of quantitative criteria of software quality; 2) the lack of unified standards for metrics - over a thousand metrics were created, each developer of "measurement" system offers own measures of software quality evaluation and proper metrics; 3) difficult interpretation of metrics values - for most users, customers and programmers the metrics and their values are not informative; 4) metrics are calculated only for the finished software (for code); 5) low level of automation of the software metrics analysis and processing - only the processes of gathering, recording and computing of metric information are automated today.

The unresolved of these issues is one of the factors that interferes to develop the defect-free and high-quality software. Difficulty of grounding of software metrics selection and interpretation does not provide to use metrics for assessing and predicting of the software characteristics of at the design stage and for improving of the software quality.

The theory of software engineering is still missing. Theory is needed as a guide for researchers and developers. That theory would provide the selection of metrics for evaluation of the results at each stage of the life cycle and would provide the prediction of developed software characteristics. Certainly, there are some fundamental research (works of Boehm, Dijkstra, Meyer), but finished, tested and approbated theory is missing.

From the results of the analysis of software evaluation methods the conclusion follows, that the perspective research direction to improve the software quality is development of intelligent methods (IM) and systems (IS). IM and IS will analyze and process the design stage metrics, will evaluate the project and will provide the prediction of the characteristics of designed software.

2. Software Metrics at the Design Stage

At the design stage the number of requirements on software complexity and quality is important to provide: requirements on software structure, on navigation by software, on design of user interfaces, on multimedia components of software, on usability; technical requirements.

The answer to the question "How software system will be implemented its requirements?" is formed at this stage.

The information flows of the design stage: software requirements (information, functional and behavioral analysis models). Information model describes the information that must be processed by software according to customer. Functional model defines the list of functions and the list of modules of software system. Behavioral model captures the software modes. The results of the design stage are: developed data, developed architecture and procedural software development.

2.1. Software Complexity Metrics

From the analysis of software complexity metrics and information flows of the design stage the conclusion follows, that the following software complexity metrics with exact or predicted values appropriate to use at the design stage (table 1) [1].

Table 1. Software complexity metrics at the design stage.

№	Software Complexity Metrics With Exact Values at the Design Stage	Software Complexity Metrics With Predicted Values at the Design Stage
1	Chepin's metric	Expected Lines of Code (LOC)
2	Jilb's metric (absolute modular complexity)	Halstead's metric
3	McClure's metric	McCabe's metric
4	Kafur's metric	Jilb's metric (relative modular complexity)
5		Expected quantity of program statements
6		Expected estimate of interfaces complexity

So, at the design stage 10 basic software complexity metrics we will use - 4 of them have the exact values and the other 6 metrics have the predicted values.

2.2. Software Quality Metrics

The analysis of software quality metrics and information flows of the design stage provides the conclude that next software quality metrics with exact or predicted values are applicable at the design stage (table 2) [1].

Table 2. Software quality metrics at the design stage.

№	Software Quality Metrics With Exact Values at the Design Stage	Software Quality Metrics With Predicted Values at the Design Stage
1	2	3
1	Cohesion metric	Software design total time (in working days)
2	Coupling metric	Design stage time (in working days)
3	Metric of the global variables calling	Software realization productivity (in minutes for code line)
4	Time of models modification (in working days)	Software quality audit cost (in USD)
5	Quantity of found bugs in models	Software design cost (in USD)
1	2	3
6		Program code realization cost (in USD)
7		Functional points (FP)
8		Effort applied by Boehm (in man-months)
9		Development time by Boehm (in working days)

Therefore the 10 basic software complexity metrics and

14 basic software quality metrics were used at the design stage. Other metrics are derived from selected basic metrics.

The processing of above 24 software complexity and quality metrics with exact and predicted values is the basis for obtaining the evaluation of design results and prediction of software complexity and quality characteristics of the developed for the project software.

3. Neural Method for Design Results Evaluating and Software Characteristics Prediction (NMEP)

NMEP provides the evaluation of the project and prediction of designed software charateristics on the basis of complexity and quality metrics with exact and predicted values at the design stage, listed in the previous section.

NMEP is based on processing of the following sets:

1) the set of complexity metrics with the exact values at the design stage

$$CMEV = \{cmev_i \mid i = 1..4\};$$

2) the set of quality metrics with the exact values at the design stage

$$QMEV = \{qmev_j \mid j = 1..5\};$$

3) the set of complexity metrics with the predicted values at the design stage

$$CMPV = \{cmpv_k \mid k = 1..6\};$$

4) the set of complexity metrics with the predicted values at the design stage

$$QMPV = \{qmpv_n \mid n = 1..9\}.$$

The results of these sets processing are:
1) project complexity estimate PCE;
2) project quality evaluation PQE;
3) designed software complexity prediction SCP;
4) designed software quality prediction SQP.

The basis of project complexity estimate are elements of set $CMEV$. The basis of project quality evaluation are elements of sets $CMEV$ and $QMEV$. The basis of designed software complexity prediction are elements of set $CMPV$, but elements of sets $CMEV$ and $QMEV$ are taken into account. The basis of designed software quality prediction are elements of sets $CMPV$ and $QMPV$, but elements of sets $CMEV$ and $QMEV$ are taken into account.

The problem of identifying the correlation between metrics values and quality and complexity of project and software should be solved for the software quality and complexity evaluation and prediction on the basis of metric analysis results. One of the means, which makes it possible to summarize the information and identify dependencies between input data and resulting data, are artificial neural networks.

Metric analysis results we will to process using artificial neural network (ANN), that performs the approximation of software metrics and provides an estimate of complexity and quality of the project and predict of complexity and quality characteristics of developed for the project software.

NMEP consists of next stages:

1) the preparation of metrics with exact and predicted values at the design stage to the inputs of ANN;

2) the checking of obtained metrics values on the subject of exceeding of ANN inputs ranges limits;

3) the processing of metrics values by artificial neural network;

4) the analysis of ANN output values;

5) the forming of conclusion about the complexity and quality of project and designed software on the basis of ANN output values.

Input data for ANN are: the sets of complexity and quality metrics with the exact values at the design stage and the sets of complexity and quality metrics with the predicted values at the design stage.

The results of ANN functioning are 4 characteristics: project complexity estimate; project quality evaluation; designed software complexity prediction; designed software quality prediction.

NMEP concept is represented on Fig.2.

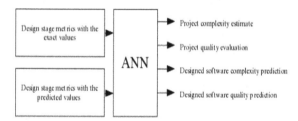

Figure 2. *NMEP conception.*

The multilayer perceptron was chosen as a result of analysis of the artificial neural networks architectures to analyze the software metrics at the design stage and to predict of software quality characteristics.

ANN has 9 one type inputs for the quantitative values of exact metrics at the design stage and 15 another type inputs for the quantitative values of predicted metrics at the design stage. If a certain metric is not determined, then -1 is given on the proper ANN input.

The conclusion about the project quality and complexity and the expected quality and complexity of designed software is based on an analysis of 4-th obtained results. Project complexity estimate, project quality evaluation, designed software complexity prediction, designed software quality prediction are values in the range [0, 1], where 0 - proper metric was not determined, approximately 0 - the project or designed software has a high complexity or low quality and 1 - the project or software is simple (non-complexity) or high quality.

The ANN has 24 neurons of the input layer, 14 neurons of approximating layer and 8 neurons of the adjusting layer and 4 neurons of the output layer.

ANN has 4 input vectors for giving the values of metrics:

1) Input1 vector consists of 4 elements - software complexity metrics with exact values at the design stage;

2) Input2 vector consists of 5 elements - software quality metrics with exact values at the design stage;

3) Input3 vector consists of 6 elements - software complexity metrics with predicted values at the design stage;

4) Input4 vector consists of 9 elements - software quality metrics with predicted values at the design stage.

Output vector Y consists of 4 elements: project complexity estimate, project quality evaluation, software complexity prediction, software quality prediction, therefore ANN has 4 neurons of the fourth (output) layer.

Architecture of neural network component of NMEP is shown on Fig.3.

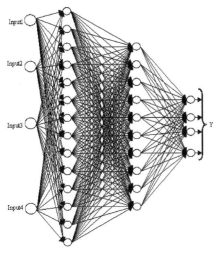

Figure 3. *Architecture of neural network component of NMEP.*

The described ANN has been implemented in Matlab [1]. Structural scheme of the ANN layers in Simulink is shown on Fig.4.

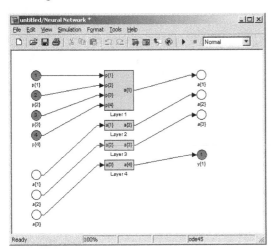

Figure 4. *ANN layers structural scheme in Simulink.*

The above dependences the resulting estimates of the input metrics sets are considered in training of the neural network.

Realized neural network was trained with training sample

of 1935 vectors and tested with testing sample of 324 vectors. The research [1] demonstrates that the smallest training performance was obtained with the mean squared error w/reg performance function (msereg); optimal number of neurons in second hidden layer is 14 neurons. The ANN training and testing performance on average is approximately $\xi = 0,102197$.

4. Intelligent System of Assessment and Prediction of Software Characteristics (ISAP)

Usually when alternatives of the same software project are available, the choice of a particular version is performed by the criteria of cost and development time. The cost and development time may have similar or equal values, but significant differences in the quality of future software may exist. Therefore, when choosing of software project version, the number of other factors must be considered, including the software complexity and quality. The effective mean of this problem solving is intelligent system of assessment and prediction of software characteristics (ISAP) [1]. The basis for the development of this system is neural method for design results evaluating and software characteristics prediction (NMEP).

Quantitative exact and predicted values of metrics are given to the ISAP inputs, and conclusions about the project and designed software complexity and quality are the results of the system functioning. Structure of ISAP represented on Fig.5.

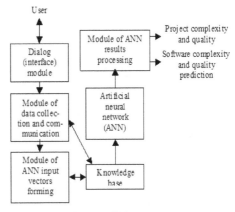

Figure 5. *ISAP structure.*

ISAP consists of modules:

1) dialog (interface) module;

2) module of data collection and communication;

3) knowledge base;

4) module of ANN input vectors forming;

5) artificial neural network;

6) module of ANN results processing.

The dialog (interface) module visualizes the functioning of module of data collection and communication, displays the system functioning and produces the messages to user in an understandable form for him.

The module of data collection and communication reads the user information about the quantitative exact and predicted values of software metrics, saves the obtained information in the knowledge base and transmits its to the module of ANN input vectors forming.

Knowledge base contains the quantitative exact and predicted values of software metrics at the design stage, the ANN input vectors and the rules of ANN results processing.

The artificial neural network (ANN) provides the approximation of software metrics and gives the quantitative evaluation of project complexity and quality and prediction of designed software complexity and quality by NMEP.

The module of ANN input vectors forming prepares the metrics values from the knowledge base for the ANN inputs.

The module of ANN results processing makes the conclusions about the project quality and complexity and the expected quality and complexity of designed software on the basis of ANN results.

For this purpose 12 production rules were developed:

1) if $PCE = 0$, then complexity metrics with the exact values at the design stage were not determined;

2) if $PCE \rightarrow 0$, then the project is complicated to realization;

3) if $PCE \rightarrow 1$, then the project is simple to realization;

4) if $PQE = 0$, then quality metrics with the exact values at the design stage were not determined;

5) if $PQE \rightarrow 0$, then project is a low quality

6) if $PQE \rightarrow 1$, then the project satisfies the customer requirements in quality;

7) if $SCP = 0$, then complexity metrics with the predicted values at the design stage were not determined;

8) if $SCP \rightarrow 0$, then designed software will have significant complexity;

9) if $SCP \rightarrow 1$, then designed software is expected simple;

10) if $SQP = 0$, then quality metrics with the predicted values at the design stage were not determined;

11) if $SQP \rightarrow 0$, then designed software is low quality;

12) if $SQP \rightarrow 1$, then high quality software is expected.

Using these rules, ISAP gives the evaluation of project complexity and quality and the prediction of the complexity and quality of developed for the project software Nhese evaluation and prediction help the customer to make the right decisions about project selection.

For example, the input data of ISAP are the results of metric analysis of 3 projects developed by the same requirements to solve one problem by a software company "STU-Electronics", Khmelnitskiy, Ukraine (table 3).

Table 3. The Processing of Results of Metric Analysis at the Design Stage by ANN of ISAP.

№	Complexity Metrics with Exact Values	Quality Metrics with Exact Values	Complexity Metrics with Predicted Values	Quality Metrics with Predicted Values	ANN of ISAP Results
1	Chepin's metric = 1690 Jilb's metric = 158	Cohesion metric =10 Coupling metric = 1	Expected LOC = 3280 Halstead's mtric = 73500 Jilb's metric = 0,051	Software design total time = 26 Software design cost = 975 Functional points = 120	Y1=0,94 Y2=1 Y3=0,94 Y4=0,96
2	McClure's metric = 90020 Kafur's metric = 376930 Chepin's metric = 24540	Cohesion metric = 3 Coupling metric = 7 Metric of the global variables calling = 0,72	Expected LOC = 40130 Halstead's metric = 124926 McCabe's metric = 1905	Software design total time = 397 Software design cost = 19000 Functional points = 2222	Y1=0,24 Y2=0,31 Y3=0,21 Y4=0,24
3	Chepin's metric = 14538 Jilb's metric = 1121	Cohesion metric = 7 Coupling metric = 4	Expected LOC = 25533 Halstead's metric = 781231 Jilb's metric = 0,52	Software design total time = 217 Software design cost = 10762 Functional points = 1212 Software quality audit cost = 1100	Y1=0,56 Y2=0,61 Y3=0,5 Y4=0,58

According to the obtained results: the project №1 is simple and has high quality, the future software is expected as a simple and high quality too; the project №2 is quite complicated and has a low quality, the future software is expected as a complicated and low quality also, the project №3 has medium complexity and quality, the future software is expected as medium complexity and quality too.

ISAP conclusions provide the comparison of different versions of projects, where the cost and development time approximately equal. ISAP help make the right choice and realize the project №1 with the best complexity and quality evaluations.

5. Conclusions

The conclusions by neural method and intelligent system of software characteristics assessment and prediction provide the assessment of project and the prediction of characteristics of the developed software for the project. These conclusions are based on the software complexity and quality metrics with exact or predicted values at the design stage. The NMEP and ISAP conclusions also provide a comparison of different versions of project.

The proposed neural method and intelligent system of assessment and prediction of software characteristics provide to customer the information to selection of the software project and to comparison the different versions of the project. NMEP and ISAP are the basis for making grounded and motivated decision on the choice of the project and its version with regard the characteristics of complexity and quality of the project and the developed software.

When developing NMEP and ISAP problems were occurred, the main reasons are:

1) absence of a fundamental theory of software engineering (special international organization SEMAT trying to solve this problem);

2) lack of the necessary theoretical and methodological principles of development and implementation of intelligent information technologies for management of the software characteristics;

3) absence of theory and methodology of assessment and prediction of software quality and complexity at the design stage.

Further efforts of authors will be directed to the solving of the aforementioned problems.

References

[1] V.Mishchenko, O.Pomorova, T.Hovorushchenko. CASE-assessment of Critical Software Systems. Volume 1. Quality / Kharkiv: The National Aerospace University "KhAI", 2012. - 201 p. [in Russian].

[2] William J. Brown, Raphael C. Malveau, Hays W. McCormick, Thomas J. Mowbray. AntiPatterns: Refactoring Software, Architectures, and Projects in Crisis - Wiley, 1998 - 336 p.

[3] Nancy Leveson, Clark S. Turner. An Investigation of the Therac-25 Accidents // IEEE Computer, Vol. 26, No. 7, July 1993, pp. 18-41.

[4] When Software Catastrophe Strikes. Ariane 5 explosion (1996) // http://images.businessweek.com/slideshows/2012-08-07/when-software-catastrophe-strikes.html#slide2.

[5] Stephen Turner. Expertise and Political Responsibility: the Columbia Shuttle Catastrophe // http://link.springer.com/chapter/10.1007%2F1-4020-3754-6_6.

[6] F-22 Squadron Shot Down by the International Date Line // http://www.defenseindustrydaily.com/f22-squadron-shot-down-by-the-international-date-line-03087/

[7] GLONASS Triple Satellite Launch Suffers Rare Failure // http://www.insidegnss.com/node/2399

[8] Russian rocket launch fails as engine shuts down // http://in.news.yahoo.com/russian-rocket-launch-fails-engine-shuts-down-105005395.html

[9] Cost of a bug within a software lifecycle // http://www.testically.org/2012/02/09/cost-of-a-bug-within-a-software-lifecycle/

[10] PVS-Studio description [in Russian] // http://www.viva64.com/ru/pvs-studio/

[11] CAST Application Intelligence Platform // http://www.castsoftware.com/products/cast-application-intelligence-platform

[12] IBM Security AppScan Source // http://www-01.ibm.com/software/rational/products/appscan/source/

[13] SofCheck Inspector 2.1268 // http://sofcheck-inspector.findmysoft.com/

[14] Visual Studio Team System Features // http://www.learnvisualstudio.net/series/visual_studio_team_system_features/

[15] Stacy J. Prowell; Carmen J. Trammell; Richard C. Linger; Jesse H. Poore. Cleanroom Software Engineering: Technology and Process - Addison-Wesley Professional, 1999 - 416 p.

[16] IBM Rational Logiscope // http://www.ibm.com/developerworks/rational/products/logiscope/

[17] Locate a Test Center // http://www.pearsonvue.com/vtclocator/

[18] Rational Purify // http://www-01.ibm.com/software/awdtools/purify/

[19] IBM Rational Software: Accelerate product and service innovation // http://www-01.ibm.com/software/rational/

8

Survey of software components to emulate OpenFlow protocol as an SDN implementation

Mohammed Basheer Al-Somaidai, Estabrak Bassam Yahya

Dept. of Electrical Engineering, Mosul University, Mosul, Iraq

Email address:

mohammedbasheerabdullah@uomosul.edu.iq (M. B. Al-Somaidai), eng_est_1990@yahoo.com (E. B. Yahya)

Abstract: Software Defined Networks (SDN) is the next wave in networking evolution. It may be considered as a revolution rather than an evolution since; many concepts of conventional network protocols are reshaped. OpenFlow protocol is the most widely deployed protocol in SDN. Emulation of OpenFlow based network projects facilitates the implementation of new ideas and driving the development of the protocol. In this paper, a summary of many software components related to OpenFlow is presented. Most of these software components were tested by the researchers in order to simplify the choice for other researchers considering the implementation of OpenFlow projects. These tests showed that there are differences in performance for the controllers that support OpenFlow 1.0 and OpenFlow 1.3. Furthermore, the tested controllers differs in the applications they support.

Keywords: Software Defined Network, OpenFlow, Emulation, Mininet

1. Introduction

A new paradigm in the field of networking is the software defined networks a promising architecture, which is gaining rapid attention of researchers and vendors as well [1-3]. This is so because; the unlimited development of network applications and the extensive demands of an explosive growth in network users are driving conventional network devices to their limits. SDN introduces a new way to handle the vast amount of packets traversing the network. Many packets belong to a single flow; thus, handling that flow and distributing the actions to be taken to all its packets would numerously speed up their forwarding. This is only one of many other benefits of a centralized control of the network. The most widely deployed SDN architecture is the OpenFlow protocol. Many gigantic Internet vendors including Google are considering the application of OpenFlow protocol in their data centers [4]. A gradual implementation of SDN and OpenFlow suggests the co-existence of OpenFlow networks with conventional networks. This requires extensive studies and projects to investigate the limitations and possibilities of these protocols.

Simulation and emulation of network projects provide a solid base to determine their pros and cons. Emulation is more realistic than simulation since, it must be carried out in real time and could provide a way to some real devices running real operating systems to interact with some simulated devices [5].

B. Lantz, et. al. [6] analyzed the performance of Mininet emulator to develop, interact with, and customize the SDN concept with OpenFlow protocol. This study showed Mininet ease of use, scalability, and limitations.

S. Wang, et. al. [5] introduced the EstiNet OpenFlow network simulator and emulator, and studied its performance to design SDN networks. They compared EstiNet behavior, capabilities and scalability with Mininet and ns-3 platforms.

A. Shalimov, et. al. [7] proposed a method to test and compare popular open source SDN/OpenFlow controller. They analyzed throughput, latency, scalability and security by developing new framework called Hcprobe based on Cbench framework.

B. Nunes, et.al. [8] provided historic review about programmable network idea from its beginning time down to the SDN revolution. The study presented the architecture of SDN and discussed OpenFlow features, application and related software to deploy and develop SDN networks based on OpenFlow.

A. Lara, et. al. [9] discussed the architecture of OpenFlow

network to understand SDN, and centralized control concept by using different controllers' platform. In addition, studies have measured the performance of OpenFlow networks through modeling and experimentation. The researchers clarify the challenges facing the large-scale OpenFlow networks and applications.

The rest of this paper is structured as follows: in section 2 we briefly discuss software defined network architecture. Section 3 introduces an overview of OpenFlow protocol, its fundamental concepts and messages. Some SDN and OpenFlow platforms are presented and compared in section 4; while, sections 5 and 6 give a survey of OpenFlow software controllers and switches respectively. Any OpenFlow project could make use of some tools that are presented in section 7. Finally, section 8 contains some concluding remarks and future work suggestions.

2. Software Defined Networks (SDN)

The adaptation of packet switching in networking made each network device such as gateway, router, or switch a standalone device. These devices manage themselves independently even if this management was according to a certain routing protocol or administration policy. Each data packet undergoes the same parsing and processing efforts at each network node even if it belongs to the same flow. This conventional architecture of networks may fail to support the dramatically increase in users' requirements and the fast deployments of new network applications.

Segregating the control plane and the management plane from the data forwarding plane in network devices is what software defined network (SDN) about [10,11]. In such a paradigm, a central controller is responsible for managing many forwarding devices that lay under its supervision. Such configuration would results in efficient, faster innovative, and more scalable networks that meet users' demands. Software defined network is managed through a network operating system implemented at the controller to make all the subsequent switches work in harmony and more flexibility.

These switches need not be in the same geographical area; the management of many planet wise distributed data centers that belong to a cloud service provider is an example of this diverse distribution of forwarding devices [2]. Fig. 1, shows the architecture of a software defined network. It is worth to mention that SDN is not a protocol; but it is an operational and programming architecture. Albeit, SDN uses certain protocols for making the network programmable. These could be OpenFlow [12], I2RS, PCE-P, BGP-LS, NetConf/Yong, and OMI [11]. In this paper, we are focusing on the widely deployed OpenFlow protocol.

3. Open Flow

OpenFlow started at Stanford University in 2008 [13]. The aim of the project was to give researchers a tool to implement their experimental protocols in networks. OpenFlow network consists of three major components: a

controller, an OpenFlow switch, and the OpenFlow protocol. The Open Networking Foundation (ONF) a non-profit

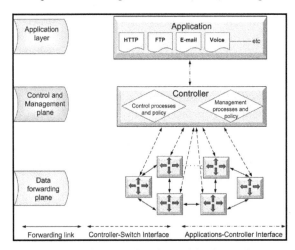

Fig 1. Architecture of a software defined network.

organization was created in 2011 by a group of vendors [14]. It is dedicated to coordinating the development of SDN standards and solutions in order to accelerate the delivery of SDN products, services, and applications. Since then ONF had published each new version of OpenFlow standard. Up to the date of writing this paper (March 2014) the last version of OpenFlow switch specification is 1.4 and it was published in October 2013 [12]. According to this specification, the architecture of an OpenFlow switch should contain the blocks shown in Fig. 2, each OpenFlow switch contains one or more flow tables processed in pipeline, a single group table, a single meter table; and a various types of ports. Each table and port in the OpenFlow switch is associated with many counters that could gather various statistics describing the events that the switch is subjected to. The controller creates all the tables and their entries; the data packets that traverse the OpenFlow switch update the counters.

The corner stone in the OpenFlow protocol is the flow table, which has 256 entries. Each entry in the flow table contains six sections as shown in Fig. 3.

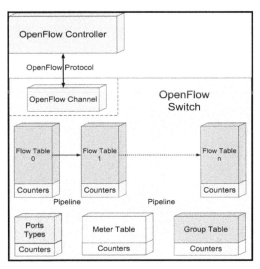

Fig 2. Architecture of an OpenFlow switch

Matching Fields	Priority	Counters	Instructions	Timeouts	Cookie

Fig 3. OpenFlow switch flow table entry fields.

The matching fields section is used to match the packet with the entry according to various packet header fields. When more than one entry match a packet the priority field determines the flow table entry that will be executed and the per flow table entry counters are updated.

The instructions section contains among other things the actions that will be acted upon the matched packet. The timeouts field specifies the maximum amount of hard time and idle time before the flow table entry expires. A zero value in any of them disable the corresponding timer. The hard timeout determines the maximum amount of time in seconds before the flow table entry expires; while the idle time out causes the expiration of the entry if it has matched no packet in the given number of seconds. The cookie field is used by the controller to filter flow statistics, flow modification, and flow deletion. Each flow table must support a table-miss flow entry clarifying the action that should be taken upon the unmatched packet either sending it to the controller, dropping it, or directing it to the subsequent flow table in the pipeline [12].

OpenFlow protocol has three types of messages to communicate between the controller and the OpenFlow switch over a secure channel or over a TCP channel as shown in Fig.4. They are classified according to the initiator of the message into controller to switch messages, asynchronous (switch to controller) messages, and symmetric messages. The controller to switch messages are used to assert its control upon the switch, reading the switch status, and modifying the switch states which includes editing the switch flow tables.

The switch to controller messages are used to inform the controller about a new incoming flow, a change in a switch state; or a request for modifying a flow table entry. Either the controller or the switch could initiate the symmetric messages. They include hello messages, echo messages, error messages, and experimenter message that identify the vendor of the controller or the switch [12]. Table 1. shows a summary of OpenFlow switch standards specification properties. It can be observed that almost every year there is a new version in the 1.x numbering of the standard, and although OpenFlow protocol is still in its 1.x version, there is huge development every year.

4. SDN Development Platforms

There are many platforms that could be used by researchers to emulate and/or simulate their SDN projects. Researchers use these tools to perform experiments, study the behavior of the network, and develop new methods to support different applications. In this section, a description of these currently available SDN platforms is presented emphasizing on the rapidly developed and deployed Mininet platform. Table 2. gives an overview of some properties of these platforms.

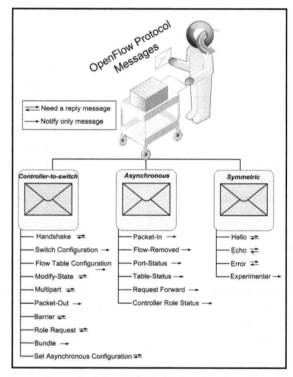

Fig 4. OpenFlow protocol messages.

Table 1. OpenFlow switch standards properties.

Version / Property	1.0	1.1	1.2	1.3	1.4
Publication date	Dec. 31, 2009	Feb. 28, 2011	Dec. 5, 2011	Jun. 25, 2012	Oct. 15, 2013
Widely deployed	Yes	No	No	No	No
Flow table	single	multiple	multiple	multiple	multiple
Group table	No	Yes	Yes	Yes	Yes
Meter table	No	No	No	Yes	Yes
VLAN and MPLS Tag	No	Yes	Yes	Yes	Yes
Controller connection failer	Emerg-ency	Stand alone /	Stand alone / secure	Stand alone /	Stand alone /
IPv6 support	No	No	Yes	Yes	Yes
Multiple controller	No	No	Yes	Yes	Yes
Eviction /Vacancy/Synchronization	No	No	No	No	Yes
Optical ports	No	No	No	No	Yes

Table 2. Properties of SDN platforms

Platform	Mininet	EstiNet	ns-3	Trema
Last version	2.1.0+	8.0	3.19	0.4.6
Vendor	Stanford University, ON. Lab	EstiNet Technologies Inc.	ns-3 Project	NEC Corporation
Web site	www.mininet. org	www.estinet. com	www.nsnam. org	io/trema/ Trema.github.
Operating system	Ubuntu, Fedora	Linux Fedora (14,17)	GNU/Linux, Windows, FreeBSD, Mac, OSX	GNU/ Debian, Ubuntu, Fedora
OpenFlow versions	1.0 – 1.3	1.0, 1.1, 1.3, 1.3.2	0.89	1.0, 1.3, 1.3.1
GUI	VND*, Miniedit	EstiNet GUI	VND*	VND*
Emulation mode	Yes	Yes	No	Yes
Simulation mode	No	Yes	Yes	No
Free / Proprietary	Free	Proprietary	Free	Free

*VND: Visual Network Description, to be mentioned in section 7

4.1. Mininet

Mininet is a network emulation platform that supports rapid development in SDN using OpenFlow protocol. It is the most popular SDN platform used by SDN researchers due to its simplicity, availability, and flexibility. Furthermore, Mininet is entirely devoted to OpenFlow architecture [6].

Mininet uses Linux kernels along with Python language scripts to construct a virtual network of large number of hosts network, OpenFlow switches, and controllers in any network topology the researcher employs over a single desktop or laptop station.

Mininet could use its built-in software tools to develop such networks through Command Line Interface (CLI), or adapts to a third-party software tools that implement other controllers or Graphic User Interface (GUI) engines [15, 16]. It has the flexibility of adding many controller types that will be mentioned in section 5.

4.2. EstiNet

EstiNet is an emulation and simulation platform of many network protocols; one of them is OpenFlow protocol. It also supports some of the controllers of section V. EstiNet is a proprietary software tool and it uses the company servers to run the simulation or the emulation projects. This cloud service is referred to as Simulation as a Service [17].

EstiNet has good simulation properties among them are accurate and repeatable result with a graphical user interface and packet animation along with good presentation of the simulation statistics as a graph for each node in the network [5].

4.3. ns-3

ns-3 is a well established network simulator usually compared to OPNET for providing simulation environment to a wide range of network protocols. ns-3 supports OpenFlow protocol and its switches in simulator environment but it cannot readily run a real OpenFlow controller such as NOX, POX, or Floodlight without

modifications. This is why ns-3 has implemented its own OpenFlow controller as a C++ module with a different performance from the above real controllers.

Another drawback of using ns-3 is that it until now supports version 0.89 of OpenFlow protocol only, this limits the researchers' ability to test and develop projects that are compatible with the new versions of OpenFlow protocol [5]. It could be used to introduce the concepts of SDN and OpenFlow to beginners who are used to ns-3.

4.4. Trema

Trema is an OpenFlow framework that includes everything the researcher needs to conduct an OpenFlow project. The source tree includes basic libraries and functional modules that work as an interface to OpenFlow switches. Several examples of sample applications are also provided.

It has an integrated testing and debugging environment that manage, monitor, and diagnose the entire system with a network emulator and a diagnostic tool chain (Trema shark, Wireshark plug-in) [18]. The lack of a graphical user interface and the use of the programming languages C and Ruby may limit the popularity of this platform.

5. Controller Software

A block diagram of the controller; which is the brain of any software defined network is shown in Fig. 5. The controller communicates with the forwarding devices through an SDN protocol such as OpenFlow. This link is also called the southbound Application Programming Interface (API). From the other side the controller uses a northbound API to deal with various applications. If we made an analogy for the network as an orchestra then the controller plays the role of the maestro. In fact, some SDN implementations use these designations to refer to SDN and the controller [11, 19].

As the basic concept of SDN is to decouple the control

plane and the management plane from the data-forwarding plane then the controller has to bear all the burden of controlling and managing all the data forwarding devices. It should maintain and update through the rule-placement algorithm information about all the forwarding devices that are under direct responsibility of the controller including their flow tables, links, and states. The routing policy is another task of the controller any change in any forwarding device state causes the controller to reshape the routing path of all flows traverse that device resulting in updates to a large number of switches' flow tables. Security strategies along with end devices policy are also, placed in the controller.

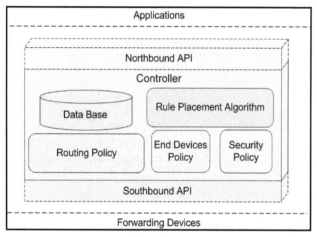

Fig 5. Block diagram of the controller.

As mentioned above the controller plays a vital role in the OpenFlow network; therefore multi controllers could establish communication with a forwarding device (switch) provided that only one of them has the master role upon the switch and the others should be in the slave role. Having multiple controllers improves reliability, as the switch can continue to operate in OpenFlow mode if one controller or controller connection fails. The hand-over between controllers is entirely managed by the controllers themselves, which enable fast recovery from failure and controllers load balancing [12]. Many software implementations of the controller are summarized in Table 3.

5.1. NOX

NOX controller was the original controller of OpenFlow. It is written in C++ language and its first version provided an API for Python scripts, but last version of NOX has dropped this API and supported C++ only. NOX provides a high-level programmable interface upon forwarding devices and applications. It is designed to support both small networks of a few hosts and large enterprise networks of hundreds of switches and hosts.

NOX's core has features of fast, asynchronous I/O, topology discovery, host tracking possibility, and learning

switch feature [20]. NOX combined with Mininet provides a platform for academic research in networking [21]. It supports now many features of OpenFlow protocol specification 1.3, but the researchers when implement this version discovered the Iperf command which determine the bandwidth utilization does not work properly.

5.2. POX

POX controller is another SDN control platform and it is considered an active development tool. POX was derived from NOX controller platform with the main difference is using Python programming language instead of C++ platform. POX uses Python API (version 2.7) to support network virtualization, SDN debugging, and different application such as layer-2 switch, bridge, hub, etc [22]. NOX and POX controllers support the same GUI and visualization tools to setup, configure controllers, and flow tables. POX still does not support OpenFlow 1.3, which many other controllers support now.

5.3. Floodlight

Floodlight is a very popular SDN controller. It is a contribution from Big Switch Networks and it uses Java based platform (API) thus it runs within a Java Virtual Machine (JVM) and it is considered suitable with continuous increase in number of network devices (switches) that deal with OpenFlow concept [11,23].

Floodlight controller realizes a set of common functionalities to control and inquire an OpenFlow network. The controller has features of simple to extend and enhance, easy to setup with minimal dependencies, support for Open Stack Quantum cloud, topology management, and it deals with mixed OpenFlow and non-OpenFlow network. Floodlight supports applications that include a learning switch, hub application, firewall, and static flow push applications [21]. Floodlight as POX does not support OpenFlow 1.3.

5.4. OpenDaylight

OpenDaylight is an OpenFlow controller. It has open and reference framework for programmability and control through open source SDN, it uses JVM so it can be used with any platform or operating system that supports Java 1.7+. It is a modular, extensible, scalable and multi-protocol controller infrastructure built for SDN deployment on modern heterogeneous multi-vendor networks [21, 24].

OpenDaylight enables users to reduce operational complexity, extend the lifetime of their testing network infrastructure, and enable new services and capabilities. In our test of OpenDaylight, it proved to have an excellent GUI, but Iperf command undergo the same problems that we faced with NOX when dealing with controller.

Table 3. Controller software implementations.

Name	Vendor	Progra-mming language	OpenFlow versions	GUI	Operating system
NOX	Nicira	C ++	1.0, 1.3	NOX GUI	Linux
POX	Nicira	Python	1.0	NOX GUI	Linux, Windows, Mac
Floodlight	Big Switch Networks	Java	1.0	Flood-light web UI, Avior	Linux, Mac
OpenDaylight	Linux Foundation Collaborative Project	Java	1.0, 1.3	Open-Daylight web UI	Linux, Windows
Ryu	Nippon Telegraph and Telephone Corporation	Python	1.0, 1.2, 1.3 and Nicira extension	VND	Linux
Mul	kulcloud	C	1.0, 1.3.1	VND	Linux
Beacon	Stanford University	Java	1.0	VND	Windows, Linux, OSX

5.5. Ryu

Ryu is a component-based, open source framework implemented entirely in Python. Nevertheless, the Ryu messaging service does support components developed in other languages [25].

The goal of Ryu is to develop an operating system for SDN that has high quality enough for use in large networks.

Ryu controller includes event management, in-memory state management, application management, and series of reusable libraries (e.g NetCOONF library, sFlow/NetFlow library and OF-Config library). Additionally, it supports applications such as OpenStack Quantum, layer-2 switch, Generic Routing Encapsulation tunnel interface (GRE), and tunnel abstractions. As well, as services about topology and statistics [11].

5.6. Mul

Mul is an OpenFlow SDN controller and it uses C based multi-threaded infrastructure at its core and it is designed to provide good services and ensure reliability through the network [26]. Mul supports OpenFlow 1.3.1and did not work in our test with OpenFlow 1.3 switches such as Open vSwitch.

5.7. Beacon

Beacon is an OpenFlow SDN controller and it uses Java based API. Beacon has features of rapid development, fast and dynamic performance in order to code bundle features [27].

5.8. Special Purpose Controllers

There is a type of controllers; that operates with general purpose controllers such as FlowVisor, and RouteFlow [21]. FlowVisor acts as a proxy between an OpenFlow switch and multi controllers. So that it directs the first packet of a new flow to the appropriate controller according to application, port, MAC, or IP address. This would results in the separation of the network or applications into slices where each slice is controlled by a different controller [28]. It does not support OpenFlow 1.3 yet.

RouteFlow can be considered as a network application on top of general OpenFlow controllers. The major objective of RouteFlow is to build up an open source framework for virtual IP routing solution over product hardware implementing the OpenFlow API [29].

6. Switch Software

OpenFlow switch is an important component of software defined network, switch connects with controller and when a packet arrives to the switch; the switch performs a number of processes, compares the packet header with flow entries, and identifies the actions to be implemented as illustrated in prior sections. Mininet can support different type of switches such as:

6.1. Open vSwitch (OVS)

Open vSwitch is a production quality open source software switch designed to be used as a virtual switch in large scale virtualized environments. Open vSwitch supports many flavors of Linux operating systems such as Debian, Ubuntu, and Fedora. Furthermore, it supports Windows and FreeBSD operating systems [30].

Open vSwitch uses OpenFlow protocol to support the efficient management, virtual switch configuration, and QoS policies need to be applied across a large number of hosts. Open vSwitch supports OpenFlow versions 1.0, 1.1, 1.2, 1.3. As well, it supports other standard management protocols such as SNMP or NETCONF. Additionally, Open vSwitch provides interfaces to monitoring protocols such as sFlow and NetFlow [31]. Open vSwitch is commonly used with Mininet emulator for testing networks that use OpenFlow protocol [21].

6.2. OFSoftSwitch13

OFSoftSwitch13 is an OpenFlow 1.3 compatible user-space software switch implementation. This project is supported by Evicsson Innovation center/Brazil [21].

Mininet users can install the switch software, NOX controller that supports OpenFlow version 1.3, and download useful documentation to run and configure OFSoftSwitch13 from public Github web site [32].

6.3. LINC

LINC is an open source project that supports OpenFlow protocol versions 1.2, and 1.3. LINC is architected to use generally available commodity, x86 hardware and runs in various operating systems such as Linux, Windows, Mac, etc [21]. Mininet user can install this switch software from Github web site [33].

6.4. Indigo Virtual Switch (IVS)

Indigo project is an open source project, which supports OpenFlow protocol on physical and hypervisor switches. It is designed for high performance and minimal administration and it uses the hardware feature of Application Specific Integrated Circuit (ASICs) of Ethernet switch to run OpenFlow at line speed [21].

Indigo Virtual Switch is a lightweight high performance virtual switch support OpenFlow version 1.0 only. It is designed to enable virtualization in big networks applications as it is used with floodlight controller [34].

7. Tools

Mininet emulator can be integrated with a number of open source tools to meet and implement the different needs of Mininet users, such as: editors, GUI, and benchmarks, ..etc.

7.1. Editors

Mininet user can use one of the Integrated Development Environment (IDE) supported by Mininet environment such as Python IDLE version 2.7, Python IDLE version 3.2, GNU Emacs editor, and Nano editor as a text editor for writing code to build and configure the network topology.

7.2. Graphic User Interface (GUI)

There are a number of GUIs that are used to configure network elements (controller, switches, and hosts) and display network topology. They include many component such as:

7.2.1. Miniedit

Miniedit is a simple Python script presented with Mininet examples. It is used as GUI to construct network topology and emulate it.

Miniedit was developed to add new features and capabilities for the purpose of forming a networks, such as the use of the remote controller and multi controllers, select properties of the links, controller, switches, and hosts, provide command line interface terminals for each node, use monitoring protocols (sFlow, NetFlow), and export python script for network topology [15].

7.2.2. Visual Network Description (VND)

Visual Network Description-SDN version is an online GUI used to form network topology and configure node properties, link type and properties, setup switches flow table entries, and export network topology and its configuration as a Python script to Mininet emulator and OpenFlow controllers or as a C++ script to ns-3 simulator [16].

7.2.3. Avior

Avior is a GUI used with floodlight controller. It provides features of eliminating dependency on using Python script and API in order to manipulate network and monitoring its behavior [35].

Avior has flow manager tools and could give a summery about controllers, switches, and hosts. Controllers summery provides information about host names, JVM memory bloat and other controllers information. Switches summery provides information about port, counters, match header fields, and switch flow entries (add/ delete). On the other hand, host summery provides information about the attached switch Data Path ID (DPID) and the switch port connect to it [21].

7.2.4. Web User Interface (UI)

It is one of the GUI used with some controllers such as Floodlight, and OpenDaylight. It is an online GUI; where user can access it after installing and running the controller using the URL address (http://localhost:8080). Web UI displays topology of network run in Mininet, network node (switches, hosts) information such as IP, MAC, and DPID, flows outline and add/remove switches flow tables entries,..etc.

7.3. Benchmarks

In order to test network performance, many benchmarks could be used. The following are examples for benchmarks.

7.3.1. OFtest

It is a framework and collection of testes for validating OpenFlow switches. OFtest provides a connection as a controller to the OpenFlow switch and send messages to test OpenFlow basic functionalities. It supports OpenFlow specification versions (1.0-1.3) [21].

OFtest uses Python and Scapy as a pre-requisites, where Scapy is a powerful interactive packet manipulation program; used to decode packets, match requests with replies. It also can handle tasks like scanning, and trace routing [36].

7.3.2. OFlops

It is an OpenFlow testing platform used to focus on OpenFlow protocol behavior by implementing basic measurement tests that allow developers to specify and study the capabilities of OpenFlow devices [37].

OFlops tests are used to assess performance of OpenFlow switches in network by utilizing multi-threading parallelism [21]. OFlops has features of modularity, low overhead with minimum delay in processing to support parallelism, and heterogeneity by being compatible with a number of packet generation and capturing tools such as Cbench and Wireshark.

7.3.3. Cbench

It is a program for testing OpenFlow controllers by generating packet-in messages and waits for flow-mods messages to receive. Cbench has two emulated modes: latency mode and throughput mode. Cbench can be used to measure controller performance by changing its arguments such as number of switches, number of MACs per switch (hosts), number of tests and time of test [7]. Cbench supports OpenFlow 1.0 only, but the Mul controller vender Kulcloud introduced a modified version of Cbench that supports OpenFlow 1.3 and is called Kcbench, albeit, it worked with Mul controller only in our test.

7.4. Linux Kernel Programs

Because Mininet emulator uses Linux kernels, it supports a number of Linux programs and commands such as Dump, Ping, Pingall, Iperf, and plot programs like Gnuplot program; which supports many types of plots in 2D and 3D. The Dump command illustrates network nodes with their interfaces connections. Ping and Pingall test network connectivity and latency. Iperf determines bandwidth utilization and retransmission of packets in TCP applications. It also measures loss and jitter for UDP applications.

7.5. Frenetic

Frenetic is a domain-specific language used to program software defined networks [38]. It has features of high-level abstractions. Therefore, it is useful to replace the low-level interfaces available today. Frenetic offers a suite of information about network state, identity, forwarding policies, and updating policies [39].

7.6. Wireshark

Mininet supports Wireshark packet analyzer and uses it to capture packets traverse the network nodes and analyze these packets to study performance of the network and obtain statistical measurements about its behavior [40]. OpenFlow messages could be displayed and studied using Wireshark. Wireshark version 1.11 and above supports a new filter for OpenFlow 1.3 packets.

8. Conclusions and Future Works

Many SDN protocols are available now, but employing the OpenFlow protocol is highly recommended due to its open source nature, rapid development, and wide deployment.

The proper use of emulation software components in developing OpenFlow and SDN projects would save a lot of time and money compared to practical testbeds since real hardware devices are still expensive and support primitive versions of OpenFlow standard only.

In this paper, we examined many software components

related to OpenFlow protocol. Most of them were downloaded, installed, and operated successfully. OpenDaylight, Floodlight, and OFSoftSwitch13 proved to have good properties like good documentation and flexibility.

Observing the rapid development of OpenFlow standards predicts that a major breakthrough is expected in version 2.0, but for the time being the use of software components that supports version 1.3 like NOX, OpenDaylight, and Mul is recommended since no software component supports the new 1.4 version yet.

Most of the tested software components are standalone components. The need for a frame that gather the installation and operation of switches and controllers into a single platform with a certain GUI and benchmark would facilitate the development of OpenFlow projects. EstiNet is a good example of such a platform. An emulation projects to test the compatibility of OpenFlow protocol with WLAN and IPv6 deployment is under consideration by the researchers.

References

[1] M. Mendonca, B. Nunes, K. Obraczka, and T. Turletti, "Software defined networking for heterogeneous networks," IEEE COMSOC MMTC E-Letter United States, vol. 8, no. 3, pp. 36-39, May 2013.

[2] S. Jain, A. Kumar, S. Mandal, J. Ong, L. Poutievski, A. Singh, S. Venkata, J. Wanderer, J. Zhou, M. Zhu, J. Zolla, U. Holzle, S. Stuart and A. Vahdat, "B4: experience with a globally-deployed software defined WAN," SIGCOMM'13 Hong Kong, China, pp. 3-14, August 2013.

[3] D. Drutskoy, E. Keller, and J. Rexford, "Scalable network virtualization in software-defined networks," IEEE Internet Computing, vol.17, pp. 20 – 27, March-April 2013.

[4] Migration Working Group, "Migration use cases and methods," Open Networking Foundation (ONF), February 2014.

[5] S. Wang, C. Chou, and C.Yang, " EstiNet OpenFlow network simulator and emulator," IEEE Communications Magazine, vol. 51, pp. 110-117, September 2013.

[6] B. Lantz, B. Heller, and N. McKeown, "A network in a lap-top: rapid prototyping for software-defined networks," In Proceedings of the 9th ACM SIGCOMM Workshop on Hot Topics in Networks New York,2010.

[7] A. Shalimov, D. Zuikov, D. Zimarina, V. Pashkov, and R. Smeliansky, "Advanced study of SDN/OpenFlow controllers,"CEE-SECR'13 Proceedings of the 9th Central & Eastern European Software Engineering Conference in Russia, November 2013.

[8] B. Nunes, M. Mendonca, X. Nguyen, K. Obraczka, and T. Turletti, "A survey of software-defined networking: past, present, and future of programmable networks," IEEE Communications Surveys & Tutorials, in press, January 2014.

[9] A. Lara, A. Kolasani, and B. Ramamurthy, "Network innovation using OpenFlow: a survey," IEEE Communications Surveys & Tutorials, vol. 16, pp. 493 – 512, February 2014.

[10] Open Network Foundation (ONF), "Software-defined networking: the new norm for networks," April 2012. Available at: https://www.opennetworking.org/images/stories/downloads/openflow/wp-sdn-newnorm.pdf, accessed on 23/3/2014.

[11] T. Nadeau and K. Gray, SDN: Software Defined Networks, 1st ed., O'Reilly Media, Inc., August 2013.

[12] Open Network Foundation (ONF), "OpenFlow switch specification, version 1.4.0 (wire protocol 0x05)," October 2013. Available at:

[13] https://www.opennetworking.org/images/stories/downloads/sdnrsources/onf-specifications/openflow/openflow-spec-v1.4.0.pdf, accessed on 23/3/2014.

[14] N. McKeown, T. Anderson, H. Balakrishnan, G. Parulkar, L. Peterson, J. Rexford, S. Shenker, and J. Turner, "Openflow: enabling innovation in campus networks," SIGCOMM Comput. Commun. Rev., vol. 38, no. 2, pp. 69–74, March 2008.

[15] Open Networking Foundation (ONF), "Open networking foundation," Available at https://www.opennetworking.org/images/stories/downloads/about/onf-what-why.pdf.

[16] Tech and Trains, available at: http://gregorygee.wordpress.com/category/miniedit/.

[17] Visual Network Description (VND), available at: http://www.ramonfontes.com/visual-network-description/.

[18] EstiNet Technologies Inc., "The GUI user Manual for the EstiNet 8.0 Network Simulator and Emulator", January 2013.

[19] T. Dietz, "Trema tutorial," NEC Corporation, March 2012. Available at: http://www.fp7-ofelia.eu/assets/Uploads/201203xx-TremaTutorial.pdf, accessed on 23/3/2014.

[20] Z. Cai, A. Cox, T. Eugene Ng, "Maestro: balancing fairness, latency and throughput in the OpenFlow control plane," Rice University Technical Report TR11-07, 2011.

[21] NOX, http://www.noxrepo.org/nox/about-nox/.

[22] S. Azodolmolky, Software Defined Networking with OpenFlow, Packt Publishing, 1st ed., October 2013.

[23] POX, http://www.noxrepo.org/pox/about-pox/.

[24] Floodlight, http://www.projectfloodlight.org/floodlight/.

[25] OpenDaylight, http://www.opendaylight.org/software/.

[26] Ryu, http://osrg.github.io/ryu/.

[27] Mul, http://sourceforge.net/projects/mul/.

[28] Beacon, https://openflow.stanford.edu/display/Beacon/Home.

[29] FlowvisorExecise, https://github.com/onstutorial/onstutorial/wiki/Flowvisor-Exercise.

[30] RouteFlow, https://sites.google.com/site/routeflow/.

[31] Open vSwitch, http://openvswitch.org/.

[32] A. Clemm, and R. Wolter, "network-embedded management and applications understanding programmable networking infrastructure," Springer New York, 2013.

[33] OpenFlow 1.3 Tutorial, available at: https://github.com/CPqD/ofsoftswitch13/wiki/OpenFlow-1.3Tutorial.

[34] LINC, https://github.com/FlowForwarding/LINC-Switch.

[35] Indigo, https://github.com/floodlight/indigo.

[36] Avior, https://github.com/Sovietaced/Avior.

[37] Scapy, http://www.secdev.org/projects/scapy/.

[38] OFLops: user manual, available at: http://archive.openflow.org/wk/images/3/3e/Manual.pdf.

[39] Frenetic, http://www.frenetic-lang.org/overview.php.

[40] N. Foster, M. Freedman, A. Guha, R. Harrison, N. Katta, C. Monsanto, J. Reich, M. Reitblatt, J. Rexford, C. Schlesinger, A. Story, D. Walker, "Languages for software-defined networks," IEEE Communications Magazine, vol. 51, pp. 128 – 134, February 2013.

[41] R. Shimonski, Analyzing and Troubleshooting Network Traffic, Elsevier Inc., 1st ed., 2013.

9

An approach to modeling domain-wide information, based on limited points' data – part I

John Charlery, Chris D. Smith

Dept. of Computer Science, Mathematics & Physics, Faculty of Science and Technology, University of the West Indies, Cave Hill Campus, Bridgetown, Barbados BB11000

Email address:

john.charlery@cavehill.uwi.edu (J. Charlery),chris.smith@mycavehill.uwi.edu (C. D. Smith)

Abstract: Predicting values at data points in a specified region when only a few values are known is a perennial problem and many approaches have been developed in response. Interpolation schemes provide some success and are the most widely used among the approaches. However, none of those schemes incorporates historical aspects in their formulae. This study presents an approach to interpolation, which utilizes the historical relationships existing between the data points in a region of interest. By combining the historical relationships with the interpolation equations, an algorithm for making predictions over an entire domain area, where data is known only for some random parts of that area, is presented. A performance analysis of the algorithm indicates that even when provided with less than ten percent of the domain's data, the algorithm outperforms the other popular interpolation algorithms when more than fifty percent of the domain's data is provided to them.

Keywords: Data Modeling, Interpolation, Data Prediction, Sparse Data Analysis

1. Introduction

There are numerous methods for making predictions based on sparse data. Some of these methods provide well-documented forms of interpolation between the known data points. Among the more popular approaches are methods such as Inverse Distance Weighting to a Power [1], Kriging [2, 3, 4, 5], Triangulation with Linear Interpolation [6], Natural Neighbour [7], and Minimum Curvature [8]. In should be noted that in this work, the term prediction and its other derivatives, are used with a purely statistical definition and is not meant to allude to a future event.

Although it would be very handy to predict the future behaviour of events, in this study, the concentration is to address the issue of predicting existing domain-wide information when the data required to draw such conclusions are significantly lacking. In setting up the premise, the strengths and weaknesses of the popular methods just mentioned, are drawn upon to formulate an algorithm which will address the stipulated intent.

The primary goal of this work therefore, is to develop an algorithm for making predictions over an entire domain area, where data is known only for some random parts of that area. In other words, to provide domain-wide information, based upon sparse and random point data. The fundamental approaches used by other authors such as Fisher [1], Stein [4], Lee [6], Laurent [7] and Smith [8] among others, have been to use physical rules and/or interpolations to produce the data values of the missing locations. This work seeks to go further to refine this approach by incorporating the historical data from all the available data points (or what will be hitherto referred to as "stations") in the domain area and to try to establish relationships in a pair wise fashion between all the stations. After these relationships are established, then a determination of the strengths or weaknesses of the paired stations are determined. Equations defining the relationships will then be created for each pair of data stations based on the historical data, so that it would be possible to predict the value of one station when given the value of the other station that makes up the pair.

Algorithms will be developed to determine which pairs of data stations would be selected to facilitate the global (or domain-wide) predictions. (We define a domain or universe, as the geographical area within whose physical boundaries that data value predictions will be made.) These algorithms would also use the strength factors of the selected pairs to make the most accurate (or strongest) predictions.

(Heretofore, the term 'global' will be used to represent coverage of the entire defined domain.)

In this first part of the research (Part I), we present the background and algorithms to the proposed methodology. Implementation of the methodology, through two very contrasting cases studied, is presented in the second part of the research (Part II).

2. Methodology

The foundations to the process of effecting the global predictions are therefore as follows:

1. Every station within the domain is paired to each other.
2. Each paired station is plotted on a Scatterplot diagram, to determine what type of relationship (if any) exists between the two stations.
3. The strength or weakness of the association between the stations is calibrated.
4. An equation is developed to compute the value of one station when the value of its pair is known.
5. As the stations' values become known, these known stations would be used as the basis for further predictions of the unknown stations. The prediction algorithms then incorporate this 'new' data to determine which predicted value is likely to be the most accurate for any station within the domain.

In order to accomplish this, the methodology employs the techniques of Scatterplots, Pearson's Correlation, Linear Regression and the Straight line equation.

3. Established Interpolation Methods

Over the years, many methods have been developed for the interpolation of unknown values based on known ones which lie in the region of interest. There are advantages and disadvantages to each method. The strengths and weaknesses of the different approaches depend on the nature of the data that is being examined and hence the accuracy of the different methods varies depending on the dataset being used. Following is a list and brief description of some of the more popular interpolation methods that are used extensively today.

3.1. Inverse Distance Weighting to a Power

The Inverse Distance Weighting to a power method is implemented through different strategies. In this work the method proposed by Shepard [9] is used to implement the Inverse Distance Weighting (IDW). IDW is a simple method of assigning values to unknown points by using values from known points. The influence on an unknown point is inversely proportional to the distance between that unknown point and a point that is known.

3.2. Kriging

Sierra [10] describes Kriging as a modified linear regression technique that estimates a value at a point by assuming that the value is spatially related to the known values in a neighborhood near that point. Kriging computes the value for the unknown data point using a weighted linear sum of known data values. The weights are chosen to minimize the estimation error variance and to eliminate any bias in the sampling. Unlike other techniques for scalar values, kriging bases its estimates upon a dynamic neighborhood point configuration and treats those points as regionalized variables instead of random variables. Regionalized variables assume the existence of a region of influence on the data.

3.3. Triangulation with Linear Interpolation

As Lee [6] showed, one of the most common triangulation method is the Delauney triangulation. In triangulation, the known data points have lines drawn between them in such a way so as to create a network of triangles. When these triangles are formed, no triangle's edges are intersected by any other triangle. The result is a patchwork of triangular faces over the extent of the data region. These triangles look somewhat like a tiled mosaic over the region of interest.

Each triangle may have several data points with unknown values within it. The values of the unknown points which lie in the triangle is determine by using a weighted average of the vertices of that specific triangle. Each triangle creates a data plane, which has tilt and elevation so the value of the known points would depend on where it is located in the triangle.

Triangulation with linear interpolation works best when the known points are evenly distributed over the entire region of interest. However, it should be noted that unknown points, which lie outside of the network of triangles, would not have values predicted for them.

3.4. Natural Neighbour

Natural Neighbour is a weighted average technique that is based on the Voronoi tessellation. One definition of the Voronoi tessellation given by Parag [11] is "the partitioning of a plane with n points into n convex polygons such that each polygon contains exactly one point and every point in a given polygon is closer to its central point than to any other". The Voronoi tessellation polygon network is constructed from the triangulation of the data points.

The vertices of the Voronoi Tessellation polygons, correspond to the centroids of the circumcircles of the triangles connecting the known data points. A circumcircle is a triangle's circumscribed circle. In other words, it is the unique circle that passes through each of the triangle's three vertices.

The way natural neighbour interpolation works to get an unknown value for a point x, is by inserting the point x into it's actual location in the defined network. After point x is inserted, the Voronoi Tessellation polygon network must be rearrange to accommodate this new point, since the new point must have its own Voronoi Tessellation polygon. This accommodation is facilitated by shrinking the polygons, which surround the new polygon. The value of x is then determined from the proportion of the intersections of the original polygons surrounding the newly inserted one.

3.5. Minimum Curvature

Smith [8] describes Minimum Curvature as a technique, which generates an interpolated surface that is like a thin elastic plate, which passes through each of the known data points with a minimum amount of bending. Minimum curvature tries to produce the smoothest possible surface while attempting to honour the known data as closely as possible.

In this method a two-dimensional cubic spline function is applied to fit a smooth surface to the set of input data values. The computation requires a number of iterations to adjust the surface so that the final result has a minimum amount of curvature.

4. The Algorithm

The prediction algorithm is a technique, which is used to make the best global prediction based on a subset of data stations, while taking into consideration the historical relationships, which exist between the various data stations in the region of interest.

The first step in the technique is to establish the historical relationships. This is achieved by having the data stations organized in a pair-wise fashion, where each station is paired with all other stations in the domain area. When the existing historical data from the paired stations are plotted on the scatter plot, there are four possible simple scenarios:

1. One station's values are high while the other station's values are low.
2. One station's values are low while the other station's values are high.
3. The values between the stations alternates from being higher and lower.
4. Both stations have the same values.

In each case a linear or quasi-linear relationship can be modeled between the pairs. The predictions for a station could then be obtained using those linear equations for stations where data are available.

As an example, if there are n stations in the domain area, then there will be a total of n(n-1) paired combinations. In other words, given a set of stations A, B and C, then the pairs would be AB, AC, BA, BC, CA and CB. All of these paired names are then stored in the primary key field of individual records in a lookup file. The records in the lookup file also store the correlation between the two stations, the distance between the two stations, the equation which defines the relationship between the two stations as well as some other data which will be discussed in the subsequent sections.

The algorithm implements a lookup file to store the information dynamically derived, which define the relationships existing between the stations. The lookup file is employed as follows:

Given the value of a station, say station A, the algorithm searches the lookup file for all the records that have its primary field value starting with the station name A (i.e. AB, AC, as in the example provided above). From the selected records, it is now possible to predict the values for the other stations in the pair, based on the value for the known station (station A in this case), since there would exist in the selected records an equation which defines their statistical relationship with the known station (station A) respectively. When another station's value becomes available (e.g. station B), it then becomes possible to predict the value of the other stations, not only from the previously known stations (e.g. station A) but also from the new station's record (Station B) in the lookup file. In all likelihood, it is quite possible that the different predictions for a station, whose data value is not known, by stations with known values, would not be perfectly identical. In such a case, the precedence portion of the algorithm, which forms the secondary nucleus of this work, would then have to decide which value among the lot would be the best prediction.

The proposed algorithm has basically three processes, which work together in order to have a successful and acceptable prediction outcome. The processes are made up of:

- Input data acceptance routine
- Paired automation routine
- Precedence selection routine

A brief description of the processes, along with the various pseudocode, are presented in Sections 4.1 to 4.4.

4.1. Input Data Acceptance Routine

The historical data for the stations within the specified domain are passed to the prediction algorithm through this module. The prediction algorithm uses the historical data values of the stations during common historical instances throughout the region of interest. These historical data values represent "snapshots" of the domain during those specified instances. To get the data organized in the required manner, the data can either be entered manually into the system, one station at a time, or more appropriately, can be accepted through the use of an input file.

For the purposes of providing an implementation example, the format of Microsoft Excel file is being used for the input file. In this file, the first column contains the names of the stations; the next series of columns hold the historical values for the stations (each column holds one value for the station for each time instance), and the last two columns to the extreme right of the data values holds the X and Y coordinates respectively of the station, within the domain.

The pseudocode for the data acceptance routine, when using an input file, is as follows:

create "points" file with fields (stations x, y)
open input file (possibly in Microsoft Excel file format)

for each station in the input file do
insert station names and coordinates into "points" file
create file of current station name with field (value)
insert station's data values into newly created file of the station name
endfor

The preceding pseudocode essentially creates a file name "points" which stores the names and coordinates of all the stations. It also creates a file named after each station where the historical values of each station are stored in their respective file. After the data have been organized in this way then the next step is to develop the paired automation stage.

4.2. Paired Automation Routine

After the historical data values for all the stations in the region of interest have been entered into the system, the algorithm proceeds to organize the data stations in a pair wise fashion. This type of organization is crucial to facilitate the prediction processes, because it is from these paired relationships that the unknown stations values can then be predicted. These predictions are made possible because each station is paired with all other stations in the region of interest. On pairing the stations, a predictive equation is developed which allows one station's value, in the pair of stations, to be used to predict the value of the other station in the pair. Therefore, it becomes possible to make a prediction for all the stations when the value of only one station is known. Needless to say, predictions made of all the stations when only one station is known would provide little more than a scaled representation of the mean spatial statistical distribution over the region of interest and would therefore be considerable less accurate than when many stations are known and used in the prediction process. As the stations are paired together, various statistical calculations are preformed with the goal of extracting and saving the statistical data in a master lookup file, which can then be referenced to guide the decision process.

The development and establishment of the master lookup file is a significant underpin to the proposed algorithm. The data stored in this file allow the algorithm to calculate various predicted values for the unknown stations based on the stations that have known values and also facilitate the determination of which predicted value is the best one based on the selected criteria in the precedence portion of the algorithm. In updating the master lookup file, several fields must be addressed. These fields hold the following information:

- Paired stations identification routine
- Relationship formula between the paired stations
- Correlation between the paired stations
- Distance between the paired stations
- Statistical Deviation between the paired stations

4.3. Paired Stations Identification Routine

In this component of the algorithm, the name of each of the station is combined with all the other station names. For convenience, the compound name is created by placing a "%" character between the two names. These concatenated names are then inserted into the master lookup table. The following pseudocode illustrates the process:

create array1
create array2
store all the station names in array1
store all the station names in array2
for each name in array1 do
for each name in array2 do
concatenate array1 station name to array2 station name
insert concatenated names into master lookup file
endfor
endfor

4.4. Relationship Formula Between the Paired Stations

This component of the algorithm determines the linear relationship formula between each pair of stations. The formula takes the form of the linear equation:

$$y = a \pm bx$$

where a and b are known and x and y are unknown. Therefore, the objective of this routine is to determine the values of a and b respectively. This is achieved by using the linear regression model on the historical data. (Kleinbaun et al [12] provide a detailed description on the technique). The routine queries the master lookup file, and uses the concatenated stations' names to access the necessary files in order to get the historical data to be used in the regression model. The following pseudocode illustrates how it is done:

open master lookup file
for each record in the master lookup file do
get names of each station in the paired name
assign first part of paired name to station1
assign second part of paired name to station2
open station1 file
open station2 file
store sum of station1 values to variable sx
store sum of station2 values to variable sy
store sum of (station1 values * station2 values) to variable sxy
store sum of (station1 values * station1 values) to variable sxsq
store record count of either station1 or station2 to variable rec
store (sy * sxsq) – (sx * sxy) to variable numeratorA
store (rec * sxsq) – (sx * sx) to variable denominatorA
if denominatorA is not zero then
store (numeratorA / denominatorA) to variable A
endif
store (rec * sxy) – (sx * sy) to variable numeratorB
store (rec * sxsq) – (sx * sx) to variable denominatorB

if denominatorB is not zero then
store (numeratorB / denominatorB) to variable B
endif
insert variable A and B's values in master lookup file for pair
endfor

4.5. Correlation between the Paired Stations

This routine calculates the strength of the linear relationship of the historical data for each pair of stations. This is achieved by using the established measure of correlation known as Pearson Product Moment Correlation. (For more details on the technique, refer to [1, 12, 13, 14, 15]. The routine queries the master lookup file, and uses the concatenated stations' names to access the necessary files in order to get the historical data to use in the Pearson's Correlation formula. The following pseudocode demonstrates how the correlation is obtained:

open master lookup file
for each record in the master lookup file do
get names of each station in the paired name
assign first part of paired name to station1
assign second part of paired name to station2
open station1 file
open station2 file
store sum of station1 values to variable sx
store sum of station2 values to variable sy
store sum of (station1 values * station2 values) to variable sxy
store sum of (station1 values * station1 values) to variable sxsq
store sum of (station2 values * station2 values) to variable sysq
store record count of either station1 or station2 to variable rec
store (rec * sxy) – (sx * sy) to variable corT
store the square root of (rec * sxsq)-(sx * sx) to variable corB1
store the square root of (rec * sysq)-(sy * sy) to variable corB2
store (corB1*corB2) to variable corB
if corB is not zero then
store corT/corB to variable correlation
endif
insert variable correlation's value in master lookup file
go to next record in the master lookup file repeat above steps
endfor

4.6. Distance between the Paired Stations

In this section of the algorithm, the Euclidean distance between the paired stations in the master lookup file is calculated. This distance is required by some of the precedence algorithms which will be presented subsequently. As with the other routines, this routine also queries the master lookup file to get the names of the paired stations. It then searches for the names in the points file created by the data acceptance routine. When the stations are found in the points file, the X-Y coordinates of each station are used to calculate the relative distance between them. The following pseudocode demonstrates the procedure:

open master lookup file
for each record in the master lookup file do
get names of each station in the paired name
assign first part of name to station1
assign second part of name to station2
open points file
search for station1
store coordinate in variables X1 and Y1
search for station2
store coordinates in variables X2 and Y2
store square of X1-X2 to variable num1
store square of Y1-Y2 to variable num2
store square-root of num1+num2 to variable distance
insert variable distance value in master lookup file
endfor

4.7. Deviation Value between the Paired Stations

In this routine the deviation value among the paired stations is calculated. We define the deviation value as the absolute difference between the values predicted for a station by another station that it is paired with and the actual value observed at that particular station. This deviation value is required by one of the precedence routines which will be described later in Section 5.1. The lookup file is searched and as each record is encountered, the file associated with the paired stations is opened and the values of the first station are plugged into the associated relationship formula for the calculation of the second stations' value. The absolute difference between calculated values and the actual observed values for the second station are tallied and inserted into the lookup file for that pair. This approach is chosen to allow faster execution of the precedence portion of the algorithm, in that, the deviation calculation would not have to be computed every time the deviation value is required. The steps are illustrated in the following pseudocode:

open master lookup file
for each record in the master lookup file
get names of stations making up pair
get relationship formula
open file of the paired stations
for each record in the paired stations file do
place the first station value in relationship formula
store absolute difference between output from formula and actual
value of second station into variable deviation
insert deviation value into lookup file for the current pair
endfor
endfor

5. Precedence Selection Routines

Having each station paired with all other stations, it therefore means that each station will have a predicted value based on the station it is paired with. In other words, if there are *n* stations in the region of interest then there can potentially be as many as *n-1* different predicted values for a station. Therefore, the precedence selection is the aspect of the algorithm, which allows for the setting of criteria by which one predicted value is chosen as the best value for the unknown station. For this algorithm, four criteria settings have been developed to drive the precedence selection process. These criteria settings are:

- Least Deviating Function
- Shortest Distance
- Moving Average
- Greatest Correlation

The Greatest Correlation (GC) criterion is being set as the default precedence setting for the algorithm.

5.1. Least Deviating Function

The Least Deviating Function method searches both the list of known stations and the list of stations to be predicted. As it searches, it concatenates the known stations name with the names of the stations to be predicted and these concatenated names are searched for in the lookup file. When the record is found, the deviation value is temporarily stored. The process of searching and temporarily storing the deviation value is continued until all the known stations are compared to each other and the lowest deviation value recorded. The record which has the lowest deviation values is selected as the record to make the prediction for the unknown station. The pseudocode below demonstrates the steps involved:

```
create variable mindev
initialize mindev to 0
open list of known stations
for each record in the list of known stations do
 store name of station to variable station1
open list of unknown stations
for each record in the list of unknown stations do
store name of station to variable station2
concatenate names of station1 and station2 to variable station1-2
open master lookup file
search for station1-2
if found then
 store deviation value to variable statdev
if mindev is equal to 0
store statdev to mindev
else
if statdev is less than mindev
store statdev to mindev
store equation to variable leastdev
endif
endif
endif
```

```
endfor
update unknown stations with prediction from leastdev record
endfor
```

5.2. Shortest Distance

The Shortest Distance method is similar to the Least Deviating Function. However, instead of searching the lookup file for the record with the least deviation value, it searches for the pair of stations that has the shortest relative distance between them. The pseudocode to this process is given below:

```
create variable leastdis
open list of known stations
for each record in the list of known stations do
 store name of station to variable station1
open list of unknown stations
for each record in the list of unknown stations do
store name of station to variable station2
concatenate names of station1 and station2 to variable station1-2
open master lookup file
search for station1-2
if found then
store distance value to variable dis
if this is the first search of the lookup file
store dis to leastdis
else
if dis is greater than leastdis
store dis to leastdis
store equation to variable less
endif
endif
endif
endfor
update unknown stations with prediction from less record
endfor
```

5.3. Moving Average

With the Moving Average method, the value of an unknown station is determined by taking the mean average of the predicted values for a number of known stations that are closest to the unknown station. In order to be meaningful, the number of known stations must be at the very least equal to two. The actual number of stations used in the routine can be chosen arbitrarily. If the total number of stations is small (less than 50 for example) then it would be expected that a small number of known stations would be selected to be used in the routine (say 3 to 8 for example). However, if the total number of stations is large (say, greater than 150) then a larger number of averaging stations could be selected.

The Moving Average routine systematically moves to all the unknown stations in the region of interest. As it moves to the unknown stations, the closest neighboring stations with known data values within the specified number, are selected and the mean average of their predictions for that unknown station is calculated. The pseudocode for this routine is as follows:

    initialize variable sum to 0
    initialize variable average to 0
    get the number of stations to used in the average from user
    count number of known stations to variable kcount
    open the list of unknown station
    for each record in the list of unknown stations do
    for item going from 1 to kcount do
    concatenate known station name with station to be predicted
    open lookup file
    locate concatenated name
    insert information into temporary file
    endfor
    open temporary file
    sort file by distance in ascending order
    for record from 1 to number of stations used in average do
    concatenate known station name with station to be predicted
    open lookup file
    locate concatenated name
    calculate predicted value
    add predicted value to sum
    store sum divided by number of stations used in prediction into
    average
    endfor
    insert average into prediction value for current unknown stations
    endfor

5.4. Greatest Correlation

The Greatest Correlation routine is similar to the Least Deviating Function presented previously in Section 5.1. However, instead of searching the lookup file for the record with the least deviation value, it searches for the pair of stations that has the highest correlation value between them. The pseudocode to the process is as follows:

    create variable maxcorr
    open list of known stations
    for each record in the list of known stations do
    store name of station to variable station1
    open list of unknown stations
    for each record in the list of unknown stations do
    store name of station to variable station2
    concatenate names of station1 and station2 to variable station1-2
    open master lookup file
    search for station1-2
    if found then
    store correlation value to variable corr
    if this is the first search of the lookup file

    store corr to maxcorr
    else
    if corr is greater than maxcorr
    store corr to maxcorr
    store equation to variable maxequ
    endif
    endif
    endif
    endfor
    update unknown stations with prediction from maxequ record
    endfor

6. Conclusion

The primary objective of this work was to develop an approach to the prediction of unknown stations values when some randomly selected stations values are known. This was achieved by the implementation of an algorithm that established a historical statistical relationship between pairs of all the data stations in the region of interest. The use of a historical relationship in the prediction of unknown data stations is a "step-away" from the established interpolations methods such as Kriging, Inverse Distance and Minimum Curvature (to name a few). These established methods do not factor in any historical relationships in their formulae.

A secondary objective was to compare the results of some of the more popular interpolation methods with the proposed algorithm. This comparison is implemented through the detailed examinations of two cases studied in Part II of this paper. In these studies, it will be shown that the image distribution maps for both an objective and subjective dataset, the proposed methodology generally out-performs the other popular interpolation analyses to generate predictions for the entire domain.

References

[1]   N. I. Fisher, T. Lewis, B. J. J. Embleton, Statistical Analysis of Spherical Data, Cambridge University Press, 1987.

[2]   D. Dorsel, T. La Breche, Kriging. <http://ewr.cee.vt.edu/environmental/teach/smprimer/krigin g/kriging.html>, January 2009.

[3]   R. V. Jesus, Kriging: An Accompanied Example in IDRISI, GIS Centrum, University of Lund for Oresund, Summer University, 2003.

[4]   M.L. Stein, Interpolation of Spatial Data: Some Theory for Kriging, Springer, New York, 1999.

[5]   W.C.M. Van Beers, J. P.C. Kleijnen, Kriging Interpolation in Simulation : A Survey, in: R .G. Ingalls, M. D. Rossetti, J. S. Smith, and B. A. Peters (Eds.), Proceedings of the 2004 Winter Simulation Conference, Washington, DC, 2004, pp. 113-121.

[6]   D. T. Lee, B.J. Schachter, Two Algorithms for Constructing a Delaunay Triangulation. International Journal of

Computer and information Sciences, Vol. 9, 1980, pp. 219-242.

[7]   P-J. Laurent, Wavelets, Images, and Surface Fitting, in: A. Le Mehaute (Ed.), A.K Peters Ltd., 1994.

[8]   W. H. F. Smith, P. Wessel, Gridding with Continuous Curvature Splines in Tension, Geophysics, 55, 1990.

[9]   D. Shepard, A two-dimensional interpolation function for irregularly spaced data. Proceedings of the 23rd ACM National Conference (128), 1968, pp.517-524.

[10] R.   Sierra,   Rigid   Registration. <http://www.rsierra.com/DA/node10.html#SECTION00103 0000000000000000>, May 2009.

[11] J.   Parag,   Class   Presentation. <http://arcib.dowling.edu/~JainP/Research1/slide2.html>, May 2009.

[12] D. Kleinbaum, L. Kupper, K. Muller, Applied Regression Analysis and other Multivariable Method, Duxbury Press, 1987.

[13] Wasson J. Statistics in Educational Research - An Internet Based   Course. <http://www.mnstate.edu/wasson/ed602pearsoncorr.htm>,

April 2009.

[14] J. Deacon, Correlation, and regression analysis for curve fitting. <http://www.biology.ed.ac.uk/research/groups/jdeacon/statis tics/tress11.html >, January 2009.

[15] R.J.   Rummel,   Understanding   Correlation. <http://www.mega.nu:8080/ampp/rummel/uc.htm>, December 2009.

[16] E. Yudkowsky, An Intuitive Explanation of Bayesian Reasoning, <http://yudkowsky.net/bayes/bayes.html>, May 2009.

[17] P. E. Gill, W. Murray, Algorithms for the solution of the nonlinear least-squares problem. SIAM Journal of Numeral Analysis, 15 [5], 1978, pp. 977-992.

[18] W. R. Greco, M. T. Hakala. Evaluation of methods for estimating the dissociation constant of tight binding enzyme inhibitors, Journal of Biological Chemistry, (254), 1979, pp.12104-12109.

[19] D. F. Symancyk, Visualizing Gaussian Elimination, <http://ola4.aacc.edu/dfsymancyk/vgetalk/VGEtalkexpande d.html>, May 2006.

10

An approach to modeling domain-wide information, based on limited points' data – part II

John Charlery, Chris D. Smith

Dept. of Computer Science, Mathematics & Physics, Faculty of Science and Technology, University of the West Indies, Cave Hill Campus, Bridgetown, Barbados BB11000

Email address:

john.charlery@cavehill.uwi.edu (J. Charlery),chris.smith@mycavehill.uwi.edu (C. D. Smith)

Abstract: Predicting values at data points in a specified region when only a few values are known is a perennial problem and many approaches have been developed in response. Interpolation schemes provide some success and are the most widely used among the approaches. However, none of those schemes incorporates historical aspects in their formulae. This study presents an approach to interpolation, which utilizes the historical relationships existing between the data points in a region of interest. By combining the historical relationships with the interpolation equations, an algorithm for making predictions over an entire domain area, where data is known only for some random parts of that area, is presented. A performance analysis of the algorithm indicates that even when provided with less than ten percent of the domain's data, the algorithm outperforms the other popular interpolation algorithms when more than fifty percent of the domain's data is provided to them.

Keywords: Data Modeling, Interpolation, Data Prediction, Sparse Data Analysis

1. Introduction

In Part I of this research, we presented the background and algorithms to a proposed interpolation methodology, whose primary objective was to develop an approach to the prediction of unknown stations values when some randomly selected other stations values are known. This was achieved by the implementation of an algorithm that established a historical statistical relationship between pairs of all the data stations in the region of interest. Since other algorithms do not incorporate historical relationships in the prediction of unknown data stations, this method is a "step-away" from the other popular established interpolations methods. In this second part of the research, we present an implementation of the methodology, through two very contrasting cases study.

2. Implementation

The algorithm is being implemented through the demonstration of two case studies. The performance of the algorithm is then analyzed through the usage of the two data sets. The first case study examines rainfall data (which represents data produced as a consequence of objective and physical rules,) and the second case study examines electoral ballots data at electoral polling stations (to represent data resulting from subjective processes). In both case studies the geographical domain is the country of Barbados, which was arbitrarily selected. The data from the stations of interest are scattered throughout the island. The map of the island is overlaid by a series of vertical and horizontal grid lines, which in turn creates a series of rectangular cells into which the data stations coincide. The virtual cells that house the data stations are used to calculate the Euclidean distances of the data stations from each other.

To determine the percentage deviations of the predictions, the error value must first be obtained. For simplicity, this is determined by simply taking the difference between the predicted values and the observed values for each station. The absolute values of the differences are used to eliminate the effects of having negative values after the subtractions. These absolute values are summed up and then divided by the sum of the observed values. Finally to get the percentage deviation, the error value is simply multiplied by 100. In other words.

Error Value is . $E = \left[\dfrac{\sum\limits_{1}^{i} D_i}{\sum\limits_{1}^{i} A_i} \right]$ (1)

Deviation percentage is .

$$Y = E \times 100 \hspace{2cm} (2)$$

Where
E = Error Value
Y = Percentage Deviation
D = absolute difference between actual observations and predicted values
A = actual observation value

The prediction accuracy is given as 1 minus the error value. The maximum resulting value for the prediction accuracy is 1, which means perfect accuracy, or where the error value is zero.

2.1. Visualization of Established and Proposed Results for Case Study 1 – Rainfall Stations

The physical domain being used is 431 square kilometers and comprises of fourteen (14) data stations with monthly historical data values, which spans the period of 1960 to 2004. In the results, which are presented in Sections 6.1.1 to 6.1.3, we have arbitrarily and randomly selected one station with a known data value for January 2005, then three stations and then finally nine stations with known data values to perform the prediction for the entire domain for January 2005. A comparative analysis with some of the other popular interpolation algorithms is also presented.

2.1.1. Analysis From Using One (1) Known Data Station Value

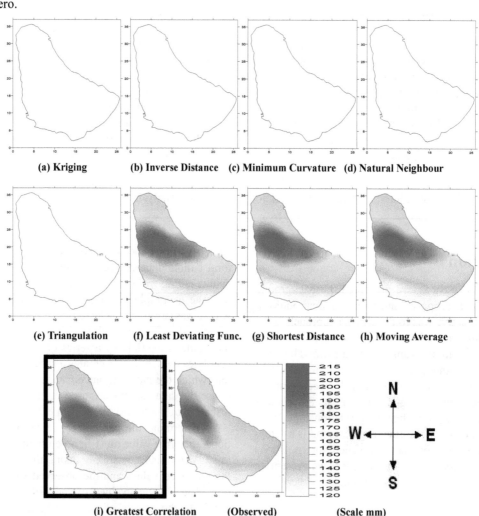

(a) Kriging   (b) Inverse Distance   (c) Minimum Curvature   (d) Natural Neighbour

(e) Triangulation   (f) Least Deviating Func.   (g) Shortest Distance   (h) Moving Average

(i) Greatest Correlation   (Observed)   (Scale mm)

Fig.. 1. Images using one known data station's value.

With only one data point is used as input data, the interpolation algorithms of kriging, inverse distance, minimum curvature, natural neighbour and triangulation are unable to generate predictions for the domain. However, the algorithms of least deviating function, shortest distance, mov-

ing average and greatest correlation, which this work has adapted to work as interpolation techniques, have been able to capture the general distribution of the rainfall over the domain. Even with only one data point provided, the analyses from these techniques mimic the observed distribution. The principal and common difference between the observed analysis and the predicted analyses is in the orientation of the distribution. For each of the three methods, the rainfall's ridge axis (reddish color) is oriented in a somewhat east/west direction while the observed rainfall's ridge axis assumes a more northwest/southeast orientation. Notwithstanding this, the area of maximum rainfall (brightest red) corresponds almost perfectly with the actual observation.

2.1.2. Analysis From Using Three (3) Known Data Stations' Values

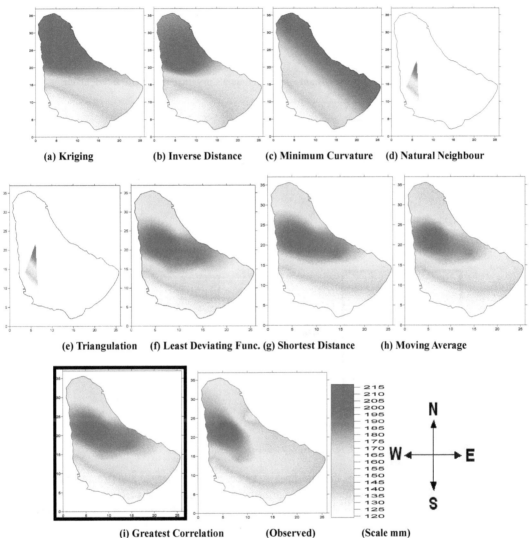

(a) Kriging   (b) Inverse Distance   (c) Minimum Curvature   (d) Natural Neighbour

(e) Triangulation   (f) Least Deviating Func.   (g) Shortest Distance   (h) Moving Average

(i) Greatest Correlation   (Observed)   (Scale mm)

Fig. 2. *Images using 3 known data stations' values.*

With three data point used as input data, the interpolation algorithms of kriging, inverse distance, minimum curvature, natural neighbour and triangulation are able to generate some predictions for the domain. However, for all three methods, when compared with the observed, their predictions are very misleading.

Kriging and inverse distance concentrate the maximum rainfall in the northern half of the island while minimum curvature concentrates the maximum rainfall in the eastern half of the island. With those three methods, neither rainfall distribution nor quantity reflects much similarity with what is actually observed. The natural neighbour and triangulation algorithms have fared better, but their predictions are limited to the zone bounded within the three data points while in both cases providing no information for the remainder of the domain.

The algorithms of least deviating function, shortest distance and moving average, maintain a similar distribution to the previous case in Section 6.1.1, although there are now some adjustments to the quantities being predicted. The analysis for greatest correlation is reflecting this tweaking and continues to generate the closest match to the observed.

2.1.2. Analysis From Using Nine (9) Known Data Stations' Values

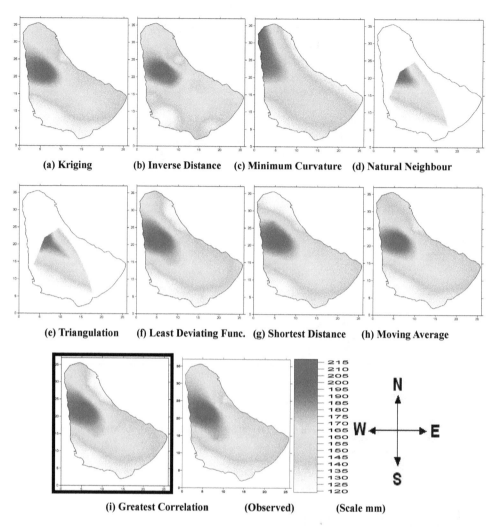

(a) Kriging   (b) Inverse Distance   (c) Minimum Curvature   (d) Natural Neighbour

(e) Triangulation   (f) Least Deviating Func.   (g) Shortest Distance   (h) Moving Average

(i) Greatest Correlation   (Observed)   (Scale mm)

Fig. 3. Images using 9 known data stations' values.

With 64% of the data now used as input in the simulation, the analyses from the interpolation algorithms of kriging and inverse distance are now beginning to show some similarity to the observed. Compared to the previous case, the results from both the kriging and the inverse distance algorithm's rainfall's ridge axis (reddish color) have contracted and shifted from a northerly direction towards a more northwest/southeast orientation. However, with the minimum curvature, the rainfall's ridge axis has shifted from its location in the extreme northern part of the island to become oriented in a north/south direction, but still locked in the northwestern part of the island. However, neither rainfall distribution nor quantity reflects much similarity with what is actually observed.

The algorithms of natural neighbour and triangulation continues to increase its coverage region with the nine known data input. The predicted values for the unknown stations in their coverage area compare favorably with the observed. However their predictions are still limited only to the zone within the nine data points, while in both cases providing no information for the remainder of the domain.

The algorithms of least deviating function, shortest dis-

tance, moving average and greatest correlation continues to maintain a similar distribution to the previous case with further minor adjustments to the quantities being predicted.

The results from the greatest correlation algorithm continue to reflect further minor tweaking in the quantities being predicted for the unknown stations and also continues to provide the closest match to the observed in terms of both rainfall quantity and distribution.

2.1.4. Summary Conclusion for Case Study 1

Although this is only a single case, some aspects of the comparison are very conspicuous and are noted as following.

Kriging, Inverse Distance and Minimum Curvature.

- No prediction was possible until at least 3 data stations were provided as input.
- With 3 data stations, predictions were made but these predictions turned out to be very misleading.
- Predictions began to show some similarity with the observed when at least 9 data stations (64% of all the stations) were used as

input. For kriging and inverse distance the predictions continued to improve steadily after more data stations were added. Minimum curvature displayed a significantly much slower rate of improvement than all the other methods.

Natural Neighbour and Triangulation.

- No prediction was possible until at least 3 data stations were provided as input.
- With 3 or more data stations used, predictions comparable to the observed were made, but these predictions were limited to the inner area created by those data points alone.

Least Deviating Function, Shortest Distance, Moving Average and Greatest Correlation.

- Captured general rainfall distribution pattern over the island with only one data point used as input.
- Predictions continued to improve with small tweaks, as more data were added as input.
- Consistently produced very good results with the greatest correlation method producing the best results at each stage.

2.2. Visualization of Established and Proposed Results for Case Study 2 – Electoral Polling Stations

For this case study, the algorithm is applied to data, which have been derived through a less rigid process, where the physical laws which determine the values are not as clearly defined. Electoral polling results for political election events in the country of Barbados are used. Far from being able to define the objective laws, which determine the casting of ballots in a democratic election, it may be more appropriate to describe this process as the result of subjective motivation. Nonetheless, it is expected that some polling stations will still have a positive relationship – even if such a relationship is weak.

The polling stations' data were provided by 225 polling stations, which span the period from 1976 to 2003 and constituted seven (7) national electoral events. For this case study, the number of stations is relatively large. Hence, in the analysis, we will observe the proposed model's performance by randomly sampling 8%, 21% and 64% respectively of known data values, and noting how "well" the model is predicting the values for the remaining unknown polling stations.

Here the choice of 8%, 21% and 64% of known data values are not a requirement for the algorithm but have been deliberate for this case. These choices will allow a percentage comparison with the rainfall data in **Section 2.1.** The historical data from 1976 to 1999 will therefore be used to derive the relationships between the stations and the observed data of 2003 will be used as the "testing values". The data presented, represent the percentage of the ballot cast for one political organization (the Barbados Democratic Party).

2.2.1. Analysis From Using 8% Of Known Data Stations' Values

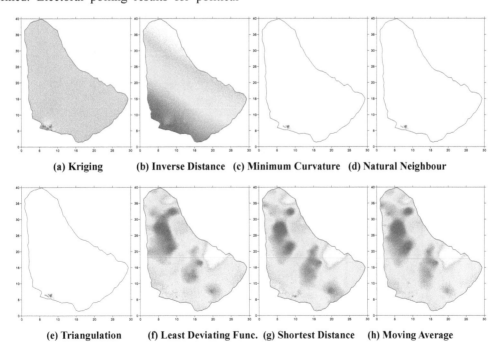

(a) Kriging   (b) Inverse Distance   (c) Minimum Curvature   (d) Natural Neighbour

(e) Triangulation   (f) Least Deviating Func.   (g) Shortest Distance   (h) Moving Average

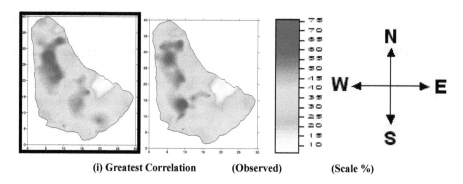

(i) Greatest Correlation   (Observed)   (Scale %)

Fig. 4. *Images using 8% of known stations.*

2.2.2. Analysis From Using 48% Of Known Data Stations' *Values*

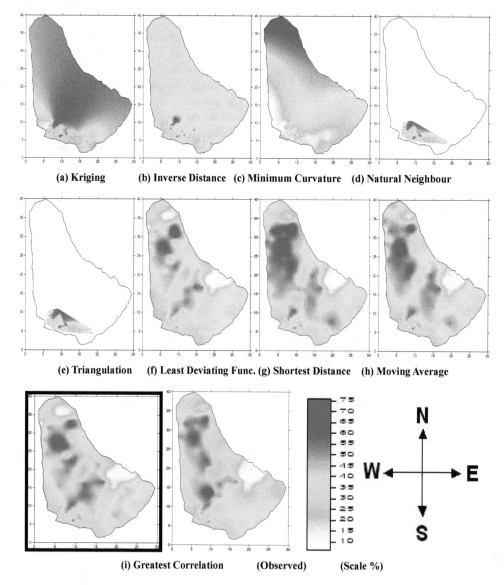

(a) Kriging   (b) Inverse Distance   (c) Minimum Curvature   (d) Natural Neighbour

(e) Triangulation   (f) Least Deviating Func. (g) Shortest Distance   (h) Moving Average

(i) Greatest Correlation   (Observed)   (Scale %)

Fig. 5. *Images using 48% of known stations.*

2.2.3. Analysis from Using 80% of Known Data Stations' *Values*

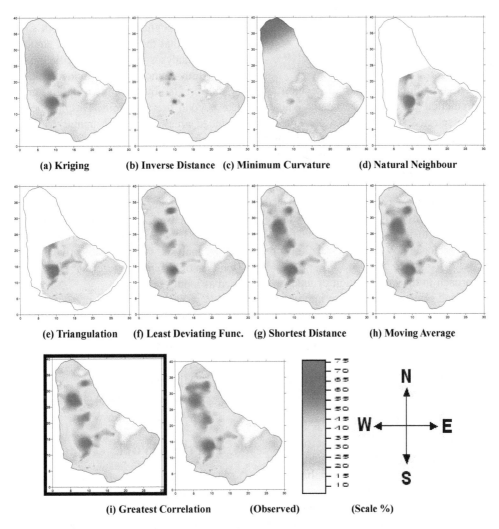

(a) Kriging   (b) Inverse Distance (c) Minimum Curvature   (d) Natural Neighbour

(e) Triangulation   (f) Least Deviating Func.   (g) Shortest Distance   (h) Moving Average

(i) Greatest Correlation   (Observed)   (Scale %)

Fig. 6. Images using 80% of known stations.

2.2.4. Summary Conclusion for Case Study 2
Kriging, Inverse Distance and Minimum Curvature.
- With almost half of the data used as input, the simulations produce results, which bear absolutely no relation to the observed.
- Between 55% and 75% of the data used as input, the values of the maxima and minima areas slowly begin to look somewhat like the observed. However, the distributions for the three models are widely varying and still not truly capturing the distribution indicated by the observed.
- Not until 80% of the data are used as input do the generated images begin to mimic a similar distribution and orientation to the observed. Even with 90% of the data used as input, there still remained many areas where the quantities are either being significantly under- or over-predicted.

Natural Neighbour and Triangulation.
- The algorithms for natural neighbour and triangulation produce a steady increase in the domain's area for which predictions are made. However, upon close examination, the maxima and minima areas did not correspond very well to those of the observed when less than 50% of the data were used as input.
- The values predicted became progressively more reliable as the input data grew beyond 50%. Even then the results provided information for only a subset of the domain.
- With over 80% of the data used as input, the images produced started to reflect the distribution of maxima and minima areas, which corresponded to the observed.

Least Deviating Function, Shortest Distance, Moving Average and Greatest Correlation.
- With as little as 8% of the data provided as input, both distributions and orientations of the analyses matched the observed fairly closely.
- Starting with using 8% of the data as input, the predictions for the entire domain continued to improve steadily as more data were added progressively to the simulations.

- Consistently produced very good results with the greatest correlation method producing the best results at each stage.

3. Conclusion

The primary objective of this work was to develop an approach to the prediction of unknown stations values when some randomly selected stations values are known. This was achieved by the implementation of an algorithm that established a historical statistical relationship between pairs of all the data stations in the region of interest. The use of a historical relationship in the prediction of unknown data stations is a "step-away" from the established interpolations methods such as Kriging, Inverse Distance and Minimum Curvature (to name a few). These established methods do not factor in any historical relationships in their formulae.

This different approach to the interpolation of unknown data stations have yielded some results that are impressive, in that it shows that irrespective of the type of data being studied, whether objective or subjective, there is a strong correlation between historical trends and the future values of the data stations.

This observation is evident in the presentation of the color distribution maps provided in the proposed algorithm's results in Section 6. These maps show that when even as few as only one station's data is used as input in the simulation of the domain's data, irrespective of either objective or subjective data, the predictions generated for the unknown stations by the proposed algorithm, have still managed to capture the quantities, distributions and general orientations of the domain's data as evidenced by the actual image map for the observed data. The differences between the predicted values for the unknown stations (as well as the analysis for the entire domain) and the actual observations became increasingly and progressively smaller as the number of known stations to be used as input increases.

The results show that the algorithm has a higher degree of accuracy when applied to objective data as opposed to subjective data. In looking at the deviation from the observed values, it can be seen that the deviation starts at a much higher comparative value for the subjective data than that for the objective data. This behaviour was expected since the engine which drives the generation of objective data is better understood and therefore more consistent over time. This consistency is therefore an ideal factor when searching for any historical significance between the data stations. On the other hand, subjective data by its own definition, is derived through a less rigid process, where the physical laws which determine the values are not as clearly defined and can therefore be inconsistent and periodically difficult to explain in quantified scientific terms.

A secondary objective of this thesis was to compare the results of some of the more popular interpolation methods with the proposed algorithm. This comparison was implemented through the detailed examinations of the two cases studied in Section 6. In the image distribution maps for both the objective and subjective data, the Natural Neighbour and Triangulation methods both showed some shortcoming, in that they were not well equipped in their interpolation analyses to generate predictions for the entire domain. Both methods only provided values within the areal bounds created by the known stations and did not extrapolate beyond these stations. Despite their skills within the bounded areas, they were unable to provide the domainwide analyses which were desired.

With the Minimum Curvature, Inverse Distance Weighting and Kriging algorithms, the results were more suited for a comparison to the proposed method. In the images produced for the objective data, it was only after 63% of the stations were used as input to the simulation did the established methods began to resemble the observed domain's analysis. With the subjective data, a similar comparison was only achieved after 88% of the stations' data were used as input.

This work has therefore presented an algorithm which can be compared favorably with the other established algorithms of.

- Natural Neighbour
- Triangulation
- Minimum Curvature
- Inverse Distance Weighting
- Kriging.

4. Further Work

The strength of this work lies in the existence of historical information to determine the relationships between data points within the domain of interest. This dependence restricts the beneficial usage of the algorithm as frequently, such historical information may either not be available or not be sufficient to truly inform the relationships between points within the domain. The scope of this work has not addressed this limitation. However, it is believed that further investigations, possibly implementing some variance of the Bayesian strategy [16] could provide an appropriate support to those cases where historical information is not available.

The need for further refinement is also being highlighted as a path for further attention to be focused. This work dealt with the historical data relationships of static stations whose data can then be used as input for the simulation. This, of course poses another limitation on the system as one may not only want to use the value of an already existing station but may want to include the available values for stations that have been newly added to the region of interest. The challenge, therefore, will be to make the system of predictions into one that is dynamic in nature or possibly to also develop relationships between zones or geographical areas. This would add a further element of complexity to the system, but will also make it more robust.

Finally, the relationships, which have been used between stations, have been for the express purpose of making predictions for the data elements, which define the relationships. Investigations into one set of data elements at one location to produce information on a different element in another location may provide better relationships between data points than that provided by the same element. For example, the humidity value at point A and the wind speed value at point B could possibly provide a better prediction relationship for rainfall at point C than rainfall values at points A and B. It is believed that this approach, particularly for subjective data, may further enhance the strength of the proposed algorithm.

References

[1] N. I. Fisher, T. Lewis, B. J. J. Embleton, Statistical Analysis of Spherical Data, Cambridge University Press, 1987.

[2] D. Dorsel, T. La Breche, Kriging. <http://ewr.cee.vt.edu/environmental/teach/smprimer/kriging/kriging.html>, January 2009.

[3] R. V. Jesus, Kriging. An Accompanied Example in IDRISI, GIS Centrum, University of Lund for Oresund, Summer University, 2003.

[4] M.L. Stein, Interpolation of Spatial Data. Some Theory for Kriging, Springer, New York, 1999.

[5] W.C.M. Van Beers, J. P.C. Kleijnen, Kriging Interpolation in Simulation . A Survey, in. R .G. Ingalls, M. D. Rossetti, J. S. Smith, and B. A. Peters (Eds.), Proceedings of the 2004 Winter Simulation Conference,Washington, DC, 2004, pp. 113-121.

[6] D. T. Lee, B.J. Schachter, Two Algorithms for Constructing a Delaunay Triangulation. International Journal of Computer and information Sciences, Vol. 9, 1980, pp. 219-242.

[7] P-J. Laurent, Wavelets, Images, and Surface Fitting, in. A. Le Mehaute (Ed.), A.K Peters Ltd., 1994.

[8] W. H. F. Smith, P. Wessel, Gridding with Continuous Curvature Splines in Tension, Geophysics, 55, 1990.

[9] D. Shepard, A two-dimensional interpolation function for irregularly spaced data. Proceedings of the 23rd ACM National Conference (128), 1968, pp.517-524.

[10] R. Sierra, Rigid Registration. <http://www.rsierra.com/DA/node10.html#SECTION00103 0000000000000000>, May 2009.

[11] J. Parag, Class Presentation. <http://arcib.dowling.edu/~JainP/Research1/slide2.html>, May 2009.

[12] D. Kleinbaum, L. Kupper, K. Muller, Applied Regression Analysis and other Multivariable Method, Duxbury Press, 1987.

[13] Wasson J. Statistics in Educational Research - An Internet Based Course. <http://www.mnstate.edu/wasson/ed602pearsoncorr.htm>, April 2009.

[14] J. Deacon, Correlation, and regression analysis for curve fitting. <http://www.biology.ed.ac.uk/research/groups/jdeacon/statistics/tress11.html >, January 2009.

[15] R.J. Rummel, Understanding Correlation. <http://www.mega.nu.8080/ampp/rummel/uc.htm>, December 2009.

[16] E. Yudkowsky, An Intuitive Explanation of Bayesian Reasoning, <http://yudkowsky.net/bayes/bayes.html>, May 2009.

[17] P. E. Gill, W. Murray, Algorithms for the solution of the nonlinear least-squares problem. SIAM Journal of Numeral Analysis, 15 [5], 1978, pp. 977-992.

[18] W. R. Greco, M. T. Hakala. Evaluation of methods for estimating the dissociation constant of tight binding enzyme inhibitors, Journal of Biological Chemistry, (254), 1979, pp.12104-12109.

[19] D. F. Symancyk, Visualizing Gaussian Elimination, <http://ola4.aacc.edu/dfsymancyk/vgetalk/VGEtalkexpanded.html>, May 2006.

11

A discussion of software reliability growth models with time-varying learning effects

Chiu, Kuei-Chen

Institute of Allied Health Sciences, College of Medicine, National Cheng Kung University, Tainan, Taiwan

Email address:

ckj0214@ms24.hinet.net

Abstract: Over the last few decades, software reliability growth models (SRGM) has been developed to predict software reliability in the testing/debugging phase. Most of the models are based on the Non-Homogeneous Poisson Process (NHPP), and an S or exponential-shaped type of testing behavior is usually assumed. Chiu et al. (2008) provided an SRGM that considers learning effects, which is able to reasonably describe the S and exponential-shaped behaviors simultaneously. This paper considers both linear and exponential-learning effects in an SRGM to enhance the model in Chiu et al. (2008), assumes the learning effects depend on the testing-time, and discusses when and what learning effects would occur in the software development process. This research also verifies the effectiveness of the proposed models with R square (Rsq), and compares the results with these of other models by using four real datasets. The proposed models consider constant, linear, and exponential-learning effects simultaneously. The results reveal the proposed models fit the data better than other models, and that the learning effects occur in the software testing process. The results are helpful for the software testing/debugging managers to master the schedule of the projects, the performance of the programmers, and the reliability of the software system.

Keywords: Software Reliability, Non-Homogeneous Poisson Process (NHPP), Learning Effects, Time-Varying Learning Effects

1. Introduction

Recently, various software reliability growth models (SRGM) have been proposed, and there has been a gradual but marked shift in the balance between acceptable software reliability and affordable software testing cost. Chiu et al. (2008) provided an SRGM that learning effects, which is able to reasonably describe the S and exponential-shaped types of behaviors simultaneously, and has good performance in fitting various data. However, the learning effects in this model are assumed be a constant, even though, in some cases they will vary. This research thus added time-varying learning effects to Chiu's model (2008), using both linear and exponential functions to explain these in the software testing process. This paper also presents numerical examples to verify the effectiveness of the proposed models, and compares other models by using four actual datasets.

2. Literatures Review

For the last few decades a number of SRGM have been developed based on the Non-homogeneous Poisson Process (NHPP). These models generally assume that each time an error occurs the fault that caused it can be immediately removed, leading to no new problems, which is usually called perfect debugging, although imperfect debugging has also been discussed (Ohba, 1984b). Gokhale and Trivedi (1999) stated that the assumption of statistical independence for the number of events occurring in disjointed time intervals is constantly violated when SRGM based on NHPP are used, and proposed an enhanced NHPP model to allow the time-varying failures in the debugging process.

In some cases, due to different testing/debugging strategies or resource allocation processes, software reliability may non-monotonically increase or decrease, due to the change-point in SRGM. Zhao (1993) identified the change-point problem, and stated that effect on software reliability should be estimated. Shyur (2003) developed a generalized reliability growth model by incorporating imperfect debugging with change-points, while Huang (2005) incorporated both a generalized logistic testing-effort function and the change-point parameter into an SRGM.

Another important issue in the field of SRGM is discovering the confidence intervals of software reliability. Yamada and Osaki (1985) stated that the maximum likelihood estimates (MLE) concerning the confidence interval of the mean value function can be estimated using as $m(T) \pm Z_{CR/2} \sqrt{m(T)}$, where CR denotes the critical region, and $Z_{CR/2}$ denotes the value providing an area $CR/2$ of the standard normal distribution. Yin and Trivedi (1999) presented the confidence bounds for the model parameters via the Bayesian approach by using the estimation method in Yamada and Osaki (1985). Huang (2005) also employed the method in Yamada and Osaki (1985) to draw a graph to illustrate the confidence intervals of the mean value function.

Some researchers in the field of software reliability consider that variations in the mean value function stem from the error detection process, and deduce the mean value function by using stochastic differential equations (SDE) (Lee *et al.*, 2004; Tamura and Yamada, 2006). Although SDE is recognized as a more effective method in evaluating the mean value function and the software testing costs, the existing models still have some problems. For instance, Yamada *et al.* (1994) proposed a simple SRGM by applying an Itô type of SDE where the error detection rate is constant, although in practice the error detection rate would vary over time. Lee *et al.* (2004) developed an SRGM by using an Itô type SDE based on the delayed S-shaped and the inflection S-shaped models proposed by Yamada *et al.* (1983) and Ohba (1984), respectively, without considering the variation in mean value function, which is a crucial factor for measuring testing costs and the variation in software reliability during the testing phase. Tamura and Yamada (2006) derived a flexible SDE model to describe the fault-detection process during the system testing phase of a distributed development environment by using an inflection S-shaped SRGM and an Itô type SDE (Karatsas and Shreve, 1997), but this model improperly presents the prediction and variance of the mean value function, and there is no complete process for obtaining the parameters in the model.

Furthermore, the notion of learning as an explicit feedback process has found its way into many areas of the social and management sciences. Learning effects usually occur when staff are involved in a production or service activity, and it is important to investigate how these will affect task times and costs. In recent years, several studies have noted that learning effects exist in the process of software testing/debugging, but few have succeeded in identify them (Smiarowski, 2006; Kapur, 2007; Chiu, 2008, 2009, 2011, 2012).

3. Method

3.1. Notations

Chiu et al. (2008) presented an SRGM that considers constant learning effects, while this paper provides an SRGM which assumes learning effects vary with testing time.

Software reliability growth models are mathematical functions that describe the error detection and removal process. The following notations will be used throughout this study:

a	:	the expected number of all potential errors in the software system
α	:	the autonomous errors-detected factor
η	:	the learning factor
$\eta_1(t)$	:	the learning effect function with linear learning effect
$\eta_2(t)$	:	the learning effect function with exponential learning effect
ξ	:	the accelerative factor with time of learning effect
τ	:	the negligent factor, which means the testing staff would cause another error when removing potential errors
$f(t)$	:	the intensity function that denotes the fraction of the errors detected at time t
$F(t)$	:	the cumulative function that denotes the fraction of the errors detected within time $(0, t)$
$m(t)$	:	the mean value function of the software error detection process, which is the expected number of errors detected within time $(0,t)$
$m_1(t)$	:	the mean value function with linear learning effects
$m_2(t)$	:	the mean value function with exponential learning effects
$\lambda(t)$	:	the intensive value function of the software error detection process, which is the expected number of errors detected at time t
$\lambda_1(t)$	:	the intensive value function with linear learning effects
$\lambda_2(t)$	:	the intensive value function with exponential learning effects
$d(t)$	:	the error detection rate per error at time t
$d_1(t)$	:	the error detection rate per error at time t with linear learning effects
$d_2(t)$	:	the error detection rate per error at time t with exponential learning effects
$R(x/t)$	:	the conditional software reliability, which is defined as the probability that no error is detected within the time interval $(t, t+x)$

Generally, the software testing/debugging process is modeled as an error counting process. A counting process $\{N(t), \ t \geq 0\}$ is said to be an NHPP with intensity function $\lambda(t)$, where $N(t)$ follows a Poisson distribution with mean function $m(t)$, this probability can be formulated as:

$$\Pr\left(N(t) = k\right) = \frac{[m(t)]^k e^{-m(t)}}{k!}, \quad k = 0, 1, 2, \dots \quad (3.1)$$

The mean value function $m(t)$, which is the expected number of errors detected within time $(0,t)$, and can be expressed as:

$$m(t) = \int_0^t \lambda(x)dx \quad (3.2)$$

The conditional software reliability $R(x/t)$ is defined as the probability that no error is detected within the time interval $(t, t+x)$, given that an error occurred at time t $(t \geq 0, \ x > 0)$. Therefore $R(x/t)$ can be formulated as:

$$R(x/t) = e^{-[m(t+x) - m(t)]}. \quad (3.3)$$

Note that the value of conditional software reliability is approximated to 1 when $t \to \infty$.

3.2. Model development

In this paper, we describe the learning effect that occurs in a software testing/debugging task and discuss the time-varying learning effects of this. Further, we explain how the time-varying learning effects influence the process of software reliability growth.

In the proposed model, the influential factors considered for finding errors in software system include the autonomous errors-detected factor α, the negligent factor τ, the learning factor η, and the accelerative factor ξ. In Chiu's model (2008), which supposes that $f(t)$ is the intensity function that denotes the percentage of the errors detected at time t, $F(t)$ is the cumulative function that denotes the percentage of the errors detected within time (0, t), and $1 - F(t)$ is the percentage of the errors as undetected yet at time t. In Chiu's model (2008), the interrelationships among the factors can be formulized as a differential equation, and which is given by:

$$f(t) = (\alpha + \eta F(t) - \tau)(1 - F(t)) \cdot \quad (3.4)$$

Where, $\alpha > 0$ and $\alpha > \tau \geq 0$ to specify that a constructive debugging activity is in process.

Equation (3.4) implies that imperfect debugging and learning effects may exist. The autonomous errors-detected factor α indicates that the testing staff/software developers spontaneously find software errors of which they were unaware. Meanwhile, the learning factor η indicates that the testing staff/software developers deliberately set out to find software errors from patterns which were previously detected. The negligent factor τ indicates that new software errors are generated while correcting the program code. The first two factors can improve the efficiency of software debugging, but the third cannot. $F(t)$ and $f(t)$ can be derived from Equation

(3.4) by using differential equation analysis to solve Equation (3.5):

$$f(t) = \frac{dF(t)}{dt} = -\eta F(t)^2 - (\alpha - \eta - \tau)F(t) + (\alpha - \tau) \cdot \quad (3.5)$$

, and the explicit solution is given by:

$$F(t) = \frac{e^{(\alpha + \eta - \tau)(t+c)} - \frac{\alpha - \tau}{\eta}}{1 + e^{(\alpha + \eta - \tau)(t+c)}} \cdot \quad (3.6)$$

Note that the number of system errors found should be zero when a system's debugging task begins, but $F(t)$ is not equal to zero when $t=0$. In view of this, we utilize the constant c to adjust the function $F(t)$, so as to let $F(0) = 0$. Based on the above discussion, the constant c can be inferred as:

$$c = \frac{\ln\left(\frac{\alpha - \tau}{\eta}\right)}{\alpha + \eta - \tau}, \quad (3.7)$$

To simplify the model, we define $\alpha' = \alpha - \tau$, and thus $F(t)$ and $f(t)$ can be rearranged as follows:

$$F(t) = 1 - \frac{1 + \frac{\eta}{\alpha'}}{\frac{\eta}{\alpha'} + e^{(\alpha' + \eta)t}}, \quad (3.8)$$

$$f(t) = \frac{(\alpha' + \eta)^2 e^{(\alpha' + \eta)t}}{\alpha'\left(\frac{\eta}{\alpha'} + e^{(\alpha' + \eta)t}\right)^2} \cdot \quad (3.9)$$

Furthermore, we need to estimate the total potential errors in the software system before the testing/debugging task starts. Here, a represents the expected number of all potential errors before the debugging task starts, which can be estimated by the size of the software system along with experience of previous testing/debugging tasks. Accordingly, the mean value function of the software error detection process can be written as:

$$m(t) = aF(t) = a\left(1 - \frac{1 + \frac{\eta}{\alpha'}}{\frac{\eta}{\alpha'} + e^{(\alpha' + \eta)t}}\right), \quad (3.10)$$

the intensity function at time t is given by:

$$\lambda(t) = af(t) = a\left(\frac{(\alpha' + \eta)^2 e^{(\alpha' + \eta)t}}{\alpha'(\frac{\eta}{\alpha'} + e^{(\alpha' + \eta)t})^2}\right) \cdot \quad (3.11)$$

In order to find the variation of the error detection rate per error at time t, we identify the error detection rate as:

$$d(t) = \frac{\lambda(t)}{a - m(t)} = (\alpha' + \eta)\left(1 - \frac{\eta}{\alpha' e^{(\alpha' + \eta)t} + \eta}\right) \cdot \quad (3.12)$$

Note that the boundary of the error detection rate is between α' and $\alpha' + \eta$ at any testing time. However, the way to distinguish the exponential and the S-shaped behaviors is whether the value of the inflection point is greater than zero or not. The proposed model behaves as S-shaped if $\eta > \alpha'$ (the value of an inflection point is positive); otherwise it behaves as exponential-shaped. The inflection point implies that learning effects exist in the process of testing/debugging, and inflection time is given by:

$$t_{\text{inflection}} = \frac{\ln(\eta) - \ln(\alpha')}{\alpha' + \eta} > 0 \cdot \quad (3.13)$$

However, in some special cases, the learning factor η may not be constant, but instead vary over time. In this study, we adopt two functions to deal with the time-varying situation, and these functions are given as (3.14), (3.15), to represent the linear and exponential growth of learning effects with time.

$$\eta_1(t) = \eta + \xi t, \text{ and} \quad (3.14)$$

$$\eta_2(t) = \eta e^{\xi t}, \quad (3.15)$$

Where ξ is the coefficient of the accelerative factor. The mean value function in Chiu's model (2008) could be improved with these two different learning styles as given by:

$$m_1(t) = a \left(1 - \frac{1 + \dfrac{\eta + \xi t}{\alpha'}}{\dfrac{\eta + \xi t}{\alpha'} + e^{\alpha' t + \eta t + \xi t^2}} \right), \text{ and} \quad (3.16)$$

$$m_2(t) = a \left(1 - \frac{1 + \dfrac{\eta e^{\xi t}}{\alpha'}}{\dfrac{\eta e^{\xi t}}{\alpha'} + e^{(\alpha' + \eta e^{\xi t})t}} \right), \quad (3.17)$$

The learning effects will be constant while $\xi = 0$, and the mean value functions (3.16), (3.17) will degenerate to Equation (3.10), flexibly.

The intensity functions with these two different learning styles are given by:

$$\lambda_1(t) = \left\{ a \left[\frac{\left(1 + \dfrac{\eta + \xi t}{\alpha'}\right)\left(\dfrac{\xi}{\alpha'} + (\alpha' + \eta + 2\xi t)e^{\alpha' t + \eta t + \xi t^2}\right)}{\left(\dfrac{\eta + \xi t}{\alpha'} + e^{\alpha' t + \eta t + \xi t^2}\right)^2} - \frac{\xi}{\alpha'\left(\dfrac{\eta + \xi t}{\alpha'} + e^{\alpha' t + \eta t + \xi t^2}\right)} \right] \right\}$$

, and

$$(3.18)$$

$$\lambda_2(t) = \left\{ a \left[\frac{\left(1 + \dfrac{\eta + e^{\xi t}}{\alpha'}\right)\left(\dfrac{\xi e^{\xi t}}{\alpha'} + (\alpha' + \eta e^{\xi t} + \eta \xi t e^{\xi t})e^{\alpha' t + \eta e^{\xi t}}\right)}{\left(\dfrac{\eta + e^{\xi t}}{\alpha'} + e^{\alpha' t + \eta e^{\xi t}}\right)^2} - \frac{\xi}{\alpha'\left(\dfrac{\eta + e^{\xi t}}{\alpha'} + e^{\alpha' t + \eta e^{\xi t}}\right)} \right] \right\}$$

$$(3.19)$$

, and the functions of the error detection rate with the two different learning styles are given by:

$$d_1(t) = \frac{\alpha'\left(e^{(\alpha' + \eta + \xi t)t}\left((\alpha' + \eta + \xi t)(\alpha' + \eta + 2\xi t) - \xi\right) + \xi\right)}{(\alpha' + \eta + \xi t)\left(e^{(\alpha' + \eta + \xi t)t}\alpha' + \eta + \xi t\right)},$$

$$(3.20), \text{ and}$$

$$d_2(t) = \frac{\alpha'\left(e^{(\alpha' + \eta e^{\xi t})t}\alpha'^2 + \xi \eta e^{\xi t} + \eta e^{(\alpha' + \xi + \eta e^{\xi t})t}\left(\alpha'(2 + \xi t) - \xi\right) + e^{(\alpha' + 2\xi + \eta e^{\xi t})t}(1 + \xi t)\eta^2\right)}{(\alpha' + \eta e^{\xi t})\left(e^{(\alpha' + \eta e^{\xi t})t}\alpha' + \eta e^{\xi t}\right)}$$

$$(3.21)$$

Since the learning effects can change over time, the proposed model can provide more flexibility in the graphic mapping of the mean value function.

3.3. Parameter estimation

Least squares estimation (LSE) is adopted to validate the proposed model as this is effective when the corresponding equations are complex and must be solved numerically. Fitting the proposed models to actual error data involves estimating the model's parameters from the datasets. The parameters a, α', η, and ξ can be obtained by using numerical methods.

4. Results

4.1. Model comparisons

Chiu et al. (2008) evaluated the effectiveness of the SRGM from the perspective of constant learning effects by using eight datasets from eight published papers, and compared the proposed model with six others by using the *MSE, MAE, AE,* and *Rsq* comparison criteria. This paper improved Chiu's model (2008) by including time-varying learning effects, as in equations (3.14) and (3.15), and evaluated its effectiveness by using the recent four datasets in Zhang and Pham (1998), Pham (2003), Bai, Hu, Xie, and Ng (2005), and Jeske and Zhang (2005) (see Table 4.1).

Table 4.1. Sources of the datasets

Reference	Dataset
Zhang and Pham (1998)	Failure data of Misra system
Pham (2003)	Failure data of a real-time control system
Bai, Hu, Xie, and Ng (2005)	Failure data of space program
Jeske and Zhang (2005)	Failure data of wireless data service system

Furthermore, this study compared the proposed models with three others (see Table 4.2) using the *Rsq* comparison criteria.

Table 4.2. Summary of m(t) for the various models

Model	Mean value function
Huang (2005)	$m(t) = a(1 - e^{-rW^*(t)})$; $W(t) = \dfrac{N}{\sqrt[\kappa]{1 + Ae^{-\alpha\kappa t}}}$, $W^*(t) = W(t) - W(0)$

Pham and Zhang (2003)	$m(t)=\dfrac{1}{1+\beta e^{-bt}}\left[(a+c)(1-e^{-bt})-\dfrac{ab}{b-\alpha}(e^{-\alpha t}-e^{-bt})\right]$
Chiu (2008)	$m(t)=aH(t)=a\left(1-\dfrac{1+\dfrac{\eta}{\alpha}}{\dfrac{\eta}{\alpha}+e^{(\alpha+\eta)t}}\right)$
Proposed linear learning model	$m_1(t)=a\left(1-\dfrac{1+\dfrac{\eta+\xi t}{\alpha'}}{\dfrac{\eta+\xi t}{\alpha'}+e^{\alpha' t+\eta t+\xi t^2}}\right)$
Proposed exponential learning model	$m_2(t)=a\left(1-\dfrac{1+\dfrac{\eta e^{\xi t}}{\alpha'}}{\dfrac{\eta e^{\xi t}}{\alpha'}+e^{(\alpha'+\eta e^{\xi t})t}}\right)$

4.2. Data analysis

The results of parameters estimated for the proposed models and other models with these four datasets presented as Table 4.3 and the results showed better fitting than other models (see Table 4.4).

Table 4.3. Parameters estimated for different datasets and models

The Sources of Datasets	The comparison models	
	Pham and Zhang (2003)	Huang (2005)
Zhang and Pham (1998)	$a=120.98$ $b=0.139304$ $c=14.883203$ $\alpha=0.13856$ $\beta=0.01$	$a=145.67$ $\kappa=1.02074$ $r=0.987034$ $\alpha=0.04297$ $A=0.163192$ $N=27.37$
Pham (2003)	$a=131.14$ $b=0.04507$ $c=1E\text{-}12$ $\alpha=1E\text{-}12$ $\beta=1E\text{-}12$	$a=132.21$ $\kappa=1.055028$ $r=0.256651$ $\alpha=0.015564$ $A=0.2127$ $N=88.23$
Bai, Hu, Xie, and Ng (2005)	$a=20.17$ $b=0.30462$ $c=0.000001$ $\alpha=0.30462$ $\beta=0.000001$	$a=20.62$ $\kappa=1$ $r=3.44794$ $\alpha=0.173252$ $A=0.029234$ $N=24.35$
Jeske and Zhang (2005)	$a=21.73$ $b=0.717$ $c=0.562066$ $\alpha=0.178759$ $\beta=0.41241$	$a=23.45$ $\kappa=1.14$ $r=0.657484$ $\alpha=0.540129$ $A=3.556583$ $N=6.37$

The Sources of Datasets	The proposed models	
	Linear Learning model	Exponential Learning model
Zhang and Pham (1998)	$a=135.97$ $\alpha=0.138257$ $\eta=3.36E\text{-}10$ $\xi=0.00001$	$a=135.97$ $\alpha=0.138257$ $\eta=3.36E\text{-}10$ $\xi=1$
Pham (2003)	$a=131.2$ $\alpha=0.045059$ $\eta=1E\text{-}13$ $\xi=0.00001$	$a=131.2$ $\alpha=0.045059$ $\eta=1E\text{-}13$ $\xi=0.35$
Bai, Hu, Xie, and Ng (2005)	$a=19.11$ $\alpha=0.0001$ $\eta=0.35186$ $\xi=0.00001$	$a=19.11$ $\alpha=0.0001$ $\eta=0.35186$ $\xi=0.03$
Jeske and Zhang (2005)	$a=22.25$ $\alpha=0.4922166$ $\eta=0.333534$ $\xi=0.002$	$a=22.25$ $\alpha=0.4922166$ $\eta=0.333534$ $\xi=0.007$

The *Rsq* increase to 0.975, 0.987, 0.976, and 0.989 with linear-learning effects as in Equation (3.14), and to 0.986, 0.989, 0.968, and 0.989 with the exponential-learning effects, as in Equation (3.15) (see Table 4.4). Figure 4.1 shows the predicted and actual data for cumulative errors, Table A.1~A.4 presented the actual data and the predicted values of the models. More detail data of model comparisons show in Appendixes A.

Table 4.4. The models fitting results with the Rsq

Model	The Sources of Datasets			
	Zhang and Pham (1998)	Pham (2003)	Bai (2005)	Jeske and Zhang (2005)
Pham and Zhang (2003)	0.966	0.975	0.914	0.988
Huang (2005)	0.973	0.982	0.953	0.988
Chiu (2008)	0.966	0.975	0.930	0.989
Proposed linear learning model	0.975	0.987	0.976	0.989
Proposed exponential learning model	0.986	0.989	0.968	0.989

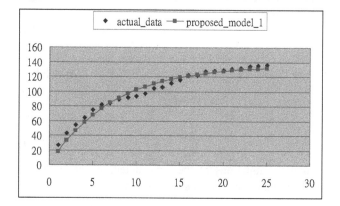

(1)   The fitting results of proposed linear learning model for the dataset in Zhang and Pham (1998) ($R^2=0.975$)

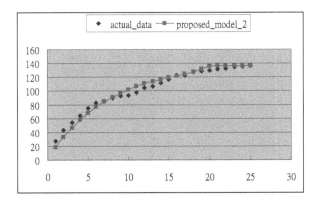

(2) The fitting results of proposed exponential learning model for the dataset in Zhang and Pham (1998) (R^2=0.986)

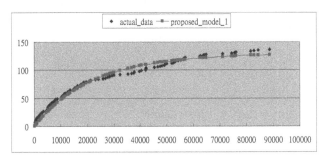

(3) The fitting results of proposed linear learning model for the dataset in Pham (2003) (R^2=0.987)

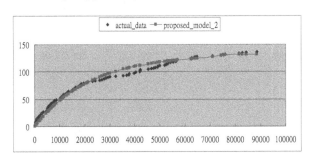

(4) The fitting results of proposed exponential learning model for the dataset in Pham (2003) (R^2=0.989)

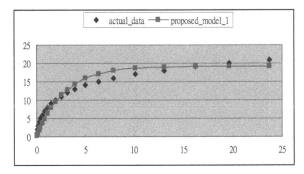

(5) The fitting results of proposed linear learning model for the dataset in Bai (2005) (R^2=0.976)

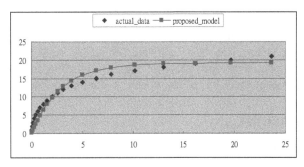

(6) The fitting results of proposed exponential learning model for the dataset in Bai (2005) (R^2=0.968)

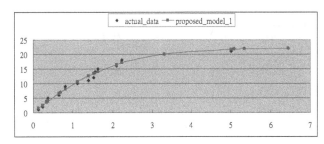

(7) The fitting results of proposed linear learning model for the dataset in Jeske and Zhang (2005) (R^2=0.989)

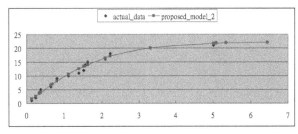

(8) The fitting results of proposed exponential learning model for the dataset in Jeske and Zhang (2005) (R^2=0.989)

Figure 4.1. Fitting results for different datasets

5. Conclusion

This study improved Chiu's model (2008) by including time-varying learning effects, including linear and exponential functions to describe the time variation of learning effects, which described the software testing behavior more reasonably. This paper evaluated the effectiveness of the proposed models using various published datasets, and compared with other models by using the *Rsq* comparison criteria. The results enhanced with both the linear and exponential-shaped learning effects. These proposed models only added one parameter, the accelerative factor ξ, in the original model and enhanced the *Rsq* to fitting better for actual datasets, event the *Rsq* shows good outcome in the original model and shows better fitting than other models, and the proposed models can still present the suitable region of the original model when $\xi = 0$.

This research predicted errors occurred in software

testing process with two mean value functions, individually. We will refine the proposed models by taking account of the change-point problem, which is concerned with a change in the factors that affect software debugging, resulting in variations in the software error intensity function and the subsequent precision of the model prediction to consider

two mean value functions, simultaneously. By model comparisons, the results show better fitting than those others, and the results are helpful for the managers managing the schedule of the software testing/debugging projects, the performance of the programmers, and the reliability of the software system.

Appendix

The results of model comparisons

Table A.1. Model comparisons of partial Misra failure data (the dataset in Zhang and Pham (1998))

Testing time (per hour)	*Defects found*	Total defects predicted by the following models				
		Pham and Zhang (2003)	Huang (2005)	Chiu (2008)	Proposed linear learning model	Proposed exponential learning model
1	27	17.515178	18.753639	17.527226	17.527305	17.527226
2	43	32.789511	34.611824	32.795171	32.795691	32.795171
3	54	46.105543	48.073478	46.095057	46.096522	46.095057
4	64	57.711199	59.544218	57.680570	57.683470	57.680571
5	75	67.823776	69.354962	67.772696	67.777430	67.772700
6	82	76.633546	77.776637	76.563933	76.570776	76.563948
7	84	84.306973	85.031825	84.221968	84.231067	84.222016
8	89	90.989586	91.304011	90.892873	90.904255	90.893015
9	92	96.808530	96.744969	96.703889	96.717483	96.704300
10	93	101.874820	101.480660	101.765860	101.781512	101.767016
11	97	106.285370	105.615980	106.175330	106.192839	106.178534
12	104	110.124690	109.238530	110.016420	110.035532	110.025130
13	106	113.466510	112.421750	113.362390	113.382835	113.385768
14	111	116.375100	115.227370	116.277050	116.298563	116.339097
15	116	118.906460	117.707460	118.816010	118.838314	118.978846
16	122	121.109420	119.906050	121.027700	121.050527	121.449567
17	122	123.026490	121.860500	122.954300	122.977408	124.023841
18	127	124.694700	123.602620	124.632560	124.655724	127.209285
19	128	126.146320	125.159520	126.094480	126.117512	131.484050
20	129	127.409420	126.554440	127.367970	127.390682	135.255654
21	131	128.508460	127.807290	128.477290	128.499548	135.971130
22	132	129.464730	128.935240	129.443630	129.465296	135.974000
23	134	130.296760	129.953060	130.285400	130.306378	135.974000
24	135	131.020680	130.873580	131.018670	131.038874	135.974000
25	136	131.650520	131.707870	131.657420	131.676788	135.974000

Table A.2. Model comparisons of the real-time control system failure data (the dataset in Pham (2003))

Testing time (per 1000 hours)	Defects found	Total defects predicted by the following models				
		Pham and Zhang (2003)	Huang (2005)	Chiu (2008)	Proposed linear learning model	Proposed exponential learning model
0.0030	1	0.017736	20.532290	0.017734	0.017734	0.020000
0.0330	2	0.194966	20.587930	0.194943	0.194942	0.190000
0.1460	3	0.860387	20.798600	0.860285	0.860280	0.860000
0.2270	4	1.335288	20.950680	1.335132	1.335122	1.340000
0.3420	5	2.006560	21.168110	2.006326	2.006305	2.010000
0.3510	6	2.058948	21.185200	2.058708	2.058686	2.060000
0.3530	7	2.070587	21.189000	2.070345	2.070323	2.070000
0.4440	8	2.599045	21.362460	2.598743	2.598706	2.600000
0.5560	9	3.246486	21.577500	3.246111	3.246047	3.250000
0.5710	10	3.332949	21.606420	3.332565	3.332496	3.330000
0.7090	11	4.125672	21.874010	4.125199	4.125079	4.130000
0.7590	12	4.411676	21.971610	4.411172	4.411028	4.410000
0.8360	13	4.850864	22.122570	4.850311	4.850124	4.850000
0.8600	14	4.987442	22.169790	4.986874	4.986672	4.990000
0.9680	15	5.600220	22.383260	5.599585	5.599306	5.600000
1.0560	16	6.097319	22.558380	6.096631	6.096276	6.100000
1.7260	17	9.818094	23.926760	9.817020	9.815605	9.820000
1.8460	18	10.472720	24.178420	10.471580	10.469867	10.470000
1.8720	19	10.614090	24.233210	10.612930	10.611153	10.610000
1.9860	20	11.231990	24.474550	11.230770	11.228666	11.230000
2.3110	21	12.976210	25.172530	12.974830	12.971595	12.970000
2.3660	22	13.268870	25.292100	13.267460	13.264002	13.270000
2.6080	23	14.547970	25.823260	14.546450	14.541899	14.550000
2.6760	24	14.904890	25.973980	14.903330	14.898440	14.900000
3.0980	25	17.095570	26.923790	17.093820	17.086445	17.090000
3.2780	26	18.017380	27.336480	18.015550	18.006919	18.020000
3.2880	27	18.068380	27.359540	18.066540	18.057834	18.070000
4.4340	28	23.762520	30.094030	23.760240	23.740384	23.760000
5.0340	29	26.628490	31.597540	26.626020	26.598015	26.630000
5.0490	30	26.699150	31.635750	26.696670	26.668446	26.700000
5.0850	31	26.868550	31.727580	26.866050	26.837283	26.870000
5.0890	32	26.887350	31.737800	26.884860	26.856025	26.880000
5.0890	33	26.887350	31.737800	26.884860	26.856025	26.880000
5.0970	34	26.924950	31.758230	26.922450	26.893499	26.920000
5.3240	35	27.986180	32.341620	27.983610	27.951070	27.980000
5.3890	36	28.288060	32.509930	28.285480	28.251860	28.290000
5.5650	37	29.101040	32.968480	29.098400	29.061780	29.100000
5.6230	38	29.367540	33.120480	29.364890	29.327243	29.360000
6.0800	39	31.443210	34.333490	31.440440	31.394149	31.440000
6.3800	40	32.782730	35.144360	32.779900	32.727366	32.780000
6.4770	41	33.211990	35.408970	33.209130	33.154485	33.210000
6.7400	42	34.366440	36.132330	34.363520	34.302917	34.360000
7.1920	43	36.318820	37.395260	36.315820	36.244158	36.320000
7.4470	44	37.402860	38.118510	37.399810	37.321459	37.400000

Testing time (per 1000 hours)	Defects found	Total defects predicted by the following models				
		Pham and Zhang (2003)	Huang (2005)	Chiu (2008)	Proposed linear learning model	Proposed exponential learning model
7.6440	45	38.231840	38.682430	38.228760	38.145018	38.230000
7.8370	46	39.036880	39.239190	39.033770	38.944562	39.030000
7.8430	47	39.061800	39.256570	39.058680	38.969304	39.060000
7.9220	48	39.389220	39.485720	39.386090	39.294420	39.390000
8.7380	49	42.703860	41.892110	42.700630	42.583457	42.700000
10.0890	50	47.930660	46.019710	47.927330	47.760892	47.930000
10.2370	51	48.484140	46.481510	48.480800	48.308457	48.480000
10.2580	52	48.562380	46.547170	48.559040	48.385845	48.560000
10.4910	53	49.425480	47.278000	49.422130	49.239406	49.420000
10.6250	54	49.917770	47.700140	49.914410	49.726097	49.910000
10.9820	55	51.214880	48.830920	51.211520	51.007928	51.210000
11.1750	56	51.907480	49.445750	51.904120	51.692037	51.900000
11.4110	57	52.746250	50.200660	52.742880	52.520205	52.740000
11.4420	58	52.855760	50.300060	52.852400	52.628311	52.850000
11.8110	59	54.147660	51.487300	54.144300	53.903139	54.140000
12.5590	60	56.701470	53.913600	56.698130	56.420691	56.700000
12.5590	61	56.701470	53.913600	56.698130	56.420691	56.700000
12.7910	62	57.476220	54.670480	57.472900	57.183772	57.470000
13.1210	63	58.564380	55.749780	58.561080	58.254988	58.560000
13.4860	64	59.749250	56.946440	59.745970	59.420671	59.750000
14.7080	65	63.577210	60.961880	63.574040	63.181228	63.570000
15.2510	66	65.211680	62.743390	65.208580	64.784319	65.210000
15.2610	67	65.241410	62.776140	65.238300	64.813460	65.240000
15.2770	68	65.288950	62.828550	65.285840	64.860059	65.290000
15.8060	69	66.841450	64.557480	66.838420	66.381192	66.840000
16.1850	70	67.931200	65.790510	67.928220	67.448034	67.930000
16.2290	71	68.056510	65.933300	68.053530	67.570665	68.050000
16.3580	72	68.422470	66.351420	68.419520	67.928743	68.420000
17.1680	73	70.672390	68.957900	70.669570	70.128328	70.670000
17.4580	74	71.458160	69.881820	71.455380	70.895756	71.460000
17.7580	75	72.260290	70.831660	72.257560	71.678750	72.260000
18.2870	76	73.648550	72.490310	73.645920	73.032909	73.650000
18.5680	77	74.372630	73.362180	74.370060	73.738701	74.370000
18.7280	78	74.780840	73.855570	74.778300	74.136448	74.780000
19.5560	79	76.846930	76.370680	76.844550	76.147877	76.840000
20.5670	80	79.267310	79.345450	79.265150	78.500589	79.260000
21.0120	81	80.298200	80.617880	80.296140	79.501457	80.300000
21.3080	82	80.972550	81.450970	80.970570	80.155783	80.970000
23.0630	83	84.791210	86.157540	84.789660	83.855222	84.790000
24.1270	84	86.963490	88.805080	86.962220	85.955305	86.960000
25.9100	85	90.378070	92.875650	90.377290	89.250153	90.380000
26.7700	86	91.929480	94.673240	91.928950	90.744732	91.930000
27.7530	87	93.630680	96.596960	93.630430	92.381941	93.630000
28.4600	88	94.808460	97.895650	94.808410	93.514447	94.810000
28.4930	89	94.862520	97.954560	94.862480	93.566413	94.860000

Testing time (per 1000 hours)	Defects found	Total defects predicted by the following models				
		Pham and Zhang (2003)	Huang (2005)	Chiu (2008)	Proposed linear learning model	Proposed exponential learning model
29.3610	90	96.256040	99.450350	96.256260	94.905360	96.260000
30.0850	91	97.377400	100.620500	97.377830	95.982089	97.380000
32.4080	92	100.738000	103.927200	100.739100	99.205639	100.740000
35.3380	93	104.504500	107.230900	104.506500	102.814533	104.510000
36.7990	94	106.204700	108.568900	106.207200	104.443146	106.210000
37.6420	95	107.136000	109.259300	107.138700	105.335318	107.140000
37.6540	96	107.149000	109.268800	107.151700	105.347776	107.150000
37.9150	97	107.430100	109.471000	107.432900	105.617088	107.430000
39.7150	98	109.281100	110.732600	109.284500	107.391262	109.280000
40.5800	99	110.118600	111.262800	110.122200	108.194536	110.120000
42.0150	100	111.438000	112.046400	111.442000	109.460999	111.440000
42.0450	101	111.464700	112.061600	111.468700	109.486627	111.470000
42.1880	102	111.591300	112.133400	111.595400	109.608322	111.600000
42.2960	103	111.686500	112.187000	111.690600	109.699723	111.690000
42.2960	104	111.686500	112.187000	111.690600	109.699723	111.690000
45.4060	105	114.236600	113.499000	114.241600	112.153850	114.240000
46.6530	106	115.162900	113.917400	115.168200	113.047836	115.170000
47.5960	107	115.829600	114.199500	115.835100	113.692421	115.840000
48.2960	108	116.306500	114.391600	116.312200	114.154161	116.310000
49.1710	109	116.881800	114.612800	116.887700	114.712049	116.890000
49.4160	110	117.038900	114.671100	117.044900	114.864524	117.050000
50.1450	111	117.496100	114.836100	117.502300	115.308833	117.500000
52.0420	112	118.617800	115.210400	118.624500	116.402030	118.630000
52.4890	113	118.868500	115.288200	118.875200	116.646996	118.880000
52.8750	114	119.080900	115.352500	119.087800	116.854817	119.090000
53.3210	115	119.321800	115.423600	119.328700	117.090739	119.330000
53.4430	116	119.386800	115.442400	119.393800	117.154501	119.400000
54.4330	117	119.901700	115.586800	119.908900	117.659911	119.920000
55.3810	118	120.373600	115.711500	120.381100	118.124480	120.390000
56.4630	119	120.888200	115.839200	120.895900	118.632572	120.910000
56.4850	120	120.898400	115.841700	120.906100	118.642666	120.920000
56.5600	121	120.933100	115.850000	120.940800	118.677006	120.960000
57.0420	122	121.153400	115.901800	121.161200	118.895147	121.180000
62.5510	123	123.359000	116.338000	123.368000	121.101578	123.470000
62.6510	124	123.394200	116.343700	123.403200	121.137185	123.510000
62.6610	125	123.397800	116.344300	123.406700	121.140737	123.510000
63.7320	126	123.764700	116.402400	123.773800	121.512953	123.930000
64.1030	127	123.887800	116.421100	123.897000	121.638151	124.070000
64.8930	128	124.143000	116.458400	124.152300	121.898543	124.380000
71.0430	129	125.847800	116.662100	125.858100	123.666055	127.320000
74.3640	130	126.589700	116.727400	126.600500	124.455703	129.710000
75.4090	131	126.801100	116.743600	126.812100	124.683715	130.390000
76.0570	132	126.927300	116.752700	126.938400	124.820530	130.720000
81.5420	133	127.859900	116.809300	127.871600	125.851762	131.200000
82.7020	134	128.029200	116.817600	128.041100	126.043632	131.200000

Testing time (per 1000 hours)	Defects found	Total defects predicted by the following models				
		Pham and Zhang (2003)	Huang (2005)	Chiu (2008)	Proposed linear learning model	Proposed exponential learning model
84.4000	135	128.283500	116.828900	128.295500	126.309827	131.200000
88.6820	136	128.774800	116.847000	128.787200	126.910967	131.200000

Table A.3. *Model comparisons of Space program failure data (the dataset in Bai (2005))*

Testing time (per 100 hours)	Defects found	Total defects predicted by the following models				
		Pham and Zhang (2003)	Huang (2005)	Chiu (2008)	Proposed linear learning model	Proposed exponential learning model
0.020	1	0.020000	0.020000	0.020000	0.134009	0.134009
0.060	2	0.060000	0.060000	0.060000	0.399217	0.399217
0.150	3	0.150000	0.150000	0.150000	0.982463	0.982463
0.270	4	0.270000	0.270000	0.270000	1.731950	1.731949
0.410	5	0.410000	0.410000	0.410000	2.567288	2.567286
0.580	6	0.580000	0.580000	0.580000	3.527846	3.527841
0.830	7	0.830000	0.830000	0.830000	4.840065	4.840052
1.160	8	1.160000	1.160000	1.160000	6.404571	6.404540
1.520	9	1.520000	1.520000	1.520000	7.916391	7.916333
2.000	10	2.000000	2.000000	2.000000	9.656157	9.656050
2.560	11	2.560000	2.560000	2.560000	11.347247	11.347074
3.140	12	3.140000	3.140000	3.140000	12.780608	12.780362
3.900	13	3.900000	3.900000	3.900000	14.266173	14.265837
4.980	14	4.980000	4.980000	4.980000	15.798014	15.797580
6.330	15	6.330000	6.330000	6.330000	17.050816	17.050322
7.850	16	7.850000	7.850000	7.850000	17.904163	17.903672
10.150	17	10.150000	10.150000	10.150000	18.573490	18.573088
13.040	18	13.040000	13.040000	13.040000	18.916101	18.915842
16.240	19	16.240000	16.240000	16.240000	19.047183	19.047047
19.650	20	19.650000	19.650000	19.650000	19.091105	19.091042
23.680	21	23.680000	23.680000	23.680000	19.105433	19.105410

Table A.4. *Model comparisons of failure data on wireless data service system (the dataset in Jeske and Zhang (2005))*

Testing time (per 10000 hours)	Defects found	Total defects predicted by the following models				
		Pham and Zhang (2003)	Huang (2005)	Chiu (2008)	Proposed linear learning model	Proposed exponential learning model
0.1340	1	1.521959	3.772587	1.454990	1.455015	1.455020
0.2350	2	2.625657	4.238855	2.522079	2.522206	2.522228
0.3360	4	3.690907	4.747994	3.562210	3.562564	3.562624
0.3690	5	4.030500	4.923709	3.897220	3.897680	3.897758
0.6380	6	6.640963	6.524091	6.512037	6.514079	6.514426
0.6720	7	6.950800	6.746603	6.822095	6.824428	6.824825
0.8060	9	8.128076	7.662513	8.024262	8.027967	8.028599
1.1090	10	10.536260	9.907183	10.501810	10.509663	10.511013
1.3810	11	12.410300	11.997960	12.439310	12.451716	12.453862
1.5160	12	13.245140	13.010750	13.309990	13.324786	13.327354
1.5500	14	13.445870	13.259970	13.517680	13.533075	13.535749
1.6180	15	13.836150	13.749470	13.921290	13.937882	13.940769

Testing time (per 10000 hours)	Defects found	Total defects predicted by the following models				
		Pham and Zhang (2003)	**Huang (2005)**	**Chiu (2008)**	**Proposed linear learning model**	**Proposed exponential learning model**
2.0930	16	16.175690	16.714350	16.331870	16.356094	16.360353
2.2350	18	16.755810	17.418800	16.925040	16.951144	16.955746
3.3050	20	19.782540	20.380550	19.917420	19.949350	19.955094
5.0120	21	21.711430	21.294340	21.662110	21.684046	21.688088
5.0850	22	21.751920	21.303590	21.696310	21.717669	21.721608
5.3410	22	21.877470	21.329520	21.801240	21.820601	21.824182
6.4390	22	22.204640	21.376840	22.068540	22.080424	22.082643

References

[1] Achcar, J.A., Dey, D.K., and Niverthi, M. (1997) "A Bayesian approach using nonhomogeneous Poisson Process for software reliability models", *In Frontiers in Reliability*, Basu et al. (Eds).

[2] Adam Smiarowski , Jr. , Hoda S. Abdel-Aty-Zohdy , Mostafa Hashem Sherif , Hemal Shah (2006) "Wavelet Based RDNN for Software Reliability Estimation", *11th IEEE Symposium on Computers and Communications* (ISCC'06), iscc,pp.312-317.

[3] Bai, C.G. (2005) "Bayesian network based software reliability prediction with an operational profile", *The Journal of Systems and Software*, 77: 103-112.

[4] Bai, C.G., Hu, Q.P., Xie, M., and Ng, S.H. (2005) "Software failure prediction based on a Markov Bayesian network model", *The Journal of Systems and Software*, 74: 275-282.

[5] Bunea, C., Charitosb, T., Cooke, R. M., and Beckerd, G. (2005) "Two-stage Bayesian models—application to ZEDB project", *Reliability Engineering and System Safety*, 90: 123-130.

[6] Chin-Yu Huang, Sy-Yen Kuo, Michael R. Lyu, (2000) "Effort-Index-Based Software Reliability Growth Models and Performance Assessment," *Computer Software and Applications Conference, Annual International*, The Twenty-Fourth Annual International Computer Software and Applications Conference, 0:454.

[7] Chiu, K.-C., Huang, Y.-S., and Lee, T.-Z. (2008) "A Study of Software Reliability Growth from the Perspective of Learning Effects," Reliability *Engineering and Systems Safety*, Vol. 93, No. 10, pp. 1410-1421.

[8] Chiu, K.-C., Ho, J.-W., and Huang, Y.-S. (2009) "Bayesian Updating of Optimal Release Time for Software Systems," *Software Quality Journal*, Vol. 17, No. 1, pp. 99-120.

[9] Cid, J.E.R. and Achcar, J.A. (1999) "Bayesian inference for nonhomogeneous Poisson processes in software reliability models assuming nonmonotonic intensity functions", *Computational Statistics & Data Analysis*, 32: 147-159.

[10] Dietmar Pfahl (2001) "An Integrated Approach to Simulation-Based Learning in Support of Strategic and Project Management in Software Organisations*" , PhD Theses in Experimental Software Engineering*, Fraunhofer-Institut für Experimentelles Software Engineering, 8:27-40.

[11] Goel, A.L. and Okumoto, K. (1979) "Time-varying fault detection rate model for software and other performance measures", *IEEE Transactions on Reliability*, 28: 206-211.

[12] Gokhale, S. S. and Trivedi, K. S. (1999) "A time/structure based software reliability model", *Annals of Software Engineering*, 8: 85-121.

[13] Ho, J.W., Fang, C.C. and Huang, Y.S. (2008) "The Determination of Optimal Software Release Times at Different Confidence Levels with Consideration of Learning Effects," *Software Testing, Verification and Reliability*, 18(4): 221-249. (SCI)

[14] Hossain, S.A. and Dahiya, R.C. (1993) "Estimating the Parameters of a Non-homogeneous Poisson-Process Model for Software Reliability", *IEEE Transactions on Reliability*, 42: 604-612.

[15] Hu, Q.P., Xie, M., Ng, S.H. and Levitin, G. (2007) "Robust recurrent neural network modeling for software fault detection and correction prediction", *Reliability Engineering & System Safety*, 92: 332-340.

[16] Huan-Jyh Shyur (2003),"A stochastic software reliability model with imperfect-debugging and change-point",*The Journal of Systems and Software*, 66,p.135–141

[17] Huang, C.-Y. (2005) "Performance analysis of software reliability growth models with testing-effort and change-point", *Journal of Systems and Software*, 76: 181-194.

[18] Jeske, D.R. and Zhang, X. (2005) "Some successful approaches to software reliability modeling in industry". *Journal of Systems and Software*, 74: 85-99.

[19] Jing Zhao, Hong-Wei Liu, Gang Cui and Xiao-Zong Yang (2006),"Software reliability growth model with change-point and environmental function". *Journal of Systems and Software*, Volume 79, Issue 11, November ,P. 1578-1587

[20] Kapur, P.K. and Bhalla, V.K. (1992) "Optimal release policies for a flexible software reliability growth model", *Reliability Engineering & System Safety*, 35: 49-54.

[21] Karatsas, I., Shreve, S. (1997) *Brownian Motion and Stochastic Calculus*, 2nd ed. Springer-Verlag: New York.

[22] Katrina Maxwell, Luk Van Wassenhove, and Soumitra Dutta (1999) "Performance Evaluation of General and Company Specific Models in Software Development Effort Estimation", *Management Science* , 45: 787-803.

[23] Kimura, M., Toyota, T. and Yamada, S. (1999) "Economic

analysis of software release problems with warranty cost and reliability requirement", *Reliability Engineering & System Safety*, 66: 49-55.

[24] Kuo, L., Lee, J.C., Choi, K., and Yang, T.Y. (1997) "Bayes inference for S-shaped software reliability growth models", *IEEE Transactions on Reliability*, 46: 76-80.

[25] Kuo, L. and Yang, T.Y. (1996) "Bayesian computation for nonhomogeneous Poisson processes in software reliability", *Journal of the American Statistical Association*, 91: 763-773.

[26] Lee, C.H., Kim, Y.T., Park, D.H. (2004) "S-shaped software reliability growth models derived from stochastic differential equations", *IIE Transactions*, 36: 1193-1199.

[27] Littlewood, B. (2006) "Comments on 'Evolutionary neural network modeling for software cumulative failure time prediction", *Reliability Engineering & System Safety*, 91: 485-486.

[28] Melo, A.C.V. and Sanchez, A.J. (2008) "Software maintenance project delays prediction using Bayesian networks", *Expert Systems with Applications*, 34: 908-919.

[29] Moran, P.A.P. (1969) "Statistical inference with bivariate gamma distribution", *Biometrika*, 56: 627-634.

[30] Nalina Suresh, A.N.V. Rao, A.J.G. Babu (1996) "A software reliability growth model", *International Journal of Quality & Reliability Management*, 13:84-94.

[31] Ohba, M. (1984a) "Inflexion S-shaped software reliability growth models", in *Stochastic Models in Reliability Theory*, Osaki, S. and Hatoyama, Y., Eds. Berlin, Germany: Springer-Verlag, 144-162.

[32] Ohba, M. (1984b) "Software reliability analysis models", *IBM Journal of Research and Development*, 28: 428-443.

[33] Özekici, S. and Soyer, R. (2003) "Reliability of software with an operational profile", *European Journal of Operational Research*, 149: 459-474.

[34] P.K. Kapur, D.N. Goswami, and A. Bardhan (2007) "A General Software Reliability Growth Model with Testing Effort Dependent Learning Process", *International Journal of Modeling and Simulation*, 205:4401

[35] Pham, H. and Zhang, X. (1999) "A software cost model with warranty and risk costs", *IEEE Transactions on Computers*, 48: 71-75.

[36] Pham, H. and Zhang, X. (2003) "NHPP software reliability and cost models with testing coverage", *European Journal of Operational Research*, 145: 445-454.

[37] Pham, H. (2003) "Software reliability and cost models -

Perspectives, comparison, and practice", *European Journal of Operational Research*, 149: 475-489.

[38] Shyur, H.-J. (2003) "A stochastic software reliability model with imperfect debugging and change-point", *The Journal of Systems and Software*, 66: 135-141.

[39] T. P. Wright. (1936) "Factors Affecting the Cost of Airplanes", *Journal of the Aeronautical Sciences*, February:3

[40] Tamura, Y., Yamada, S. (2006) "A flexible stochastic differential equation model in distributed development environment", *European Journal of Operational Research*, 168: 143-152.

[41] Tian, L. and Noore, A. (2005) "Evolutionary neural network modeling for software cumulative failure time prediction", *Reliability Engineering & System Safety*, 87: 45-51.

[42] William J. Stevenson. (1999) "Production Operations Management", Irwin/McGraw-Hill, 349-358.

[43] Yamada, M. Kimura, H. Tanaka and S. Osaki. (1994) "Software reliability measurement and assessment with stochastic differential equations", *IEICE Transactions on Fundamentals of Electronics, Communications and Computer Sciences* E77-A: 109-116.

[44] Yamada, S., Ohba, M., and Osaki, S.(1983). "S-shaped software reliability modeling for software error detection". *IEEE Transactions on Reliability*, 32: 475-484.

[45] Yamada, S., Osaki. S. (1985) "Software reliability growth modeling: Models and applications", *IEEE Transactions on Software Engineering*, 11: 1431-1437.

[46] Yamada, S., Tokuno, K. and Osaki, S. (1992) "Imperfect debugging models with fault introduction rate for software reliability assessment", *International Journal of Systems Science*, 23: 2241-2252.

[47] Yin, L., Trivedi, K.S. (1999) "Confidence Interval Estimation of NHPP-Based Software Reliability Models", *Proceedings of the 10th International Symposium on Software Reliability Engineering*, November: 6-11.

[48] Zhang, X. and Pham, H. (1998) "A software cost model with warranty cost, error removal times and risk costs", *IIE Transactions*, 30: 1135-1142.

[49] Zhang, X. and Pham, H. (2006) "Software field failure rate prediction before software deployment", *The Journal of Systems and Software*, 79: 291-300.

[50] Zhao, M. (1993) "Change-point problems in software and hardware reliability", *Communications in Statistics Theory and Methods*, 22: 757-768.

12

A framework for evaluating model-driven architecture

Basel Magableh[1],Butheyna Rawashdeh[2], and Stephen Barrett[3]

[1]School of Computer Science and Informatics,University College Dublin,Ireland

[2]Faculty of Computer Science and Information, Ajloun University College, AL-Balqa Applied University, Ajloun, Jordan

[3]School of Computer Science and Statistics, Trinity College, University of Dublin, Ireland

Email address:

basel.magableh@ucd.ie (B. Magableh), butheyna.rawashdeh@bau.jo (B. Rawashdeh), stephen.barrett@tcd.ie (S. Barrett)

Abstract: In the last few years, Model Driven Development (MDD) has become an interesting alternative for designing the self-adaptive software systems. In general, the ultimate goal of this technology is to be able to reduce development costs and effort, while improving the modularity, flexibility, adaptability, and reliability of software systems. An analysis of model-driven methodologies shows them all to include the principle of the separation of concerns as a key factor for obtaining high-quality and self-adaptable software systems. Each methodology identifies different concerns and deals with them separately in order to specify the design of the self-adaptive applications, and, at the same time, support software with adaptability and context-awareness. This research studies the development methodologies that employ the principles of model-driven architecture in building self-adaptive software systems. To this aim, this article proposes an evaluation framework for analyzing and evaluating the features of those development approaches and their ability to support software with self-adaptability and dependability in highly dynamic contextual environment. Such evaluation framework can facilitate the software developers on selecting a development methodology that suits their software requirements and reduces the development effort of building self-adaptive software systems. This study highlights the major drawbacks of the proposed model-driven approaches in the related works, and emphasize on considering the volatile aspects of self-adaptive software in the analysis, design and implementation phases of the development methodologies. In addition, we argue that the development methodologies should leave the selection of modeling languages and modeling tools to the software developers.

Keywords: Model-Driven Architecture, Self-Adaptive Application, Context Oriented Software Development, Evaluation Framework Of Model-Driven Architecture.

1. Introduction

There is a growing demand for developing applications with aspects such as context awareness and self-adaptive behaviors. Context awareness [1] means that the system is aware of its context, which is its operational environment. Hirschfeld et al. [2] considered context to be any information that is computationally accessible and upon which behavioral variations depend. A self-adaptive application adjusts its behavior according to context conditions arising during execution. A self-adaptive application modifies its own structure and behavior in response to changes in its operating environment [3].

In recent years, a significant number of model-driven architecture approaches were proposed for the construction of context-dependent and self-adaptive applications. The Object Management Group (OMG) presented Model Driven Architecture (MDA) as a set of guidelines for building software systems based on the use of the MDD methodology [4]. MDA focuses primarily on the functionality and behavior of a distributed application or system deployed across many platforms. In MDA, the functionality and behavior are modeled once and only once. Thus, MDA defines the notions of a Computation Independent Model (CIM), Platform Independent Model (PIM) and Platform Specific Model (PSM). CIM describes the software requirements in computational free fashion. A PIM describes the components of the software that do not change from one platform to another, and a PSM describes the implementation of the software components independently from the platform configurations [4].

This article contributes to the knowledge by providing an evaluation framework for most popular model-driven approaches that were proposed to support the development of self-adaptive software systems. Such evaluation framework can facilitate software developers on selecting the best development approach that suits their needs and the software requirements.

This research studies the MDA approaches that used for building self-adaptive mobile software. For this aim, we focus on studying the features of those modeling approaches and comparing their impact on the software development. This can help the software developer in selecting the best methodology that suits their needs.

This article is structured as follows: the self-adaptive software and their self-* properties are defined in Section II. Section III provides a detailed description of model-driven approaches that were proposed for facilitating the development of self-adaptive software systems. Section IV proposes an evaluation framework for analyzing and evaluating those model-driven approaches. Section V illustrates the evaluation results, followed by the conclusions of this study.

2. Self-Adaptive Software

Mobile computing infrastructures make it possible for mobile users to run software systems in heterogeneous and resource-constrained platforms. Mobility, heterogeneity, and device limitations create a challenge for the development and deployment of mobile software. Mobility induces context changes to the computational environment and therefore, changes to the availability of resources and services. To overcome those challenges mobile software can be more dynamic and adaptive by enabling the software to be able to adapt their functionality/behavior to the context changes in the mobile environment [5]. This requires implementing mobile software to be more self-adaptive and reliable.

Self-adaptive applications have the ability to modify their own structure and behavior in response to context changes in the environment where they operate [3]. Self-adaptive software offers the users with context-dependent and context-independent functionality. Context-independent functionality (also called base functionality) refers to software functionality whose implementation is unaffected by the context changes. For example, the map view and user login forms in mobile map application are context-free functionality (i.e. context changes would not change their functionality). The context-dependent functionality refers to software functionality, which exhibits volatile behavior when the context changes. Self-adaptive software can be seen as a collaboration of individual features spanning the software modules in several places [2], and they are sufficient to qualify as heterogeneous crosscutting in the sense that different code fragments are applied to different program parts [6].

Before encapsulating crosscutting context-dependent behaviors into a software module, the developers must first identify the behaviors in the software requirements. This is difficult to achieve because, by their nature, context-dependent behaviors are entangled with other behaviors, and are likely to be included in multiple parts (scattered) of the software modules [7]. Using intuition or even domain knowledge is not necessarily sufficient for identifying their volatile behavior; instead, a formal procedure is needed for analyzing and separating their individual concerns [8].

Implementing a self-adaptive software system in a resource-poor environment faces a wide range of variance in platforms' specifications and Quality of Services (QoS) [9]. Mobile devices have different capabilities in terms of CPU, memory, and network bandwidth [9]. Everything from the devices used and resources available to network bandwidths and user context can change extremely at runtime [11].To face those challenges, the concept of MDA were employed of building self-adaptive software as an attempt to overcome the variability of context changes and reduces the development efforts, besides increasing the software ability to change its architecture and/or behaviors at runtime.

In general, using MDA for building self-adaptive softwarefaces several challenges such as maintaining the correspondence between architectural models and software implementation in order to ensure that behavioraladaptation is appropriately executed. The second issue is providing the necessary facilities for implementing the software in wide-range of platforms, specifically in mobile computing the same application can be executed in several platforms. The following section focuses on describing MDA approaches for modeling self-adaptive software systems that proposed to suit mobile computing platform.

3. Modeling Self-Adaptive Software

In the classical view of object-oriented software development, the modular structure for software systems has rested on several assumptions. These assumptions mayno longer characterize the challenge of constructing self-adaptive software systems that are to be executed in mobile computing environments [13]. The most important assumptions in object-oriented development methodologies are that the decision to use or reuse a particular component/object is made at the time the software is developed. However, the development of a variety of modern self-adaptive software architectures such as mobile/ubiquitous computing, and component-based and context-oriented software has emphasized on deferring these decisions about component selection until runtime. This might increase the software capabilities in terms of variability, adaptability, and maintainability, and increase the anticipatory level of the software by loading a particular component/service that can handle unforeseen context changes dynamically.

Supporting the development of self-adaptive software systems raises numerous challenges. These challenges include: 1) the development processes for building them, 2) the design of their building blocks (i.e. component model, service model or code fragments) and the adaptation engine, which describes the design patterns that can be employed by the middleware designers to support adaptability, 3) the adaptation mechanism that describes the best adaptation action that can be used under the limited resources of the computational environment. This requires the model-driven approach to maintain the correspondence between architectural models and system implementation in order to ensure the adaptation action is appropriately executed. 4) Providing the necessary configurations that suit the deployment platforms.

An appropriate way to study those challenges is to classify them on the basis of adaptation features that they support and how they manage software variability in the architecture level [12]. In the following sections, several model-driven approaches that target engineering self-adaptive software systems are discussed.

3.1. Model Driven Development and AOP

Carton et al. [8] proposed the Theme/UML, a model driven approach supported by Aspect-Oriented Programming (AOP) in an attempt to model various crosscutting concerns of context-aware applications at an early stage of the software development. Crosscutting concerns refers to aspects of a program that affect other concerns. These concerns often cannot be cleanly decomposed from the rest of the system in both the design and implementation. Theme/UML provides a systematic means to analyze the software requirements in order to identify the base and crosscutting concerns, and the relationships between them.

The Theme/UML approach was based on the use of the Meta Object Facility (MOF) extension and the ECORE [14]. The MOF meta model for the development of context-aware mobile applications proposed by de Farias et al. [15] was structured according to the core and service views of thesoftware system. This approach provides a contextual model that is independent from the application domain. However, it does not provide high-level abstraction of the software models, which express conceptual characteristics of the context-dependent behaviors. From a software developer's perspective, it does not take into account the architectural or deployment issues of the target platform;there is no clear process that describes the deployment configurations and the platform specific model of the software. In addition, it has focused on the model-to-model transformation for generating the software composition. Such approach increases the development effort, as the developers have to write and configuremany MOF scripts for the software. The Theme/UML methodology limits the development of self-adaptive applications to a very specific framework that supports the AspectJ and Eclipse Modeling Framework (EMF) [16]. Extending this paradigm for another platform requires a specific compiler that supports Aspect-Oriented Programming (AOP) and toolset that follow the process of EMF.

Plastic is another development approach, which uses the MDD paradigm for developing and deploying adaptable applications, implemented in Java language [5]. The Plastic development process focuses on the model verification and validation and service composition of java service stubs. The methodology shows a very interesting feature of runtime model verification and validation mechanism. Unfortunately, the generated software is tightly coupled with the target deployment platform and cannot be used with a standard development process supported by a standard object-oriented language other than the JAVA and AspectJ languages. However, the two-paradigm Theme/UML and Plastic face challenges with regard to the model manipulation and management. These challenges arise from problems associated with (1) defining, analyzing, and using model transformations, (2) maintaining traceability linksbetween model elements to support model evolution and round-trip engineering, (3) maintaining consistency among viewpoints, (4) tracking versions, and (5) using models during runtime [17].

3.2. A-MUSE

Daniele et al. [18] proposed an MDA-based approach for the refinement andmodeling of software systems, called Architectural Modeling for Service Enabling in freeband (A-MUSE).The A-MUSE approach focuses on the decomposition of the PIM model into three levels; each level is used forautomating a behavioral model transformation process. Daniele et al. [18] applied their approach to a Mobile System Domain Specific Language (DSL) (called M-MUSE). Therefore, the platform independent design phase has been decomposed into service specification, and platform-independent service design. The platform-independent service design model is a refinement of the service specification, which implies correctness and consistency of the originalbehavioral model. Such correctness and consistency are addressed in the transformation process. However,when trying to realize this refinement transformation, there is a gap between the service specification and the platform-independent service model, so that correctness and consistency were hard to guarantee in a single transformation process. Daniele et al. approach this problem by proposing multiple rounds of the transformation between the PIM and PSM, which requires the developers to switch simultaneously between the PIM, PSM and the service specifications several times during the software development.

3.3. CAMEL

Context Awareness modeling Language (CAMEL) is an MDD-based approach proposed by Sindico and Grassi [19]. The approach uses a domain-specific language called JCOOL, which provides a metamodel for context detection;a context model designed using the JCOOL metamodel supports CAMEL. However, Sindico and Grassi implemented the context binding as the associate relationship between context value and context entity. On the other hand, context-driven adaptation refers to a structure or behavior elements, which are able to modify the behavior based on context values. The structural or behavioral insertion is accomplished whenever a context value changes; it uses AOP inter-type deceleration, where the behavioral insertion is accomplished by means of an AOP advice method to inject a specific code into a specific join point.

The CAMEL paradigm provides insufficient details with regard to the underlying component model or the application architecture. The authors used their former domain-specific language to support the Context-Oriented Programming (COP) approach proposed by Hirschfeld et al. [2]. Moreover, CAMEL has no formal MDD methodology that possesses a generic life cycle that a developer can use. Irrespective of these problems, JCOOL is specific to an AOP framework called the Simple Middleware Independent LayEr (SMILE) [20]. SMILE platform used for distributed mobile applications [20]. The model approach in JCOOL supports only ContextJ, which is an extension of the Java language proposed by Appeltauer et al. [21]. The CAMEL methodology requires the software to be re-engineered whenever a new context provider is introduced into the context model. The developers must build a complete context model for the new values and maintain the underlying JCOOL DSL and the Unified Modeling Language (UML) model. The CAMEL methodology has adapted AOP and the EMF to produce a context-oriented software similar to the layered approach proposed by Hirschfeld et al. [2]. This makes CAMEL limited to the EMF tool support and the ContextJ language [22]. From our point of view CAMEL tightly coupled the software with modeling language, modeling tool and the target deployment platform configurations.

3.4. MUSIC MDD

The MUSIC development methodology [23]–[25] adapts a model-driven approach to construct the application variability model. In MUSIC, applications are built using a component framework, with component types as variation points. The MUSIC middleware is used to resolve the variation points, which involves the election of a concrete component as a realization for the component type. The variability model defines the component types involved in the application's architecture and describes their different realizations. This comprises either a description of collaborating component types and rules for a composite realization, or a reference to a concrete component for an atomic realization. To allow the realization of a component type from an external services, the variability model can include a service description, which is used for service discovery and invocation in the variability model.

The software architecture in MUSIC is a pluggable architecture, which means composing the software from multiple plug-ins developed separately. To support dynamic adaptation, a middleware is proposed for facilitating a generic and reusable context management system. The architecture supports context variation and resource utilization by separating low-level platform-specific context from higher-level application-specific context. The resource utilization is improved through intelligent activation and deactivation of context-related plug-ins based on the needs of the active application. The MUSIC middleware architecture defines multiple components that interact with each other to seamlessly enable self-adaptive behavior in the deployed applications. These components include context management, adaptation reasoned, and a plug-in lifecycle management based on the Open Services Gateway initiative framework (OSGI) [26].

At runtime, a utility function is used to select the best application variant; this is the so-called 'adaptation plan'. The utility function is defined as the weighted sum of the different objectives based on user preferences and QoS. Realistically, it is impossible for the developer to predict all possible variations of the application when unanticipated conditions could arise. In addition, mobile computing devices have limited resources for evaluating many application variations at runtime and can consume significant amounts of device resources. Theoutcome of this isthe adaptation benefits aredefeated by the big loss of the allocated resources[12].

3.5. Paspallis MDD

Paspallis [27] introduced a middleware-centric development of context-aware applications with reusable components. Essentially, his work is based on the MUSIC platform [28]. According to Paspallis, an MDA-based context-aware application is built by separating the concerns of the context provider from those of the context consumer. For each context provider, a plug-in or bundle is modeled during the design phase. At runtime, a utility function is used to consider the context state and perform the decision of which plug-in should be loaded. Once the plug-in is selected to be loaded into the application, the MUSICmiddleware performs dynamic runtime loading of the plug-in.

However, it is impossible for the developers to predict all the context providers that might produce context information at runtime. In addition, using this methodology means that the developer is required to design a separate plug-in architecture for each context provider, which is proportional to the available number of context providers. Additionally, this methodology does increases the development effort as each plug-in requires a separate development process.

3.6. U-Music MDD

Khan [29] proposed U-MUSIC methodology. U-MUSIC adapts a model-driven approach to construct self-adaptive applications and uses a component model for achieving unanticipated adaptation. However, the author has modified the MUSIC methodology to support semi-anticipated adaptation; also called planning-based adaptation, which enables the software to adapt to foreseeable context changes. U-MUSIC enables developers to specify the application variability model, context elements, and data structure. The developers are able to model the component functionalities and QoS properties in an abstract, platform-independent model. In U-MUSIC, dynamic decision-making is supported by the MUSIC middleware mentioned above. However, this approach suffers from a number of drawbacks. First, it is well known that correct identification of the weight for each goal is a major difficulty for the utility function. Second, the approach hides conflicts between multiple goals in its single, aggregate objective function, rather than exposing the conflicts and reasoning about them. Finally, it assumes that the code generation process can produce high quality of code based on the variability models in automatic and unsupervised process by the software developers.

3.7. CAUCE

CAUCE proposed as a model-driven development approach [30]. The authors defined an MDA approach that focuses on three layers of models. The first layer confirms to the computational independent model for capturing the conceptual properties of the applications. The second layer defines three complementary points of view of the software systems. These views include deployment, architecture and communication. The third layer focuses on converting the conceptual representation of the context-aware application into a software representation using a multi model transformation. The Atlas Transformation Language (ATL) is used to interpret the model and convert them into a set of models conforming to the platform independent model. The final model is transformed using the MOF Script language based on the EMF paradigm [14]. The CAUCE methodology focuses more on the CIM by splitting this layer into three layers of abstraction, which confirms to the tasks, social and space meta models. The task model focuses on modeling a set of tasks and the relationships among them that any entityin the system is able to perform. The social metamodel defines the social environment of the entities in the system and is directly related to the entity task and entity information that identify the context-aware application behavior. The space metamodel defines the physical environment of the entities in the system. Therefore, this metamodel is directly related to the physical conditions, infrastructure and location characteristics of the context-aware applications.

However, the CAUCE methodology provides a complete development process for building context-aware applications. Despite that, CAUCE is limited to specific modeling tool and language, in this case the UML is integrated with EMF. The generated application can only be implemented using Java language as the ATL and MOF Script languages support it. However, it is impossible for the developers to adapt CAUCE for building heterogeneous and distributed mobile applications, which might have multiple deployment platforms that require variant numbers of implementation languages.

3.8. ContextUML

Generally, UML profiles and metamodels are used to extend the UML language semantics. ContextUML was one of the first approaches that targeted the modeling of the interaction between context and web service applications [31]. Prezerakos et al. [32] extended ContextUML using aspect-oriented programming and service-oriented architecture to fulfill the needs for dynamic adaptation in service-oriented architecture. However, contextUML used a UML metamodel that extended the regular UML by introducing appropriate artifacts that used to create context-aware applications. The contextUML produces a class diagram, which corresponds to the context class and to specific services. They mitigate the UML relationship and dependency to express the interaction between the context information and the respective services. A means of parameters injection and service manipulation are used to populate specific context-related parameters in the application execution loop.

However, the UML profiles and metamodels lack from several features required for modeling the self-adaptive software system. Ignoring the heterogeneity of the context information, they based their claims on the nature of the context values, which can fluctuate and evolve significantly at runtime. It is not feasible to this study how the behavior is modeled when multiple context values have changed at the same time.

3.9. COCA-MDA

According to the COCA-MDA approach, the software self-adaptability and dependability can be achieved by dynamically composing software from context-oriented modules based on the context changes rather than composing the software from functional-oriented modules. Such composition requires the design of software modules to be more oriented towards the context information rather than being oriented towards the functionality. The principle of context orientation of software modules was proposed in the COCA-MDA [33]. COCA-MDA proposes a decomposition mechanism of software based on the separation between context-dependent and context-independent functionality. Separating the context-dependent functionality from the context-independent functionality enables adaptability and dependability of software systems with the aid of middleware technology. The middleware can adapt the software behavior dynamically by composing interchangeable context-dependent modules based on context changes. COCA-MDA proposes that software self-adaptability is achieved by having both adaptive middleware architecture and a suitable decomposition strategy, which separates the context-dependent functionality from the context-independent functionality of the software systems.

COCA-MDA was proposed as a generic and standard development paradigm towards constructing self-adaptive software from context-oriented components, which enables a complete runtime composition of the context-dependent behaviors and provides the software with capabilities of self-adaptability and dependability in mobile computing environment. The context-oriented component model encapsulates the implementation of the context-dependent parts in distinct architectural units, which enables the software to adjust its functionality and/or behavior dynamically. This differs from the majority of existing work, which seeks to embed awareness of context in the functional implementation of applications. The context-oriented software is developed using a COCA-MDA. Afterwards, the context-oriented software is manipulated at runtime by a COCA-middleware that performs a runtime behavioral composition of the context-dependent functionality based on the operational context. The self-adaptive software dependability is achieved through the COCA-middleware capability in considering its own functionality and the adaptation impact/costs. A dynamic decision-making based on a policy framework is used to evaluate the architecture evolution and verifies the fitness of the adaptation output with the application's objectives, goals and the architecture quality attributes.

The COCA-MDA follows the principles of OMG model-driven architecture. In MDA, there are three different views of the software: the Computation Independent View (CIV), the Platform Independent View (PIV), and the Platform Specific View (PSV). The CIV focuses on the environment of the system and the requirements for the system, and hides the details of the software structure and processing. The PIV focuses on the operation of a system and hides the details that are dependent on the deployment platform. The PSV combines the CIV and PIV with an additional focus on the details of the use of a specific platform by a software system [34]. COCA-MDA partitioning the software into three views: the structure, behavior, and enterprise viewpoints. The structure view focuses on the core component of the self-adaptive application and hides the context-driven component. The behavior view focuses on modeling the context-driven behavior of the component, which may be invoked in the application execution at runtime. The enterprise view focuses on remote components or services, which may be invoked from the distributed environment. The COCA-MDA provides the developers with the ability to specify the adaptation goals, actions, and causes associated with several context conditions using a policy-based framework. For each COCA-component, the developers can embed one or more Decision PoLicys (DPLs) that specify the architecture properties. A state-machine model is used to describe the DPL by specifying a set of internal and external variables, and conditional rules. The rules determine the true action or the else part of the action based on the variable values. The action part of the state diagrams usually involves invoking one or more of the component's layers. A single layer is activated if a specific context condition is found, or deactivated if the condition is not found.

COCA-MDA was used for building self-adaptive applications for indoor wayfinding for individuals with cognitive impairments as proposed in [35]. Evaluating the COCA-MDA productivity among the development cost and effort using the Constructive Cost Model II (COCOMO II) [36] was demonstrated in [37]. This article focuses on evaluating the features of COCA-MDA against other MDA approaches as shown in the following section.

4. Feature Analyses And Comparative Study Of MDA-Based Approaches

From the software developer's perspective, it is vital to know the features of the development paradigm, which might be used in constructing a self-adaptive application. Feature evaluation of the development methodology can assist the developers in selecting among the proposed methodologies in the literature for achieving adaptability and dependability of the software systems. Improving the development of self-adaptive software systems using model driven approach has attained several research efforts. The target was in general to introduce software with adaptability and variability while focusing on reducing the software complexity and optimizing the development effort.

The examination of software system performance, dependability and availability is of greatest importance for tuning software system in conjunction with several architecture quality attributes. Such performance analysis was considered by the modeling Specification and Evaluation Language (MOSEL) [38]. The system modeling using MOSEL illustrates how easily it can be used for modeling real-life examples from the fields of computer communication and manufacturing systems. However, extending the MOSEL language towards the modeling and performance evaluation of self-adaptive software system can estimate several qualityattributes of model-based architecture and provides early results about how efficient is the adaptation action.

Kitchenham et al. in [39] proposed the DESMET method, which evaluates software development methodologies using an analytical approach. Asadi et al. have adapted the DESMET method to analyze several MDA-approaches. The authors adapted several evaluation criteria that can be used to compare MDA methodologies based on MDA-related features and MDA-based tool features [40].

However, Calic et al. [41] proposed an evaluation framework to evaluate MDA-based approaches in terms of four major criteria groups, as follows: I) MDA-related features: The degree to which the proposed methodologies are compliant with OMG's MDA specification [42]. II) Quality: Evaluation of the overall quality of the MDA-based approaches including their efficiency, robustness, understandability, ease of implementation, completeness, and ability to produce the expected results [39]. III)

Usability: Simplicity of use and ease of implementation by the developer, which covers clear information about the impact of the methodology on the development effort [43], [44]. IV) Productivity: The quality of benefits derived from using the methodology and its impact on the development time, complexity of implementation, code quality, and cost effectiveness [41]. Calic et al. [41] presents the COPE tool, to evaluate the MDA productivity by automating the coupled evaluation of metamodels and model by recording the coupling history in a history model.

Lewis et al. [45] have evaluated the impact of MDA on the development effort and the learning curve of the MDA-based development tools based on their own experiences. The authors concluded that the real potential behind MDA is not completely employed either by current tools or by the proposed MDA approaches in the literature. In addition, the developers have to modify the generated code such that it is suitable for the target platform. The MDA tools can affect the level of maintenances required for the generated codes. In the same way, the developer's level of understanding of MDA tasks and their familiarity with the target platform have direct impacts on MDA productivity.

The COCOMO II [36] emerged as software cost estimation model, which considers the development methodology productivity. The productivity evaluates the quality of benefits derived from using the development methodology, in terms of its impact on the development time, complexity of implementation, code quality, and cost effectiveness [41]. COCOMO II allows estimation of the effort, time, and cost required for software development. The main advantage of this model over its counterparts such as the Software Life-cycle Management (SLIM) model [46] and the System Evaluation and Estimation of Resources Software Estimation Model (SEER-SEM) [47] is that COCOMO II is an open model with various parameters which effect the estimation of the development effort. Moreover, the COCOMO IImodel allows estimation of the development effort in Person-Months (PM) and the Time to Develop (TDEV) a software application. A set of inputs such as software scale factors (SF) and 17 effort multipliers is needed. A full description of these parameters is given in the COCOMO II model definition manual, which can be found in [36]. An example of an evaluation of MDA approaches with COCOMO II can be found in [48].

In this research, we intend to use an evaluation framework that can test and qualify the ability of MDA-based approaches to produce the expected results [39] in terms of dynamic adaptation in general, and self-adaptability, in specific. These features are evaluated in the following sections.

4.1. Existence of MDA-related Features

Table 1. *MDA-related features.*

Group criteria	Features	Criterion Type	Description of level	UML-based meta model	CAMEL	A-MUSE	MUSIC	Paspalis	U-MUSIC	CAUCE	COCA-MDA
Existence of MDA-related Features	Tool suit and implementation:	Scale form	**A.** The methodology does not provide a specific tool and there are no explicit guidelines as to how to select an appropriate alternative. **B.** The methodology does not provide a complete toolset, or only general guidelines are provided for selecting alternative tools. **C.** The methodology provides a complete toolset, or provides precise guidelines for selecting appropriate alternative tools.	A	A	A	C	B	B	A	A
	Computational independent model	Scale form	**A.** Production of the model are not addressed by the methodology. **B.** The methodology provides general guidelines for creating the model; creation steps are not determined precisely. **C.** The methodology explicitly describes steps and techniques for creating the model.	A	A	A	B	B	B	C	C
	Platform independent model	Scale form		B	B	B	C	B	C	C	C
	Platform specific model	Scale form		B	B		C	B	C	C	C
	Verification and validation	Scale form	**A.** The activity is not defined and is devolved to the developers. **B.** The activity is defined by the methodology, but not in detail. **C.** The methodology provides explicit and detailed guidelines and techniques for performing the activity.	B	A	B	C	A	A	A	B
	Source model. Target model synchronization	Scale form		A	A	B	C	A	B	A	A
	Use of UML profiles	Narrative	**Involved:** the Methodology depend on the UML Profile **Devolved:** Methodology is not using UML profile	Involved	Involved	Devolved	Devolved	Devolved	Devolved	Devolved	Devolved

MDA features refers to the degree to which the proposed methodologies are compliant with the OMG's MDA specifications; these specifications can be divided into the support of CIM, PIM, PSM, model validation, and transformation [42]. In terms of MDA features, we adapt the criteria proposed by Asadi and Ramsin [40], which highlights the methodology's conformance to the original OMG standard, as shown in Table 1. Feature analysis can be performed in two ways: scale form and narrative form. The scale form attaches the methodology compliant to a specific feature, which is divided into three ranks, from A to C, as shown in each table. The narrative form captures whether the methodology covers a specific feature based on the level of involvement.

4.2. Tool-related Feature Analysis

The major challenges arise from concerns associated with providing support for creating and using an appropriate modeling abstraction for analyzing and designing the software [17]. A second challenge posed by Asadi and Ramsin [40], that each development methodology generates more specific technical details that suit the underlying modeling language or modeling tool they used, as each tool requires a learning curve, and it might have some limitation with regard to the platform and the number of implementation languages they support [45]. This implies that a MDD approach should be decoupled from using a specific tool or modeling language. The developers have to be free on selecting the tool(s) that fits their needs and the software under development.

On the other hand, MDD approaches should focus more on describing standard development processes without relaying on a specific technology or platforms like EMF and ECORE. In terms of the tools the methodology used, the features that highlight the methodology dependency on the modeling languages and tools are shown in Table 2.

***Table 2.** Modeling tools-related features.*

Criterion Name	Feature	Description of level	UML-based meta model	CAMEL	A-MUSE	MUSIC	Paspalis	U-MUSIC	CAUCE	COCA-MDA
Existence of tool-related	Model To Model transformation	Involved : The methodology explicitly participates in the activity and provides precise techniques/ guidelines	Devolved	Involved	Involved	Involved	Involved	Involved	Involved	Involved
	Model to code transformation		Devolved	Devolved	Involved	Involved	Involved	Involved	Involved	Involved
	Meta-model maintainability		Devolved	Involved	Involved	Involved	Devolved	Involved	Devolved	Involved
	Verification of the generated model and code		Devolved	Devolved	Devolved	Involved	Involved	Involved	Devolved	Involved
	Traceability between models	Devolved: The activity is developed to the tools and the methodology does not prescribe the steps that should be performed by the tools	Devolved	Devolved	Involved	Involved	Involved	Involved	Devolved	Involved

4.3. Quality of the MDA-based Approaches

Quality refers to the overall quality of the MDA-based approaches, including their efficiency, robustness, and understandability, In addition the ease of implementation, completeness, and the software ability to produce the expected results are included [39]. However, in this research, we have focused on the ability of the MDA-based approaches to provide the expected results that support the adaptability of the generated software, whether these results are derived from the code or the architecture. Moreover, we have split these criteria into four groups: requirements engineering, unanticipated awareness, context model, and modeling context-dependent behavioral variations.

4.3.1. Requirements Engineering of Context-dependent Behavioral Variations

Requirements engineering refers to the causes of adaptation, other than the functional behavior of the self-adaptive system. Whenever the system captures a change in the context, it has to decide whether it needs to adapt. The MDA-based approaches in the related work were evaluated regarding whether they support the modeling of context requirements as a specific feature and whether they support the requirements engineering in general, as shown in Table 3.

In addition, the methodology's ability to analyze and models the context-dependent behavior variations requires the MDD supports at three levels. The first is the requirement analysis at the computational independent model. The second is the representation of these requirements by means of UML objects at the platform independent model and platform specific model. The third is the representation of the context-dependent behavior as runtime objects, which are a code representation of these requirements [49,50]. However, the evaluation of these criteria is shown in Table 3.

4.3.2 Unanticipated Awareness

This feature captures whether a context change can be predicted ahead of time [51]. Anticipation can be classified into three degrees: foreseen, foreseeable, and unforeseen changes. Foreseen refers to the changes that are handled in the implementation code. Foreseeable refer to the context changes that were predicted at the software design.

Unforeseen refers to the changes that are not modeled at the design or the implementation stage, but are to be handled at runtime [52]. The evaluation criteria are shown in Table 4 with their related scale form.

Table 3. *Supporting context-dependent behavior variations on the analysis, design and implementation.*

Criterion Name	Features	Criterion Type	Description of level	UML metmodel	CAMEL	A-MUSE	MUSIC	Paspallis	U-MUSIC	CAUCE	COCA-MDA
Context-dependent variations management	Requirements analysis in the CIM	Narrative	Involved : The methodology supports context-dependent behaviour concerns. Devolved : The methodology does not support context-dependent behaviour concerns.	Devolved	Involved	Devolved	Devolved	Involved	Devolved	Devolved	Involved
	Modelling Context-dependent behaviour at PIM	Narrative	Involved : The methodology has supports for modelling the context-dependent behaviours at the PIM. Devolved : The methodology has no supports for modelling the context-dependent behaviours at the PIM.	Devolved	Involved	Devolved	Devolved	Devolved	Devolved	Devolved	Involved
	Modelling Context-dependent behaviour at PSM.	Narrative	Involved : The methodology has supports for modelling the context-dependent behaviours at the PSM. Devolved : The methodology has no supports for modelling the context-dependent behaviours at the PSM.	Devolved	Involved	Devolved	Devolved	Devolved	Devolved	Involved	Involved

Table 4. *Anticipation of context change-related criteria and evaluation results.*

Criterion Name	Features	Criterion Type	Description of level	UML metamodle	CAMEL	A-MUSE	MUSIC	Paspallis	U-MUSIC	CAUCE	COCA-MDA
unanticipated awareness	Foreseen changes	Scale form	A. The methodology takes care of the context changes implicitly by the code. B. The methodology takes care of the context changes explicitly by means of UML model C. The methodology takes care of the context changes explicitly by enabling the developer to model them in abstract level.	B	A	B	C	B	C	C	C
	foreseeable changes	Scale form	A. The methodology enables the developer to plane for the context changes implicitly by maintaining the code. B. The methodology planned for the context changes explicitly by the variation model supported by planning-based adaptation at runtime. C. The methodology takes care of the context changes and enables the developer to model them in an abstract level.	B	A	B	C	B	C	B	C
	Unforeseen Changes	Scale form	A. The methodology anticipates the context changes implicitly by maintaining the code to handle them , static adaptation. B. The methodology anticipates the context changes explicitly and enables the developer to specify several application variations models supported by refining the base model. C. The methodology anticipates the context changes at runtime by means of requirements' reflection and allows the developers to represent them as runtime objects.	A	A	B	B	B	B	B	C

4.3.3 Context Model

This captures the ability of the methodology to incorporate the context information using the 'separation of concerns' technique between the context information model and the business logic. The first criterion focuses whether the methodology supports/uses the separation of concerns in the development processes. The second criterion refers to the ability to bind the context source to the context provider, as proposed by Sen and Roman [53] and Broens et al. [54] and Paspallis [55]. The binding mechanism enables the developers to map each context cause to the affected architectural units. The binding mechanism also enables the

application to determine which part has to manage the context changes, by means of the adaptation mechanism.

The evaluation criteria for the context model are shown in Table 5.

Table 5. Context model-related criteria and evaluation results.

Criterion Name	Features	Criterion Type	Description of level	UML metmodel	CAMEL	A-MUSE	MUSIC	Paspallis	U-MUSIC	CAUCE	COCA-MDA
Context model	Separation of concerns between the context model and the business logic code.	Narrative	Implicitly: The context model is implicitly handled by the generated code. Explicitly: The context model is explicit separated from the generated code.	Implicitly	Implicitly	Implicitly	Explicitly	Explicitly	Implicitly	Implicitly	Explicitly
	Context Binding	Narrative	Involved : The methodology binding the context information to architectural units Devolved: The methodology is does not support context binding	Involved	Involved	Devolved	Devolved	Involved	Devolved	Devolved	Involved

4.3.4 Modeling Context-dependent Behavior

These criteria refer to the ability of the model to capture the impact of context changes on the self-adaptive application's behavior. However, Hirschfeld et al. [2] classified these changes into three kinds of variations: actor dependent, system dependent, and environment dependent behavioral variations. This behavioral variation requires a separation between their concerns, by separating the

context handling from the concern of the application business logic. In addition, a separation between the application-dependent parts from the application-independent parts can support behavioral modularization of the application, thereby simplifying the selection of the appropriate parts to be invoked in the execution, whenever a specific context condition is found. The behavioral modeling criteria are shown in Table 6.

Table 6. Modeling context-dependent behaviors.

Criterion Name	Features	Criterion Type	Description of level	UML metmodel	CAMEL	A-MUSE	MUSIC	Paspallis	U-MUSIC	CAUCE	COCA-MDA
Modelling Context-dependent Behaviour	Actor-dependent behaviour	Scale form	A. The methodology does not capture the actor-dependent behaviour B. The methodology capture actor-dependent, implicitly by means code weaving and advise. C. The methodology capture actor-dependent behaviour in abstract level, manipulating the behaviour performed at runtime by means of compositional reflection	A	A	A	A	A	A	A	C
	System-dependent behaviour	Scale form	A. The methodology does not capture the system-dependent behaviour. B. The methodology capture system-dependent, implicitly by means of code weaving and advise methods. C. The methodology capture system-dependent behaviour in abstract level, manipulating the behaviour performed at runtime by means of compositional reflection	A	A	A	B	A	B	B	C
	Environment-dependent behaviour	Scale form	A. The methodology does not capture the environment-dependent behaviour B. The methodology capture environment-dependent, implicitly by means of code weaving and advise methods. C. The methodology capture environment-dependent behaviour in abstract level, manipulating the behaviour performed at runtime by means of compositional reflection	A	A	A	A	A	A	A	C

5. Evaluation Results

Based on the analysis results shown in Tables 1, 2, 3, 4, 5, and 6, we find that the discussed methodologies in the related work suffer from several critical failings in terms of

their conformance to the OMG's guidelines for MDA methodology [4].

First, it is well known that correct identification of the weight of each goal is a major difficulty for the utility functions as shown in the MUSIC, U-MUSIC and Paspallis methodologies.

Second, these approaches hide conflicts among multiple adaptation goals by combining them into a single, aggregate objective function, rather than exposing the conflicts and reasoning about them. On the other hand, it would be optimistic to assert that the process of code generation from models can become completely automatic or that the developer's role lies only in application design, as discussed in the above with regard to CAMEL and A-MUSE.

Third, it is impossible for the developers to predict the possible application variations, which will extend the application behavior when unanticipated conditions arise, this applied to all methodologies mentioned in the above.

In addition, mobile devices have limited resources for evaluating many application variations at runtime, which might consume significant amounts of the allocated resources. As a result, the benefits gained from the adaptationprocess areachieved by drained the allocated resources because theadaptation processneedlong processing time to achieve the adaptation. Fourth, the previously mentioned methodologies produce an architecture with a tight coupling between the context provider and the context consumer, which may cause the middleware to notify multiple components about multiple context changes. Finally, all the methodologies seem to generate an architecture that is tightly coupled with the target platform for deployment and the modeling tools they used.

In addition, the developers have to explicitly predict the final composition of the software and the possible variations of the application, whether at the platform independent model or through the model transformation. Moreover, the developers have to modify the generated code to be suitable for deployment on the target platform and to be integrated with the middleware implementation, which is in the best case made a huge gap between the middleware designer and the application developer. Understandings the modeling tasks and the target platform configurations have limited software developers from employing MDA-approaches in several platforms.

6. Conclusions

The MDD-based approaches evaluated in thisstudy suffer from a number of drawbacks. First, there is no guaranty that the code generation process and model transformation of the software models can become completely automatic and unsupervised by the software developer's. Alternatively model-checking techniques are used to check the validity of the generated code or software models. Second, it is impossible for the developer to predict all possible variations of the application when unanticipated conditions will arise. In addition, mobile devices have limited resources for evaluating many application variations at runtime and can consume significant amounts of the allocated resources. As result of

that, the advantages from the adaptation processareoverwhelmed by the overhead required to achieve the adaptation output. Third, each development methodology generates more specific technical details that suit the underlying implementation language or modeling tool they used. Fourth, the impact of MDA-approach over the development cost must be consider by the software developers for selecting the most appropriate methodology for their project. We found that COCA-MDA is more capable to meet the requirements of self-adaptive systems and allows the software developers to adapt it in wide range of execution platforms.

Acknowledgement

Research presented in this paper was funded by a Strategic Research Cluster grant (07/SRC/I1168) by Science Foundation Ireland under the National Development Plan. The authors gratefully acknowledge this support.

References

[1] Parashar, M., Hariri, S.: Autonomic computing: An overview. Unconventional Programming Paradigms (2005) 257–269.

[2] Hirschfeld, R., Costanza, P., Nierstrasz, O.: Context-oriented programming. Journal of Object Technology 7(3) (March 2008) 125–151.

[3] Oreizy, P., Gorlick, M., Taylor, R., Heimhigner, D., Johnson, G., Medvidovic, N., Quilici, A., Rosenblum, D., Wolf, A.: An architecture-based approach to self-adaptive software. Intelligent Systems and Their Applications 14(3) (1999) 54–62.

[4] Kleppe, A.G., Warmer, J., Bast, W.: MDA Explained: The Model Driven Architecture: Practice and Promise. Addison-Wesley Longman Publishing, Boston, MA, USA (2003).

[5] Inverardi, P., Tivoli, M.: The future of software: Adaptation and dependability. In Lucia, A., Ferrucci, F., eds.: Software Engineering. (2009) 1–31.

[6] Apel, S., Leich, T., Saake, G.: Aspectual mixing layers: aspects and features in concert. In: Proceedings of the 28th international conference on Software engineering. (ICSE '06), Shanghai, China, ACM (2006) 122–131.

[7] Lincke,J.,Appeltauer,M.,Steinert,B.,Hirschfeld,R.:Anopeni mplementationfor context-oriented layer composition in contextjs. Science of Computer Programming 76 (December 2011) 1194–1209.

[8] Carton, A., Clarke, S., Senart, A., Cahill, V.: Aspect-oriented model-driven development for mobile context-aware computing. In: Proceedings of the 1st International Workshop on Software Engineering for Pervasive Computing Applications, Systems, and Environments. (SEPCASE '07), Washington, DC, USA (2007) 5–10.

[9] Kuwadekar, A., Joshi, A., Al-Begain, K.: Real time video adaptation in next generation networks. In: Proceedings of Fourth International Conference on Next Generation Mobile

Applications, Services and Technologies (NGMAST 2010). Volume 1 of LNCS., Amman, Jordan (july 2010) 54 –60.

[10] A. Kuwadekar, C. Balakrishna, and K. Al-Begain, "Genxfone: design and implementation of next-generation ubiquitous sip client," in Proceedings of the Second International Conference on Next Generation Mobile Applications, Services and Technologies, ser. (NGMAST '08), Cardiff, UK, sept. 2008.

[11] Belaramani, N.M., Wang, C.L., Lau, F.C.M.: Dynamic component composition for functionality adaptation in pervasive environments. In: Proceedings of the Ninth IEEE Workshop on Future Trends of Distributed Computing Systems. (FTDCS '03), San Juan, Puerto Rico (May 2003) 226–232.

[12] Salehie, M., Tahvildari, L.: Self-adaptive software: Landscape and research challenges. ACM Transactions on Autonomous and Adaptive Systems (TAAS) 4 (May 2009) 14:1–14:42.

[13] Harrison, W.: Modularity for the changing meaning of changing. In: Proceedings of the tenth international conference on Aspect-oriented software development. (AOSD '11), Porto de Galinhas, Brazil (2011) 301–312.

[14] Eclipse: Eclipse modeling framework. http://www.eclipse.org/modeling/emf/ (November 2012) [Online; accessed 1-November-2012].

[15] de Farias, C.R.G., Leite, M.M., Calvi, C.Z., Pessoa, R.M., Filho, J.G.P.: A mof metamodel for the development of context-aware mobile applications. In: Proceedings of the 22nd Annual ACM Symposium on Applied Computing. (SAC '07), Seoul, Korea (2007) 947–952.

[16] Kiczales, G., Hilsdale, E., Hugunin, J., Kersten, M., Palm, J., Griswold, W.: An overview of aspectj. In: Proceedings of the 15th European Conference on Object-Oriented Programming, (ECOOP 2001). Volume 2072 of LNCS., Budapest, Hungary (2001) 327–354.

[17] France, R., Rumpe, B.: Model-driven development of complex software: A research roadmap. In: Proceedings of the Future Of Software Engineering. (FOSE '07), Washington, DC, USA (2007) 37–54.

[18] Daniele, L.M., Ferreira Pires, L., Sinderen, M.: An mda-based approach for behaviormodeling of context-aware mobile applications. In: Proceedings of the 5th European Conference on Model Driven Architecture Foundations and Applications. (ECMDA-FA '09), Birmingham, UK (2009) 206–220.

[19] Sindico, A., Grassi, V.: Model driven development of context aware software systems. In: Proceedings of International Workshop on Context-Oriented Programming. (COP '09), Genova, Italy (2009) 7:1–7:5.

[20] Bartolomeo, G., Salsano, S., Melazzi, N., Trubiani, C.: Smile: simple middleware independent layer for distributed mobile applications. In: Proceedings of the Wireless Communications and Networking Conference. (WCNC 2008), Las Vegas, USA (31 2008-april 3 2008) 3039–3044.

[21] Appeltauer, M., Hirschfeld, R., Masuhara, H.: Improving the development of context-dependent java applications with contextj. In: Proceedings of the International Workshop on Context-Oriented Programming. (COP '09), Genova, Italy (2009) 5:1–5:5.

[22] Appeltauer, M., Hirschfeld, R., Haupt, M., Masuhara, H.: Contextj: Context-oriented programming with java. Information and Media Technologies 6(2) (2011) 399–419.

[23] Floch, J., Hallsteinsen, S., Stav, E., Eliassen, F., Lund, K., Gjorven, E.: Using architecture models for runtime adaptability. IEEE software 23(2) (2006) 62–70.

[24] Rouvoy, R., Beauvois, M., Lozano, L., Lorenzo, J., Eliassen, F.: Music: an autonomous platform supporting self-adaptive mobile applications. In: Proceedings of the 1st workshop on Mobile middleware: embracing the personal communication device. (MobMid '08), Leuven, Belgium (2008) 6:1–6:6.

[25] Rouvoy, R., Barone, P., Ding, Y., Eliassen, F., Hallsteinsen, S., Lorenzo, J., Mamelli, A., Scholz, U.: Music: Middleware support for self-adaptation in ubiquitous and service-oriented environments. In Cheng, B.H., Lemos, R., Giese, H., Inverardi, P., Magee, J., eds.: Software Engineering for Self-Adaptive Systems. (2009) 164–182.

[26] Osgi: the dynamic module system for java. http://www.osgi.org/Main/HomePage (November 2010) [Online; accessed 1-November-2010].

[27] Paspallis, N.: Middleware-based development of context-aware applications with reusable components. PhD thesis, University of Cyprus, Department of Computer Science (Nov 2009).

[28] Reichle, R., Wagner, M., Khan, M.U., Geihs, K., Lorenzo, J., Valla, M., Fra, C., Paspallis, N., Papadopoulos, G.A.: A comprehensive context-modeling framework for pervasive computing systems. In: Proceedings of the 8th international conference on Distributed applications and interoperable systems. (DAIS '08), Oslo, Norway (2008) 281–295.

[29] Khan, M.U.: Unanticipated Dynamic Adaptation of Mobile Applications. PhD thesis, University of Kassel, Distributed Systems Group, Kassel, Germany (may 2010).

[30] Tesoriero, R., Gallud, J., Lozano, M., Penichet, V.: Cauce. Model-driven development of context-aware applications for ubiquitous computing environments. Journal of Universal Computer Science 16(15) (July 2010) 2111–2138.

[31] Sheng, Q., Benatallah, B.: Contextuml: a uml-based modeling language for model-driven development of context-aware web services. In: Proceeding of the 4th International Conference on Mobile Business. (ICMB '05), Sydney, Australia (2003) 11–13.

[32] Prezerakos, G., Tselikas, N., Cortese, G.: Model-driven composition of context-aware web services using contextual and aspects. In: Proceedings of the IEEE International Conference on Web Services. (ICWS 2007), Utah, USA (July 2007) 320–329.

[33] Magableh, B., Barrett, S.: Context oriented software development. Journal of Emerging Technologies in Web Intelligence (JETWI) 3(4) (June 2012) 206–216.

[34] Miller, J., Mukerji, J.: Mda guide version 1.0.1. Technical report, Object Management Group (OMG) (2003).

[35] Magableh, B., Barrett, S.: Self-adaptive application for indoor wayfinding for individuals with cognitive impairments. In: Proceedings of the 24th International Symposium on Computer-Based Medical Systems. Number 1 in (CBMS '11), Bristol, United Kingdom (june 2011) 1 –6.

[36] Boehm, B.W., Clark, Horowitz, Brown, Reifer, Chulani, Madachy, R., Steece, B.: Software Cost Estimation with Cocomo II. 1st edn. Prentice Hall PTR (2000).

[37] Magableh, B., Barrett, S.: Model-Driven productivity evaluation for self-adaptive Context-Oriented software development. In: Proceedings of the 5th International Conference and Exhibition on Next Generation Mobile Applications, Services, and Technologies. (NGMAST'11), Cardiff, Wales, United Kingdom (September 2011) 158–167.

[38] Begain, K., Bolch, G., Herold, H.: Practical Performance Modeling: Application of the Mosel Language. Kluwer Academic Publishers, Norwell, MA, USA (2001).

[39] Kitchenham, B., Linkman, S., Law, D.: Desmet: a methodology for evaluating software engineering methods and tools. Computing & Control Engineering Journal 8(3) (2002) 120–126.

[40] Asadi, M., Ramsin, R.: Mda-based methodologies: An analytical survey. In: Proceedings of the Euro Conference on Model Driven Architecture Foundations and Applications. (ECMDA-FA 2008), Berlin, Germany (2008) 419–431.

[41] Calic, T., Dascalu, S., Egbert, D.: Tools for mda software development: Evaluation criteria and set of desirable features. In: Proceedings of the Fifth International Conference on Information Technology. (ITNG 2008), Istanbul, Turkey (2008) 44–50.

[42] OMG, O.M.G.: Software & systems process engineering meta-model specification. Technical report, Object Management Group (2010).

[43] Norman, D.A.: The Design of Everyday Things. Reprint paperback edition. Basic Books (September 2002)

[44] Preece, J., Rogers, Y., Sharp, H., eds.: Interaction Design: Beyond Human-Computer Interaction. John Wiley and Sons (January 2002).

[45] Lewis, G., Wrage, L.: Model problems in technologies for interoperability: Model-driven architecture. Technical report, Software Engineering Institute (2005).

[46] Estell, R.G.: Software life cycle management. International Journal of Management Reviews 5 (August 1976) 2–15.

[47] Galorath, D.D., Evans, M.W.: Software Sizing, Estimation, and Risk Management. Auerbach Publications (2006).

[48] Achilleas: Model-Driven Petri Netbased Framework for Pervasive Service Creation. PhD thesis, University of Essex (2010).

[49] Bencomo, N., Whittle, J., Sawyer, P., Finkelstein, A., Letier, E.: Requirements reflection: requirements as runtime entities. In: Proceedings of the 32nd ACM/IEEE International Conference on Software Engineering, (ICSE '10). Volume 2 of LNCS., CAPE TOWN, South Africa (2010) 199–202.

[50] delmos,R.,Giese,H.,Mu¨ller,H.,Shaw,M.,Andersson,J.,Baresi ,L.,Becker,B., Bencomo, N., Brun, Y., Cikic, B., Desmarais, R., Dustdar, S., Engels, G., Geihs, K., Goeschka, K.M., Gorla, A., Grassi, V., Inverardi, P., Karsai, G., Kramer, J., Litoiu, M., Lopes, A., Magee, J., Malek, S., Mankovskii, S., Mirandola, R., Mylopoulos, J., Nierstrasz, O., Pezz`e, M., Prehofer, C., Scha¨fer, W., Schlichting, W., Schmerl, B., Smith, D.B., Sousa, J.P., Tamura, G., Tahvildari, L., Villegas, N.M., Vogel, T., Weyns, D., Wong, K., Wuttke, J.: Software engineering for self-adaptive systems: A second research roadmap. In: Proceedings of Dagstuhl Seminar, Software Engineering for Self-Adaptive Systems. (Dagstuhl Seminar '11), Dagstuhl, Germany (2011) 1–26.

[51] Cheng, B.H., Giese, H., Inverardi, P., Magee, J., de Lemos, R., Andersson, J., Becker, B., Bencomo, N., Brun, Y., Cukic, B., Serugendo, G.D.M., Dustdar, S., Finkelstein, A., Gacek, C., Geihs, K., Grassi, V., Karsai, G., Kienle, H., Kramer, J., Litoiu, M., Malek, S., Mirandola, R., Mu¨ller, H., Park, S., Shaw, M., Tichy, M., Tivoli, M., Weyns, D., Whittle, J.: Software engineering for self-adaptive systems: A research road map. In: Proceedings of Dagstuhl Seminar, Software Engineering for Self-Adaptive Systems. (Dagstuhl Seminar '08), Dagstuhl, Germany (2008) 1– 26.

[52] Laprie, J.: Basic concepts and taxonomy of dependable and secure computing. IEEE Transactions on Dependable and Secure Computing 1 (Apr 2004) 11–33.

[53] Sen, R., Roman, G.: Context-sensitive binding, flexible programming using transparent context maintenance. Technical report, Department of Computer Science and Engineering Washington University in St. Louis (2003).

[54] Broens, T., Quartel, D., Van Sinderen, M.: Capturing context requirements. In: Proceedings of the 2nd European conference on Smart sensing and context. (EuroSSC '07), Kendal, England (2007) 223–238.

[55] Paspallis, N.: Software engineering support for the development of context-aware, adaptive applications for mobile and ubiquitous computing environments. http://www.cs.ucy.ac.cy/paspalli/phd/thesis-proposal.pdf (2010) "[online accessed 1-December-2010]".

13

A cohesion measure for C in the context of an AOP paradigm

Zeba Khanam, S. A. M Rizvi

Jamia Millia Islamia, New Delhi

Email address:

zebs_khan@yahoo.co.in(Z. Khanam)

Abstract: Cohesion measures the relative functional strength of a module and impacts the internal attribute of a function such as modularity. Modularity has become an accepted approach in every engineering discipline. The concept of modular design has considerably reduced the complexity of software design. It represents the strength of bond between the internal elements of the modules. To achieve effective modularity, design concepts like functional independence are considered to be very important. Aspect-oriented software development (AOSD) has emerged over the last decade as a paradigm for separation of concerns, which aims to increase the modularity. Therefore the presence of aspects affects the cohesiveness of a module. Like any new technology, aspect-oriented programming (AOP) was introduced to solve problems related to object-orientation (OO), and more in particular Java .It was noticed that AOP's ideas were not necessarily tied to OO (and Java) but also to less modular paradigm like imperative programming. Moreover, several metrics have been proposed to assess aspect-oriented systems quality attributes in an object oriented context. However, not much work has been done to assess the impact of AOP on imperative style of programming (also called procedural paradigm, such as C language). Therefore, metrics are required to measure quality attributes for AOP used with imperative programming. Cohesion is considered an important software quality attribute. In this context, this paper presents an approach for measuring cohesion based on dependence analysis using control flow graphs (CFG).

Keywords: Cohesion Measures, Procedural Paradigm, Software Metrics, Aspect Oriented Programming

1. Introduction

Module cohesion is a property of a module that represents unity of purpose. It describes the degree to which elements of a module are associated with each other. Aspect-oriented (AO) software development is a paradigm that provides new abstractions and mechanisms to support separation of concerns and the modularization of crosscutting concerns through the software development [Figueiredo etal 2005].Though there have been a number of researches on the evaluation of this design technique and it has been claimed that applying an AOSD method will eventually lead to quality software in the field of object oriented programming, however efficient evaluation in a quantitative manner about the role of AOSD in the area of procedural programming is still ignored. Moreover, phenomenon like scattering and tangling, the usual indicators for crosscutting concerns, equally arises in less modular paradigms like imperative programming. Therefore, in order to establish the significance of AOSD in

improving the software attributes: maintainability, reusability and reliability of systems developed using aspect oriented techniques, software measures are required. Software engineers have assumed that the most impacted property of an aspect-oriented system is separation of concerns. However, some recent studies (e.g. [Garcia, A. et al., 2005][Garcia, A. et al.2004]) have shown that other fundamental software engineering principles, such as low coupling and high cohesion, need to be assessed in conjunction with separation of concerns issues. Cohesion describes the degree to which the actions performed within the module contribute to single behavior/function.

Module cohesion has been associated to the quality of software. Cohesion is the measure of strength of the association of elements within a module. Modules whose elements are strongly and genuinely related to each other are desired. Stevens etal. and Page-Jones claimed that cohesion is associated with effective modularity, a desirable quality of software, and has predictable effects on external software quality attributes such as modifiability, maintainability, and understandability [Yourdon and Constantine,1978][Stevens,etal 1974]. Booch has defined modularity as the property of a system whose modules are cohesive and loosely-coupled .Fenton stated that modularity is the internal quality attribute of the software system [Melton, 2007][Fenton,1994]. Karstu indicated that there appears to be a correlation between module cohesion and number of changes made to a module [Karstu, 1994] such that highly cohesive modules are less likely to need change. Though a number of papers have addressed different measures for evaluating the cohesion in procedural software[BiemanandOtt.1994][Kang &Bieman,1996] and object oriented software [Chidamber &Kemerer,1994][Briand,1998][Kiczales,1997][Chae.etal.2 000] but not much work is done when it comes to assessing the software components developed using aspect oriented programming.

In order to study the impact of aspect-oriented software development (AOSD) on evolution, one has to study its impact on software characteristics such as evolvability, maintainability, understandability, and quality. This paper addresses a measure for module cohesion for procedural software modified or refactored with Aspect oriented design and implementation .For this purpose we have used C language with AspectC as the AOP language for the quality of implementations.

The assessment of relevant attributes of aspect-oriented design and implementation is a prerequisite for achieving high-quality AO software, and that exploiting those attributes will open up a broader design evaluation, which is essential to allow the AO software engineers reason about and make a proper trade-off analysis between different solution alternatives.

The rest of the paper is organized as follows. Section 2 briefly describes the related work. Section 3 introduces Aspect oriented programming and Aspect. Section 4 depicts the application of AOP in procedural software. Section 5 presents member dependency in aspect oriented scenario. Section 6 defines a cohesion measure suite based on the dependence criteria. Section 6

2. Related Work

There are number of research work dedicated to measure and analyze the complexity of software systems [Chidamber, 1994] [Buse, 2008] [McCabe, 1976] [Halstead, 1979]. Several metrics have been proposed in the literature in order to assess quality attributes (complexity, coupling, cohesion, etc.)Software metrics measures the complexity of software systems for software cost estimation, software development control, software assurance, software testing, and software maintenance. Several software metrics exist based on different categories [Meyer, 2009]:

Size-related software metrics: NCLOC, Memory footprint, Number of classes / headers, Number of methods, Number of attributes, Size of compiled code, etc.

Quality-related software metrics: Cyclomatic complexity,

Number of states, Number of bugs in LOC, Coupling metrics, Inheritance metrics, etc.

Process-related software metrics: failed builds, defect per hour, requirement changes, programming time, number of patches after release, etc.

There are currently more than 200 metrics with many different purposes [Meyer, 2009], but currently, the existing procedural metrics [Henryan&Kafura, 1981][McCabe,1976] are only applicable on the procedural software not aspect oriented code therefore if the aspect oriented constructs are intercepting the source files it is necessary to evaluate their impact because they tend to affect the cohesion and coupling between the modules and the introduced advice. McCabe measures the number of linearly independent paths through a program's source code.[McCabe 1976] proposed complexity measures based on the number of local information flows entering and exiting in each module. Presently, a number of papers have addressed the metrics related to aspect-oriented programs quality [Zhao&Xu,2004][Kang&Bieman,1996][Gélinas,2006][Ce ccato&Tonella,2004][Anna.etal.2003].One of the first approaches in the field of cohesion measurement for AOP was given by Zhao. It is based on a dependency model for aspect-oriented software that consists of a group of dependency graphs. According to Zhao and Xu's approach, cohesion is defined as the degree of relatedness between attributes and modules. Zhao and Xu present, in fact, two ways for measuring aspect cohesion based on inter-attributes (γa), inter-modules (γm) and module-attribute (γma) dependencies. Further, this approach was modified by [Gélinas etal, 2006].They analyzed that the approach was complicated and the cohesion(x) computation was based on some arbitrary constants $\beta 1$, $\beta 2$, and $\beta 3$.

(Where $x = \beta 1* \gamma a + \beta 2* \gamma m + \beta 3 * \gamma ma$, k the number of attributes and n the number of modules in aspect A). [Gelinas etal 2006] deviced a measure for cohesion computation based on data-module and module-module connection criteria. Therefore, the Aspect cohesion (ACoh) was computed as:

ACoh represents the relative number of connected modules: ACoh(Aspecti) = NC(Aspecti) / NM(Aspecti) $\in$ [0,1].

Where NM(Aspecti) is the total number of modules pairs in an aspect and NC(Aspecti) is the number of connections between modules. The target AOP language was AspectJ.

In [Anna.etal, 2003] a method for the computation of LCOM was derived from the well-known LCOM (Lack of Cohesion in Methods) metric developed by [Chidamber&Kemerer,1994].A more synonymous extension of C&K metric suite [Chidamber&Kemerer,1994] has been made in [Cecatto&Tonella,2004] but it is again a measure for object oriented software designed using AspectJ as the aspect oriented language. Therefore all the measures are basically devised for aspect oriented systems developed in an object oriented environment. We are inspired by some approaches proposed for cohesion measurement [Briand, 1998][Garcia A.etal,2004][Zhao&Xu,2004][Gélinas,etal 2006]. As none of the existing metrics tend to target the AO code in AspeCt C we have devised a measure for computing cohesion in AOP used with C software.

3. Aspect-Oriented Programming and Aspect-Oriented C

In this paper we use C and AspectC as the aspect oriented language to show the basic ideas of coupling measurement in AO systems. AspectC is an aspect-oriented extension to C by adding some new concepts and associated constructs. The current ACC language design adapts the ideas of AOP introduced by Kiczales [Kickzales1997] to the C programming language. These concepts and associated constructs are called join points, pointcut, advice, intype and introduce declaration, and aspect. The AspeCt-oriented C compiler processes the advice declaration from the aspect file and the core program from the core file and generates C sources that contain information from both files. This step is referred to as aspect compilation. That is the advice specified in the aspect file is woven into the core to result in a program that reflects both programs' intends.

The major construct of AspectC is the advice, which is just like function but are executed when a join point is matched by a pointcut defined inside the code part of a pointcut declaration. They are different from the aspects in AspectJ, as the aspects are just like classes that encapsulate functionalities that crosscut other classes.

4. Applicability of AOP in Procedural Software

We have used an example from an encryption program to make a reusable aspect that checks the file opening result. Below is an example to depict a simple encryption function. In order to encrypt or decrypt the file, it needs to be opened and the file check operation has to be done to ensure that the file pointer doesn't return null.

The check is done after each call to fileopen().Hence all the operations to be carried on the file uses the above code fragment that is almost identically scattered across the whole system. This is a very important check that needs to be performed but at the same time the code unnecessarily distracts from the principal program logic. This is an example of an aspect. This therefore reduces the understandability of the code and also if the code needs updation it needs to be done at several places, which unnecessarily creates complications.

Example: It is common practice to check the return value after opening a file for any use to ensure the return value is non null. This code often looks as follows:

```
void encrypt()
1.{ FILE *fp,*fp1;
2.char name[20],temp[20]={"Temp.txt"},c;
3.printf("Enter the filename to Encrypt:");
4.scanf("%s",name);
5.fp =fopen(name,"r+");
6. if( fp==NULL)
7.{ printf("The file %s can't be open",name);
8.   exit();}
9. fp1=fopen(temp,"w+");
10.if(fp1==NULL)
11. {   printf("The file Temp can't be open");
12.   exit();}
13. c=fgetc(fp);
14.while(c!=EOF) {
15.fputc((c+name[0]),fp1);printf("%c",c+name[0]);
16.c=fgetc(fp); }
17.fclose(fp);
18.fclose(fp1);
19.remove(name);
20.rename(temp,name);
21.printf("The file is Encrypted:"); }
```

Figure 1. *Code snippet from file encryption program*

Thus a better option is to isolate the concern that would improve maintainability and would also better modularize the system. In the above example the file checking logic would be extracted into an aspect file, as follows:

```
void encrypt{ FILE *fp, *fp1;
2.char name[20],temp[20]={"Temp.txt"},c;
1 .printf("Enter the filename to Encrypt:");
2. scanf("%s",name);
3. fp=fopen(name,"r+");
4. fp1=fopen(temp,"w+");
5 .c=fgetc(fp);
6. while(c!=EOF)
   {
7.
fputc((c+name[0]),fp1);printf("%c",c+name[0]);getch()
;
8.  c=fgetc(fp); }
9. fclose(fp);
10 . fclose(fp1);
11 .remove(name);
```

Figure 2. *Aspect to handle the checking logic*

```
after (void * s) : (call($ fopen(...)) && result(s) {
File * result = ( File*)(s);
if(result == NULL) {
/* routine to handle the case */
printf("The file can't be open");
.....
.... exit();
}
}
```

Figure 3. *File Encryption Code after removing the file check routine*

A similar situation arises when malloc( ) and calloc( ) functions are used for memory allocation. After each call to malloc ( ) it is a common practice to check if the value returned after memory allocation is null or not null. The memory checking concern is scattered throughout the entire program hence crosscutting each function, therefore the AspectC offers a good solution by the extraction of the concern in an advice that should be invoked after each call to these functions.

5. Member Dependency in an Aspect Oriented Scenario

As illustrated in the previous section, different cohesion measures have been proposed by Zhao, Ceccato and Jean. But all these measures are specially designed for AspectJ but AspectC has different constructs and the structure of the procedural program too is different from the object oriented constructs so none of these measures can be applied directly. However, in the context of the measures defined by Zhao we have defined the member dependencies in C and AOP and subsequently the measure to quantify cohesion.

Our basic concepts will be illustrated using AspectC. AspectC introduces several new language constructs such as: join points, pointcuts, advice as well as intype declarations. Join points are well-defined points in the structure and dynamic execution of a system. Examples of join points are method calls, method executions, and field sets and reads. Pointcuts describe join points and context to expose. Advice is a method-like abstraction that defines code to be executed when a join point is reached. Pointcuts are used in the definition of an advice. Inter-type declarations define how an aspect modifies a program's static structure, namely, the members and the relationship between components. Pointcuts and advice dynamically affect program flow, and inter-type declarations statically affect a program's class hierarchy.

Since in a procedural language a program is written using functions or procedures, therefore cohesiveness is defined on a software module/function/procedure. Therefore cohesion in a function is an internal software attribute that measures the degree to which its members are bounded together. Cohesion can be a measure to identify the poorly designed function or advice. A function that has probably been assigned unrelated concerns will depict a low cohesion value. Thus such a function will be difficult to understand, to test, to reuse and to maintain but if a concern is extracted into an advice and is separated from the original function then the function exhibits higher cohesiveness and if the advice handles a single concern then it is also supposedly highly cohesive.

The cohesion measure is defined on the basis of dependence analysis. We define cohesion on the basis of inter attribute dependence. Therefore we present the dependency between the attributes defined in a function or an advice and the dependencies are depicted using Control flow Graph (CFG) of a module.

The associations (or relationships) between the processing elements of a module are defined in terms of control and data dependencies between the variables of a module. These dependencies are computed from a directed graph called Control Flow Graph (VDG). Control flow analysis is defined as:

Definition 1: The control flow graph, or simply a flow graph, of a program is a directed graph where the nodes correspond to the basic blocks of the program and the edges represent potential transfer of control between two basic blocks [Aho86, Hecht77].

Dependence Definition: Consider a directed Control Flow Graph (CFG) of a module M (i.e. a module is used for a function or an advice) GM where the nodes represent the basic blocks of the module and the edges represent the control transfer between the 2 blocks. A basic block is a group of statements such that no transfer occurs into a group except to the first statement in that group, and once the first statement is executed, all statements in the group are executed sequentially [Hecht77]. If there are n attributes a1, a2,…an in the module, then any attribute a1 ∈ GM is said to be related to ai ∈ GM if they both lie on the same edge of the GM and is denoted as a1 → ai.

Therefore, the relatedness or the dependence of an attribute ai to the other attributes of the module is computed at every edge of the CFG GM.

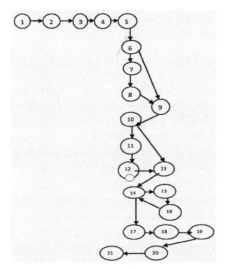

Figure 4. *Contror Flow Graph For Encrypt().*

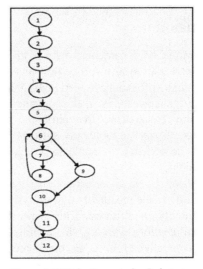

Figure 5. *CFG for Encrypt after Refactoring*

6. A Cohesion Measure

The cohesion is about tightness between attributes in a module. Based on the introduced dependence criteria, we define the cohesion of a module (advice/function) by the degree of relatedness of its attributes or data. We are inspired by some approaches proposed for aspects and class cohesion measurement [Zhao,2003][Zhao&Zu,2004][Gélinas, etal 2006]. To compute the cohesion for a module, we define it as follows:

Definition: For each attribute ai of module M, a set $R_M(a)$ contains the attributes on which 'a' depends or is related to by the dependence criteria defined above. Thus

$R_M(a)=\{ai|\ a\rightarrow ai, a\neq ai\}$　where i=1,2…..k such that k is the number of attributes present in the module M. We define the degree of relatedness of 'a'　to the other attributes of the module 'M' on the graph 'GM' with 'E' edges as follows:

$$DR\ (a)=1/e\sum_{i=1}^{e}|\ R_M(a)|/(k-1)$$

k represents the number of attributes:- e　represents the blocks that are not declarative statements.

Thus we define the cohesion measure as:

$$Ca(M) =\{\ 0\ k=0\ 1\ k=1\ 1/k\ \sum kj=1\ DR(aj)\ k>1\ \}$$

The cohesion is measured on the basis of attributes present. If the attribute is zero then the inter attribute cohesion is 0 if there is a single attribute then the cohesion is 1 and　one attribute itself is tight.

Example 1: The degree of cohesion is computed through the CFGs available (Fig.4 and Fig.5). For the function encrypt, before refactoring Ca (encrypt) is .705(.705/5=.141) based on the above definition of cohesion. After refactoring the cohesion measure is Ca (encrypt) =.179 and can be observed that it has increased. As we compute the aspect cohesion for the advice we may notice that there is a single attribute in the function so therefore the inter attribute cohesion is 1 for the advice.

6. Conclusion

The application of a particular metrics to software is dependant upon the system properties that are to be assessed. Modular software has several advantages such as maintainability, manageability, and comprehensibility. As described many researchers, five attributes are closely related to modularity in software systems which are coupling / dependency, complexity, cohesion, and information hiding.

Thus, cohesion is an important internal attribute of a software that affects the modularity of a software and hence the maintainability of software. This paper proposes a cohesion measure for assessing the cohesiveness of a module (function/advice) in C in the context of AOP (AspectC) environment. The proposed cohesion measure is basically defined for procedural software using an aspect oriented environment. Cohesiveness Measure Ca(M) of a

module (advice/function)　is defined on the basis of　its inter attribute dependence, as attributes form the basic building blocks of a module and their correlation forms the functionality of the module and　is the most significant aspect for establishing the tightness of a module. We had also discussed the criteria of attribute dependence and have depicted an AOP scenario with an example to compute its cohesion measure.

Most of the metrics suites for Aspect oriented software are defined in the context of object oriented programming. Therefore, we believe that our approach can be a good measure to assess the cohesion of a procedural module in an AOSD context. In future, we intend to perform more empirical studies in order to establish the tradeoff between advantages and disadvantages obtained by using the AOP approach in terms of other software attributes.

References

[1]　E. Figueiredo, A. Garcia, C. Sant'Anna, U. Kulesza, and C. Lucena, Assessing Aspect-Oriented Artifacts: Towards a Tool-Supported Quantitative Method, Wkshp. on Quantitative Approaches in OO Software Engineering, 2005.

[2]　S.R. Chidamber and C.F. Kemerer, A Metrics suite for object Oriented Design, IEEE Transactions on Software Engineering, Vol. 20, No. 6, pp. 476-493, June 1994.

[3]　J.Bieman and L. Ott.Measuring Functional Cohesion. IEEE Transactions of Software Engineering.Vol.22,No.10,August 1994.

[4]　L.C. Briand, J. Daly and J. Wusr, A unified framework for cohesion measurement in object-oriented systems, Empirical Software Engineering, Vol.3, No.1, pp. 67-117, 1998.

[5]　G.Kiczales, J.Lamping, A.Mendhekar,C.Maeda,C.Videara Lopes,J.M. Loingtier and J.Irwin,Aspect Oirented Programming. In ECOOP,1997.

[6]　H.S. Chae, Y. R. Kwon and D H. Bae, A cohesion measure for object-oriented classes, Software Practice and Experience, No. 30, pp. 1405-1431, 2000.

[7]　Garcia, A. et al.: Modularizing Design Patterns with Aspects: A Quantitative Study. In Proc. of the AOSD'05, Chicago, USA, (2005), pp. 3-14.

[8]　Garcia, A. et al.: Separation of Concerns in Multi-Agent Systems: An Empirical Study. In Software Engineering for Multi-Agent Systems II, Springer, LNCS 2940, (2004).

[9]　J. Zhao, Coupling Measurement in Aspect-Oriented Systems, Technical-Report SE-142-6, Information Processing Society of Japan (IPSJ), July 2003.

[10]　J. Zhao and B. Xu, Measuring Aspect Cohesion, Proceeding of International Conference on Fundamental Approaches to Software Engineering (FASE'2004), LNCS 2984, pp.54-68, Springer-Verlag, Barcelona, Spain, March 29-31, 2004.

[11]　B.Kang and Bieman, Design Level Cohesion Measures:Derivation,Comparisons and Applications,Computer Science Technical Report CS-96-103,Colorado State University,1996.

[12] J.F. Gélinas, L. Badri and M. Badri, A Cohesion Measure For Aspects, in Journal of Object Technology, vol. 5, no. 7, September - October 2006, pp. 97 – 114 http://www.jot.fm/issues/issue_2006_09/article5.

[13] Henry, S., Kafura, Software Structure Metrics Based on Information Flow D. IEEE Transactions on Software Engineering Volume SE-7, Issue 5, Sept. 1981 Page(s): 510 - 518

[14] McCabe,T.,A Software Complexity Measure,IEEE Transactions on Software Engineering,Vol 2,Issue 4,pp 308-320,1976.

[15] Meyer B., Oriol M., & Schoeller B. (2009), "Software engineering: lecture 17-18: estimation techniques and

[16] software metrics", Chair of Software Engineering Website, available: http://se.inf.ethz.ch/teaching/2008-S/se 0204/slides/15-Estimation-and-metrics-1-6x.pdf , accessed: 18 January 2009.

[17] N. E. Fenton.(1994) "Software Measurement: A necessary scientific basis", IEEE Trans. Software Eng., vol. 20,no. 3, March 1994, pp. 199-206.

[18] Mariano Ceccato and Paolo Tonella,(2004) " Measuring the Effects of Software Aspectization", In Cd-rom Proceedings of the 1st Workshop on Aspect Reverse Engineering (WARE 2004). November, 2004. Delft, The Netherlands.

[19] C. Sant"Anna, A. Garcia, C. Chavez, A. von Staa, and C. Lucena. On the reuse and maintenance of aspect oriented software: An evaluation framework. In 17o. Simpsio Brasileiro de Engenharia de Software, pages 19–34,2003.

[20] Yourdon, E. and Constantine, L. L., Structured Design, Yourdon Press, 1978.

[21] Stevens, W. P., Myers, G. J. and Constantine, L. L., "Structured Design," IBM Systems Journal, Vol. 13, No. 2, May 1974.

[22] Karstu , S., An Examination of the Behavior of Slice Base Cohesion Measures, Master's Thesis, Michigan Technological University, Department of Computer Science, August 1994.

14

R language in data mining techniques and statistics

Sonja Pravilovic[1,2]

[1]Montenegro Business School, "Mediterranean" University, Montenegro
[2]Dipartimento di Informatica, Università degli Studi di Bari "Aldo Moro", Italy

Email address:
ksonja@t-com.me sonja.pravilovic@uniba.it (S. Pravilovic)

Abstract: Data mining is a set of techniques and methods relating to the extraction of knowledge from large amounts of data (through automatic or semi-automatic methods) and further scientific, industrial or operational use of that knowledge. Data mining is closely related to the statistics as an applied mathematical discipline with an analysis of data that could be defined as the extraction of useful information from data.The only difference between the two disciplines is that data mining is a new discipline that is related to significant or large data sets. R is an object-oriented programming language. This means that everything what is done with R can be saved as an object. Every object has a class. It describes what the object contains and what each function does. Application of R as a programming language and statistical software is much more than a supplement to Stata, SAS, and SPSS. Although it is more difficult to learn, the biggest advantage of R is its free-of-charge feature and the wealth of specialized application packages and libraries for a huge number of statistical, mathematical and other methods. R is a simple, but very powerful data mining and statistical data processing tool and once "discovered", it provides users with an entirely new, rich and powerful tool applicable in almost every field of research.

Keywords: R Language, Data Mining Techniques, Statistics

1. Introduction

Data mining is a set of techniques and methods relating to the extraction of knowledge from large amounts of data (through automatic or semi-automatic methods) and further scientific, industrial or operational use of that knowledge. Data mining is closely related to the statistics as an applied mathematical discipline with an analysis of data that could be defined as the extraction of useful information from data.

The only difference between the two disciplines is that data mining is a new discipline that is related to significant or large data sets.

In essence, data mining is a mathematical analysis carried out on large databases. The term data mining became especially popular in the 90's, and today it has a double meaning:

- using advanced analytical techniques to extract implicitly hidden information knowledge already structured in data in order to make it available and directly useful,
- research and analysis of large amounts of data, performed automatically or semi-automatically, with the aim of discovering significant patterns.

In both cases, the concepts of information and its meaning are closely related depending on the domain of data mining and the application of these data in a particular area. Today, data mining is a crucial activity in many areas of scientific research, but also in other areas (for example, in market research, economics, finance, medicine, agriculture, meteorology, etc.). In the professional world, it is used to solve various problems ranging from customer relationship management (CRM), fraud identification, consumer behavior, web pages optimization, etc.

The main factors that contributed to the development of data mining are:

- large amounts of data in the electronic form,
- cheap data storage,
- new methods and techniques of analysis (machine learning, pattern recognition).

Data mining techniques are based on specific algorithms. Patterns can be identified, the starting point for new hypotheses can be set, and then the causal relationship between the events can be tested, which can be further used in a statistical sense for the production and prediction of new data.

Among the most commonly used techniques are the following:

- grouping;
- neural networks,
- decision trees,
- associative analysis (identification of simultaneously purchased products), etc.

One of the most widespread techniques is learning through classification.

There are numerous packages for statistical data processing: SAS, SPSS, Stata, R. Certainly, it is a very good idea to have a number of tools available, but in the end they users themselves should decide which of them to apply. The technical reports of the strengths and weaknesses of these packages rarely take into account the accuracy in choosing the statistical software. In some models, such as nonlinear regression, it is the accuracy that will have a bigger problem of practical importance than others.

Data mining techniques allow easier analysis, and a high level of knowledge of analytical skills is highly attractive and sought after in many successful companies. R represents an ideal solution for many challenging tasks associated with data mining. It offers a breadth and depth of computational statistics, and is much more than what is offered by commercially closed source products. R is primarily a programming language for highly qualified statisticians.

2. R-in Data Mining

Data mining combines the concepts, tools and algorithms of machine learning and statistics to analyze very large data sets, so as to gain insight, understanding and effective knowledge and it is applied for this purpose in many companies.

R is a statistical software, and an object-oriented high-level programming language used for data analysis, which includes a large number of statistical procedures such as t-test, chi-square test, standard linear models, instrumental variables estimation, local regression polynomials, etc. Besides, R provides high-level graphics capabilities.

R is an object-oriented programming language. This means that everything what is done with R can be saved as an object. Every object has a class. It describes what the object contains and what each function does. For example, plot (x) does not give the same output if the regression result is x or vector.

The objective of the R style as a programming guide is easier reading, using and verification of the code.

3. Creation of R

The elegant and widely accepted S language, as a permanent software system with an outstanding comprehensive conceptual solution is the result of the effort and hard work of John Chambers. In 1998, the Association for Computing Machinery (ACM) presented it with its Software System Award as "the S system" and forever changed the way people would analyze, visualize and manipulate data. R is inspired by the S environment developed by John Chambers, and significant contributions of Douglas Bates, Rick Becker, Bill Cleveland, Trevor Hastie, Daryl Pregibon and Allan Wilks.[1].

R was initially written by Ross Ihaka and Robert Gentleman at the Department of Statistics, University of Auckland, New Zealand. After that, a large group of individuals contributed to R by sending codes and so-called bug reports. The current R is a result of a collaborative effort with contributions from around the world. In mid-1997 a core of the group known as the R Core Team was formed, whose members can change the archive of the R source code.

R is a dialect of the S language. The S language was developed at Bell Labs as a computing environment for data analysis and graphical display. The graphical display and interactivity, which can be found in R, are powerful tools for data research since they provide an understanding of data in the easiest way.

4. R Language

In the last ten years, the language R statistics has exploded in popularity and functionality and has become an election tool of scientists around the world. Today, R is used by more than 2,000,000 analysts. Since it has completely unveiled its elegance and power to the academic community so far, the members of the academic community have embraced the R language for solving their most challenging problems in the fields ranging from computational biology, quantitative finance to training people in these fields.

The result is the explosion of the R analytics and applications, which has led to enthusiasm and acceptance of R as a primary analytical method in companies such as Google, Facebook and LinkedIn. R is now available to everyone and is becoming a powerful and revolutionary support in any workplace, improving productivity.

Each technique of data analysis is now at hand instead of limiting the analysis and features with paid added modules. R encompasses virtually all data manipulations, statistical models, dates, and charts, that is, everything that a modern scientist needs. Even when the predictive model doesn't give excellent results, it is simple and easy to find help by assuming and using the most modern community of reviews of the methods in statistics and predictive modeling of leading scientists, absolutely free of charge.

To make a beautiful and unique visualization of the date by presenting the complex data and charts is just one of the essential elements of the process of data analysis. R surpasses the traditional bar charts and line plots, and facilitates the extraction of meaning from multidimensional data with a multi-panel scale, 3-D surfaces and much more.

Instead of using the point-and-click menu or inflexible black box procedures, R is a programming language designed specifically for data analysis. Experienced programmers of R have created a data analyzer which is faster, more efficient and flexible than the inherited user-friendly statistical software in creating the mix and match models for the best results. The R code is automated and easily repeatable in research and implementation. [4]

As a successful open-source project, R is supported by a community of more than 2 million users and thousands of programmers around the world. Whether the use enables optimizing portfolios, analyzing genomic sequences or predicting a certain component in the failure, experts in every field have made resources, applications and the code available online free of charge.

The basis of the R language consists of: data entry, data-frames, graphical display of 2D and 3D data, tables, mathematics and mathematical functions, the classical tests of data mining, statistical models, regression, analysis of variance, covariance, general linear models, count data, count data in the tables, the proportions of data, binary variable, general models, mix-effect models, tree models, time series analysis, multivariate models, spatial statistics, simulation models, and many others. [1]

R is a high-level language with the environment designed for the analysis and graphical representation of data. Here, the term "environment" is used to characterize it as a fully planned and coherent system, and not a system that is gradually supplemented with specific and inflexible programming tools, which is very often the case with other data analysis programs.

R can be easily and considerably expanded by the installation through packages or libraries. There are more than 3000 packages in the Cran data warehouse (repository). The R language design was influenced by the schemes of two existing languages: Becker, Chambers and Wilks's and Sussman's.

The existing R language is very similar in appearance to S, but sublevels of implementation and the semantics are derived from this scheme.

R certainly has a very rich environment that can be enjoyed by beginners, intermediate-level users and experts in disciplines ranging from scientific activities, economics, finance, sociology, political science, agriculture, medicine and engineering.

R includes the packages for preparation, processing, data display, graphics, mathematical functions, a wide range of statistical techniques, from the basic conventional tests, through regression and analysis of variance and general linear modeling, to more specialized topics such as spatial statistics, multivariate methods, tree models, mix-effective models and analysis of time series, as well as many others.

The idea is to offer R to users with very little knowledge of statistical theory, assuming that they do not know the basics of mathematics and / or statistics in order to assist them in their assumptions behind the tests, and encore a critical approach to statistical modeling.

The question that may be asked is why users should begin to deal with R instead of implementing a perfectly appropriate statistical package to solve their problems? If the intention is to implement a very limited range of statistical

tests, and not to do more (or otherwise) in the future, then it is absolutely fine not to switch to R.

However, the main reason for switching to R is to take advantage of the coverage and availability of new applications where R is the best in the areas such as effective generalized mixed models, as well as other general and additional models. Another reason for learning R may be the desire of users to understand the literature, as more people in various fields of sciences publish their research results in the context of R. Thirdly, if some research is made in the field of data mining, then it is very easy to notice that today the best known researchers in this discipline have become highly specialized in using R. In addition, a large number of the world's leading statisticians use R, so of course, this also contributes to the importance of knowing R.

Another very important reason for learning R is a quality of back-up and support. There is a premium network dedicated to research and Web wizards are eager to answer the questions of users. If the user intends to invest enough effort in becoming a good computer statistician, the structure of R and the easiness of writing one own's functions are the main attractions. The last, but certainly not the least important reason is that the R product, as one of the best integrated software in the world, is available for free.

Resembling methods (bootstrapping, random permutation tests, etc.) are very useful and easy to operate (function within the for loop). In addition, it enables a direct access to packages through the network or via the mailing list. Eg: through install.packages (name) you get a package called name (assuming that the computer running R is connected to the Internet), which makes R good, in collaboration with other programs, and widely available.

R runs on Windows, Macintosh, Linux and Unix platforms and the installation is free of charge and easy through http://cran.r-project.org/ . However, although the R language has a lot of benefits it is difficult to learn for users who have had no experience in programming. For users who have worked with data in other programming languages, switching to R makes everything incredibly easier and faster.

Working in R can sometimes be problematic, since it requires that all objects are stored in memory, indicating the limited size of data sets. Optimization routines in R such as optim or nlm require passage through a function whose argument is a vector of parameters (eg. log-likelihood). However, the function object may depend on a variety of other things in addition to its parameters (data). In writing the optimization code, the existence of bonding parameters is desirable in order to allow the access to the user.

R has functions to access databases. A typical solution with large data sets is the storage of data in the database and the entry of those that are necessary to R, as needed. Another weakness is the lack of coherent documentation that covers the entire R.

5. Organization of R

The "official" R consists of several packages that are created by the core R team. In addition, there are hundreds of packages that have been enriched by the users. Some of these packages represent the latest statistical research library. Most statistical research is first conducted in the R language.

R is not supported in the same way as the commercial software, but many users are finding better support through the R-help or through the network, rather than from commercial enterprises. Users will often use R because of its simple and clear graphical environment.

Many users use R as a statistics system, although it is much more than that. The R environment incorporates classical and modern statistical techniques and / or packages and libraries.

There is a significant difference in approach between S (toward R)and other statistical systems. For example, in S, a statistical analysis is usually conducted in a series of steps, storing the intermediate results of individual steps in objects. [3].

For example, SAS and SPSS give more extensive results from a regression or discriminant analysis. R, however, gives the minimal output and stores the results within certain objects, so they can be accessed by further functions for subsequent interrogation.

R is started within the graphical environment (Figures 1, 2, 3, 4) and through a windowing system, and the programming code can be written directly within the window or copied from another editor. The results and code, input or output data, can be saved and loaded in various forms, such as. *.txt, *.dat. *.r data files.

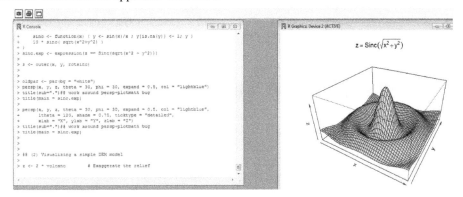

Figure 1. *Display of the 3D function in R.*

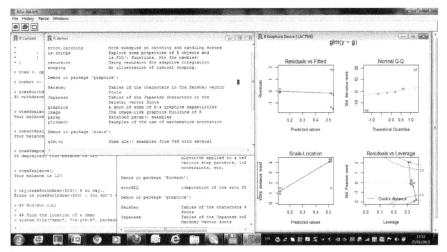

Figure 2. *Display of the window in R.*

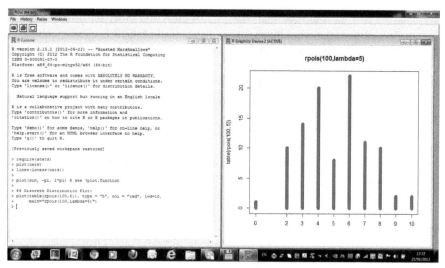

Figure 3. *Display of the window in R.*

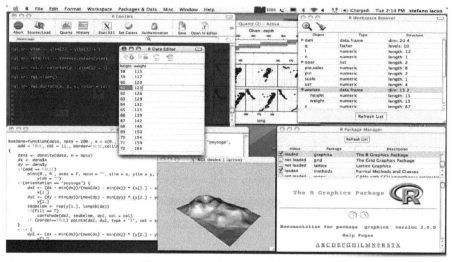

Figure 4. *View of the window in MacOS.*

Since R has a rich set of facilities and the programming language, it is, of course, difficult to master for the customers, but once learned, it is very easy to extend, amend, enhance, and apply in another field or find a simpler solution in R.

It is particularly difficult for users who are accustomed to working within the framework of statistical packages, since they have high expectations. There are hundreds of R packages, but only a few of them may be suitable for a given problem for a particular client.

Individual users have a much easier task. They need some basic knowledge of R, and then they need to learn some specific techniques that are related to the problems in their area. After solving the problem, the user can only retain an insight into how to solve the problem and try new packages within R that could help achieve even simpler solution. [2]

Functions in the research are "first class objects", which means that they can be treated like any other R object. It is important that the results of the function can be input arguments in new functions. Functions can be nested, which means that they can be contained within one another. The output value of the function is the last expression in the body of the function.

The object functions can be "created" so as to contain all the arguments necessary for evaluating the function. There is no need for the transfer of long arguments of the list, which are useful for interactive and research work within the program. The code can be relieved and cleaned using comparametrisation.

R has a vast amount of information available, is rich in the user databases and functionality. In addition, R is very suitable for the creation of reports on daily, weekly, yearly schedule, while the level of documentation is much higher than the average open source software, even than some commercial packages (eg, SPSS).

6. Conclusion

The aim of this study was to point to the application of modern programming languages and statistical packages without which modern science and research work in many areas of economics, finance, medicine, meteorology, engineering, and data mining cannot be imagined today.

Application of R as a programming language and statistical software is much more than a supplement to Stata, SAS, and SPSS. Although it is more difficult to learn, the biggest advantage of R is its free-of-charge feature and the wealth of specialized application packages and libraries for a huge number of statistical, mathematical and other methods. R is a simple, but very powerful data mining and statistical data processing tool and once "discovered", it provides users with an entirely new, rich and powerful tool applicable in almost every field of research.

References

[1] M. J. Crawley, The R book, Imperial College London at Silwood Park, UK, John Wiley and Sons, Ltd 2007.

[2] Dalgaard, P. Introductory Statistics with R, New York, Springer-Verlag, 2002.

[3] Krause, A. and Olson, M. The Basics of S and S-PLUS, New York, Springer-Verlag, 2000.

[4] McCulloch, C.E. and Searle, S.R. Generalized, Linear and Mixed Models, New York: John, 2001.

15

A systematic review of fault tolerance in mobile agents

Bassey Echeng Isong[1], Eyaye Bekele[2]

[1]Deptmemt of Computer Science, University of Venda, Thohoyandou, South Africa
[2]School of Computing, Blekinge Institute of Technology, Karlskrona, Sweden

Email address:
bassey.isong@univen.ac.za(B. Isong), eyayeb@gmail.com (E. Bekele)

Abstract: Mobile agents have engrossed substantial attention in recent years, especially in fault tolerance researches and several approaches have emerged. Fault tolerance design tends to put a stop to incomplete or complete loss of the agent in the face of failures. Despite these developments, reliability issues still remain a critical challenge. Moreover, there is no comprehensive detail bringing together, summaries of the existing efforts of researches in order to focus attention where it is needed most. Therefore, our objective in this systematic literature review (SR) is to explore and analyze the existing fault tolerance implementations in order to bring about the state-of-the-art and the challenges in mobile agent's fault tolerance approaches. We used studies from a number of relevant article sources, and our results showed the existence of twenty six articles. Our analysis indicates that the existing approaches are not generic and each focuses on a specific aspect of the problem, usually in one or two specific fault models which impacts on agent's reliability. The implication of the study is to give a clear direction to future researchers in this area for a better reliable and transparent fault tolerance in mobile agents.

Keywords: Mobile Agents, Fault Tolerance, Replication, Check-Pointing, Systematic Review, Platforms

1. Introduction

In the last few decades the field of mobile agents in distributed computing has witnessed substantial attention in both academia and industrial fields. This is known to be stimulated by the exponential growth of the Internet and system dependability. However, in spite of all, mobile agent's reliability is still a critical issue. Due to their nature, mobile agent's reliability and execution is not failure-free in the environments they operate. The growth of distributed heterogeneous environments such as the Internet naturally exposes them to abnormal conditions originating from migration request failure, communication exceptions or security violation [3],[4],[6]. Hence, providing reliability is of the essence to integrate agent-driven systems into today's industrial applications. Mobile agents have to be made reliable through fault tolerance to withstand adverse environmental situations in today's industrial applications. Fault tolerance is designed to provide reliable execution of mobile agents even in the presence of system failure.

Achieving mobile agent's fault tolerance requires the adherence to the non-blocking and exactly-once execution [7]. Presently in literature, several mobile agents' fault tolerance approaches exist in variety of mobile agent platforms. These approaches used different mechanisms to provide the reliability mobile agents' execution needs especially in the failure detection and recovery aspects. Moreover, majority of the recent approaches are based on optimizations, hybrid-based, while others are based on exception handling. In general, the existing fault tolerance schemes are categorized as either curative in nature (e.g. exception handling) or preventive [8], [9], [10]. The preventive schemes are further categorized into check-pointing and replication-based schemes but in some cases a hybrid of both schemes [8].

Despite several efforts and interest in this field, there is no comprehensive detail bringing together, summaries of these efforts. The main gap in this research area lies in the fact that the existing approaches are not generic and each focuses on a specific aspect of the problem, usually in one or two specific fault modes which is known to have huge impacts on agent's reliability. To improve the reliability of a system, faults originating from different forms need to be addressed in the fault tolerance measure. Unfortunately, there is no fault tolerance framework in the existing literature that serves as a guideline for realizing the state-of-the-art in mobile agent's fault tolerance. Therefore, bringing together fault tolerance approaches in mobile agent will assist researchers in closing the gaps identified in this study. The objective of this systematic literature review (SR) is to explore the existing fault tolerance approaches in mobile agents system to identify the current state of research, the techniques and approaches used, and the factors that influence the execution reported in recognized fault tolerance implementations research.

The rest of this article is organized as follows. An overview of mobile agents is given in Section 2. The research methodology of this SR is described in Section 3. The analysis of the results in accordance with the research questions is presented in Section 4. Section 5 provides the study discussions while the conclusions and recommendations are in Section 6.

2. Overview of Mobile Agents

Mobile agents are encapsulated pieces of executing program that have the ability to travel from one host to another and perform certain task autonomously [3]. It is a technology that aimed at shifting computation towards the data other than the other way round [1]. Mobile agents have characteristics that are distinct, thus making them flexible in deployment and desirable for use in distributed applications than other technological paradigms such as client-server, peer-to-peer, and others [2]. (see Figure 1.) These features include ability to naturally operate in heterogeneous environments [9], act autonomously [8], move independently from one host and can effectively make execution decision 14]. Mobile agents heavily rely on the underlying protocol for communications by way of interactions and message exchanges in order to successfully carry out and execute certain task in the   in the agent system [9].

Based on their characteristics, mobile agents provide several benefits such as bandwidth conservation [15], asynchronous and autonomous interactions [8], extended flexibility in disconnected data operations [16] and can improve network latency with better response time [16], robust and fault tolerant [17]. Mobile agents are generally independent of the computer-layer and transport-layer but dependent only on their execution environment [18], and have better scalability [16].

Today, the concept of mobile agents is receiving considerable attention in both research and industrial fields. Several platforms exist that provides operating environments for mobile agents such as Aglets, Agent Tcl, Knowbots, Telescript, Voyager, Mole, Tacoma, Grasshopper, James, Swarm and others [1], [2], [13]. Moreover, they have applications in several areas such as e-commerce and m-commerce, network monitoring and management, distributed information retrieval, telecommunications, remote device control and configuration, Internet computing, etc [2],[5],[8],[19],[20],[22].   To this end, despite the flexibility offered by mobile agents, agents are not isolated from several challenges such as malicious or errant hosts, erratic Internet behaviors or resource scarcity [6]. These therefore, calls for reliability and security mechanisms to be in place [9],[12]. The reliability issue is being addressed by

fault tolerance mechanisms, which is the focus of this study.

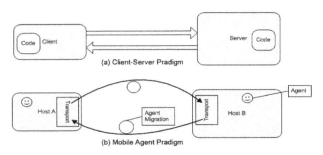

Figure 1. *Client-server vs. mobile agent paradigm*

3. Research Method

Systematic review is a methodology aimed at minimizing the inconsistencies associated with less scientifically rigorous review methodologies through strict qualitative research methods resulting to objective and unbiased results. In this study, we have applied SR to explore the state-of-the-art of fault tolerance in mobile agents by following the guidelines in [23]. The steps involves are discussed in subsequent sections.

3.1. Research Questions

This SR aimed to summarize the existing mobile agent's fault tolerance approaches in recent years. It would provide a list of reported and recognized techniques and approaches, influencing factors, platform supports and challenges in mobile agent's fault tolerance. Therefore, the research questions are:

SRQ1. What is the state-of-the-art in research of the recognized mobile agent's fault tolerance?

SRQ2. What available fault models are considered in designing fault tolerance protocols?

SRQ3. What are the available approaches and their design elements in the available recognized mobile agent's fault tolerance in current state of research?

SRQ4. What factors influences mobile agent's fault tolerance execution?

SRQ5. How much supports are offered by the mobile agent's platforms used in implementing the fault tolerance features?

SRQ6. What challenges exist and how do they affects the implementation of the fault tolerance in mobile agents?

3.2. Search Strategy

A search strategy is designed to ensure that all relevant studies other than irrelevant ones appear in the search result. In this SR, our literature search is limited over the scopes of: publication time period and publications that discusses fault tolerance in mobile agents. We considers the review of 10-years' efforts in mobile agents fault tolerance, that spanned from January 1998 to December 2008. We selected these periods in order to obtain relevant and sufficient information that are of the essence to this study and provide evidences of the trends in mobile agent fault tolerance then.

Therefore, any paper published after 31 December, 2008 is not included in our search result. We limited our searches to the electronic databases: Compendex/Inspec, IEEE Xplorer, Google Scholar, ACM digital library, Springer link and Scirus since they contain peer-reviewed works published in journals, digital libraries, conferences, proceedings and workshops which are of recognized quality within the software engineering research community. In this study, the quality of each selected research article was evaluated against a number of checklist questions. Each of questions is answered based on three options along assigned weights: Yes=1, Partial=0.5 and No=0. The maximum score a particular publication can get is 8.(see Table 1)

Table 1. List of selected publications by publisher and methodology

Ref.	Authors	Year	Publisher	Published in	Methodology	Quality Score
[25]	Summiya	2006	IEEE	Conference	Model and Simulation	4.5
[26]	Leung, Kwai Ki	2005	IEEE	Conference	Model and Simulation	6
[14]	Kyeongmo Park	2004	Springer	Conference	Model and Experiment	5
[5]	Guiyue Jin	2004	Springer	Conference	Model and Simulation	5
[27]	Lyu, M.R.	2003	IIIS	Conference	All	5.5
[28]	Sehl Mellouli	2007	Springer	Conference	Model and Experiment	4.5
[29]	Assis, Silva, F.M.;	1998	Springer	Workshop	Model	3
[30]	Osman, Taha	2004	IEEE	Journal	Model	3
[31]	Meng, Xuejun	2006	IEEE	Conference	Model and Experiment	5
[32]	Jong-Shin Chen	2008	IEEE	Conference	Model and Simulation	3
[33]	Marin, Olivier	2005	Springer	Workshop	Model and Experiment	8
[34]	Lyu, Michael R.	2004	IEEE	Journal	Model and Simulation	4.5
[35]	Youhei Tanaka	2006	IEEE	Conference	Model and Simulation	3
[36]	Silva, Luís Moura	2000	IEEE	Conference	Model and Experiment	6
[7]	Pleisch, Stefan	2003	IEEE	Journal	Model and Experiment	7
[38]	Rothermel, Kurt	1998	IEEE	Conference	Model	3.5
[39]	Alan Fedoruk	2002	ACM	Conference	Model and Experiment	6.5
[40]	Taesoon Park	2004	Springer	Conference	Model and Experiment	5.5
[41]	Taesoon Park	2004	Springer	Conference	Model and Experiment	6
[42]	Mohammadi, K.	2005	IEEE	Conference	All	5
[44]	Yang, Jin	2005	Springer	Conference	Model and Simulation	5
[46]	Park, Taesoon	2004	Springer	Conference	Model and Experiment	5
[47]	Tomoaki Kaneda	2005	ACM	Conference	Model and Experiment	5
[48]	Park, Taesoon	2006	Springer	Conference	Model and Simulation	3
[43]	Johansen, D.	1999	IEEE	Conference	Model and Experiment	5.5
[45]	Milovan Tosic	2005	Springer	Conference	Model and Experiment	4.5

The study selection process was individually carried out by the authors involved and any differences were settled by consensus. The search strategies we adopted were iterative in nature and the inclusion/exclusion decisions were checked at least twice and discussed at each stage of execution. We adopted a multi-stage process in selecting the studies in accordance with the guidelines in [23], using different selection criteria. All search terms we created were applied on the selected databases and a total of 6,901 results were found. In the first stage, 6788 articles were excluded based on the relevance of their title or abstract. Furthermore, the titles and abstract of the left over 113 were read and the basic inclusion and exclusion criteria applied, leaving a total of 86 studies. In the second stage, 55 out of the 86 articles were selected based on the application of the detailed inclusion and exclusion criteria - abstract, the conclusion and in some cases the introduction was reviewed to apply the exclusion criteria. The exclusion criteria were based on inaccessibility, formal or mathematical description, and exception handling. Lastly, in the third stage, we based the selection process on the detailed research questions while the exclusion criteria was based on issues of duplication, application of mobile agents in a different study area, and mobile agent's platforms articles. As a result, 26 unique studies were selected as primary studies for this SR and 29 studies were discarded.

3.3. Data Extraction and Synthesis

The data extraction strategy was developed in accordance with the research questions, quality assessment checklist, general information associated with the study identification and certain common characteristics in the studies. During the extraction, the authors also checked and re-checked the extracted data to get rid of uncertainties. To assist us find and validate the extracted information and resolve inconsistencies quickly, we tinted all important lines and paragraphs in the selected studies. Accordingly, difficulties encountered were resolved via discussion among the authors. For multiple articles of the same information, articles with the most complete and latest information were used to avoid unbiased findings. To extract relevant information, we created and used data extraction form with the following fields: Title, Authors names, Journal/Conference/Workshop, Year, Research Methodology, Moble agent fault tolerance Scheme, Protocol, Fault model, Assumptions Detection, Recovery, Fault Tolerance execution, Agent types, Communication, Factors affecting the performance of the proposed model and experiment variables, Platform type, Platform support and Challenges.

With the extracted data from the extraction forms coupled with the nature of this study, we performed descriptive synthesis of the data since it is the only suitable method in such heterogeneous data format.

4. Analysis

In this section, we present analysis of the results of this SR by answering the research questions as follows:

4.1. Mobile Agents Fault Tolerance Research

RQ1: What is the state-of-the-art in research of recognized mobile agent's fault tolerance?

To answer this research question, analysis will be based on publication years, the qualities of the articles and the methodology used. Table 1 presents list of selected publications by publisher and Methodology as well as the quality score for each study.

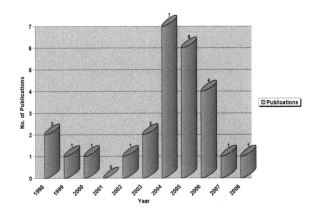

Figure 2. Studies by year of publication.

4.1.1. Year of Publications

We found 26 studies related to mobile agent fault tolerance where 21 studies were published in conference proceedings, 2 studies in Journals and 3 studies in workshops. Analysis shows that the field of mobile agent fault tolerance was active in research in those periods. Further analysis indicates that years between 2004 and 2006 have showed a remarkable increase in number of publications, though the trend seems to be going down in the last three years (2006 - 2008). Figure 2 and Table 1 show studies by year of publication.

4.1.2. Publication Quality Scores

Analysis shows that more than 75% of the selected publications scored 4.5 or more. Articles with more than 4 as score in the quality assessment generally are selected on the basis of having the most vital information such as detailed description of a model and some form of proof such as results from a real experiment or simulation to support their findings. (see Figure 3)

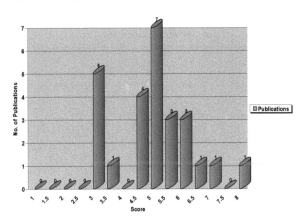

Figure 3. Publications by quality assessment scores

4.1.2. Methodology

In this study, we noticed that the number of studies on fault tolerance in mobile agents that were supported by simulation or experiment has improved over the years. Analysis indicates that about 46% studies are with experiments, 31% is simulation only, while a combination of experiments and simulations has 8%. Only 12% of the studies discussed fault tolerant models with no experiments or simulations. (see Figure 4).

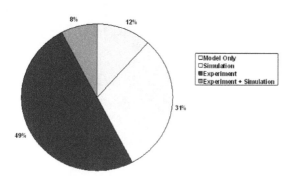

Figure 4. *Primary studies research methodology*

4.2. Fault Models

SRQ2. What available fault models are considered in designing fault tolerance protocols?

In the 26 studies, we found that the ability to observe the agents and detect failure during execution is one of the cardinal features of any fault tolerance in mobile agent approach. This is because mobile agents or its environments are not failure-free. We noticed '*fault model*' is used to define which set of observations are categorized as failure and which are acceptable operation modes. Analysis shows that all the existing approaches have fault models and there are three classes of agent's failures: *communication, crash* and *agent software* failure. Moreover, we found that most of the studies are designed to either cater for one of the stated failures or multiple of them. Table 2 presents the existing implementations of each study and the failure types designed for them.

Table 2. *Failure Types*

Failure Types		
Communication	**Crash**	**Agent/Agent Software**
[25],[30],[31],[32], [42],[36],[38],[39], [43], [44], [45]	[5],[7],[25],[26],[27], [29],[30],[31],[32], [34],[42],[35],[36], [38],[40],[41],[14], [44],[46],[47],[43], [45]	[25], [26], [5], [27], [28], 29],[30],[31],[32], [33], [42], [7], [36], [38], [39], [40], [41], [44], [46], [47], [45],[48]

Based on Table 2, the distribution of fault models in the studies presented in Figure 5 denotes that fault models for communication failures were least addressed (43%). This could depend on the assumption that the network is reliable or agents can eventually resume service even if the network fails. Crash and agent software fault models seem to be supported in most of the existing implementations (84%). Only about 35% of the studies supported all three fault models [44], [27], [38], [30], [31], [32], [42], [36], [45],

while 12% of these studies considered the issue of network partitioning and suggested a solution to it [44], [38],[30].

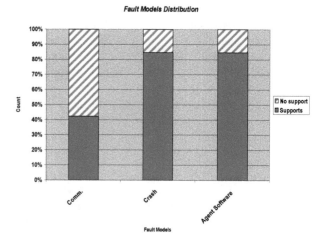

Figure 5. *Fault Model distribution*

4.3. Mobile Agents Fault Tolerance Approaches and Design

SRQ3. What are the available approaches and their design elements in the available recognized mobile agent's fault tolerance in current state of research?

This research questions will be answered based on the different approaches of mobile agent's fault tolerance, the available protocols and the design of the available implementations.

4.3.1. Fault Tolerance Schemes

One of the key features of fault tolerance approach is the ability to recover from failure. In this study, we found that the existing fault tolerance schemes that deal with sources of system failures and recovery were categorized as either the replication-based, checkpoint-based or a hybrid schemes [16], [9], [49]. In this study, we only considered the two most widely used schemes: check-pointing and replication for analysis. The different studies that used these approaches in the perspective of transactional and non-transactional approach are shown in Table 3.

Table 3. *Fault tolerance schemes and execution modes*

Agent's Execution Modes		
Scheme	Transactional	Non-transactional
Checkpoint	[5], [38], [36], [27], [30], [26], [42]	[34], [45], [48], [46], [32]
Replication	[29], [39], [7], [47], [35]	[43], [40], [41], [33], [44], [25], [28]
Hybrid	[14], [31]	-------

Further analysis shows that both check-pointing and replication-based schemes are used almost equally over the years of consideration (see Figure 6).

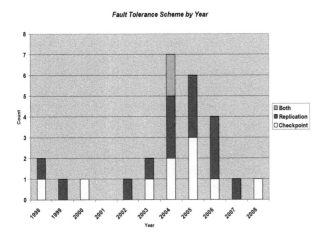

Figure 6. Fault tolerance scheme distribution

4.3.2. Replication Scheme Types

For replication-based schemes: active and passive, analysis in this study shows that the trend of distancing away from active replication-based schemes is quite evident. (See Figure 7) In addition, about 72% of the replication-based approaches used either the passive or semi-active replication, but the semi-active to passive ratio within the passive replication-based category is 3:7. This indicates that semi-active techniques are not used often either. It could be as a consequence of high computation and communication cost they incur. The computation overhead in active replication is higher even among the implementations that support both replication types.

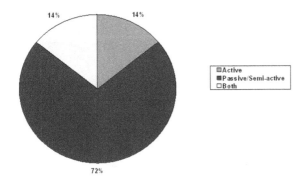

Figure 7. Replication scheme types distribution

4.3.3. Execution Modes

We found that execution mode in existing agents fault tolerance are either transactional or non-transactional. From all indication, we noticed that the distribution of the transactional and non-transactional executions is someway balanced (see Figure 8), though the transaction-based executions are slightly higher with about 54% than non-transaction-based modes with 46%. The analysis indicates there is no noticeable shift in trend over the years. However, transactional executions are more reliable in maintaining the exactly-once property of agent execution, while its counterpart maintain lower computation overhead. But we recommend transactional execution for application domains that require higher level of consistency.

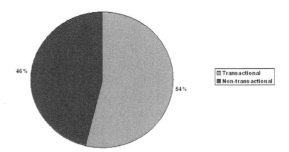

Figure 8. Agent's execution modes

4.3.4. Communication Modes

In this study, we found that there are only two communication modes in fault tolerant mobile agent dominated by the asynchronous mode. Analysis shows that about 92% of the studies implemented asynchronous mode execution while only 8% of the studies are both synchronously and asynchronously. (see Figure 9) There was no implementation that solely works on synchronous mode. We believe this could be as a result of the characteristics of the agent's environment where they are autonomous and migrate usually in open networks with latency. In addition, there is high performance overhead with synchronous when compared to asynchronous.

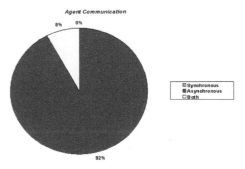

Figure 9. Agent's communication mode distribution

4.3.5. Fault tolerance Protocols

In this SR, we found that protocols in mobile agents fault tolerance implementation model are mostly achieved through effective message passing to coordinate and ensure reliable agent failure detection and recovery. In addition, categorizing these protocols into classes is not easy since some of them exist in association with other protocols. However, they can only be organized with respect to the two execution properties of mobile agents: the exactly-once or non-blocking. Figure 10 shows the class of existing protocols in mobile agents fault tolerance implementation model.

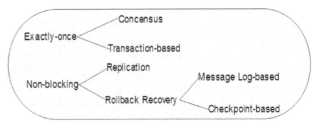

Figure 10. Agent's proptocols

4.3.5.1. Exactly-onec Protocols

This protocol guarantees that an agent must execute the desired action not more and not less than once in a host. This protocol includes the consensus and the transaction-based approaches.

A. Consensus Protocol: This protocol provides a means of achieving agreement between the primary agent process and the replicas in the case of failure. This is usually achieved by voting on a certain result by all the participating agents where a consensus is reached when all the participants agree on one outcome. In this case, a replica can become the new primary through its own consensus for either being the first to detect or having the highest priority when the primary fails.

B. Transaction-Based Protocol: Similar to consensus, but uses the transaction commits/abort to reduce the effect of failures on the availability of operational sites during distributed transaction. Commit and abort are both irreversible and unlike consensus, transaction can only be committed if all participating sites vote or agree to commit, otherwise, the transaction is aborted. In this study, analysis shows that most of the studies used the basic transaction-commit protocol such as centralized transaction commit by [26] while [7],[27],[30],[35],[36],[47] used the transaction commit protocol. A hybrid approach of both consensus and transaction-based protocol were implemented by [29],[47],[7],[38].

4.3.5.2. Non-Blocking Protocols

These protocols are used basically for overcoming blocking problems pose by the exactly-once protocols. It is achieved by either restarting a failed process or use duplicate agents that are able to take over in time of primary agent failure without voting. Protocols under this category include the rollback recovery protocols and the replication-based protocols.

A. Rollback Recovery Protocol: This approach tries to reduce the amount of loss in computation by avoiding the restarting of computation from the beginning. It provides a technique that requires a process to periodically record its consistent state, known as check-pointing, into a stable storage. Most of the existing rollback recovery approaches are based on message passing: checkpoint-based and message logging-based.

1. Checkpoint-based: This approach depends strictly on regularly saving agent's process states and code to a stable storage for future restoration or recovery in the event of failure. Protocols in this category include coordinated, uncoordinated, communication-induced, lazy and the timer-based protocol. In this study we found that most of the rollback-based protocols used this protocol to provide fault tolerance behavior such as communication-induced check-pointing [42] independent check-pointing with receiver-based logging [46], checkpoint-based scheme to restore agents processes back to its consistent state during failure, and checkpoint-based with reliable publisher/subscriber messaging layer[45].

2. Message Log-base: This is the logging of non-deterministic actions preset as determinants in combination with check-pointing to achieve fault tolerance recovery behavior. Protocols under this category include the pessimistic and optimistic logging protocol [7]. Pessimistic execution ensures that changes are applied only if no agent crashes and there is no erroneous result, while in optimistic execution the place modifications can be immediate and transparent but undoing modifications is a complex task [7].

B. Replication-based Protocols: In this approach, there is a live backup agent, either as a duplicate of the primary or as a standby, even before failure is detected. One drawback is that it requires synchronization of replicas with the primary, which is very expensive both in computation and communication. However, several optimizations have been suggested in the studies we considered such as formed a group of replicas and a proxy that communicates with the primary on behalf of the multiple replicas by [39], dynamic adaptive replication scheme by [33] and the sliding window protocol by [25], a technique that controls the number of backup or replicated agents in order to minimize bandwidth consumption.

3.3.6. Implementation Models

In the studies we found in this SR, we noticed that there were several approaches used in designing mobile agent fault tolerance models. These approaches are either integrated into the underlying agent's codes or platforms. Further analysis shows that most of the approaches are a hybrid of a variety of the protocols but some also include preventive techniques. Figure 11 presents the design approaches of existing implementations.

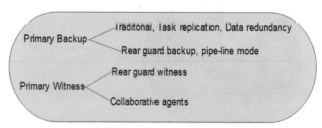

Figure 11. *Fault tolerance design approach*

4.3.6.1. Primary Back-up Model

The primary back-up model (PBM) design requires the replication of the agents or server into primary component (worker component) and one or more observer components (backups/replicas component). The primary component takes charge of execution while the backup components monitor the primary's computation for any possible failure.

A. Traditional Primary-Backup/Task replication/Data redundancy: In this design, the traditional primary-backup model relies on the replication of system components, task, data, etc. in order to achieve fault tolerance in mobile agents.

B. Rear Guard Agents as Backup: It is chiefly based on the primary-backup principle but instead the backup agent resides on the previously visited host. The backup monitors the primary agent and perform recovery actions to resume the computation when it detects failure of the primary agent especially in a stage-based partition network. We found several forms of these approaches such as multiple rear-guard in [5] and parallel processing of replicas by [44]. Others are optimizations to the approaches by [43] based on rear-guard protocol and reliable broadcast protocol with election protocol, while [7] discusses the pipe-line mode.

4.3.6.2. Primary Witness Model

The primary witness model (PWM) approach is very similar to the PBM, but here the backup agent is a different type of agent usually for monitoring and creating a backup agent when the primary agent fails. The backup agent that replaces the failed primary agent is only created after the detection of a failure. These approaches include rear guard agents as witness and the collaborative agents.

A. Rear Guard Agents as Witness: The witness agent involves a different type of agent that cannot on its own take over as a primary agent during recovery. The primary agent takes charge of the natural execution while the witness only monitors and recovers. In this case, it creates a new primary and restores normal execution. We found this approach in studies such as Monitor Agent (MA) which detects failure of Execution Agent (EA), it creates Repair Agent (RA) for fixing the error in the EA host [31], and the actual and witness agents that creates a probe agent for recovering log during recovery[27], [34].

B. Collaborative Agents: Here, three or more types of agents with designated responsibilities in the detection and recovery processes work together for achieving fault tolerance action with a clear division of labor. The approach involves the primary agent in charge of the execution, while others participate for specifically task such as monitoring, tracking, checking path, recovering, creating another type of agent, etc. Other agents cannot assume the primary agent position during recovery. In this study, studies that used this approach are [25] using three agent types: observer agents, ping agents and transaction agent used for monitoring, path checking and executing transactions respectively. Also, [26] uses three types of agents which are worker, monitor and tracker.

4.4. Mobile Agents Fault Tolerance Performance Factors

SRQ4. What factors influences mobile agent's fault tolerance execution?

We noticed in this study that mobile agent's fault tolerance execution is affected by several factors leading to a decrease in their performance as reported in most studies' experimental data. However, we only focused on the factors rather than the actual figures from the experiments due to unique scenarios and measurements that cannot be quantitatively compared across the studies. From these studies, the influencing factors are as follows:

4.4.1. Agent Size

Agents are affected by the size of their code and the payload data it takes with itself during mobility. In this study, more than 50% of the experimental studies reported agent size as a performance factor and that the execution time of the agents linearly increases with the increase in size of the agent [14], [40], [41], [42], [36], [46], [7]. In addition, increase in size also lead to replication process having overheads [7],[40].

4.4.2. Numbers of Replica

Also more than 50% of the replication based schemes reported that the number of replica affects their performance especially in the synchronous replication schemes [40]. For instance, a design with consensus requires an increase in agent's replicas leading to agents spending longer time than expected. In this SR, the studies that reported number of replica/witness factor in their findings are [40], [41], [36], [46], [39], [28], [34].

4.4.3. Message Size

In this SR, over 30% of the experimental studies consider message size as a factor influencing agent's performance which in turn contributes significantly to network traffic. Increase in the time spent to send a message, increases the size of the messages. We found that, the cost is relatively higher in synchronous communication models than in asynchronous model. Studies that reported message size factor in their findings are [14], [38], [45], [34].

4.4.4. Number of Messages

The number of uncontrolled messages can overwhelm fault detection capability and reducing number of messages can produce performance gain [7]. Some studies that reported the number of messages factor in their findings are [44], [39],[31],[34].

4.4.5. Number of Hops/Host

With agent's characteristics, their survivability decreases with increase in the number of servers the agent's have to visit [34]. This is believed to have impact on reaching a timeout when the execution time takes a long time especially for schemes that relies on timeout and can initiate an unnecessary recovery process that would affect the performance of the system negatively. In this SR, studies that reported this problem in their findings are [7], [26], [27], [44].

4.4.6. Frequency of Check-pointing

Lastly, another important influencing factor is the degree at which check-pointing are taken. An increase in check-pointing frequency increases overhead while infrequent check-pointing brings about much re-computation in the event of recovery [6],[5].

4.5. Platforms Supports

SRQ5. How much supports are offered by the mobile agent's platforms used in implementing the fault tolerance features?

A platform in this context is an executing environment for mobile agents. In this SR, we found varieties of agent's platforms which are mostly built from Java. In addition, most of the existing platforms provide partial or incomplete facilities for fault tolerance mechanisms. We noticed that several academic and commercial systems are available which differs in their features, architecture and implementations, but more or less offer common facilities for the support of agent migration, inter-agent communication, various forms of security and programming or interpreted languages etc.

Analysis here is based on a qualitative comparison of the current agent platforms. Table 4 presents the various platforms used and the nature of fault tolerance support they have in their implementation.

Table 4. Qualitative comparison of Platforms support for fault tolerance

Platform	Prog. Lang.	Mobility	Communication	Fault Tolerance Feature
Aglet [58]	Java	Weak	Asynchronous, Synchronous, Proxy	NA
Concordia [59]	Java	Weak	Asynchronous	Yes (Checkpoint, Transactional message queue, Proxy)
FIPA-OS [60]	Java	Weak	Asynchronous	Yes (Replication(clone) Transactional message queue, Proxy)
Grasshopper [61] **	Java	Weak	Synchronous, Asynchronous, Multicast, Dynamic method invocation	NA
JADE [62]	Java	Weak	Asynchronous	NA
JAMES [21]	Java	Weak	JavaSpace	Yes (Checkpoint)
MadKit [63], [64]	Java	Weak	asynchronous message passing	Yes (congestion management, agent monitoring mechanisms)
MOLE [65]	Java	Weak	Asynchronous, Synchronous, Sessions	Yes (Transactional message queue)
Naptel [66]	Java	Weak	asynchronous message passing	Yes (agent monitoring mechanisms, cloning)
Tacoma [68]	C/C++, ML, Perl, python	Weak	Asynchronous, Synchronous	Yes (Rear guards)
Voyager [69]	Java, C#, C++	Weak	Asynchronous, Synchronous, Multicast, Proxy	NA

Note: NA (Not Applicable) implies that either the information or the feature is unavailable. ** Authors have stopped updating the platform

4.6. Challenges

SRQ6. What challenges exist and how do they affects the implementation of the fault tolerance in mobile agents?

There are lots of challenges that faced in existing fault tolerance implementations that has limited their efficiency or the direct application of fault tolerance strategies. Some of the challenges found in this SR are discussed as follows:

4.6.1. Reliable Fault Detection

The key challenge in fault detection is when a fault tolerance process wrongly detects fault and acts upon it. In such cases, an agent is wrongly assumed failed and a replacement agent is created in place of the failed agent leading to the violation of the *"exactly once"* property of agent execution [25]. In this study, we see that existing fault tolerance schemes, rely on techniques such as timeout, periodical exchange of heartbeat message, call backs, etc. for reliable detection of faults but none is absolute in detecting the occurrence of failures. Only 20% of the studies specifically mention this problem and considered it as a very critical attribute.

4.6.2. Network Partition

This is due to communication failure where agent's implementations execute in stages and internal network partitioned into stages or domains. In the event of communication failure, the various stages will be unable to communicate either to advance to the next stage or complete the assigned task, which results in blocking. In this study, only about 12% of the studies specified network partition as a challenge while most studies regard it as a temporary problem.

4.6.3. Lack of Full Process State Capture/Restore

This study found that majority of the existing agent platforms are Java-based systems using the Java Virtual Machine (JVM). With these platforms, analysis indicates that about 90% of them do not allow the capturing and restoring of the full execution state of a process which in turn affects strong mobility support.

4.6.4. Lack of Interoperability

This study noticed fault tolerant agents developed for one agent platform cannot be ported easily to a different agent platform, which impacts the adoption and full realization of fault tolerance. We found few standards such as Foundation for Intelligent Physical Agents (FIPA) and Mobile Agent System Interoperability Facility (MASIF) and steps have been taken to realize this issue in the future.

4.6.5. Lack of Full Transactional Support

This study found that there is no full transactional support in existing fault tolerant framework especially for various types of failure situations. This could be due to the active nature of mobile agent systems which is somewhat incompatible with the concept of transactions that forces several agents to remain in the same transaction as long as it does not commit or abort [6], [29],[69].

4.6.6. Scalability

This study found that all the studies are from the academia and the implemented mobile agent's fault tolerance were not large scale. Analysis shows that most experiments and simulations performed are on a small scale setup, though some promise scalability [26], [33], [41], [44]. In all the studies, we did not find large scale experiments.

4.6.7. Lack of Transparency

In majority of the studies we noticed that developers viewed the fault tolerance platforms as not being transparent since it requires the modification of the underlying platform to accommodate the protocols.

5. Discussion

Despite the importance of mobile agents in distributed environments coupled with the increase in research activities in both academia and industry, we found several issues that still affect the complete realization of reliable fault tolerance in mobile agents. In this study, we noticed that the distribution of the publications by year shows sharp increase between 2003 and 2004 and more than 65% of the studies were conducted between 2004 and 2006. This could be due to the increased interest in the area of mobile agents from the research community. However, the trend seems to be going down resulting in only 23% of the studies being conducted in the last three years, which we think is related to the problem of trust in mobile agents as a result of increasing threat from viruses and network worms. Accordingly, the number of studies that were supported by simulation or experiment improved over the years. They provide detailed description of a model used and reporting some results from a real experiment or simulation to support their findings. Also the existing implementations have classified agent's failures into communication, crash and agent software failure. Each study provides mechanism to detect these failures based on their fault model strategy, but no known fault model can detect and recover from all types of failures in the existing implementations.

It is evident that different approaches exist that deals with the recovering from failure of mobile agents. These approaches include the check-pointing, replication schemes or the hybrid approach and both were used almost equally over the years of consideration. Among the replication-based schemes, most of the studies tend to favor inactive replication due to it lower computation overhead. In the same vein, the mode of agent's communication in existing implementations is mostly asynchronous, as well as there appears to be a balance between transactional or non-transactional execution of mobile agents. The reasons could be from the fact that transactional executions are more reliable in maintaining the exactly-once property, while the non-transactional maintain lower computation overhead. In all the studies we considered, there were other elements such as fault tolerance protocols and their design models. Protocols were based on the exactly-once or non-blocking properties, while the implementation design models were based on hybrid approaches dominated by preventive techniques of agent's replications: primary backup and witness approaches. Each approach has its own strategy to implement fault tolerance.

Other issues we observed were challenges emanating from platform supports and the general challenges in terms of performance affecting mobile agent's fault tolerance that has not been addressed. Variety of mobile agent platforms exist and are dominated by Java which does not support strong mobility of agents which affects full capturing of the state of collaborating processes. Also, the numbers of replicas, messages, size, etc. were among the factors reported as having impacts on the performance of mobile agent's execution.

The consequence of this study is that investigating intensely in the state-of-the-art fault tolerance approaches and the challenges in mobile agent will serve as a starting point and give a clear direction to future researchers who will work in this area to improve the existing implementations.

5.1. Strengths and Weaknesses

In this SR, we have covered several numbers of articles, whose authors are listed in Table 1.We are pretty sure that this study truly covers fault tolerance in mobile agents that have been published to date we considered. We have strictly followed Kitchenham et al. [23] guidelines starting from the planning to the reporting of the review results. However, possible threats or weaknesses in this SR could be related to bias in publication, selection of the included studies and the inaccuracy in data extraction.

For publications, we used sources that are credible and trusted by the research community and also conducted trial searches. We also believe publications from 2009 till date that were not considered will not affect the validity of our study since another study will be performed to compare the trends. In addition, though is possible that some relevant papers may have been missed and if they do, we are sure they are not many and their absence has no significant effect to the information reported in this study. Another issue is the search terms we used. If the search terms/strings formulated were not sufficient and effectively utilized, we believe it has no counter effect on this study. However the two authors worked in collaboration with a librarian and all the selected studies analyzed. In addition, all decisions and results were checked and re-checked.

6. Conclusions

With the increase in system dependability and the exponential growth of the Internet, there is an increasing need to develop reliable mobile agent's fault tolerance techniques capable of withstanding unfavorable and unpredictable behavior of today's systems. Several well known approaches and models for failure detection and recovery schemes have been designed, but none is generic. When deciding on how to develop a reliable fault tolerance in mobile agents, it is important to have the knowledge of the existing techniques, and to be able to make a good decision, taking into account the strong and weak points of diverse approaches against each other. To this effect, this SR identifies the existing fault tolerance mobile agent's approaches and studied them from the perspectives of: establishing facts in the directions of fault tolerance in mobile agents, recognized techniques/approaches, influencing factors, platform supports and challenges. These were chosen because they together helped in giving a good understanding of the existing findings, identify gaps in existing research and provide recommendations for new research activities.

We have analyzed the existing studies implementations in order to realize the state-of-the-art in mobile agent fault tolerance and trends. In this study, we present the found fault tolerance in mobile agents existing implementations in Table 1. In addition, we have developed taxonomy of the existing protocols and the design model used (Figure 10 and 11). Based on the analysis and results obtained, the study takes a closer look at the available mobile agent's fault tolerance strategies and the challenges that affects its realization. The cardinal findings are:

- Agent's fault tolerance fault models generally fall into the three failure types, namely communication, crash and agent software failure though, stated differently in different studies. For instance, place failure, node crash, hardware failure, server failure, host failure; etc were all described as crash failure in the studies.
- Fault tolerance strategies can not address all single-point-of-failures in a system with respect to faults resulting from communication, agent software and crash failures. The complexity and cost of addressing all single-point-of-failures makes the fault tolerance process virtually incomplete. Thus, single-point-of-failures are inevitable in mobile agent and no approach is considered the best in all failure situations.
- Fault tolerance in mobile agent systems can be achieved in a number of ways: replication schemes, check-pointing schemes or a combination of both replication and check-pointing schemes called hybrid

approach. However, there is no fault tolerance scheme that is best for all situations since the suitability of an approach heavily depends on the application domain.

- Performance overhead of a fault tolerance strategy is inversely related to recovery time. That is the shorter the recovery time the higher performance overhead. Fault tolerance strategy should try to make a balance between recovery time and performance overhead.
- Mobile agent's fault tolerance faces enormous challenges such as lack of adequate support from agent's platforms as well as lack of resource control capabilities which impacts greatly the realization of a reliable agent execution and need to be drastically addressed.
- Fault tolerant mobile agent is gathering momentum without a clear general framework in its agent system. The existing fault tolerance designs are designed to handle a particular set of fault models and not faults in all situations.

Future work includes proposing a general framework for fault tolerance in mobile agents. This will contribute positively to a high level of system dependability and in addressing the challenges and influencing factors affecting the existing fault tolerance models. In addition, we will validate and implement the framework, perform a more in-depth analysis to investigate challenges outside the framework and investigate fault tolerance in other areas.

Based on the above finding, our recommendations are as follows:

- A generic fault tolerance in mobile agents should be designed and developed since it is difficult to measure the completeness of a fault tolerance approach. The fact is that the existing implementations found in this study focus on partial list of failure types, indicating agents cannot tolerate failure of all types. Thus, issues of all single-point-of-failures should be addressed if high reliability or availability is to be achieved.
- Larger scale tests in real world applications other than simulations should be applied to the available fault tolerance schemes so as to better demonstrate their reliability, capabilities and effectiveness. This is because the maturity of fault tolerance approaches depends highly on the level of acceptance of the approaches. The more the approaches are used, the more the approaches evolve and develop and proved that they work.
- The effects of very long itinerary, many collaborative agents, many replicas, many uncommitted transactions, etc during scalability would need to be investigated so as to increase support for the dependability of fault tolerance techniques.
- Existing platforms should be improved by standardizing and including some of the vital fault tolerance protocols such as cloning and resource monitoring in order to reduce interoperability. Moreover, it will be more flexible to detect runaway agents from within the platform than building a

separate architecture on top of the platforms.

- A better flexibility is if the platforms have a mechanism to selectively apply a fault tolerance protocol to a specific agent or agent place as needed since not all fault tolerance protocols are needed at all times. Developers of agent systems should be able to pick their suitable protocol within their application domain.

- Researchers should focus more on carefully analyzing the unique characteristics of existing agent systems and the applications that are built on them in order to avoid the selection of unsuitable methodology for the recovery of the applications running the agent from faults that affects agents' execution, migration, and interaction.

- Additional fault tolerance features should be introduced for a better reliability.

- Also, alternative agent's design approaches should consider minimizing resource consumption such as using existing code in previously visited hosts instead of re-transporting code improve the reusability of code.

- Lastly, developers should have in mind that the application of fault tolerance approach in the real world applications could also introduce a different set of challenges that have never been thought of.

References

[1] W. Qu and H. Shen, Analysis of Mobile Agents' Fault-Tolerant Behavior, *IEEE/WIC/ACM, Proceedings of International Conference on Intelligent Agent Technology*, 2004, pp 377 – 380, ISBN: 0-7695-2101-0

[2] L. L. Pullum, Software Fault Tolerance Techniques and Implementation, *Artech House*, 2001, ISBN 1-58053-137-7

[3] N. M. Karnik and A. R. Tripathi, Design Issues in Mobile Agent Programming Systems, *IEEE Concurrency*, Vol. 6 , No. 3, 1998, pp 52-61, ISSN:1092-3063

[4] W. Dake and C.P. Leguizamo and K. Mori, Mobile Agent Fault Tolerance in Autonomous Decentralized Database Systems, *IEEE, Proceedings of the Autonomous Decentralized System on The 2nd International Workshop*, 2002, ISBN:0-7803-7624-2

[5] G. Jin, B. Ahn and K. D. Lee, A Fault-Tolerant Protocol for Mobile Agent, *Springer, Proceedings of International Conference on Computational Science and Its Applications*, 2004, pp. 993–1001, ISBN 978-3-540-22057-2

[6] G. Serugendo and A. Romanovsky, Designing Fault-Tolerant Mobile System, *Springer, International Workshop on Scientific Engineering for Distributed Java Applications*, 2003, pp 185-201, ISBN: 978-3-540-00679-4

[7] S. Pleisch, and A. Schiper, Fault-tolerant Mobile Agent Execution, *IEEE, IEEE Transactions on Computers*, Vol. 52 , Nr. 2, 2003, ISSN: 0018-9340

[8] T. Park, I. Byun, H. Kim and H. Y. Yeom, The Performance of Checkpointing and Replication Schemes for Fault Tolerant Mobile Agent Systems, *IEEE Computer Society, Proceedings of 21th IEEE Symposium on Reliable Distributed Systems*, 2002, ISBN:0-7695-1659-9

[9] W. Qu, H. Shen and X. Defago, A Survey of Mobile Agent-Based Fault-Tolerant Technology, *IEEE, Proceedings of the Sixth International Conference on Parallel and Distributed Computing Applications and Technologies*, 2005, pp 446-450, ISBN:0-7695-2405-2

[10] J. P. Briot, S. Aknine, I. Alvarez and Z. Guessoum, Multi-Agent Systems and Fault-Tolerance: State-of-the-art Elements, *EuroControl Technical Report, LIP6 & MODECO- CReSTIC*, 2007

[11] S. Pleisch, State-of-the-art of Mobile Agent Computing: Security, Fault Tolerance, and Transaction Support, *Research Report, IBM Research, Z. R. Lab. Switzerland*, 1999

[12] S. Pleisch and A. Schiper, FATOMAS-A Fault-Tolerant Mobile Agent System Based on the Agent-Dependent Approach, *IEEE, Proceedings of the 2001 International Conference on Dependable Systems and Networks*, 2001, pp 215-224, ISBN:0-7695-1101-5

[13] L. M. Silva, G. Soares, P. Martins, V. Batista and L. Santos, The Performance of Mobile Agent Platforms, *IEEE, Proceedings of First International Symposium on Third International Symposium on Mobile Agents*, 1999, pp. 270-271, ISBN: 0-7695-0340-3

[14] K. Park, A Fault-Tolerant Mobile Agent Model in Replicated Secure Services, *Springer, Proceedings of International Conference Computational Science and Its Applications*, Vol. 3043, pp 500-509, 2004, ISBN 978-3-540-22054-1

[15] P. Braun, and W. Rossak, Mobile Agents: Basic Concepts, Mobility Models, and the Tracy Toolkit, *Morgan Kaufmann*, 2005, ISBN-13: 978-1558608177

[16] R. S. Gray, D. Kotz, G. Cybenko, and D. Rus, Mobile Agents: Motivations and State-of-the-Art Systems, *Dartmouth College, Technical Report: TR2000-365*, 2000

[17] D. Kotz and R. S. Gray, Mobile Agents and the Future of the Internet, *ACM, ACM SIGOPS Operating Systems Review*, Vol. 33, Nr. 3, 1999, pp 7-13, ISSN: 0163-5980

[18] D. B. Lange and M. Oshima, Seven Good Reasons for Mobile Agents, *ACM, Communications of the ACM*, Vol. 42, Nr. 3, 1999, pp 88-89, ISSN:0001-0782

[19] M. Eid, H. Artail, A. Kayssi, and A. Chehab. Trends in Mobile Agent Applications, *Journal of Research and Practice in Information Technology*, Vol. 37, No. 4, November 2005

[20] R. Boutaba and J. Xiao, Network Management: State of the Art, *Kluwer, B.V., Proceedings of the IFIP 17th World Computer Congress - TC6 Stream on Communication Systems: The State of the Art*, 2002, pp 127-146, ISBN: 1-4020-7168-X

[21] L. M. Silva, P. Simões, G. Soares, P. Martins, V. Batista, C. Renato, L. Almeida and N. Stohr, JAMES: A Platform of Mobile Agents for the Management of Telecommunication Networks, *Springer, Proceedings of Third International Workshop Intelligent Agents for Telecommunication Applications*, Vol. 1699, 1999, pp 76-95, ISBN 978-3-540-665397

[22] O. Kachirski and R. Guha, Intrusion Detection Using Mobile

Agents in Wireless Ad Hoc Networks, *IEEE, Proceedings of the IEEE Workshop on Knowledge Media Networking*, 2002, pp 153-158, ISBN:0-7695-1778-1

[23] B. Kitchenham and S. Charters, Guidelines for performing Systematic Literature Reviews in Software Engineering, *Keele University and Durham University Joint Report, Tech. Rep. EBSE 2007-001*, 2007

[24] J. W. Creswell and Dana L. Miller, Determining Validity in Qualitative Inquiry, *Theory Into Practice*, 1543-0421, Volume 39, Issue 3, 2000, Pages 124 – 130

[25] S. Summiya, K. Ijaz, U. Manzoor and A. A. Shahid, A Fault Tolerant Infrastructure for Mobile Agents, *IEEE, Proceedings of the International Conference on Computational Intelligence for Modelling Control and Automation and International Conference on Intelligent Agents Web Technologies and International Commerce*, 2006, pp 235-235, ISBN:0-7695-2731-0

[26] K. K. Leung and K. W. Ng, A fault-tolerance mechanism for mobile agent systems, *Proceedings. 2006 International Conference on Intelligence For Modelling, Control and Automation. Jointly with International Conference on Intelligent Agents, Web Technologies and Internet Commerce*, 2005, pp.7 ISBN-10: 0 7695 2504 0

[27] M.R. Lyu and T. Y. Wong, A progressive fault tolerant mechanism in mobile agent systems *SCI 2003. 7th World Multiconference on Systemics, Cybernetics and Informatics Proceedings*, 2003, pp. 299-306 , Vol.9 ISBN-10: 980 6560 01 9

[28] S. Mellouli, A reorganization strategy to build fault-tolerant multi-agent systems *Advances in Artificial Intelligence. 20th Conference of the Canadian Society for Computational Studies of Intelligence, Canadian AI 2007. Proceedings 2007, Vol.4509*, pp. 61-72, ISBN-10: 3 540 72664 0

[29] F. M. A. Silva and R. Popescu-Zeletin, An Approach for Providing Mobile Agent Fault Tolerance, *Springer, Proceedings of Second International Workshop on Mobile Agents*, Vol. 1477, 1998, pp 14-25, ISBN: 978-3-540-64959-5

[30] T. Osman, W. Wagealla and A. Bargiela, An Approach to Rollback Recovery of Collaborating Mobile Agents, *IEEE, IEEE Transactions on Systems, Man, and Cybernetics, Part C: Applications and Reviews*, Vol. 34, Nr. 1, 2004, pp 48-57, ISSN: 1094-6977

[31] X. Meng and H. Zhang, An efficient fault-tolerant scheme for mobile agent execution *First International Symposium on Systems and Control in Aerospace and Astronautics*, 2006, pp.5, ISBN-10: 0 7803 9395 3

[32] J. Chen; H. Shi; C. Chen; Z. Hong; P. Zhong, An efficient forward and backward fault-tolerant mobile agent system, *Eighth International Conference on Intelligent Systems Design and Applications*, 2008, pp.61-6, ISBN-13: 978-0-7695-3382-7

[33] M. Olivier, B. Marin , S. Pierre, G. Zahia and B. Jean-Pierre, DARX - A Self-healing Framework for Agents, *Springer, Third International Conference*, 2007, Vol. 4322/2007, pp. 88-105, ISBN: 978-3-540-71155-1

[34] M.R. Lyu, X. Chen and T. Y. Wong, Design and Evaluation of a Fault-Tolerant Mobile-Agent System, *IEEE, Intelligent Systems*, Vol. 19 , Nr. 5, 2004, pp 32-38, ISSN: 1541-1672

[35] Y. Tanaka, N. Hayashibara, T. Enokido and M. Takizawa, Fault-tolerant distributed systems in a mobile agent model, *Seventeenth International Conference on Database and Expert Systems Applications*, 2006, pp.5, 2006 ISBN-10: 0 7695 2641 1

[36] L. M. Silva, V. Batista and J. G. Silva, Fault-Tolerant Execution of Mobile Agents, *IEEE, Proceedings International Conference on Dependable Systems and Networks*, 2000, pp 135-143, ISBN: 0-7695-0707-7

[37] FIPA, http://www.fipa.org, [Accessed August 26, 2009]

[38] K. Rothermel and M. Strasser, A fault-tolerant Protocol for Providing the Exactly-Once Property of Mobile Agents, *Proceedings Seventeenth IEEE Symposium on Reliable Distributed Systems 1998, pp.* 100-8, ISBN-10: 0 8186 9218 9

[39] A. Fedoruk and R. Deters, Improving Fault-Tolerance by Replicating Agents, *ACM, Proceedings of the first international joint conference on Autonomous agents and multiagent systems: part 2*, 2002, pp 737-744, ISBN:1-58113-480-0

[40] T. Park, I. Byun and H. Y. Yeom, Lazy Agent Replication and Asynchronous Consensus for the Fault-Tolerant Mobile Agent System, *Springer, Proceedings of Third International IFIP-TC6 Networking Conference*, 2004, pp 1060-1071, ISBN: 978-3-540-21959-0

[41] T. Park and I. Byun, Low Overhead Agent Replication for the Reliable Mobile Agent System, *Springer, Proceedings of 9th International Euro-Par Conference*, Vol. 2790, 2003, pp 1170-1179, ISBN 978-3-540-40788-1

[42] H. Hamidi and K. Mohammadi, Modeling Fault Tolerant and Secure Mobile Agent Execution in Distributed Systems, *Idea Group, International Journal of Intelligent Information Technologies*, Vol. 2, Nr. 1, 2006

[43] D. Johansen, K. Marzullo, F.B. Schneider, K. Jacobsen, and D. Zagorodnov, NAP: practical fault-tolerance for itinerant computations, *Proceedings. 19th IEEE International Conference on Distributed Computing Systems 1999, pp.* 180-9, ISBN-10: 0 7695 0222 9

[44] J. Yang, J. Cao, W. Wu and C. Xu, Parallel algorithms for fault-tolerant mobile agent execution, *Distributed and Parallel Computing. 6th International Conference on Algorithms and Architectures for Parallel Processing, ICA3PP. Proceedings*, 2005, pp. 246-56, ISBN-10: 3 540 29235 7

[45] M. Tosic and A. Zaslavsky, Reliable multi-agent systems with persistent publish/subscribe messaging, *18th Industrial and Engineering Applications of Artificial Intelligence and Expert Systems, IEA/AIE 2005. Proceedings, 2005 Vol. 3533*, pp.165-74, ISBN-10: 3 540 26551-1

[46] P. Taesoon and Y. Jaehwan, The K-Fault-Tolerant Checkpointing Scheme for the Reliable Mobile Agent System, *Parallel and Distributed Computing: Applications and Technologies. 5th International Conference, PDCAT 2004. pp.*577-81, ISBN-10: 3 540 24013 6

[47] T. Kaneda, Y. Tanaka, T. Enokido and M. Takizawa, Transactional agent model for fault-tolerant object systems, *Proceedings of the ACM Symposium on Applied Computing*, 2005, Vol. 2, pp. 1133-1138

[48] T. Park, J. Youn and D. Kim, Using adaptive agents for the fault-tolerant mobile computing system, *6th International Conference, Proceedings* 2006, Vol. 3993, pp. 807-814 ISBN-10: 3540343830

[49] H. K. Yeom, H. Y. T. Park and H. Park, The Cost of Checkpointing, Logging and Recovery for the Mobile Agent Systems, *Proceedings of Pacific Rim International Symposium on Dependable Computing*, 2002, pp 45-48, ISBN: 0-7695-1852-4

[50] J. Briot, Z. Guessoum, S. Charpentier, S. Aknine, O. Marin and P. Sens, Dynamic Adaptation of Replication Strategies for Reliable Agents, *Proceeding of 2nd Symposium on Adaptive Agents and Multi-Agent Systems*, 2002, pp 10-19

[51] M. Q. Patton, Qualitative Research & Evaluation Methods, *Sage Publications, Inc; 3rd edition*, 2001, ISBN-10: 0761919716

[52] E. N. (Mootaz) Elnozahy, L. Alvisi, Y. Wang and D. B. Johnson, A Survey of Rollback-Recovery Protocols in Message-Passing Systems, *ACM, ACM Computing Surveys*, Vol. 34, Nr. 3, 2002, pp 375-408, ISSN:0360-0300

[53] S. Mishra and P. Xie, Interagent Communication and Synchronization Support in the DaAgent Mobile Agent-Based Computing System, *IEEE, IEEE Transactions on Parallel and Distributed Systems*, Vol. 14, Nr. 3, 2003, ISSN:1045-9219

[54] L. Bettini and R. D. Nicola, Translating Strong Mobility into Weak Mobility, *Springer, Proceedings of the 5th International Conference on Mobile Agents*, Vol. 2240, 2001, pp 182-197, ISBN:3-540-42952-2

[55] N. Suri, J. M. Bradshaw, M. R. Breedy, P. T. Groth, G. A. Hill and R. Jeffers, Strong Mobility and Fine-Grained Resource Control in NOMADS, *Springer, Proceedings of the 2nd International Symposium on Agents Systems and Applications and the 4th International Symposium on Mobile Agents*, 2000, pp 2-15, ISBN:3-540-41052-X

[56] R. A. Bourne, A. L. G. Hayzelden, Rachel Bourne and P. Buckle, Agent Technology for Communication Infrastructures, *Wiley*, 2001, ISBN: 0471498157

[57] Aglet, http://aglets.sourceforge.net/, [Accessed May 21, 2009]

[58] T. Walsh, N. Paciorek and D. Wong, Security and Reliability in Concordia, *IEEE, Proceedings of the Thirty-First Annual Hawaii International Conference on System Sciences*, Vol. 7, 1998, pp 44-53, ISBN: 0-8186-8255-8

[59] FIPA-OS   Tutorial, http://fipa-os.sourceforge.net/tutorials.htm,   [Accessed August 26, 2009]

[60] Agents Technology in Europe, *ACTS project InfoWin*, 1999

[61] JADE - Java Agent DEvelopment Framework, http://jade.tilab.com/, [Accessed August 26, 2009]

[62] MadKit, http://www.madkit.org, [Accessed May 21, 2009]

[63] MadKit: A generic Multi-agent platform, *ACM*, 2000.

[64] J. Baumann, F. Hohl, K. Rothermel, M. Strasser and W. Theilmann, *MOLE: A Mobile Agent System*, John Wiley & Sons, Software—Practice & Experience, Vol. 32, 2002, pp 575–603

[65] Naptel, http://www.ece.eng.wayne.edu/~czxu/software/naplet.html, [Accessed August 26, 2009]

[66] A. Grimstrup, R. Gray, D. Kotz, M. Breedy, M. Carvalho, T. Cowin, D. Chacón, J. Barton, C. Garrett and M. Hofmann, Toward Interoperability of Mobile-Agent Systems, *Springer, Proceedings of 6th International Conference on Mobile Agents*, 2002, pp 106-120, ISBN: 978-3-540-00085-3

[67] D. Johansen, R. V. Renesse, F. B. Schneider, N. P. Sudmann and K. Jacobsen, A Tacoma Retrospective, *John Wiley & Sons, Software—Practice & Experience*, Vol. 32, Nr. 6, 2002, pp 605-619, ISSN:0038-0644

[68] Voyager 3.1.1 Developer Guide, *Object Space*, 1999

[69] M. J. Fischer, N. A. Lynch and M. S. Paterson, Impossibility of Distributed Consensus With One Faulty Process, *ACM, Journal of the ACM*, Vol. 32, Nr. 2, 1985, pp 374-382, ISSN: 0004-5411

16

Using the semantic Web services to build a virtual medical analysis laboratory

Houda El Bouhissi[1], Mimoun Malki[1], Djamila Berramdane[1], Rafa E. Al-Qutaish[2]

[1] Dept. of Computer Sciences, EEDIS Laboratory, Sidi-Bel-Abbes University, Algeria
[2] Dept. of Software Engineering & IT, ÉTS, University of Québec,1100 Notre-Dame West, Montreal, Québec, H3C 1K3, Canada

Email address:

houda.elbouhissi@gmail.com (H. E. Bouhissi), mimoun.malki@gmail.com (M. Malki), berramdane@gmail.com (D. Berramdane),
rafa@ieee.org (R. E. Al-Qutaish)

Abstract: In medical analysis field, patients often must visit a multitude of laboratories related web sites in order to check availability, booking, prices, result duration, and find the nearest laboratory. Thus, these varieties of reasons to visit the web sites make limitations on the usability of them. However, to overcome these limitations, this paper proposes a Virtual Medical Analysis Laboratory (VMAL) prototype system which will be based on applying the Semantic Web Services (SWSs) for scheduling outpatient tests in order to discover the suitable laboratory. Furthermore, the proposed prototype will also be based on the Web Service Modeling Ontology (WSMO).

Keywords: Ontology, Web Services, Semantic Web Services, WSMO

1. Introduction

Web Services are software components that are accessible via the Web. However, their concomitant descriptive languages and Web Services Description Language (WSDL) do not offer sufficient semantic richness that can be processed by machine [1]. Furthermore, human intervention is often needed to interpret the meanings in order to discover, compose, and invoke Web services, but this can be time consuming and error-prone [2].

The semantic Web researchers propose many approaches to augment the Web services with a semantic description of their functionality in order to facilitate their discovery and integration [3]. These approaches consist of a combination of Web services with semantic Web technology, and are referred to as Semantic Web Services (SWSs). In addition, the SWSs have the potentiality to modify the knowledge and business services which are given and used on the web [4].

Discovery is one of the central reasoning tasks in Service-Oriented Architecture (SOA) systems, concerned with the detection of usable Web services for a specific request or application context. SWS discovery helps to discover an appropriate service according to user requirements in such scenario. This is the first step towards service selection and composition in order to complete a specific task especially in business environment. Therefore, this paper aims at discovering the suitable SWS taking into account the existing approaches.

In addition, it will propose a prototype system by applying the SWSs for scheduling outpatient tests (blood tests, urine, etc.). Then, this prototype system could be used to discover the suitable laboratory. Also, it will present a state of the art of current enabling SWS technologies and describes the proposed prototype, thus, each Web service has been implemented in a different technologies in order to make them more flexible.

The paper is organized as follows; Section 2 summarizes the main approaches related to SWSs technology. Section 3 introduces the proposed prototype in details. Finally, section 4 concludes the paper and outlines the future work.

2. Semantic Web Services Approaches

Web service technologies bring a dynamic aspect to overall Web usage. However, the current understanding about Web services fails to capture enough semantic data. Therefore, semantic services deal with such limitation by augmenting the service description with a semantic layer in order to achieve automated discovery, composition, monitoring, and execution, which are all highly desirable processes [5].

However, several approaches have already been suggested for adding semantic to Web services. Semantics can either be added to currently existing syntactic Web service standards such as Universal Description, Discovery and Integration (UDDI) [6] and Web Services Description Language (WSDL), or services can be described using some ontology based description language. The Major initiatives in the area of SWSs are documented by W3C member submissions, such as, OWL-S [7], WSMO [8] and WSDL-S [9].

Ontology Web Language for Services (OWL-S) is a description language that semantically describes Web Services using OWL ontologies. OWL-S services are mapped to WSDL operations, and inputs and outputs of OWL-S are mapped to WSDL messages.

The Web Services Description Language - Semantic (WSDL-S) is an evolutionary and backwards compatible extension of the existing Web Services standards and descriptions language, which augments the expressivity of WSDL with semantics in an arbitrary semantic representation language. In addition, it provides a means to supply semantic information, but actual semantic functionality has to be provided by additional components, which are not part of the WSDL-S initiative.

The WSDL-S proposal was replaced by Semantic Annotations for WSDL (SAWSDL) [10], a W3C recommendation, which is a simple and generic mechanism for semantically annotating Web Service descriptions. The SAWSDL is a restricted and homogenized version of WSDL-S in which annotations like preconditions and effects have not been explicitly contemplated.

The Web Services Modeling Ontology (WSMO) provides ontological specifications for the description of SWSs [11]. One of the main objectives of WSMO is to give a solution to application integration problems for Web Services by providing a conceptual framework and a formal language for semantically describing all relevant aspects of Web Services [12], Table 1 depicts the main differences between the three approaches.

Table 1. Comparison between the three approaches

	OWL-S	WSMO	WSDL-S
Scope	Description model for semantically describing Web Services	Description model & language for core elements of Semantic Web Service technologies	Semantic Annotation of WSDL description
Top Level Elements	Service Profile Process model Grounding	Ontologies Goals Web Services Mediators	Operations/ WSDL descriptions
Language	OWL	WSML	Not specified
Maturity of the approach	Strong	Medium	Medium
Mediation	Under development	Strong (MEDIATORS elements)	Not specified

WSMO is the only initiative which has an explicit notion of mediation [13]. Furthermore, WSMO is the only standard for which there exist several implementation environments which aim to support the complete standard [14]. For these reasons WSMO is used as our SWSs technology throughout the rest of this paper. In addition, WSMO model consists of both the requester and provider sides, and thus, it gives the opportunity to the requester (user) to define a goal in order to find a semantically annotated web service.

Ait-Ameur [15] proposes a semantic repository for adaptive services in which he uses a semantic registry, to store SWSs. However, this, semantic registry is equipped with an exploitation language that supports semantic based process discovery. Moreover, Belaid *et al.* [16] apply ontology and indexation based management of services and workflows to the Geological Modeling.

3. The Proposed Prototype

3.1. Motivation

It is clear that finding out the interested services without using automated mechanisms is very difficult and time consuming. This issue is similar to search in web pages without using browsers. Service consumer can be user, another service or a program. Thus, using of automated mechanisms to finding out services is very important [17].

SWSs technology can be used to optimize several processes in the domain of e-health, especially in Medical Analysis [18]. These processes are mainly related to human interactions, and consequently to the costs associated with them. Hence, the main benefit of applying SWS technology is that it could permit to develop and maintain e-health services with lower costs.

The use of SWSs technology can optimize this manual process by allowing a search in available registries, so that the new Web Services which have been deployed can be discovered easily and quickly.

Figure 1 below, presents two scenarios that motivated us to develop this prototype. In the first scenario (Scenario 1), for an outpatient test (blood test, urine test, etc.), the patient often must visit the web sites for many different laboratories in order to check availability, prices, result duration and also to find the nearest laboratory.

Using phone directories is also needed if some web sites' laboratories are not available. The patient should contact each laboratory by phone or email to get the necessary information, such as, address, distance from home, price, possible results, etc. This method is very difficult and time consumer, especially when the patient needs to visit many laboratories.

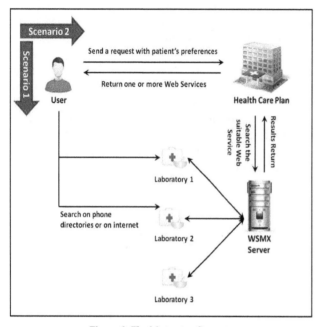

Figure 1. The Motivation Scenario

In the second scenario (Scenario 2), to overcome the limitations in the first scenario, the Virtual Medical Analysis Laboratory (VMAL) prototype system is proposed to discover the suitable Laboratory by applying SWSs for scheduling outpatient tests (blood tests, urine tests, etc.).

In order to model the scenario, we propose prototype based on Web service Modeling Ontology (WSMO), we use WSMO for modeling of services and goals (i.e. required and offered capabilities) as well as ontologies (i.e. information models on which services and goals are defined) all written in the WSML ontology language.

The scheduling of the required tests could be done through the following steps:
• The patient informs what tests she/he wants to do (blood test, urine test, etc.);
• The system discovers what laboratories can do these tests (discover web services from laboratories); and
• The system returns a list of one or more discovered Web Services to patient.

As shown in Figure 1, the patient sends a request to the portal with her/his preferences. A searching process for suitable Web Services is performed in the WSMX server where all the Web Services are stored. At last, the patient receives one or more Web Services according to her/his request. Next subsections will explain in more details the main architecture of the prototype.

3.2. The WSMO Framework

WSMO (Web service Modeling Ontology) is a formal ontology and language which identifies the following four main top-elements:
• Ontologies that provide the terminology used by other elements;
• Goals that state the intentions which should be solved by Web Services;
• Web Services descriptions which describe various aspects of a service; and
• Mediators to resolve interoperability problems.

Each of these WSMO Top Level Elements can be described with non-functional properties, such as, creator, creation date, format, language, owner, rights, source, type, etc. Furthermore, WSMO comes along with a modeling language (WSML) and a reference implementation (WSMX).

The WSML (Web Service Modeling Language) is a formalization of the WSMO ontology and providing a language within which the properties of SWSs can be described.

Whereas, the WSMX (Web Service eXecution Environment) provides an architecture including discovery, mediation, selection, and invocation. In addition, it has been designed to include all the required supporting components enabling an exchange of messages between requesters and the providers of services.

3.3. Architecture of the Prototype

The VMAL prototype could be used to help users of the medical laboratories to schedule their outpatient tests (blood tests, urine tests, etc.)

Figure 2 presents the architecture of the prototype. The patient communicates with the VLMA portal via the HTTPS protocol, which provides a secure communication channel.

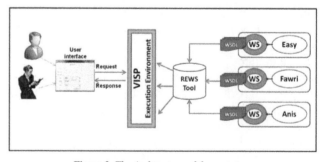

Figure 2. The Architecture of the prototype

The essential functionalities of the proposed prototype process applied to medical analysis are as the following:
• Provide a friendly interface for patient interaction.
• Discover suitable Web Services according to patient preferences (availability, distance, price, etc.).

Much of the promise of Web Services is its potential for seamless interoperability across heterogeneous systems, platforms, applications, and programming languages. Interoperability is a primary goal of web services. Web services standards facilitate interoperability, but do not ensure it.

The proposed prototype consists of three Web Services, a WSMX server and a simple interface client application implemented with Java language that communicates with the WSMX Server. The three Web Services are implemented with different platforms and programming languages. The use of several programming languages makes our prototype more flexible because we consider that the WSDL file as our only source of information and the choice of these programming languages is random. The first Web Service was implemented with the Java language and the NetBeans Platform, the second with the .NET, and the third one was implemented with PHP and MYSQL.

Service providers publish their service and made a description of it in Web Service Description Language (WSDL). WSDL provides the way through which Web Services can be described according to their functional, non-functional behavior.

All the WSDL files are submitted to the Reverse Engineering Web Service Application (REWS) tool [19] for extracting the main WSMO Web Service elements, which are written in WSML language and then will be stored in the WSMX Server.

In our prototype, the WSMX server plays the role of a UDDI directory where all Web Services elements are stored.

All semantic descriptions are provided on top of existing providers' syntactic services, making providers unaware of this semantic layer. No changes are involved in providers' services and native data formats are preserved.

The WSMX server is a computer where the WSMX is installed and configured, it acts as a transparent and intermediary layer between interacting parties for mapping and discovery. It consists of some components that fulfill Web Services tasks such as discovery, invocation, composition, etc.

The patients' desires are expressed via web forms (see Figure 3) which are mapped to appropriate Goal and expressed in WSML language.

Once a WSMO Goal with its actual values is created, then it can be sent to WSMX, where provider matching this Goal is discovered, and according to Goal and Web service choreography communication is carried out. At last, one or more Web Services are returned to the patient.

This scenario is very simple, and the use of SWS is needed in this case. The reason for choosing this scenario is to keep the implementation within the scope of the project and because it uses the most important and basic parts of WSMX.

To be able to fulfill this scenario, WSMO ontology elements must be created to provide a shared vocabulary for the different interactions.

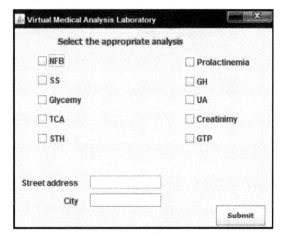

Figure 3. User interface snapshot

3.4. System Phases

According to WSMO, to develop SWS, the actual Web Service should be implemented; a WSMO Web Service should be created to describe the web service. Also, the necessary ontologies used by the Web Service should be defined. Then, to test it, a goal needs to be created, that is, to represent a request to WSMX and the ontologies used by it. The discovery process can be split into eight high-level steps, see Figure 4.

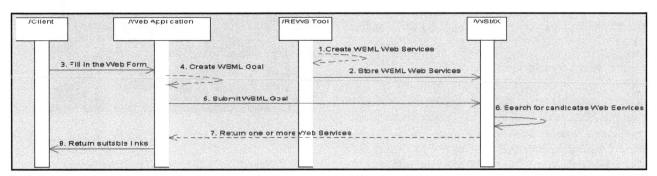

Figure 4. Sequence diagram for discovery of Web Services

The following describes, in more details, the different phases of the process.

Phase 1: Creating WSMO Web Services Elements

Providers' Web Services have to be semantically described to include lifting arbitrary XML messages in WSDL document to the semantic level by the ontology conceptualization.

In this phase, the REWS tool has been used to create WSMO Web Services elements. It takes as input WSDL File of each Web Service and generates as output the web Service Elements expressed in WSML language. Then, these elements will be stored on the WSMX server for further using. Figure 5, depicts part of a WSML file according to the first Web Service.

```
wsmlVariant _"http://www.wsmo.org/wsml/wsml-syntax/wsml-flight"

namespace {_"http://www.gsmo.org/laboratoire/laboratoire1#",
    dO _"http://www.gsmo.org/laboratoire/laboratoireOntology#",
    dc _"http://purl.org/dc/elements/1.1#"}
webService _"http://www.gsmo.org/laboratoire/laboratoire1.wsml"
    nfp
        dc#title hasValue "laboratoire1 Web Service"
        dc#contributor hasValue "Soumia Amina"
        dc#description hasValue "oran FNS"
        dc#description hasValue " oran gioimie "
    endnfp
    importsOntology _"http://www.gsmo.org/laboratoire/laboratoireOntology.wsml"
    capability webServiceAnalyseCapability
        postcondition
            definedBy
                ?noma [dO#noma hasValue "FNS"] and
            ?ville memberOf dO#ville[dO#valeur hasValue "oran"]
```

Figure 5. *Snapshot of a part of WML Web Service file*

Phase 2: Creating WSMO Goals

Patient does not have to visit multiple web sites, but can use only the friendly interface provided by the portal (see Figure 3 above) that aggregates multiple Medical analysis services, and sure it can be extended with new ones.

The requirements and behavior of the client have to be expressed as WSMO Goal. A Web application implemented with Java and NetBeans provides forms where user can specify her/his requirements and input values.

The patient has to Introduce necessary data to find Medical analysis offers.

The system accept the expression of patients' goals using Web forms that in turn are mapped to WSMO Goals, and allow them to be executed by WSMX.

In the proposed prototype, the Goals are based on a template approach where the Goal structure is defined but actual input values can be provided during the run-time by the patient. Also we create an ontology for such goal(see figure 6).

Phase 3: Matching Web Service to Goal

Now, the Goal is submitted to WSMX, whereas, the provider matching this Goal is discovered, and then according to the Goal itself and Web Service choreography communication is carried out [20].

The Discovery component of the WSMX server then starts to match the capabilities required by the goal, with the capabilities of the Web Services already registered in WSMX.

The Service Discovery component refines the suggested Web Services resulted from the discovery and chooses the most appropriate web service based on the requester's preferences

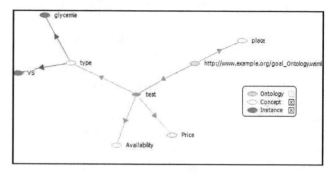

Figure 6. *Ontology according to WSMO goal*

This matching is performed by the discovery component of the WSMX platform and it can be held using different criteria that are further discussed by [21]. The default matching criteria are the Keyword-based discovery and the LightWeight discovery.

The former relies on matching the Non-Functional properties defined by the Web Service and the goal, while the latter compares the Postconditions and the Effects specified in the two interfaces.

After that the Service Discovery component refines the suggested web services resulted from the discovery and chooses the most appropriate web service based on the requester's preferences. Some user preferences can be specified using Non-Functional properties.

After the web service is chosen, a response is returned to the patient with suitable Web Services links.

WSMX takes a semi-automatic approach to this problem. Initially, three Web Services were loaded to WSMX. Then to perform the discovery, the WSMX server used both the Keyword-based and the LightWeight discoveries. Two Web Services were discovered, the first one using the Keyword discovery and the second one using the LightWeight (see figure 7 below).

The human's role is to ensure accuracy of these mappings and to adjust them if necessary.

The 2 Web Services discovered according to the goal

Figure 7. *Snapshot of the discovered Web Services*

4. Conclusion

SWSs are very powerful paradigm which could be used to transform the current syntactic Web into a dynamic and semantic one, thus, this transformation allows automating the use of the Web Services.

Especially, the discovery of SWSs has become an important when large number services are available for use on the Internet, so the acquisition of appropriate SWS is the main goal for a user who is searching for a service.

This paper describes a prototype of a Virtual Medical Analysis Laboratory (VMAL) application for demonstrating how the application of SWSs technology makes it possible for individual patients to find the suitable laboratory for scheduling outpatient tests.

As a future work, this proposed prototype could be extended to transport Web Services. In addition, such prototype could also be used with many applications in Web Services.

References

[1] W3C, *Web Services Description Language (WSDL) 1.1*, available online at: http://www/w3.org/TR/wsdl, retrieved on: March 7, 2013.

[2] L. A. Kamaruddin, J. Shen and G. Beydoun, Evaluating Usage of WSMO and OWL-S in Semantic Web Services, *In Proceedings of the 8th Asia-Pacific Conference on Conceptual Modelling (APCCM'12)*, RMIT, Melbourne, Australian, January 30 - February 2, 2012, pp. 53-58.

[3] A. Suganthy, G. S. Sumithra, J. Hindusha, A. Gayathri and S. Girija, Semantic Web Services and its Challenges, *International Journal of Computer Engineering and Technology (IJCET)*, Vol. 1, No. 2, 2010, pp. .26-37.

[4] L. Cabral, J. Domingue, E. Motta, T. Payne and F. Hakimpour, Approaches to Semantic Web Services: An Overview and Comparisons, *In Proceedings of the 1st European Semantic Web Symposium*, Heraklion, Greece, May 10-12, 2004.

[5] Antoniou, G.; van Harmelen, F., 2008. *A Semantic Web Primer*. The MIH Press, Cambridge, USA.

[6] OASIS, *UDDI Version 3.0.2*, UDDI Spec Technical Committee Draft, available online at: http://uddi.org/pubs /uddi_v3.htm, retrieved on: March 7, 2013.

[7] D. Martin, M. Burstein, J. Hobbs, O. Lassila, D.McDermott, S.McIlraith, S.Narayanan, M.Paolucci, B. Parsia, T. Payne, E.Sirin, N.Srinivasan and K. Sycara, *OWL Web Ontology Language for Services (OWL-S)*, available online at: http://www.w3.org/Submission/OWL-S, retrieved on: March 7, 2013.

[8] J.d. Bruijn, C. Bussler, J. Domingue, D. Fensel, M. Hepp, U. Keller, M. Kifer, B. König-Ries, J. Kopecky, R. Lara, H. Lausen, E. Oren, A. Polleres, D. Roman, J. Scicluna and M. Stollberg, *Web Service Modeling Ontology (WSMO)*, available online at: http://www.w3.org/Submission/WSMO, retrieved on: March 7, 2013.

[9] R. E. Akkiraju, J. Farrell, J. Miller, M. Nagarajan M. Schmidt, A. Sheth and K. Verma, *Web Service Semantics - WSDL-S*,

W3C Member Submission 7, 2005, available online at: http://www.w3.org/Submission/2005/SUBM-WSDL-S-2005 1107, retrieved on: March 7, 2013.

[10] J. Farrell and H. Lausen (eds), *Semantic Annotations for WSDL and XML Schema*. W3C Candidate Recommendation, available online at: http://www.w3.org/TR/sawsdl, retrieved on: March 7, 2013.

[11] H. El Bouhissi and M. Malki and D. Bouchiha, Towards WSMO Ontology Specification From Existing Web Services, *In Proceedings of 2nd Conférence Internationale sur l'Informatique et ses Applications (CIIA 2009)*, Saida, Algeria, May 3-4, 2009.

[12] F. Cristina and J. Domingue, *D2v1.0 WSMO Primer: CMS WG Working Draft*, available online at: http://cms-wg. sti2.org/TR/d2/v1.0/20050401, 2005, retrieved on: March 7, 2013.

[13] ESSI WSML working group, *Web Service Modeling Language WSML*, available online at: http://www. wsmo.org/wsml, retrieved on: March 7, 2013.

[14] Web Service Execution Environment, *Web Service Modeling Ontology*, available online at: http://www.wsmx.org, retrieved on: March 7, 2013.

[15] Y. Ait-Ameur, A Semantic Repository for Adaptive Services, *In Proceedings of the IEEE Congress on Services (SERVICES'09)*, Los Angeles, CA, USA, July 6-10, 2009, pp. 211-218.

[16] N. Belaid, S. Jean, Y. Ait-Ameur, J.-F. Rainaud, An Ontology and Indexation Based Management of Services and WorkFlows: Application to Geological Modeling, *International Journal of Electronic Business Management (IJEBM)*, Vol. 9, No. 4, 2011, pp. 296-309.

[17] K. Zamanifar, A. Zohali and N. Nematbakhsh, Matching Model for Semantic Web Services Discovery, *In Proceedings of the International Conference on Advanced Information Networking and Applications Workshops*, Bradford, United Kingdom, May 26-29, 2009.

[18] L. J. Cox, *Feature-Oriented Domain Analysis for Semantic Web Services*, M.Sc. Thesis, Athabasca University, Athabasca, Alberta, Canada, December 2010.

[19] H. El Bouhissi and M. Malki, Reverse Engineering Existing Web Service Applications, *In Proceeding of the 16th Working Conference on Reverse Engineering (WCRE'09)*, Lille, France, October 13-16, 2009, pp. 279-283.

[20] H. El Bouhissi and M. Malki, Semantic Web Services: WSMO Goal Based Architecture, *In Proceedings of the International Conference on Information and Communication Systems (ICICS'11)*, Irbid, Jordan, May 22-24, 2011.

[21] M. Herold, *Evaluation and Advancement in Context of a Tourist Information System*. http://www.fhwedel.de/ fileadmin/mitarbeiter/iw/Abschlussarbeiten/Masterarbeit Herold.pdf, 2008. Retrieved on March 7, 2013.

17

Simulation of traffic lights for green wave and dynamic change of signal

Güney GORGUN, Ibrahim Halil GUZELBEY*

Department of Mechanical Engineering, University of Gaziantep, Gaziantep, Turkey

Email address:

gorgunguney@hotmail.com (G. GORGUN), guzelbeyih@gantep.edu.tr (I. H. GUZELBEY)

Abstract: In this study a traffic light system has been considered and simulated on Matlab to create hierarchical and logical model. This model is designed over five junctions to solve traffic jam in big cities by simulation of continuous flow of traffic lights. This simulation includes Green Wave flow and dynamic change of traffic lights due to change traffic volume. The simulation secures the continuous traffic flow by updating the light time for providing green wave flow.

Keywords: Matlab, Simulation, Traffic Lights, Green Wave Flow and Traffic Volume

1. Introduction

The history of traffic light starts with an idea of an engineer from, a Rail Way Engineer, John Peak Night, who specialized in designing signal systems for Britain's rail way. He realized no reason why these couldn't be adapted to roads. On 9 December 1868, the world's first traffic lights were set up at the junction of Bridge Street and George Street. Later on the first 4-way three color traffic lights were installed in 1920 in Detroit [1].

When it is investigated the technological development of traffic signal and control systems, it can be easily recognized remarkable improvement of signal systems. For example *fuzzy systems* deal with complex systems where imprecise, uncertain or ambiguous information is available, where the real world problems are nonlinear or where expert knowledge is expressed vaguely in natural language and fuzzy system was easily suited for traffic signal control. The general rule base for traffic signal control will develop with time, and also the fuzzy controller will become better with time [2-4]. Model formulation and solution of linear optimization problem for multiple intersections in a network was worked by explicit constraints capturing traffic movement on the links connecting the intersections [5].

Development technology has come a long way for detecting of cars in the traffic. It guides for organizing of traffic signal incase traffic congestion. For example AMR sensor (The anisotropic magneto resistive) is used for detection of ferrous object like cars [6]. In addition to them, an adaptive traffic control system was developed where the traffic load is continuously measured by loop detectors connected to a microcontroller-based system which also performs all intersection control functions [7] and Real-time Recognition and Re-identification of Vehicles from Video Data with high Re-identification [8]. But still world has traffic jam problem parallel to increasing population and vehicle number especially in big cities.

Nowadays people spent their time in traffic. It is called as "rush-hours." This time is non-productive time which stolen from people life. In addition to rush hours, the negative effect of exhaust emission occurs during waiting in the traffic jam. Finally, vehicle fuel consumption and emissions at or near street intersections are usually higher than on other street segments because the intersection frequently causes vehicles to slow, stop, accident and accelerate. [9-13]

This paper aims to simulate four-way traffic lights and green wave flow over the five junctions. It has also dynamic change of traffic signal due to traffic volume at critical intersections together with updating green wave time in every cross to safe passing of vehicles without stop. This study will be guided for problem solving of traffic jam.

2. Simulation of Traffic Lights

2.1. Cycle Time Arrangement and Simulation

Cycle time is an important parameter for organizing of traffic flow on junctions. Sometimes, this time is shared between cross randomly. When it is shared without numerical values of volume distribution, sometimes, vehicles on one junction, have to wait signal which let them pass even there is no vehicle on other junction. This situation makes "rush-time" and waste of money. In big cities, which has crowded junctions must be arranged the

cycle of time with analyzing of traffic volume distribution.

This section includes discussion of cycle time and sharing between crosses which depends on volume distribution of vehicle as shown in Figure 1 which includes 4-way and five crosses application in an isolated area.

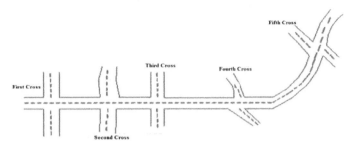

Figure 1. 4-way and Five Crosses Traffic Road in an Isolated Area

There is a relation between cycle time for signal and volume distribution on a cross;

, $\in Z^+$ there is five cross simulation so $imax= 5$ and $imin= 1$,

Cycle time without yellow signal (seconds), (Ti -2).

So green signal or red signal can be calculated below,

$$Gij= \frac{Vij}{\sum_{j=1}^{2} Vij} \times (Ti - 2) \qquad (1)$$

$$Rij=(Ti-2)- Gij \qquad (2)$$

It can be embedded to simulation of traffic light. State duration can be explained as below;

S'ijm=Rij seconds   if m=1 and j=1 or   S'ijm=Gij+3 seconds if m=1 and j=2

S'ijm=Gij-1seconds if m=2 and j=1   or   S'ijm=Rij-1seconds if m=2 and j=2

This will be shown in Figure 3.

There is an unbalance time cycle due to default transition. After a while, distortion occurs during simulation. It can be

easily heal by self transition in every Ci' cross. This transition is used after $Ti+ 4$ seconds on specified crosses, Ci' state exits after that time and goes inside its state instantaneously. It is repeated in every cycle. The system renews itself with self transition. It will be discussed and can be shown in Figure 3.

Cycle time division includes some steps as shown in Figure 2. This figure is also representation of Matlab model of isolated area. Only first cross cycle time division is represented shown in this figure. The other four crosses will be same as shown in Figure 2. The time input firstly goes inside "Matlab function" and arranges time per one cycle equation(1) which depends on vehicles volume of whole junctions and this value is assigned to signal time for red. After that, the signal time for red goes into second "Matlab function 1" and it is recalculated then it is assigned to signal for green. Thus when it is changed cycle time, the dividing cycle time ratio between one cross to another will be always same.

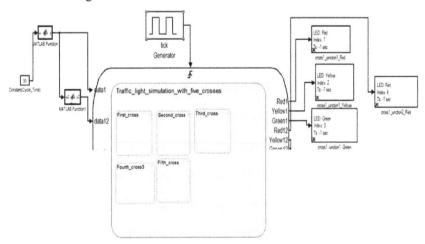

Figure 2. Pictorial Representation of Main State with Sub States, Input Cycle Time and LEDs

In Figure 2 it can be also seen the representation of main states which has sub-charts. These sub-charts are working parallel when the program is executed [14].

When one of these main states, in Figure 2, is opened it

can be seen new states of one junction as shown in Figure 3. It is called as *state_1*. This state is parallel states which make it to simulate simultaneously with other states. This state reserves one state which calls as *First_cross*. This state has two parallel states which include the situation of lights on two different junctions at one cross. *First_junction_cross1* starts its default state with *Stop1* lights red led, at the same time *Second_junction_cross1* starts its default state of *Go12* and it lights green led. The transitions between states depend on *data_1* and *data_2* parameters. After *data_1-1, seconds, Go12* exits state and program runs to *Stop12* state. After one second this event, *Stop1* is finished and the program runs to state *Ready1* which has two parallel states lights *Red1* and *Yellow1*on same junction simultaneously. After 2 seconds of entering *Ready1,* the first junction lets vehicle to pass. After passing *data12-1 seconds,* the first junction light turns to red and

finishes first cycle. In every cycle, the balance of lights time gradually distortion.

It is mentioned before that after a while, the green led lights simultaneously on different junctions because of unbalance transition time between junctions due to default states. This is a big mistake but it could be fixed and healed as to create self transition in *First_cross*. After *data1+data12+4 seconds* the state of *First_cross* turns to its first situation like the program turns beginning situation. Every that time, it means that the program completes its one cycle and repeat this transition according as the program works. Now the system works properly.

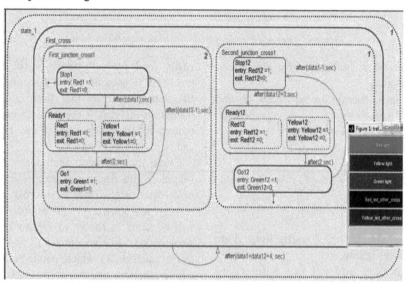

Figure 3. *States of First Junction and Simulation (Day Cycle)*

2.2. Green Wave Application and Simulation

New researchers have already suggested improving traffic globally. The new approaches make vehicles passed in the traffic without stopping under velocity constrain from one arterial to another arterials. It is called as *"Green Wave"*. A green wave is a kind of pattern such that if vehicles travels at a certain velocity from specified junction to others, they will not hit any red lights. But the signal between specified crosses must be synchronized. There are lots of main reasons using green wave in big cities which have traffic jam problem. Traffic network congestion causes delays which add substantial costs to society and businesses on a daily basis and also increase emissions and the risk of accidents. The study mentioned above reports that in 2002 people where spending 100,000 hours in total in queues in the Greater Copenhagen road infrastructure, this corresponds to an economic loss of more than 750 million Euros [10]. This kind of problems and hazardous consequences can be reduced by optimization of green wave [15,16].

There are many investigations about vehicle fuel consumption and emission at signalized intersection where signal causes vehicles slow, stop and accelerate. This situation makes vehicle consume excess fuel and produce

more emission. Analytical Fuel Consumption Model was worked by The University of Texas at Austin, USA and experimental study was done which was called as TEXAS model (Traffic Experimental and Analytical Simulation model) in 1998. This model was compared with Webster (1958) who derived optimal cycle time using his empirically developed delay equation [9].

According to these studies, Green wave application is an important criterion for fuel consumption and emissions at intersections and discusses in this section.

Simulation of green wave will be discussed in this model which has five different arterials (4-way), as shown in Figure 1, are synchronized together for adapting of green wave. All crosses in this simulation can be thought run on with their own clock. As shown in Figure 4 the simulation starts with sleeping mode in the night. We can adjust sleeping mode from night to day and also from day to night.

After *night_cycle seconds* the state *night 1* exits its state goes in new state which is day cycle. It is represented in Figure 3. When the program finishes its day cycle, the lights on junction take it sleeping mode again.

To adjust proper green wave we should start with sleeping mode. Distance and cycle of time is shown in Table 1.

Table 1: *Distance Between Crosses and Time for Green Wave Depends on Vehicle Velocity*

traffic cross	distance(m)	Green wave(km/h)	vehicle velo.(m/s)	spent time(sec)	cycle of time(sec)
1st cross					50
2nd cross	500	45	12.5	40	50
3rd cross	400	45	12.5	32	50
4th cross	300	45	12.5	24	50
5th cross	250	45	12.5	20	50

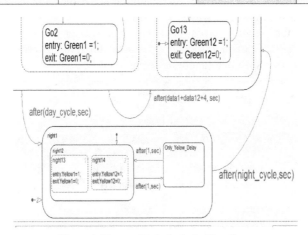

Figure 4. *Sleeping Mode Cycle for First Cross*

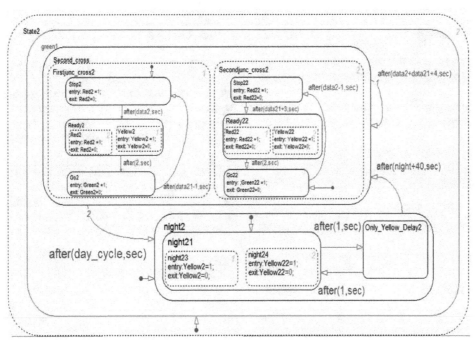

Figure 5: *Sleeping Mode Cycle and Optimization of Green Wave for Second Cross*

It is mentioned before that every cross uses its own clock and simulation starts from night to day state in this simulation. Normally night cycle for each crosses are same but in this simulation night cycle on specific cross is different than others for green wave. Also cycle time and vehicle velocity should be constant as shown in Table 1. Now distance is only variable parameter for synchronization of green wave. It is explained before Ci, as number of cross. New variable is;

Distance between cross (meter), Cik , $\sum_{i=1}^{n}$, n ∈ N and k=i+1, for example when i=5;

C56 means that distance between fifth and sixth crosses.

Spend time from one cross to other (seconds), Sik

$$Sik = \frac{Cik}{Vehicle\ Velocity} \qquad (3)$$

It can be embedded to simulation which has five different crosses as shown in Figure 1. Crosses must be delayed to turn day cycle except first cross for green wave. For example: in Figure 6, second cross time for night cycle is *night+40 seconds.* Sik is equal to 40 as calculated in equation (3) shown in Table 1 and i=1.

When the program is executed, the simulation begins sleeping mode which let vehicles pass without red light hit at nights, and after *night_cycle* it is going on day cycle. The night cycle for cross one is equal to *night_cycle* but the rest of crosses are not if it is wanted to modify green wave, it must be set up night cycle for second cross as *night_cycle*+40 seconds. The day cycle starts for second cross after that time and the second cross specified junction

is joined to green wave as shown in Figure 6. We should also set up night cycle time for other crosses with adding spent time which is calculated equation (3) as shown in Table 1

Green wave application is set up only second junctions of all crosses which were assumed critical. The rest of three crosses for green wave can be modified like in Figure 6 just adding green spent time in Table 1. After *night + 40 seconds* the simulation represents lights of led as shown in Figure 7a. After night seconds, the first cross starts its day simulation. In Figure 7b we can see the day simulation of all crosses after passing specified time in Table 1. And all second junctions of crosses were modified to green wave situation.

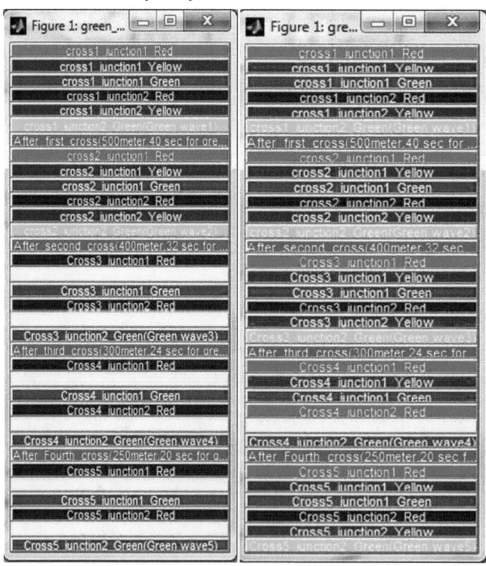

a. *After night−40 seconds*   b. *After Total Specified Time for Green Wave*

Figure 6. *Simulation of LEDs for Green Wave Application*

2.3. Dynamic Change of Signal and Modified to Green Wave

Dynamically change of signal in the traffic is an important situation over the past years in the parallel of

increasing vehicle on the roads. Developing technology help to learn number of passing vehicles at intersection and getting data for processing to the next intersection on the traffic. This data can be used to modify signal for next intersections to prevent drivers from traffic jam. Some kind of counters are video cameras; Real-time Recognition and Re-identification of Vehicles from Video Data with high Re-identification Rate[8] and metallic mass detector, the sensing element is placed just below the road [6].

This section is about representation dynamical change of signal depends on traffic volume at one intersection and modified the simulation again depends on green wave. So, the flow of traffic and green wave mustn't be affected by changing dynamically and instantaneously.

Dynamical change should be updated specified cross. For example, first cross. New variable will be defined for representation number of vehicle on specified cross and junction shown in Figure 8. There is a slider picture called as "*traffic volume at first cross.*"

Mathematical model of dynamic change;

Traffic volume on specified cross for dynamical change of signal, $Vdyna$,

Dynamic green wave time (seconds), Di;   i: cross number.

In this simulation critical vehicle volume is 40 as shown in Figure 7 as "*dynamic1>40*". It can be also thought number of vehicle waits for green signal on specified junction.

If $Vdyna,i$= 40, i=1 then turns signal to red for other junction which lights green led and turns signal to green for this junction (i=1) then let vehicles pass. For green wave update; Sik should be modified which was defined before as "*Spend time for green wave from one cross to other*" to update green wave synchronization.

If Vdyna,i = 40 then

$$Di=\sum_{i=1}^{n} Sik - 1, \quad i : number of cross \quad (4)$$

This will be used for new transition to update green wave as shown in Figure 9.

D3= $\sum_{i=1}^{3} Sik - 1$ means S12 +S23 -1 equal to 71 seconds as shown in transition.

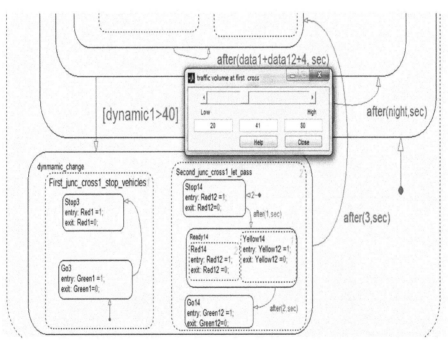

Figure 7. Representation of Dynamical Change of Traffic Volume on First Cross

Using dynamical gain box, as shown in Figure 7, program can be thought like a counter of vehicle. It was been specified range of vehicle number before the simulation. During the simulation a junction which is specified before turns its light to red and after a while the number of vehicle at this junction increase dramatically then it will slide dynamic gain as if sending digital signal from vehicle counter machine to signal process port. This change of signal triggers states as shown in Figure 8 and let the signal turns to green at specified junction.

After change of traffic volume at first junction, the rest of junctions should be affected to modify this simulation for green wave. Figure 7 represents what would happen on third cross when traffic volume at first junction was changed.

It was discussed about sleeping mode previous section. After sleeping mode of traffic light, state of simulation works properly for green wave application. *Dyna3* in Figure 8 simulates its default states parallel with main states simulation. From default state to *adjust_green_wave* depends only *[dynamic1>40]*. When traffic volume changes at first cross it means that volume is larger than 40 vehicles. Dynamic slider, in Figure 7, is moved to the right. Then the main state on first cross goes in to sub state, *dynamic_change,* at the same time default *dyna3* on third cross go in to *adjust_green_wave* in Figure 8. In the sub state of first cross, first junction lights green led and second junction lights red led, then first cross' light turns red light after 1 second and second junction lights green led after 3 seconds to let vehicles pass. After 3 seconds of triggering dynamic gain the first cross turns to initial condition again it means that red led for first junction and green led for second junction on cross one. The rest of other main crosses don't affect this condition until specified time. They progress their duty of modifying green wave but it is not correct because of broken of green wave time with chancing signal at first cross at any time. Analyze of 3rd cross in Figure 8. Why it was specified *71 second*? After 3 seconds of dynamical change 1st cross turns its initial condition. On 3rd cross to turn its initial condition takes 75 seconds. Difference seconds between these cross is 72 seconds, in Table 1, which make 3rd cross modify for green wave after 1st cross start simulation. Preventing of accident it should be modified other crosses for example after

changing traffic volume it is not known which led lights after 71 second for 3rd cross. It is better to create if transition after specified time as shown in Figure 8. If *Green3==1* then go into *Adjust_green_cross3_1* change *Go3* to *Red3* for first junction and after 2 seconds change *Red32* to *Ready32 and* 2 seconds after change *Ready32* to *Green32*. After 4 seconds coming into *day3* turn to initial condition and join to green wave. If *Green3* doesn't equal to 1 means that *Green32* led lights and go on to light green led for *Green32* until 4 second then turn to initial condition and join green wave. It can be seen that total spend time for initial condition for 3rd cross is 75 seconds.

In summary, it be can modified the conditions and states for other crosses and make sure for green wave synchronize.

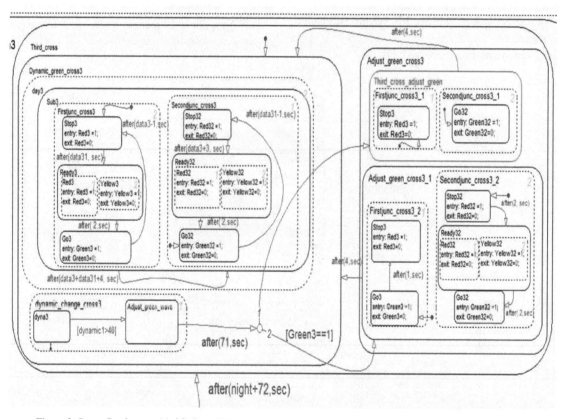

Figure 8: *States Condition to Modify Green Wave on Second Cross after Dynamically Change of Specified Intersection*

3. Conclusion

This study has presented a model for simulation of traffic control and signal. Application and simulation of green wave and dynamical change of signal depends on traffic volume at essential intersection.

In the section of simulation of traffic light, it was firstly discussed about importance of cycle time. The cycle time of one intersection is one of the most important parameters for proper planning and flowing of traffic. Also in this section, it was defined input cycle time and let it changed depending on traffic volume at intersection via using Matlab function as shown in Figure 3. Then it was mentioned about five crosses simulation which execute concurrently in away using parallel states. In this section

we also demonstrated simulation of one cross in hierarchy as shown in Figure 4. After that it was dealt with how green wave application works and mentioned about its benefits in addition to them it was mentioned how people's life is affected in a good way by green wave application. Then it was discussed how to modify our state flow chart to green wave.

Finally, it was adjusted state flow chart to change signal dynamically at specified intersection and learnt how to overcome problems due to dynamical change of signal at any time causes to spoil green wave cycle.

As a result, Matlab/Simulink/Stateflow suits well to representation, simulation and adjustment of dynamic changes. This study may be guided for development of future projects about traffic signal and control systems.

Nomenclature

i : Specified cross, $i \in Z^+$

j: number of junction on specified cross.

: Number of cross

: Volume distribution on a junction weekly or monthly; $j=1$ first junction, $j=2$ second junction

: Cycle time in each cross (seconds)

: Signal time for red light (seconds)

: Signal time for green light (seconds)

$C'i$: Cross in simulation

$S'ijm$: State duration in simulation (seconds); $m=1$ for red light, $m=2$ for green light

: Distance between crosses (meter); $k=i+1$

: Spent time for green wave one cross to other cross

$Vdyna$, : Traffic volume on specified cross for dynamical change of signal

: Dynamic green wave time (seconds)

References

[1] http://www.ideafinder.com/history/inventions/trafficlight.htm

[2] J. Niittymäki, M. Pursula. Signal Control Using Fuzzy Logic; *Fuzzy Sets and Systems,* Vol. 116(1), 2000, pp. 11–22

[3] A.S.M. Rahman, N.T. Ratrout. Review of the Fuzzy Logic Based Approach in Traffic Signal Control: Prospects in Saudi; *Journal of Transportation Systems Engineering and Information Technology*, Vol. 9(5), 2009, pp. 58–70

[4] I. Kosonen. Multi-Agent Fuzzy Signal Control Based on Real-Time Simulation; *Transportation Research Part C: Emerging Technologies*, Vol. 11(5), 2003, pp. 389–403

[5] W. M. Wey. Model Formulation and Solution Algorithm of Traffic Signal Control in an Urban Network; *Computers Environment and Urban Systems*, Vol. 24(4), 2000, pp.355-378

[6] M. J. Caruso, L. S. Withanawasam. Vehicle Detection and Compass Applications using AMR Magnetic Sensors; *Sensors Expo Proceedings*, May 1999, pp.477-489.

[7] K. Tavladakis, N. C. Voulgaris. Development of Autonomous Adaptive Traffic Control System in ESIT'99; *The European Symposium on Intelligent Techniques*, 1999.

[8] Rate, Woesler, Richard. Real-time Recognition and Reidentification of Vehicles from Video Data with high Reidentification; *8th World Multiconference on Systemics*, 2004, pp.347-352

[9] T. Y. Liao, R. B. Machemehl. Development of an Aggregate Fuel Consumption Model for Signalized Intersections; *Transportation Research Board of the National Academies*, Vol. 16(41), 1998, pp.9-18

[10] A. Warberg, J. Larseny, R. M. Jorgensen. Green Wave Traffic Optimization- A survey Informatics and Mathematical Modelling; *Technical University of Denmark*, DTU, 2008, pp.1-23

[11] H. Rakha, Y. Ding, Impact of stops on vehicle fuel consumption and emissions; *Journal of Transportation Engineering*, Vol.129 (1), 2003, pp.23–32,

[12] I. D. Greenwood C. R. Bennett. The Effects of Traffic Congestion on Fuel Consumption; *Road & Transport Research*, Vol. 5, No. 2, June 1996, pp. 18-31.

[13] C.Gershenson. Self-organizing Traffic Lights; *Complex Systems*, Vol.16 (1), 2005, pp.29-53

[14] Stateflow User's Guide the Math Works, Inc.

[15] http://www.wired.com/wiredscience/2010/09/traffic-lights-adapt/

[16] D.Greenwood, B. Burdiliak, I. Trencansky, H. Armbruster. Green Wave Distributed Traffic Intersection Control; *Proceedings of the 8th International Conference on Autonomous Agents and Multiagent Systems*, Vol.2, 2009, pp.1413-1414.

18

Models and frameworks for a successful virtual learning environment (VLE) implementation

Ayman Ahmed AlQudah

Deanship of E-Learning and Distance Learning, University of Dammam, Ad Dammam, Saudi Arabia

Email address:
alqudah@hotmail.com

Abstract: E-learning has become one of the major components in education processes, and it is one of the most important elements in which universities can attain a competitive advantage. Virtual learning environment (VLE), which is considered as a subpart of the LMS, allows educators and educational systems to go beyond place and ti.me in communication with every student. For this reason universities focus on having LMS, for it helps users access educational sources that is not only reliable, but also has the possibility to be integrated with other systems available at the university. The paper highlights and explores the different theories and methodologies related to implementing and switching virtual learning environment successfully. Many previous studies, framework, theories and models have been reviewed; those models and frameworks identify how successful the implementation of virtual learning environments is in higher educational institutes.

Keywords: E-Learing, Virtual Learning, Educational Sources Online

1. Introduction

Virtual learning environment (VLE) does not refer to or specifically mean educational site, nor a system including 3D or virtual reality classes and rooms. It is not also restricted to distance learning or to well-structured information spaces, its purpose is to enrich class room activities also use multiple pedagogical approaches, and different technologies should be integrated to create the VLE. It is not synonymous to a virtual campus; a virtual campus is the sub part of VLE (Beastall and Walker, 2007). Between these over general and over-specific definitions the VLE could be a mixture of these definitions, which are social space that contains text-based interfaces to the most complex 3D, and the integration of multiple tools which reproduce most functions thatcan be found on a real campus. These points illustrate the fact that implementing VLE is a big challenge, and this is the core aim of this paper: to implement and change management processes related to switching from one VLE to another or adapt a new VLE that will be assessed and critically evaluated in the next pages.

2. Proposed Frameworks Provided by Alhogail and Mirza (2011), to Successfully Implement VLE on a Higher Educational Institution

This model represents the summary while relying on approaches, research and ways that certain universities conduct to create and build a model that is appropriate for their needs and is cost effective. Some of these universities are York University, the University of Lincoln, H.P. University, and Oxford Books university as shown in table 1 below:

Table 1. A comparison of the carrying out of each task of the frame work in four universities VLE implementation case, Alhogail and Mirza (2011)

The Task	York University	University of Lincoln	Oxford brooks University	H.P. University
Analysis of institutional context			✓	✓
Sufficiency of resources				✓
Selection of the VLE that support the language of academic staff and student	None of these came across this task as in all the four universities cases ,language was not problem			
Getting people support and ownership	✓	✓	✓	✓
Creation of the user coalition group that cover all stakeholders	✓	✓	✓	
Design training programs to empower people to effect change	✓	✓	✓	✓
Creation of the change agent to communication the change vision	✓		✓	✓
Increasing the awareness the of the selected VLE	✓	✓	✓	✓
Setting of clear targets			✓	
Establishing VLE help desk	✓	✓		
Gradual implementation of the VLE across the university	✓			

This model (Figure1) has been built in accordance with actual experience and practices, and is built by higher educational institutions that implemented VLE successfully. This model consists of eight distinguished, but interactive functions, and were applied correctly. As a result of proper implementation, their success is expected. The following paragraphs provide a brief summary about each stage of the models:

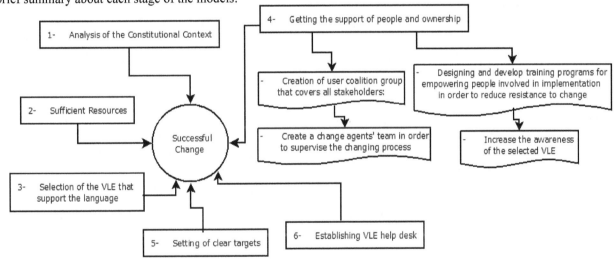

Figure 1. Frameworks to successful implement VLE in higher education institution that is based on change management approach

2.1. Analysis of the Constitutional Context

This primary stage is considered to be an important stage due to its analysis of environmental change, which is counted as a vital phase in any changing process (Sharpe et al, 2006). An analysis of weakness, strength and opportunity in the institution's objectives and plans are necessary in order to be compatible with the expected changes made by the institution. The institution determines for initiatiation, especially in VLE change.

This change is based on a proposed framework, initiated according to a bottom-up planning strategy, which means that each faculty dean is aware of it, and participates in the changing process. In addition, there are deans who are aware of changing benefits and are obliged to see it through.

2.2. Sufficient Resources

According to Beastall, and Walker (2007), prior change process intuition must be assured of having the necessary element that leads to the project or change required by the institution's determination to initiate; such elements include

the solid infrastructure available in an institution, and skilled operators' training, technical support, and financial resources. Lacking one of them may lead to the failure of the VLE project.

2.3. Selection of the VLE that support the language

It is the process of selecting VlE that supports multiple languages. In addition, this must be taken into serious consideration when it is chosen for countries in which the English language is a second language. Thus, a language barrier should not affect the implementation of VLE and limits its effectiveness (Ardito et al, 2005).

When selecting VLE, there are some critical elements which must be taken into consideration in order to have a successful project. These elements include desirable functions such as video chat, white board, lecture capturer, and calendar. Some countries use the lunar calendar such as Saudi Arabia, while others use the solar calendar (Alhogail and Alhogail, 2011). Thus, the chosen VLE must overcome such elements which may hinder its success.

2.4. Getting the support of people and ownership

It is natural to have resistance to change especially when it comes to replacing IS, or selecting a particular VLE (Cook, 2009). Therefore, such resistance must be taken seriously by VLE developers, and make their best effort to reduce such resistance in order to provide a smooth transition (Dublin, 2004). The model shown below suggests some steps that may be considered by developers to achieve this objective

- Creating a user coalition group that covers all stakeholders: the main objective of this step according to the model is to gather as much possible information as we can from all personnel that may be affected, and be involved in the project especially in the system change and adoption, such as technical people, students, instructors, involved managers, registrars and others in order to reveal the expected problems. Hence, suggested solutions will be provided; furthermore, providing these information to a senior management with all ongoing developments will guide the process, and assure the senior management what these stakeholders want from the system, what benefits they may obtain, and how to deal with their concerns as well.
- Designing and developing training programs for empowering people involved in implementation will reduce resistance to change. The objective of the suggested empowering programs provide staff with necessary computer skills in order to handle the system properly such as: Workshops, seminars, training programs etc. Computer skills are not limited to creation of the content in the VLE, chat discussion groups, and others.
- Changing the agents' team in order to supervise the changing process: every successful project change should have a team whose sole purpose is to supervise the change process (Russell, 2009) by opening all communication channels with the people involved and with top managements. The process facilitates the change project while eliminating or reducing obstacles; thus, achieving the major goals that perceives the vision of the people and management involved with change.
- Increasing the awareness of the selected VLE: this step involves online engagement between students and instructors. The purpose of this step is to minimize resistance to change.

2.5. Setting clear targets

- The availability of benchmarks and quantitative measurements are vital to the success of any project in order to determine the success of VLE's implementation strategy (sharp et al 2006). For example, we have a clear target by determining the number of courses which must be implemented and uploaded to the institution's VLE system by the end of a specific date (by the end of June 15, we must

have 50 courses implemented on VLE). While taking into consideration any difficult problems arising at this stage, the problem should be detected and solved.

2.6. Establishing VLE help desk

The aim of this step is to provide assistance for those who encounter problems with the new system. Gradual implementation of VLE across the institution aims at building new systems gradually while making use of the stakeholder's feedback in every step. By doing so, there will be a chance at solving arising problems and facilitating the implementation (Alhogail and Alhogail, 2011).

2.7. Model Evaluation and Critical Review

The above explained model aims at how to manage and support the change towards the implementation of VLE, which focuses on the importance of bottom-up change strategy. By doing so, resistance of change is reduced and allows the stakeholders at the bottom of the hierarchy to discuss the changes, aims, and challenges. Furthermore, this model provides a road map on how to implement VLE in the institution while taking into consideration change management and stakeholders who are involved in the process of change by granting them an opportunity to express their opinion and concerns.

Although, this model was reviewed properly, several previous studies were conducted on actual experiments done by universities that initiated change; however, it does not determine the project's implementation realistically. In order to have strong evidence that this model adds to the value of strategies implemented on higher educational institutions throughout the world, it is important to gather all types of stakeholders with different backgrounds that may not lead to a homogeneous response and understanding. Plus, having these stakeholders share their skills and experiences on how to implement VLE may constitute a challenge and difficulty (Ward et al, 2010).

3. IEEE Draft Standard for Learning Technology, Learning Technology Systems Architecture LTSA

IEEE, Institute of Electrical and Electronics Engineers, is considered to be one of the most important and largest establishments that set forward influential standardizational bodies at word level (Derntl and Motschnig-Pitrik, 2004), Electronic Education Technology is one of the applications that IEEE has put forward, which is called the draft standard or the learning technology system architecture (LTSA) according to this standard model. This is shown in the figure below (2):

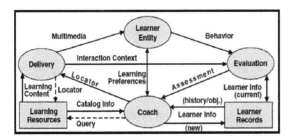

Figure 2. Learning Technology Systems Architecture (LTSA) system components. (IEEE, 2001)

This model aims at facilitating and dividing e-learning systems and its subsystems, and the ways they interact with each other. This model shows a very broad approach in creating strategy to develop and build VLE (Derntl and Motschnig-Pitrik, 2004). The model primarily focuses on the technical view point. This means if any company or individual is willing to create this system, they must make use of this model as an essential reference to deal with in the way systems interact with each other.

This system consists of three components:

  a- Process: Learning, coaching, evaluating, and delivering.
  b- Stores : Learner records and learning resources
  c- Flows: multimedia, behavior, assessment, interaction context, locator, learning content, catalogue information, etc.

These components are explained as follows:

- Learning entity: it may be a single learner, multiple learners, or a human element that process and deal with the rest of the components through multimedia. Multimedia is received in a learner's entity (Pdf, Word, etc). The learner's entity reacts with multimedia through observation and evaluation, as his or her behavior will be subjected to evaluating the entity. In other words, when actually building a system, a learner's entity needs a computer screen to submit multimedia to the learner, or by any other means that would help the learner's entity to understand and comprehend the content.
- Evaluation entity: theoretically, evaluation entity provides measurements of learning. To process or assess for instance, a coach expert uses a certain test, such as a multiple choice test, thus the functions of the evaluation entity are determined as the correct responses through an interaction context and link with a learner's current information send the results to the coach in assessment form.
- Coach entity: represents the learner's retrieval of information from various sources such as learner's information, learner's preferences, and learning content the learner receives through multimedia
- Learning resources: it's the place where the learner's educational level of students is stored, like experience, education or learning instruments such as assignments, tutorials, videos, pdf, etc. In addition, learning resources constitute primarily a place for retrieving

learning material content. To shed more light on this subject, below is an illustrative example: query an order for mathematics. The query returns a set of information relevant to mathematics, which is distributed according to certain aspects that involves mathematics as video or pdf of mathematics.

- Delivery: Represents the concept of information delivery which is obtained from learning resources to learner entity through multimedia or information learning resources in order to evaluate interactive contexts.
- Learner record: it is the place to store learner's information, such as past learning experience. The results of current assignments are recorded with the students' current performance.

3.1. Model Evaluation and Critically Review

This model provides excellent approaches and practical ones in order to understand the interaction process of the learning management system (LMS). Furthermore, a full description of the function is provided by each element for the purpose of having successful LMS software. The model primary focuses on how the system's elements interact with each other, regardless of the rest of the elements that virtual learning environment (VLE) implementation requires in pedagogical elements (Derntl and Motschnig-Pitrik, 2004).

This model is based on technical points of view while ignoring the aspects of other important elements such as social-technical and psychological aspects in VLE implementation. However, IEEE LAST standards can be used in evaluation learning management system to see whether this system is compatible with LAST standerds due to its being a pure technical point of view.

4. Saeedikiya et al. (2010) Model

According to this model, Saeedikiya suggests six stages to implement e-learning in traditional universities. Any process of establishing an e-learning system at any university should go through six major steps as shown below:

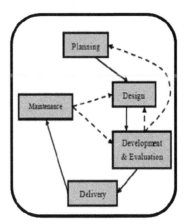

Figure 3. Sequences of stages of e-learning implementation according to Saeedikiya et al. (2010)

The Following is a Summary of the Model Steps:

1. Diagnoses: it consists of the evaluation of the current institutional status of the of E-learning system, followed by an establishment of a financial, educational and strategic plan for change. This step requires the participation and cooperation of institutional mangers, business managers, and E-learning experts.

2. Decision-making: it consists of the LMS's decision making to fulfill the university's needs. This suggests that LMS must determine and clarify the students' needs and their expectations from the system (Ardito et al, 2005). In addition, it is used to determine the financial and technical resources of the university.

3. Design: this step calls for the participation of E-learning experts, technical experts, subject matter experts, and institutional designers. The design step aims at content design learning to use the E-learning system effectively (Ssekakubo et al, 2011).

4. Development: establishing a pilot project of the system is created in order to observe the system's functions, and to resolve problems that may emerge during implementation, in addition to conducting a system evaluation after its testing. This step aims at helping students and instructors in their dealings with the system, and to ensure the accuracy of the way in which they deal with the system.

5. Post-delivery: follows up the E-learning system development through student and instructor's training, and providing them with technical support in order to have their feedback.

By understanding in steps, it is clear that the model focuses on the following items primarily when establishing E-learning systems:

- The building of an E-content must be conducted by experts, and not through arbitrary ways that depend on instructors alone. Thus, experts should participate in content building process.

- Personal training and guidance on best utility of the system.

- Have information technological staff in transformation and implementation of E-learning system, because consequently they will be the ones in charge of managing the systems at their universities.

This model is similar to another model developed by Khan, (2004). Khan's model is divided into six steps with three sequences:

- Content development consists of planning, design and development of an E-learning system.
- Content delivery consists of evaluation and delivery of the E-learning system.
- Content maintenance deals with maintenance of an E-learning system.

This model introduces a simple way in understanding the process of the E-learning system at a university level, and the role of various personnel in the building process of an E-learning, while taking into consideration the educators' role in the success of the E-learning system.

Table 2. Stages of e-learning implementation, According to saeedikiya et al. (2010) and Khan

According to Saeedikiya et al (2010)	Diagnosis	Decision Making	Design	Development	Delivery	Post Delivery
According to Khan (2004)	planning		Design	development and evaluation	Delivery	Maintenance

4.1. Model Evaluation and Critical Review

Although this model is simple and easy to use, especially in strategic planning for VLE implementation, the model needs various experts with different backgrounds such as E-learning experts, technical experts, subject matter experts, software evaluation experts, and business management experts. In addition, all of these needed experts will raise the costs, and cause contradictory points when implementing VLE.

5. Khan's Frameworks

This model provides an idea on how planning is set forward, along with E-learning development, management and assessment.

Blended learning is integrated in E-learning with traditional learning (face to face) in one framework. E-learning instruments are employed in teaching without abandoning actual and accustomed learning, which is physically attending the class room (Hameed et al 2009).

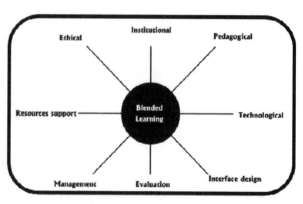

Figure 4. Khan's framework (Singh, 2003)

Khan's framework consists of the following major steps: Institutional, pedagogical, technological, recourses support, ethical, interface, design, evaluation and management. Each one of the above mentioned steps represent a set of sub steps and issues that must be dealt with in order to make blended learning successful (Khan, 2006).

5.1. Institutional: Consists of Three Dimensions

This sub step dimension focuses on examining the users' expectation from the system users such as (academic staff, students, and administrative staff) to know what users expect and reveal their demands, which are considered to be essential steps towards system development.

The second dimension focuses on academic aspects of system building and change process, in terms of the availability of electronic and scientific contents to be delivered through a system project used for developing the organization level.

The last dimension focuses on the administrative (managerial) affairs in the organization, which relates to the readiness of the organization's infrastructure. Thu author sees the significance of the availability of a strategic plan for the organization, and the extent of human resources and budget readiness in the organization can offer.

5.2. Pedagogical

It reveals the significance of the educational parameter that is extended in the building and transforming of the blended learning. This step aims at insuring the educational content which intends to provide objectivity in learning. To illustrate further, a student is requested to conduct an experiment in the chemical substance reaction, there must be an ability to program E-learning that allows students to conduct this experiment through some tools as E-simulation.

5.3. Technological

This step ensures that the organization possesses hardware and software along with technological skills are necessary for building the system and dealing with software; hardware such as servers and networks, software such as LMS (learning management system) and LCMS (learning content management system).

5.4. Interface Design

Blended learning is utilized in many universities (Hameed et al 2009). The student's lecture is online, and he attends a traditional classroom for the other. At this phase, concentration is on the general appearance which allows access to learn materials with an attractive appearance.

5.5. Evaluation

Evaluation is a standard measurement that determines errors. It is the location and extent that one reaches in a system's application. Thus evaluation is important in order to know the usability extent of the system (Nokelainen, 2006). Without conducting evaluation, the university will not be able to know whether it has reached the intended level in the E-learning system. In addition, assessments determine the barriers that obstruct the benefits of the system and

determines the defective place (Rovai et al, 2008).

5.6. Management

This step ensures that all of the steps in the system application are functioning in accordance with the project plan, and their projected timing and all that are involved in the change process are functioning integratively in order for the intended change and implementation of an E-learning system to reach a safer level.

5.7. Resources Support

This phase is intended to provide assurance to different resources available for the change process. Resources for students and instructors include online and offline material content. In addition, this phase is created for the students' convenience in learning, so they would feel comfortable in asking for help when they need their E-learning process.

5.8. Ethical

This model insists that in the process of designing and implementing the system's cultural diversity, the students' mode of learning and requirements are involved. Furthermore, this phase aims at providing system users with a good attitude, respect for privacy, and intellectual property rights (Khan, 2004).

5.9. Model Evaluation and Critical Review

Khan's framework provides a comprehensive vision on how to build and develop blended learning systems computable with learning objectives of the institutions, which are framed within a variable of "learning quality." How to achieve a flexible learning environment for a learner wherever they are? The answer to this question is the key for understanding Khan's framework. This model goes deeper into subjects and aspects with big details, for instance, the model consists of eight steps explained with extensive details, and each step has several issues. These issues have more branches and details needed to deal with. The model brings forward a new theme that is ethical in VLE implementations and adoption, when no other model or framework touches upon ethical issues.

Khan's model discusses change from different aspects as mentioned earlier; it is an extensive model that deals with the VLE's development and implementation from many angles, such as management, student-instructor interaction, and technicality. This model can be used in the strategic planning for implementing VLE.

6. Systematic Change Management Strategies for an E-learning System Ghavifekr and Hussin (2011)

Ghavifekr and Hussin (2011) provide the overview of the main, sub-themes and sub-sub themes of the systematic change management strategies for an E-learning system.

This study provides in depth analysis of management functions, including planning, organizing, guiding, and monitoring the E-learning system as shown in table 3.

This model is based on Malaysian experiences that focused on transforming into an open distance learning system. The notion of the model reflects primarily on the major elements for building an E-learning system, and they are: planning, organizing, guiding, and monitoring.

Table 3. *Main, sub, and sub-theme of systematic change management strategies for an e-learning system*

Main Theme	Sub-Themes	Sub-sub Themes
Elearning system	planning	- Elearning system continuous upgrading - E-support effectiveness - E-tools-services ,E-facilities - E-budgeting
	organizing	- E-leadership and e-environment maintenance - E-training programs and profession development strategies - E-content and E-learning materials
	Guiding	- Advanced objectives for technology management - Effective E-learning platform in ODL Organization
	Monitoring	- Monitoring the utilization and evaluate the effectiveness - Continues monitoring of the systems security and maintenance

This phase depends heavily on the availability of clear vision and strategic planning of E-learning systems.

The significance of clear vision relies on the answer of this question: "What to change?" While the strategic planning lies in the answer of "how to change? "(Bateman and Snell, 2007).

The Planning is conducted on four elements:
- E-learning System Continuous upgrading
- E-support effectiveness
- E-tools, E-services, and E-facilities
- E-sources for the entire system
- Continuous Monitoring of System's Security and Maintenance
- E-budgeting management

6.1. Organizing E-learning System in Two Elements

a- The organization of structure.
b- The organization of arrangement.

These aim to transform the organization in a way that makes it ready and acceptable to change. The infrastructure of the organization in particular relies on skilled workers, financial sources, and E-content.

Organization is achieved through the availability of these elements:
- E-leadership and E-environment maintenance
- E-training programs & professional development strategies

- E-content and E-learning materials

6.2. Guiding

Consists of two major steps:
- Advanced Objectives for Technology Management
- Effective E-learning Platform in ODL Organization

Guiding in general, E ensures that the two steps of advanced objectives and effectives of E-learning are complementing each other, aiming to achieve common goals with the presence of conflict between the two steps. Common goals are reflected in cost effectiveness and flexibility (Poole and Van de Ven, 2004).

6.3. Monitoring

The aim of monitoring is ensuring that the objective suggested in this model can be achieved, and knowing the actual performance of various departments involved in the change process will aid the progress. This can be achieved by the following two steps:
- Monitoring the utilization and evaluating effectiveness.
- Continuous monitoring of system's security and maintenance

6.4. Model Evaluation and Critical Review

The model focuses on quality of leadership and skilled management to direct the change and provide policies and strategies to help upper management ensure a successful change process. Also to focus primarily on strategic planning of E-learning without dealing sufficiently with technological matters of the issues. The focus on management of change gives the guidance and instructions the steps and policies taken into consideration, along with elements during change process sent to top and middle management.

7. Kotter's Change Model

It is possible to summarize this model by stating that the successful change in an organization is its need for sound planning, set by a solid foundation for change process in order to facilitate implementation and elevate the level of a higher success, whereas the success of organizations lie in the eight steps of the following model; thus, an organization will be able to enjoy a real change as expected:

Kotter's change model consists of eight steps, each leads to a successful change process. The first four steps focus on defreezing the organization, while the next three steps focus on change implantation, and the last step involves refreezing of a new culture in the organization.

The summary of Kotter's model is as follows:
1. Establish a sense of urgency, an occuring change, the majority of involved people will show a good favor towards it (Rovai et al, 2008). In order to have a sense of urgency, subordinates must talk and show a willingness for change.

2. Forming a powerful guiding coalition team would convince subordinates to make the change required for strong leadership with the support from upper management in an organization; whereas, it is not sufficient to mange change without leading it (Kotter, 1998). The leadership is in need for a group of influential people who promote change, by doing so, change will occur smoothly.

3. Create a clear vision expressed in simple forms; concepts and nations of change must be connected with the overall vision of the organization (Menchaca et al, 2003). The vision idea can be understood and accepted by people easily, because the clear vision facilitates the understanding of work expected from people involved.

4. Communicating the vision: primary purpose of this step is that whatever is done for this vision determines the success or failure of the organization's continuous communication of this vision throughout its organization, as it includes details in what the organization does. Thus, all employees will comprehend it entirely.

5. Empowering others to act in the vision: according to the author, following the previous steps allows one to reach an actual change. When talking about vision and establishing people's commitment at all levels of the organization with the support of top management permits the start of change.

In this step according to the author's organization, one must determine obstacles and eliminate them by doing the flowing:

- Determine the change in leaders and functions which leads to a safe change.
- Review the organization structure in order to guarantee it's appropriateness with the vision.
- Know and reward those who helped the change to occur.
- Determine those who resist changes and help them see the impotence of this change.

6. Plan for creating a short team that aims to win and succeed, this is the greatest motivator and drive (Poole et al, 2004). As a result, having short term goals will lead to long term goals. The success in short term objectives work as an additional motivational factor for all those who are involved in the change process.

7. Consolidations gain and make more changes: The early announcement for the success of change causes change failure (Kotter, 1998), where the real change must be managed deeply because swift wins are just the beginning for what must be gained in order to achieve a long term change.

8. Institutionalize the new approaches: in order to anchor the new culture caused by change in organization, change must be an essential part of organizational activates, along with the continuation of supporting change by change leaders.

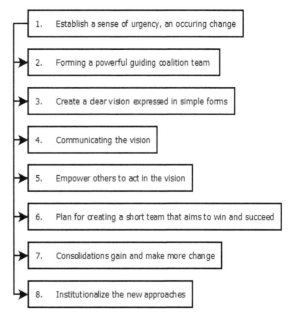

Figure 5. *Kotter's change model (1998)*

7.1. Model Evaluation and Critical Review

Although the model primarily focuses on change theories in terms of management, however, it is proper when implementing change from a management point of view. In addition, the model focuses on management and preparing individuals for implementing change. The model does not discuss technology's effects on the changes of the organization. The model provides strategic approaches for change to occur and change management. Thus, it has been utilized widely throughout the world. Talks about change from a sole and pure management perspective is what Kotter provides, he generally guides the steps required to initiate an effective change.

8. CSU Change Model

Carlo Sturt University is the first Australian university to establish an open electronic learning system on January 2008 (Uys et al, 2007). This model reflects a three years practical experience of change and innovation by the university during its development of E-learning systems from 2007 – 2009.

This model is based on Kotter's model as explained earlier, yet Kotter's model focuses on change management. The CSU model consists of eight major steps which does not need a specific order for implementation (Uys, 2010). Whereas, it is possible to start with any step without abiding to order, however, it is possible to implement these steps simultaneously.

Prior to explaining this model, it is worth mentioning that this model is characterized by two major strategic factors in establishing E-learning:

a- Building E-learning communities.

b- Sharing best practices in E-learning system's implementation.

It is worth mentioning that this model is characterized by a flowing bottom – up strategy. The above two sub steps indicate that the aim of this learning committee is to provide various topics relevant to a university's E-learning system

(CSU interact), discussing them among this committee members such as E-Learning system evaluation, visualizing online content, and attaining an E-portfolio.

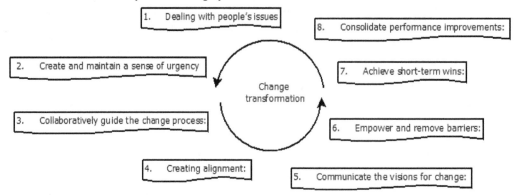

Figure 6. CSU Change model (Uys, 2010)

In regard to sharing best practices, these should be shared with others; it involves various topics relevant to E-learning systems such as course content design. Best practices are considered to be as reference to others because they express the summary of experience towards a certain topic.

Model Steps Summary:

1.   Dealing with people's issues:

It is a stage whereas the model deals with academic staff. Marshall (2004) points out that having academic staff participate or be involved with change process leads to success of change. This stage aims at examining the extent of academic staff readiness to accept the change, and change the way they teach with it; in order to being part of the change or the ownership of the academic staff, their involvement is vital.

2.   Create and maintain a sense of urgency:

This stage clarifies to employees throughout the university that the process of change and the university is in

need for such change, and this change may affect the performance of the university. The creator of this feeling is at top management (Poole et al, 2004). For instance deterring a due date which must be enabled by all academic staff has a site on the E-leaning system that carries out the course or leaning materials.

3.   Collaboratively guide the change process:

Through the activity of the guiding team in various university departments, the change process is coordinated, and this reveal its importance of the aim of this step, which is to gather as many possible of motivated people for the change process.

4.   Creating alignment:

To ensure the success of change process, this change must be harmonized with the university's plan, objectives and vision along with various faculties plan and objectify (Uys et al, 2007).

5.   Communicate the visions for change:

Have staff and students be aware always regarding to the

change and its objectives. The Carlo Sturt University implemented this step through communicating plans, which consists of four elements:

- E-mailing the occurrences of the university's E-learning system that is called CSU interaction.

- Establish communities along with stakeholders to elaborate and communicate the e-learning system.

- University adopts screen savers that display the change and whereabouts at the university.

- University utilizes blogging tools named Yammer which is an open source tool for change promotion. According to Uys (2010), all the above mentioned tools have maintained the spirit of change for three years, and promoted those who were involved and were aware of change's significance.

6.   Empower and remove barriers:

Through training sessions and workshops, computer skills have been archived, while the E-learning system is considered to be needed for many involved users, especially faculty members. This stage aims to determining that obstacles add berries to hinder the application of the system, and this must be removed, especially those elements that accept ways for success.

7.   Achieve short-term wins:

It has been noticed that the university has achieved short short-term wins during application stages throughout the running of the pilot project, which achieved tangible and clear results in regard to functions. The system is able to perform in the future at a university level.

8.   Consolidate performance improvements:

The significance of this stage lies in the assurance that the system is constantly up to date and it's able to perform tasks with competence through establishing a plan to enhance the system continuously and have it subjected to improvements.

8.1. Model Evaluation and Critical Review

The model provides a framework which helps underhand the implementation of change in VLE at the university level. Starting from a strategic vision of change, the university ends up with changes that must be occurred at an individual's level in order to achieve favorable results in VLE application. One of the model's disadvantages lies in the difficulty in establishing team or committees from various interest and different back grounds.

9. Successful System Implementation Factors by Zwass (1998)

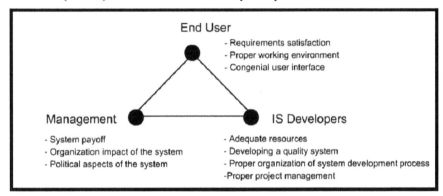

Figure 7. Key agent in information system development

According to Zwass (1998), the factors play a role in successful system implementations that are summarized as seen in figure 8. These steps or seven elements should be used by managements in order to be sure that the implementation of its system is successful, due to the fact that the seven elements represent the successful system of a company that already has the characteristics of being successful. These factors are as follows:

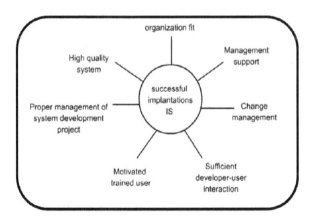

Figure 8. Factors in successful system (Zwass, 1998)

1- Organization fit:

This means to be sure that organization's objectives of the new Information system (IS), along with employees and workers who are affected by the organization orientation towards changes.

2- Management support:

Management support of IS is achieved by providing human resources, financial resources, hardware, and software due to being the essential elements for a module's successful implementation.

3- Change management:

During change occurrences, an organization goes through

According to Zwass (1998), there are three key agents in implementing the information system (IS): End user, management, and the information system developer (figure 7). Each agent has a range of issues associated with it that must be achieved and satisfied in order to accomplish successful implantations of IS. For example: One of the most important issues concerning the end user that the system provides is the desire function they want.

three stages or sequences: Unfreeze Moving, and Refreezing.

A- Unfreeze consists of motivational workers throughout the organization in regard to change, the importance of change and its benefits, along with training employees who are affected by the changes, and who will be in charge of change.

B- Moving is a phase in which the organization moves towards implementing the new system (installing the new system).

C- Refreezing is the adoption of the new system. The new system has become part of an organization. This phase should have a plenty of interaction between management and employees that are extensively used for the purpose of strengthening the system by getting people used to it, and to reduce some employee's resistance to the system (Kotter,1998); Thus, reducing employee resistance is a problem which changes management that should work and reduce it through several means such as training and participating in system implementation.

4- Sufficient interaction between developers and users:

The aim of this stage is to increase user's satisfaction with the system, thus users become independent in solving problems. In order to archieve this goal, a prototype approach should be tried to provide similar functions as the system's functioned by Zwass (1998). It is not costly and it is a fast built prototype, whereas the philosophy of prototyping is based on trying and refining, prototype is used when user's requirement is hard to determine (Richards et al, 2004), whereas it helps in solving this problem by having users participate in determining the system requirement and development.

5- Motivate and train users:

Motivation is a significant factor in the quality and functionality of the system Zwass (1998). Thus, motivating people through training them via workshops and training programs and other means of motivation is a fruitful factor.

6- Proper management of a system development project:

The adaption of the new IS is a significant project which affects many parts of the quantization and carries potential risk (Buchan, 2010), thus, it is devisable to divide the project and implement on step bases.

7- System Quality:

The system must be convenient without causing complications to its users, within a reasonable cost, thus, if a system does not help in solving users' problems or lessen their complicated functions, this system is not accessible. The quality of any system relies upon the degree of use and user satisfaction.

10. Model Evaluation and Critically Review

The model can be used in strategic planning of VLE implementation and adoption. If VLE is considered to be an IS, the model ignores several important aspects of VLE adoption such as pedagogical elements in E-learning, this model discusses how strategic implementations of IS in an organization does not specify for VLE adoption.

11. Summary

Khan's model takes into account many issues to ensure that VLM implementation and education used by LMS shall be effective and will lead to a meaningful blending, learning experience. It is an extensive model that deals with VLE development and implementation from many angles such as management, student- instructor interaction, and technicality. The model brings forward a new theme that is ethical in VLE implementations and adoption, when no other model or framework discussed in literature touches the ethical issues. The proposed model by Ghavifekr and Hussin (2011) focused on identifying how implantation and adoption of VLE is used to open distance learning (ODL). The framework proposed by Alhogail and Mirza (2011) provides comprehensive vision of how to implement and adopt VEL. But it does not determine the implementation of the project realistically or actually in order to have strong evidence from the model. The given evidence adds value to strategies implemented on higher educational institutions. The framework is not implemented on the real world to find out the suitability of the theoretical framework with a practical framework.

Although Saeedikiya et al. (2010) model is simple and easy to use, especially in strategic planning for VLE implementation. However the model insists that in order to successfully implement and adopt VLE, there must be a large number of experts involved in the process of change. Various experts with different backgrounds such as E-learning experts, technical experts, subject matter experts, software evaluation experts, and business management experts are relevant. In addition, all these needed experts would raise the costs and cause contradictory points of view in implementing VLE.

Zwass (1998) provides a framework that illustrates the factors that play a role in a successful information system IS implementation. The model ignores several important aspects of VLE adoption such as pedagogical elements in E-learning. This model discuses how to make strategic implement IS in organizations, while it does not specify for VLE adoption. The model can be used in strategic planning of VLE implementation and adopt if VLE is considered to be an IS.

IEEE Draft Standard for Learning Technology and the Learning Technology Systems Architecture LTSA aim at facilitating and dividing LMS systems and its subsystems, and the ways they interact with each other, regardless of the rest of the elements that virtual learning environment (VLE) implementation requires such pedagogical elements (Derntl and Motschnig-Pitrik, 2004). This model shows a very broad approach as to create strategy to develop and build VLE.

The CSU Model is based on Kotter's change model and reflects the Carlo Sturt University three years of practical experience of change and innovation by the university during the development of its VLE system. This study focused mainly on human issues that affect LMS using from students and staff perspective. The use of LMS is one of the core elements that affect VLE success. Khan's model consists of eight main stages to assure that the institution have a successful virtual learning environment, which provide blended learning. The stages are: Institutional, pedagogical, technological, recourses support, ethical, interface design, evaluation and management, which have been described previously in literature.

12. Conclusion

The paper highlights eight theoretical frameworks and explores the relationship between implementation and management change process, which is related to switching from one VLE to another or adapting a new VLE. All of these frameworks have been assessed and critically evaluated. Khan's frameworks can be used to manage the change process in universities that follow a blended learning way of education, Ghavifekr and Hussin (2011) propose that frmaworks can be used in case the university uses open distance learning (ODL) Saeedikiya's et al. (2010) model considers that there must be a large number of experts involved in the changing process which raises the costs of implementing VLE. Zwass (1998) and IEEE Draft Standard frameworks ignore important aspects of VLE adoption such as pedagogical elements in E-learning. As for the CSU Model, it focuses mainly on human issues that affect LMS used from students' and staff perspectives. Hence, this paper is important to highlight the needed frameworks and elaborates their importance to simplify online learning process in academia

References

[1] Alhogail, A.A. and Mirza, A.A. (2011). IMPLEMENTING A VIRTUAL LEARNING ENVIRONMENT (VLE) IN A HIGHER EDUCATION INSTITUTION: A CHANGE MANAGEMENT APPROACH. Journal of Theoretical and Applied Information Technology.approach to planning, design, instruction, evaluation, and accreditation. New York, NY: Teachers College Press.approach to planning, design, instruction, evaluation, and accreditation. New York, NY: Teachers

[2] Ardito, C., Costabile, M.F., De Marsico, M., Lanzilotti, R., Levialdi, S., Roselli, T., and Rossano, V. 2005. An approach to usability evaluation of e-learning applications. Univ. Access Inf. Soc. 2006, 4: 270–283 Published online: 8 December 2005.

[3] Bateman, T. S., & Snell, S. (2007). Management: Leading and collaborating in a competitive world (7th ed., pp. 16 -18). New York, NY:McGraw- Hill.

[4] Beastall, L. and Walker, R., "Effecting institutional change through e-learning: An implementation model for VLE deployment at the University of York", Journal of Organisational Transformational and Social Change, 3(3), (2007), 285-299.

[5] Bremer, D, Bryant, R. (2005) "A Comparison of two learning management Systems: Moodle vs Blackboard", Proceedings of the 18th Annual Conference of the National Advisory Committee on Computing Qualifications. pg135-1390CE

[6] Buchan, J. (2010). Putting ourselves in the big picture: A sustainable approach to project management for e-learning. The Journal of Distance Education, 24(1), 55-76.

[7] Bremer, D, Bryant, R. (2005) "A Comparison of two learning management Systems: Moodle vs Blackboard", Proceedings of the 18th Annual Conference of the National Advisory Committee on Computing Qualifications. pg135-1390CE

[8] Cook, D. A. 2009. The failure of e-learning research to inform educational practice, and what we can do about it. Informa, 2009, 31(2):158-162

[9] Derntl, M. & Motschnig-pitrik, R. (2004). Patterns for Blended, Person-Centered Learning: Strategy, Concepts, Experiences, and Evaluation. ACM Symposium on Applied Computing. - (-), 916-923.

[10] Dublin, L., (2004), "The nine myths of elearning implementation: ensuring the real return on your e-learning investment",Industrial and Commercial Training, 36(7),(2004), 291-294.

[11] Ghavifekr, S. & Hussin, S. (2011). Managing Systemic Change in a Technology-based Education System: A Malaysian Case Study. Procedia - Social and Behavioral Sciences. 28 (-), 455-464.

[12] Hameed, S., Fathulla, K., and Thomas, A. 2009. Extent of e-learning effectiveness and efficiency in an integrated blended learning environment. Newport CELT Journal, 2:52-62.

[13] Hameed, S., Fathulla, K., and Thomas, A. 2009. Extent of e-learning effectiveness and efficiency in an integrated blended learning environment. Newport CELT Journal, 2:52-62.

[14] IEEE. Draft Standard for Learning Technology – Learning Technology Systems Architecture (LTSA) (IEEE P1484.1/D9), 2001.

[15] Johnson, S., Aragon, S., Shaik, N. and Palma-Rivas, N. (2000). Comparative Analysis of Learner Satisfaction and Learner Outcomes in Online and Face-to-Face learning Environments. Journal of Interactive Learning Research. Vol 11(1). pp 29 – 49.

[16] Johnson, S., Aragon, S., Shaik, N. and Palma-Rivas, N. (2000). Comparative Analysis of Learner Satisfaction and Learner Outcomes in Online and Face-to-Face learning Environments. Journal of Interactive Learning Research. Vol 11(1). pp 29 – 49.

[17] Khan, B. H. (2005). ELearning Quick Checklist, Information Science Publishing , Idea Group Inc, Hershey PA,USA .

[18] Khan, B. H. (2006). Flexible Learning in an Information Society , Information Science Publishing , Idea Group Inc,Hershey PA, USA.

[19] Khan, B. H. 2004. People, process and product continuum in e-learning: The e-learning P3 model. Educational Technology, 44(5): 33-40.

[20] Kotter, J. P. 1998. "Leading change: Why transformation efforts fail." In Harvard Business Review on Change, 1–20.Boston: Harvard Business School Press.

[21] Marshall, S. J. (2004). Leading and managing the development of e-learning environments: An issue of comfort or discomfort? In Beyond the comfort zone: Proceedings ASCILITE Perth 2004.

[22] Menchaca, M., Bischoff, M., & Abrams, B. (2003). A Model for Systemic Change Management in Education. Paper Presented in International Conference on Education and Information Systems: Technology and Applications (EISTA 03), 26.

[23] Nokelainen, P. (2006). An empirical assessment of pedagogical usability criteria for digital learning material

[24] Poole, M. S., & Van de Ven, A. H. (2004). Handbook of organizational change and innovation. Oxford University Press.

[25] VanRaaij, E. M., & Schepers, J. J. L. (2008). The acceptance and use of a virtual learning environment in China. Computers and Education 50, 838-852.

[26] Richards, L, Connolly, M., & O'Shea, J. (2004). Managing the concept of strategic change within a higher education institution: The role of strategic and scenario planning techniques. Journal of Strategic Change, 13, pp. 345-359.

[27] Rovai, A. P., Ponton, M. K., & Baker, J. D. (2008). Distance learning in higher education. A programmatic

[28] Russell, C, (2009) "A systemic framework for managing e-learning adoption in campus universities: individual strategies in context",Research in Learning Technology, 7 (1), 3-19.

[29] Saeedikiya, M., Mooghali, A., and Setoodeh B. 2010. Stages of the Implementation of E-Learning in Traditional Universities, Edulearn10 Proceedings, Pp. 6620-6624.

[30] Sharpe, R., Benfield, G., and Francis, R., (2006), "Implementing a university e-learning strategy: levers for change within academic schools", Research in Learning Technology,14(2), 135–151.

[31] Sharpe, R., Benfield, G., and Francis, R., (2006), "Implementing a university e-learning strategy: levers for change within academic schools", Research in Learning Technology,14(2), 135–151.

[32] Singh, H. (2003) Building Effective Blended Learning Programs Harvey .Issue of Educational Technology, 43, (6), 51-54.

[33] Uys, P. M. & Tulloch, M. K. (2007). Appropriate change leadership for the introduction of flexible learning within university governance and strategic leadership frameworks: A comparative analysis of case studies in developed and developing countries. Integrating for Excellence 3rd International Conference. 27-28 June, Sheffield Hallam university.

[34] Uys, P.M. (2010). Implementing an open source learning management system: A critical analysis of change strategies. Australasian Journal of Educational Technology. 26 (7), 980-995.

[35] VanRaaij E.M. and Schepers J.J. (2008). The acceptance and use of a virtual learning environment in China. Computers & Education,vol. 50, pp. 838-852.

[36] Ward, M., West, S., Peat, M. and Atkinson,S., "Making it Real: Project Managing Strategic e-Learning development Processes in a Large, Campus-Based University", Journal Of Distance Education, 24(1),(2010), 21-42.

[37] www.blackbaord.com, (2012) Viewed online on 23th Jan 2012.

[38] www.ju.edu.jo (2012), Viewed online on 12th Jan 2012.

[39] www.moodle.org (2012), Viewed online on 22th Jan 2012.

[40] Zwass, A. (1998). Foundations of information systems. USA: Irwin/McGraw-Hill. 496-514.

19

Software security metric development framework (an early stage approach)

A. Agrawal[1, *], R. A. Khan[2]

[1]Department of Computer Science, Khwaja Moinuddin Chishti Urdu, Arabi-Farsi University, Lucknow, India
[2]Department of IT, Babasaheb Bhimrao Ambedkar University, Lucknow, India

Email address:
alka_csjmu@yahoo.co.in (A. Agrawal), khanraees@yahoo.com (R. A. Khan)

Abstract: This paper does an extensive survey on software security metrics and put forth an effort to characterize design time software security. Misconceptions associated to security metrics have been identified and discussed. A list of characteristics good security metrics should posses is listed. In absence of any standard guideline or methodology to develop early stage security metrics, an effort has been made to provide a strong theoretical basis to develop such a framework. As a result, a Security Metrics Development Framework has been proposed in this paper. Our next effort will be to implement the proposed framework to develop security metrics in early stage of software development life cycle.

Keywords: Software Security, Software Security Metrics, Metric Development, Design Phase

1. Introduction

The increasing use of information system led to dramatically improve the functionality with respect to safety, cost and reliability. The exponential growth of technology and the prospect of increased public access to the computing, communications, and storage resources have made these systems more vulnerable to attacks. A system cannot be considered as of high assurance if it has poor security. Security problems involving computers and software are frequent, widespread, and serious. In an era riddled with asymmetric cyber attacks, claims about system reliability, integrity and safety must also include provisions for built-in security of the enabling software.

Generally, software developed and implemented has bugs, and many of the bugs available with the software system have security implications. As reported by various researchers and practitioners, security incidents seem to have increased exponentially. Security engineering as a discipline is still in its infancy. The field is hampered by its lack of adequate measures of goodness. Without such a measure, it is difficult to judge progress and it is particularly difficult to make engineering trade-off decisions when designing systems [1]. A widely accepted management principle is that an activity cannot be managed if it cannot be measured. Software security also falls in this rubric [2]. All security vulnerabilities in software are the result of security

bugs or defects within the software. In most cases, these defects are created by two primary causes including non-conformance, or a failure to satisfy requirements, and an error or omission in the software requirements.

Software security is a concept that still lacks unambiguous definitions. It is important to understand the nature of software when developing methods for measuring software security. A common way to try to understand software security is to find different dimensions of it including confidentiality, integrity and availability [3]. Most commercial software suffers from significant design and implementation security vulnerabilities because of two most important factors including complexity and motivation. Software developers are producing more complex software and work constantly on the boundary of manageable complexity. Most of the software contains security flaws because of the complex nature. Developers are readily capable of preventing them. The second cause of software insecurity is because of the lack of motivation to the vendors for creating more secure software as the economics of the software industry provide them with little incentive [4].

Security vulnerabilities are increasingly due to software. Researchers and practitioners have carried out much work on code-level vulnerabilities including buffer overflows. But, at the same time, there is a great demand in identifying and mitigating security vulnerabilities at design level [5]. In August 2006, first-time Steve Bellovin, argued that for software, meaningful security metrics are not yet possible because 100 percent security of software is not possible, i.e., one cannot measure what cannot possible exist [6][7]. Regulatory, financial, and organizational reasons drive the requirement to measure software security performance. Software security metrics provide a practical approach to measuring security by facilitating decision making and accountability through collection, analysis, and reporting of relevant performance data [8].

2. Security Measurement

Measurement is a decision aid and what needs to be measured depends on the decision. Measurement in any science and engineering can be done by involving three main steps including data collection, data validation, and data processing. Data collection defines what to collect and how to collect the data. The kind of data to be collected is directly linked to the kind of behavior to be analyzed and to the quantitative measures to be evaluated to characterize such behavior. Data validation analyzes the collected data for correctness, consistency, and completeness. Data processing performs statistical analysis on the validated data to identify and analyze trends and to evaluate quantitative measures that characterize security [9]. Software security measurement requires [10]:

- Identifying measurable security characteristics;
- Specify security metrics to be utilized;
- Map identified measurable characteristics to security metrics;
- Associate sub-sets of security characteristics to software system entities;
- Develop or use methodology to assess security strength of system entities.

There is a noticeable difference between metrics and measurements. Measurements provide single-point-in-time views of specific, discrete factors. On the other hand, metrics are derived from comparing two or more measurements taken over time with a predetermined baseline [11]. Alger differentiates measurements from metrics and believes that measurements are generated by counting, whereas metrics are generated from analysis [12]. Software measurement is at the foundation of software engineering. Software security metrics are quantitative measurements that are important for assessing the effects of proposed improvements in security engineering. Metrics serve an equally important role in risk analysis, scheduling, planning, resource allocation, and cost estimation. This results in implications on what should and may be measured.

Actual Measurable: Security metrics are fundamental in order to specify what is actually to be measured. In a simplified manner, a metric may be defined as a framework in which raw data (measurements) are given a signification or meaning.

Aggregation: There is a common agreement between researchers and practitioners that there is no single measure available to capture the security value of software system. Thus, security measurement methods have to be able to combine several measurements into software system wide-values.

A security metric measures or assesses the extent to which a system meets its security objectives. Since meaningful quantitative security metrics are largely unavailable, the security community primarily uses qualitative metrics for security.

3. Security Metrics

Building secure software highly depends on quantitative measurement of software security. Security measurement defines the target security level and achievable security levels. Metrics and measurements are the cornerstones of any scientific discipline [13]. Software security measurement is essential in order to make good decisions about how to design security countermeasures. A measure is a dimension compared against a standard. Security measures assists in choosing alternative security architectures, and improving security during design and operations [14].

It is essential to be able to define the actual meaning while security is measured. Security metrics is a term that has been used for the purpose. The need and significance of security metrics has been emphasized by researchers [15] [16] as well as by the industry practitioners [17]. A metric is a system of related measures enabling quantification of some characteristic. Security metrics are essential to meeting organizations security objectives. Without good security metrics, it is very difficult to assert a certain level of security [13]. A security metric is a system of related dimensions enabling quantification of the degree of freedom from possibility of suffering damage or loss from malicious attack [14]. An exhaustive review of literatures on software security reveals that the field of defining security metrics systematically is too young to have a well acceptable definition. The problem behind the immaturity of security metrics is that the current practice of software security is still a highly diverse field and holistic and widely accepted approaches are still missing [18].

Plenty of work has been done in defining and proposing security metrics. Various security metrics exist in literature and are widely used by the security community. Most of the metrics proposed fall short of meeting the set objectives of quantifying the measures, as well as scientifically defining the same. A lot of attention has been devoted to metrics focusing on operational security of deployed systems, analyzing defect rates, known and un-patched vulnerabilities, configuration of systems.

Security metrics are hard to quantify because the discipline itself is still in the early stages of development. There is not yet a common vocabulary and not many documented best practices to follow [2]. Security metrics refer to the quantitative measurements of trust indicating how well a system meets the security requirements.

4. Security Metrics Collection

Security metrics is the measurement of the effectiveness of the organization's security efforts over time. Security metrics have always been difficult to evaluate. It helps in determining an organization whether it is secure. Several software security metrics have been proposed, and are under development, by researchers and practitioners. Some of the pertinent security metrics are listed in the following section.

Computer Viruses per Malicious Code (CVMC): This metrics counts the ratio of number of computer viruses to total number of malicious code caught: This metric measures effectiveness of automated antivirus controls [19].

Relative Attack Surface Quotient (RASQ): It is developed and used by Microsoft. This metric measures the attackability of a system, i.e., the likelihood that an attack on the system will occur and be successful. It is calculated by finding the root attack vectors, which are features of the targeted system that positively or negatively affect its security [7].

Relative Vulnerability Metric (RVM): This metric compares the calculated ratio of exploitable vulnerabilities detected in a system's software components when an intrusion prevention system (IPS) is present, against the same ratio calculated when the IPS is not present [7][20].

Security Incidents and Investigations (SII): This metrics counts the number of security incidents and investigations performed to find out such an incident. This metrics assists in monitoring security events [19].

Cost of security breaches (SBC): This metrics estimates total cost of security breaches. It gives a measure to true business loss related to security failures [19].

Time and materials (TMA): This gives measures to time and materials assigned to security functions. It presents a true business cost of running a security program [19].

Security Compliance (SC): This metrics measures compliance with security rules. It produces level of compliance matching security program goals [19].

Static Analysis Tool Effectiveness Metric (SATE): The metric combines the actual number of flaws with the tool's false positive and false negative rates, and then weights the result according to the intended audience for the resulting measurements [21].

Predictive Undiscovered Vulnerability Density Metric (UVD): This metrics is the extrapolation of Vulnerability Discovery Rate metrics. It gives measure to undiscovered or hypothetical vulnerabilities [22].

Flaw Severity and Severity-to-Complexity Metric (FSC): This metrics gives a rating reported software flaws as critical, high, medium, or low severity. It also determines whether it is possible to make a direct correlation between the number and severity of detected vulnerabilities and bugs and the complexity of the code that contains them [23].

Security Scoring Vector (S-vector) for Web Applications (SSV): This metrics is used to rate a web application's implementation against its requirements for technical capabilities, structural protection, procedural methods in order to produce an overall security score for the application [24].

Martin listed another set of metrics in his paper on software security evaluation based on a top-Down Mc Call-Like Approach [25][26].

Inalterability Metrics (IM): This metric defines the difficulty of illegal modification of the code by a potential hacker.

Physical Difficulty Metrics (PD): This metric measures the physical difficulty of code modification.

Checksum Efficiency Metrics (CE): This metrics measures the efficiency of the checksum algorithm.

Selftest Validity Metrics (SV): This metrics synthesizes an assessment on the validity of the whole selftest mechanism.

Diversity Metrics (DM): This metrics assess the diversity of code.

Number of Versions (NV): This metrics counts the different versions of the same mechanism. The code is difficult in every version, but the functionality remains the same.

Diversity Factors (DF): This metrics gives an estimate of the independence of the different versions.

Multiplicity Metrics (MM): This metric assess the number of invocations of the same mechanism. The more a mechanism is used, the more difficult it will be to circumvent.

Multiplicity Factor (MF): This metrics measures the difficulty of modification of the code implementing the mechanism.

Frequency of Use (FU): This metrics measures how often the mechanism is used.

Isolation Metrics (IM): This metrics is used to assess the isolation of the mechanism from the rest of the application and/or system.

Code Isolation (CI): This metrics assess the physical isolation of the code segment implementing the mechanism.

Data isolation (DI): This metrics addresses the data segment of the software implementing the mechanism.

Data Reuse (DR): This metrics addresses the difficulty of modifying the operational parameters of the mechanism when it is not in use.

Context Isolation (CI): This metrics address the isolation provided from the context.

Interruptibility Metrics (IM): This metrics addresses the resistance of the mechanism against interrupt driven attacks.

Mandatory Mediation (MM): This metrics is to assess of the mechanism is used every time it could.

Mediation Factor (MF): This metrics establishes the ratio between the effective use of a mechanism and its potential use.

Mediation Efficiency (ME): This metrics estimates the efficiency of use, taking into account that this efficiency is related to the situation of the mechanism in the total system.

Number of Mediation (NM): For each function using the mechanism, this metrics measures the number of times it is used.

Auditability Metrics (AM): This metrics is aimed to assess if the software leaves auditable traces of its use.

Listing of Access Denial (AD): This metrics evaluates the performance of the mechanism when it denies an access or any operation.

Alarm Triggering Metrics (AT): This metrics evaluates the performance of the alarm triggering mechanism.

Non Standard Behavior Detection (BD): This metrics aims at assessing the efficiency of such systems detecting when the behavior of a subject deviates from its standard.

Listing of Granted Access (GA): This metrics evaluates the performance of the system when it keeps tracks of the granted accesses.

5. Security Metrics Characteristics

It is inevitable facts that metrics are important to software security to measure the success of security policy, mechanism, or implementations. Metrics can be an effective tool for software security practitioners to measure the security strength and levels of their systems, products, processes, and readiness to address security issues they are facing. Metrics can also help identify system vulnerabilities, providing guidance in prioritizing corrective actions, and raising the level of security awareness within the organization [9]. Software security metrics are quantifiable, feasible to measure, and repeatable. They provide relevant trends over time and are useful in tracking performance and directing resources to initiate performance improvement actions [8].

Jelen believes that a good metric should be Specific, Measurable, Attainable, Repeatable and Time-dependent (SMART) [11]. Payne remarks that truly useful security metrics indicate the degree to which security goals such as data confidentiality are being met [18] [27][28]. Characteristics of good security metric should include the followings [14]:

- A good security metrics should be able to measure the right thing, for which it has been written;
- It should also provide quantitative measurement to make some decisions;
- It should be capable enough to be measured accurately;
- A good metrics should be validated in prior of its use;
- Metrics should be less expensive
- It should be available in early stage of software development life cycle;
- It should be able to predict overall security of software and vulnerability of software under development;
- The security metrics should be able to be refereed independently;
- It should be repeatable in nature so that the results are independent of the analyst performing the measuring;
- Good security metrics should be scalable from small single-computer systems to large nation-scale enterprise networks.
- It should generate reproducible and justifiable measurements
- It should measure something of value to the organization

- It should be able to determine real progress in security posture
- It should be capable of applying to a broad range of organizations while producing similar results
- It should help determining the order in which security controls should be applied
- It should determine the resources needed to apply to the security program

A measurement, by itself, is not a metric. Time has to be brought into the picture, and a metric alone is not the answer to all the organization's problems. The metrics have to enlighten the organization by showing some type of progress.

6. Security Metrics Development Process

Organizations that measure successes and failures of past and current security investments may use security metrics to justify and direct future security investments. It is well understood and common believe that metrics assists in improving accountability to stakeholders, ensuring an appropriate level of mission support, determining software security program effectiveness, and improving customer confidence [8]. In absence of any standard framework for identifying and developing security metrics, it appears to be advantageous to make an effort to design such a framework to carryout security metrics early in the development life cycle. The framework facilitates tailoring security metrics to a specific organization and to different stakeholders groups in each organization.

6.1. Generic Guidelines

The guidelines before following the process to develop the security metrics early in the development life cycle may be listed as follows:

- Assure compliance/ adherence to collect a generally-accepted set of characteristics that good design possesses.
- Identify and persist with all the security-specific issues involved in design phase.
- Identify policies and standards as a source of software security metrics.
- Assure to control somehow all the extraneous and intervening factors that may affect the outcome based prediction.

6.2. Premises

The following premises have been considered when the proposed framework is being used to develop a security metrics:

- There is no universally agreed-upon definition for each of high-level security factors.
- The set of security attributes used in the development of the framework has been defined operationally in the context.

- A common set of features for the desired metrics may be used to form the basis for its development.
- The recourse optimization in SDLC depends on the early use of procedure for metrics specification and uncovering of vulnerabilities as far as possible.
- The approach to risk estimate should be more applicable to identifying low security software than the highly secured code.

6.3. The Framework

The development process of the metrics is comprised of six phases together with prescriptive steps for each and has been depicted pictorially in Fig. 1 Such a framework has been proposed on the basis of integral and basic components for designing good security metrics. The first phase starts with the conceptualization. Planning for the desired metrics is treated as an important task and has been putforth as a second phase, followed by the phases termed as development, theoretical validation, experimental validation and packaging. An attempt has been made to symbolically represent the spirit of designing a security metric and make the framework prescriptive in nature followed by a brief description of each o f the phases comprising the depicted steps in the special reference to development of metrics.

Conceptualization: Conceptualization is one of the foremost tasks of any comprehensive problem-solving activity, where an initial brainstorming activity is undertaken to understand the problem, jot down ideas for solution and to realize problem-related facts. In this phase, the need and significance of the metrics to be developed is assessed. The developmental feasibility will also be checked. A strong theoretical basis will be prepared to develop such a metrics. Metrics attributes will be selected and features will be identified.

Planning: Planning assists to get success in a problem solving situation. A precisely defined plan provides guidance to the developer as it works as a roadmap. There is no doubt, that a metric will have little value if it is designed outside a well-developed structural framework. Strategic planning will be carried out for the metrics development. Security policies, guidelines and procedures are reviewed. Security factors are identified and design characteristics are explored. A link is established between identified security factors and design characteristics.

Development: Software security metrics are an integral part of the state-of-the-practice in software security engineering. Well designed metrics with documented objectives may help the organization to mitigate the vulnerabilities. Thus, designing is the most important and critical step towards the development of desired security metrics. As a subtask, stakeholders and interests are identified. Metrics program goals and objectives are defined. The metrics to be generated are decided. A metrics computation is established and finally a security metrics is formulated. Theoretical Validation: Theoretical validation of software security metrics provides the supporting evidence as to whether a measure really captures the internal

attributes that it purports to measure. The main goal of theoretical validation is to assess whether a metric actually measures what it supposed to measure. A theoretical basis is examined in this phase. Experts review is conducted and observations are examined critically. On the basis of the observations made, changes are identified to be incorporated.

Empirical Validation: Testing is one of the best empirical research strategies, performed through quantitative analysis of experimental data on implementation. Hence it is necessary to place the developed security metrics under testing. A viable experiment is designed and pre-tryout is performed and reviewed. Changes are identified and tryout is performed. Result from tryout is analyzed, and as a conclusion, metrics is finalized.

Packaging: This is the conclusive phase of the metric development process. During this phase the developed metric is prepared with the needed accessories to become a ready-to-use product, like any other usable product. Metrics is introduced and its all accessories are described. A usage guideline is prescribed and a typical example is worked out. An implementation mechanism is prescribed at last.

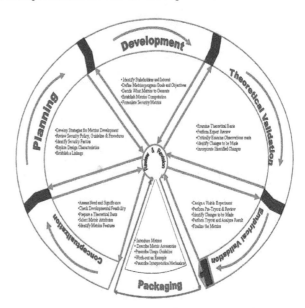

Fig 1. *Security Metrics Development Framework*

7. Conclusion

With this technological advancement, security is a relatively new concept for many of the organizations. Within the security realm, quantify security is still a relatively new theme. Every software system has security vulnerabilities and risks to certain degrees. It is critical for software security researchers and practitioners to identify these security risks, assessing the probability of their occurrences and the damage they could cause, and then develop security policy and mechanism to prevent or reduce the potential damages from the exploits of those security vulnerabilities. There are no well-established processes or methods to measure software security. To a great extent, different organizations have developed and deployed their own methods in measurements. Security Metrics provides a way to measure your security program. It facilitates collecting and documenting program status and reporting on the current situation and gap analysis. A framework to develop security metrics early in the development life cycle has been proposed. The proposed framework comprises of six steps including conceptualization, planning, development, theoretical validation, empirical validation and packaging. Our next step will be to implement the proposed framework in order to develop a design time security metrics.

References

[1] O. S. Saydjari, Risk: A Good System Security Measure, Proceedings of the 30th Annual International Computer Software and Applications Conference (COMPSAC'06) 0-7695-2655-1/06 $20.00, IEEE, 2006.

[2] S. Naqvi and M. Riguidel, Quantifiable Security Metrics for Large Scale Heterogeneous Systems, 1-4244-0174-7/06/$20.00, IEEE, pp. 209-215, 2006.

[3] W. Qu, D. Zhang, Security Metrics Models and Application with SVM in Information Security Management 1-4244-0973-X/07/$25.00, IEEE pp. 3234-3238, 2007.

[4] A. Ozment, Software Security Growth Modeling: Examining Vulnerabilities with Reliability Growth Models, in: Quality of Protection: Security Measurements and Metrics, Dieter Gollman, Fabio Massacci and Yautsiukhin, Artsiom.

[5] J. M. Wing, Software Security, First Joint IEEE/IFIP Symposium on Theoretical Aspects of Software Engineering (TASE'07), 0-7695-2856-2/07 $20.00, IEEE, 2007.

[6] Since Metricon 1.0, a second "mini-Metricon" was held in February 2007 at the University of San Francisco. See "Metricon 1.0" web page. securitymetrics.org [Last updated September 20, 2006, by Andrew Jaquith].

[7] 'Software Security Assurance", State-of-the-Art Report (SOAR) Information Assurance Technology Analysis Center (IATAC) Data and Analysis Center for Software (DACS) Joint endeavor by IATAC with DACS July 31, 2007.

[8] G. Agarwal, IT Security Metrics, 08Feb, 2008.http://cobitexpert.com/index.php?itemid=3

[9] A. J. A. Wang, Information Security Models and Metrics, 43rd ACM Southeast Conference, ACM, March 18-20 Kennesaw, GA, USA. pp. 178-184, 2005.

[10] J. Hallberg, A. Hunstad and M. Peterson, A Framework for System Security Assessment, Proceedings of the 2005 IEEE Workshop on Information Assurance and Security, United States Military Academy, West Point, NY, pp. 224-231, 2005

[11] G. Jelen, SSE-CMM Security Metrics. NIST and CSSPAB Workshop, Washington, D.C., June 2000.

[12] J. I. Alger, On Assurance, Measures, and Metrics: Definitions and Approaches. Proc. of Workshop on Information Security System Scoring and Ranking (WISSSR), ACSA and MITRE, Williamsburg, Virginia, May, 2001, proceedings published 2002.

[13] Z. Abbadi, ST13: Security Metrics: What can you test? Web Reference, 21 January, 2008.

[14] O. S. Saydjari, Is Risk a Good Security Metric? QoP'06, Alexandria, Virginia, USA. ACM 1-59593-553-3/06/0010, pp. 59-60, , October 30, 2006.

[15] ACSA (2002), Proc Workshop on information Security System Scoring and Ranking, Applied Computer Security Associates, 2002.

[16] M. Greenwald, C. Gunter, E. Knutsson, A. Sccdrov, J. Smith & S. Zdancewic, Computer Security is not a Science, Large-Scale Network Security Workshop, Landsdome, VA, 2003.

[17] Seemet, Security metrics consortium, 2004. http://www.secmet.orp

[18] Department of Homeland Security, Security in the Software Lifecycle, Making Software Development Processes—and Software Produced by Them—More Secure, DRAFT Version 1.1 - July 2006.

[19] D. A. Chapin and S. Akridge, How Can Security Be Measured? Information Systems Control Journal, Volume 2 2005.

[20] C. Cowan, Relative Vulnerability: An Empirical Assurance Metric, Presented at the 44th International Federation for Information Processing Working Group 10.4 Workshop on Measuring Assurance in Cyberspace (Monterey, CA, 25-29 June 2003).

[21] F. Stevens, Validation of an Intrusion-Tolerant Information System Using Probabilistic Modeling, MS thesis, University of Illinois, Urbana-Champaign, IL, 2004.

[22] O.H. Alhazmi, Y. K. Malaiya, and I. Ray, Security Vulnerabilities in Software Systems: a Quantitative Perspective, Proceedings of the IFIP WG 11.3 Working Conference on Data and Applications Security, Storrs, CT, August 2005.

[23] Pravir Chandra, "Code Metrics", Presented at Metricon 1.0 (Vancouver, BC, Canada, 1 August 2006).

[24] R. R. Barton, W. J. Hery, and P. Liu, An S-vector for Web Application Security Management, working paper, Pennsylvania State University, University Park, PA, January 2004.

[25] S. Martin, Software Security Evaluation Based on a Top-Down Mc Call-Like Approach, IEEE 1988, pp. 414-418.

[26] D. B. Aredo, Metrics for Quantifying the Impacts of Monitoring on Security of Adaptive Distributed Systems, Master Thesis Proposal – II, December 2005.

[27] S. C. Payne, A Guide to Security Metrics, SANS Institute Information Security Reading Room, June 2006.

[28] R. Savola, Towards a Security Metrics Taxonomy for the Information and Communication Technology Industry, International Conference on Software Engineering Advances(ICSEA 2007) 0-7695-2937-2/07,2007, IEEE.

20

Analogy-based software quality prediction with project feature weights

Ekbal Rashid[1], Srikanta Patnaik[2], Vandana Bhattacharya[3]

[1]Department of CS & E CIT, Tatisilwai,Ranchi, India
[2]Department of CS & E SOA University, Bhubaneswar, Orissa,India
[3]Department of CS & E BIT Mesra, Ranchi, India

Email address:

ekbalrashid2004@yahoo.com (E. Rashid), patnaik_srikanta@yahoo.co.in (S. Patnaik),
vbhattacharya@bitmesra.ac.in (V. Bhattacharya)

Abstract: This paper presents analogy-based software quality estimation with project feature weights. The objective of this research is to predict the quality of project accurately and use the results in future predictions. The focus includes identifying parameters on which the quality of software depends. Estimation of rate of improvement of software quality chiefly depends on the development time. Assigning weights to these parameters to improve upon the results is also in the area of interest. In this paper two different similarity measures namely, Euclidian and Manhattan were the measures used for retrieving the matching cases from the knowledgebase to increases estimation accuracy & reliability. Expert judgment, weights and rating levels were used to assign weights and quality rating levels. The results show that assigning weights to software metrics increases the prediction performance considerably. In order to obtain the results, we have used indigenous tools.

Keywords: Analogy, CBR, Effort Estimation, Software Quality Prediction, Similarity Function

1. Introduction

Software Quality estimation is an important and hard management task. This is due to the lack of information on making decisions in the early phases of the project development. Most of today's software quality estimation models are built on using data from projects of single organization. Using such data has well known benefits such as ease of understanding and controlling of collected data. But different researchers have reported contradictory results using different software quality estimation modeling techniques. It is still difficult to generalize many of the obtain results. This is due to the characteristics of the datasets being used and dataset's small size. In Case-Based Reasoning (CBR) problem solving is seen as a process, which involves the retrieval of similar prior cases from case bases using mobile agent methodology and the adaptation of retrieved cases' solutions to fit the new problem's requirements. Estimation models in software engineering are used to predict some important attributes of future entities such as software development effort, software reliability, software quality, and productivity of

programmers. Among such models, those estimating software effort have motivated considerable research in recent years [11]. Correct prediction of the software quality or maintain a software system is one of the most critical activities in managing software project. Due to the nature of the software engineering domain, it is important that software quality estimation models should be able to deal with ambiguity and indistinctness associated with such values. To serve this purpose, we propose our case-based estimation model for software quality estimation. We feel that case-based models are particularly useful when it is difficult to define concrete rules about a problem domain in addition to this, expert advice may be used to supplement the existing stored knowledge. A case-based reasoning model was developed in [13] for estimating software development effort.

In this paper, we have used features with weights, which are based on expert judgments. For example, if the difficulty level of a program increases then there is also increase in the efforts and development time. For our experiment, we have assumed weights based on expert judgment and by empirical study. We displayed the software quality relative to the lines of code retrieved from the knowledgebase in Table 4. The rest of the paper is organized as follows: Section 2 gives a brief overview of the various related work. Section 3 describes the methods. In section 4, we present research methodology. Sections 5 and 6 present the production rule and the development of models. Section 7 presents the results and analysis. Finally, section 8 concludes the paper and presents some future trends.

Table 4. *Classification used for Software Quality prediction.*

Program Scenario	Value of Q	Class		
Sl.No		Excellent	Good	Poor
1	0.195	√	×	×
2	0.028	√	×	×
3	0.030	√	×	×
4	0.037	√	×	×
5	0.088	√	×	×
6	0.600	√	×	×
7	0.090	√	×	×
8	2.99	×	√	×
9	4.067	×	√	×
10	7.036	×	×	√
11	0.014	√	×	×
12	0.092	√	×	×
13	0.142	√	×	×
14	0.037	√	×	×
15	0.074	√	×	×

2. Background and Motivation

Many researchers have used soft computing approaches for software quality estimation. Zhong et. Al in [16] have used unsupervised Learning techniques to build a software quality estimation system. Idri et. Al have implemented the COCOMO cost model using fuzzy logic in [1] and also a fuzzy logic based analogy estimation approach in [2-4]. Case based reasoning has also been used by Kadoda. Al in [5].They examine the impact of the choice of number of analogies when making predictions: They also look at different adaptation strategies. The analysis is based on a dataset of software projects collected by a Canadian software house. Their results show that choosing analogies is important but adaptation strategy appears to be less. For this reason they urge some degree of caution when comparing competing prediction systems and only modest

numbers of cases. Myrtveit et. Al in [6] and Ganesan et. Al in [7] have also studied case based approach to development effort prediction. Bhattacherjee et. Al have proposed Expert Case Based Models in [9-14]. Rashid et. Al emphasized on the importance of software quality estimation [15].

3. Methods

3.1. Hypothesis

Distance between the status of two programs p1 and p2.

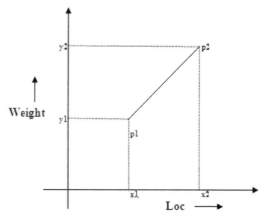

We can consider a particular parameter weight which may be dependent on LOC.

Let us take LOC =X and the hypothetical parameter weight that depends upon LOC be = Y

Then we can express the relation between the two as an ordered pair as:

$$f:NR : y=f(x)$$

Now, we can represent the two different program states by two points on the Cartesian plane. Let that be $p_1(x_1,y_1)$ and $p_2(x_2,y_2)$, then the distance between the two can be calculated using the Euclidean distance formula:ED=

$$dist (p_1,p_2)=[(x_2-x_1)^2 + (y_2-y_1)^2]^{1/2}$$

The Manhattan distance (MD) of p_1 from p_2 is:

$$MD =|abs (x_2-x_1) + abs (y_2-y_1)|$$

A small distance indicates a high degree of similarity. When a new project is estimated, its distances to each project in the historical feature database are calculated.

A fundamental question in this model is how to set the feature weights:

w_i since individual features should influence project similarity to a different degree [8]. Various approaches have been proposed:

•Set all project feature weights to identical values: w_i =1, i = 1,....l.

•Set each project feature weight to a value determined by human judgment.

• Set each project feature weight to a value obtained by

statistical analysis.

•Set each project feature weight to either 0 or 1 so that an estimation quality metric is maximized. This brute-force approach proposed by Shepperd and Schofield tries to identify a subset of important features. Once these features are identified, they are all given the same weight. We have adopted the combined approach of expert judgment and empirical study. We now present the methodology adopted for software quality estimation based on Case-Based Reasoning using project feature weights.

4. Research Methodology

The environment of our study is the university campus and students of computer science and engineering are our target group. All students are provided with same level of guidance by instructors, supported by the laboratory staffs, resources like computers, software etc.

Data collected from students included the following:
•Number of lines of code
•Number of functions
•Number of variables
•Difficulty level of program (low , medium , high)
•Number of formal parameters in each function
•Exposure to programming language and
•Programmers Experience

5. Production Rule

We have used production rules for quality rating levels. See table 2

Table 2. Quality rating levels.

Quality Score	Rating
If Q<2	Excellent
If Q >= 2 and Q<=5	Good
If Q> = 6 and Q<=10	Poor

RULE: R1 IF Q<2 THEN
EXCELLENT
RULE: R2 ELSE
IF Q>=2 AND Q<=5 THEN
GOOD
RULE: R3 ELSE
IF Q>=6 AND Q<=10 THENPOOR

6. Model Development

A knowledgebase is created and maintained to store the cases against which the matching process has to be performed. Parameters with weight related to the software are given as input and the quality is predicted by finding the best match from the knowledgebase. See Figure 1.

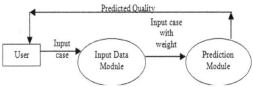

Figure 1. cuntest level diagram.

6.1. Input Data Module

This module accepts the values of various parameters from the user. It also has the provision of assigning weights to the parameters.

6.2. Prediction Module

This module predicts the quality of software for which the parameters have been given as input. The quality is calculated using different similarity measures. These measures use the knowledgebase to find the matching cases for the input parameters. Once the matching cases are generated the new results are added to the database. Depending upon the dissimilarity between two projects it calculates the quality (Q) of the module with respect to lines of code. Only those results are added that give an error of 5% or less.

The inputs to the proposed model are as follows:
•Lines of code
•Number of Functions or Procedures
•Experience of the Programmer in years
• Difficulty level of software.

7. Results and Analysis

We present the results obtained when applying the Case-based reasoning model to the data set. The accuracy of estimates is evaluated by using the magnitude of relative error MRE defined as:

$$MRE = abs\left|\frac{AP - TP}{AP}\right|$$

Where AP = Actual parameter
TP = Targeted parameter
Prediction level *Pred* is used to test the performance of the model. It is defined as:
Pred(p)= E/R
Where, R is the total size of the data set and E is the number of programs. We calculate Pred (0.10) values for the various values of weights. We have used feature

weights from wi ranging between 0 to 1. These were the values as suggested by experts, in our case, they comprised of a team of faculty members from various colleges/ institutes actively involved in software engineering research. The results of applying the different combinations of weights are displayed in Table 1, quality rating levels are shown in Table 2 and results for software quality prediction are shown in Table 3.

Table 1. *Results of applying different weight measures to the analogy-based model.*

S. No.	W1	W2	W3	W4	Pred(0.1) Euclidean	Pred(0.10) Manhattan
1	0.5	1	1	1	0.97	0.883
2	1	0.5	0.5	0.5	0.833	0.316
3	0.5	1	0.5	0.5	0.816	0.3
4	0.5	0.5	0.5	1	0.833	0.316
5	1	0.25	0.3	0.3	0.616	0.316
6	0.25	1	0.3	0.3	0.65	0.25
7	0.25	0.25	1	0.3	0.66	0.26
8	1	0.5	0.5	0.5	0.816	0.33
9	1	1	1	1	0.9	0.66
10	0.5	1	1	1	0.97	0.883
11	0.5	0.5	1	1	0.8	0.633
12	1	0.5	0.5	1	0.9	0.633
13	0.4	0.25	1	0.5	0.622	0.61
14	0.25	0.25	0.25	0.5	0.80	0.360
15	0.5	0.25	1	0.25	0.77	0.522

Table 3. *Quality of Software.*

Rules	Quality Level of Software	Class	%
R1	High	Excellent	80.1%
R2	Medium	Good	13.3%
R3	Low	Poor	6.6

8. Conclusions and Future Trends

The aim of paper is to improve in accuracy of predictions and increasing the reliability of the knowledgebase was our priority. For each program we have evaluated the students four times. Value of Q (Quality of software) is calculated by indigenous tools written in c language and graph was plotted through MATLAB 7.10.0 version which is shown in Figure 2. It can be seen in Table 3 the results are very good where quality of software is concerned because 80.1% are excellent, 13.3% are good and 6.6% are poor (As per quality rating levels). In this research paper we have used two similarity measures Manhattan Distance and Euclidean Distance. The combination (0.5, 1, 1, 1) works the best where prediction is concerned because 97% data are within 10% error for Euclidean distance and 88% data are within 10% error for Manhattan distance measure. Apart from predicting quality of software, this system can also be used to predict the development time. As part of our ongoing work, increasing the volume of knowledgebase is another objective.

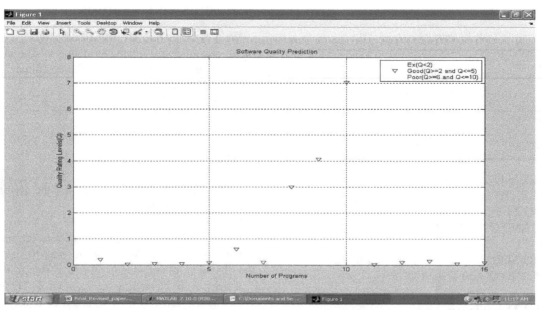

Figure 2. *Classification used for Software Quality prediction.*

References

[1]   A. Idri, L.Kjiri, and A Abran. (2000), "COCOMO Cost Model Using Fuzzy Logic", In Proceedings of the 7th International Conference on Fuzzytheory and Technology, pp.219-223. Atlantic City, NJ, USA.

[2]   A. Idri and A Abran. (2000b), "Towards A Fuzzy Logic Based Measures for Software Project Similarity", In

Proceedings of the 6th Maghrebian Conference on Computer Sciences, pp. 9-18, Fes Morroco.

[3] A. Idri and A. Abran. (2001), "A Fuzzy Logic Based Measures For Software Project similarity: Validation and Possible Improvements", In Proceedings of the 7th International Symposium on Software Metrics, pp. 85-96, England, UK, IEEE.

[4] A. Idri , A. Abran and T.M. Khoshgoftaar .(2001c), " Fuzzy Analogy: Anew Approach for Software Cost Estimation", In Proceedings of the 11th International workshop on software Measurements, pp.93-101, Montreal, Canada.

[5] G.Kadoda, M Cartwright, L Chen, and M.shepperd.(2000), "Experiences Using Case- Based Reasoning to Predict Software Project Effort", In Proceeding of EASE, p.23-28, Keele,UK.

[6] I. Myrtveit and E. Stensrud. (1999), "A Controlled Experiment to Assess the Benefits of Estimating with Analogy and Regression Models", IEEE transactions on software Engineering, vol 25,no. 4, pp. 510-525.

[7] K. Ganeasn, T.M. Khoshgoftaar, and E. Allen. (2002), "Case-based Software Quality Prediction", International journal of Software Engineering and Knowledge Engineering, 10 (2), pp. 139-152.

[8] M. Auer, A. trendowicz, B. Graser, E. Haunschmid and S. Biffl, "Optimal Project Feature Weights in analogy-based Cost Estimation: Improvement and Limitations", IEEE, TSE, Vol.32, No.2, Feb 2006, pp 83-92.

[9] S. Kumar and V.Bhattacharjee,(2005),"Fuzz logic based Model for Software cost Estimation ",In Proceedings of the international Conference on information Technology, Nov'05, PCTE, Ludhiana India.

[10] S. Kumar and V.Bhattacharjee,(2007),"Analogy and Expert Judgment: A Hybrid Approach to Software Cost Estimation", In Proceedings of the National Conference on information Technology: Present practice and Challenge, Sep'07, New-Delhi, India.

[11] V. Bhattacherjee and S. Kumar,(2004),"Software cost estimation and its relevance in the Indian software Industry", In Proceedings of the International Conference on Emerging Technologies IT Industry, Nov'05, PCTE, Ludhiana India.

[12] V. Bhattacherjee and S .Kumar,(2006),"An Expert- Case Based Frame work for Software Cost Estimation", In Proceedings of the National Conference on Soft Computing Techniques for Engineering Application (SCT-2006), NIT Rourkela.

[13] E. Rashid, V. Bhattacherjee, S. Patnaik, "The Application of Case-Based Reasoning to Estimation of Software Development Effort". International Journal of Computer Science and Informatics (IJCSI) ISSN 2231 −5292, Vol 1 Issue 3 pp 29-34 Feb 2012.

[14] V. Bhattacherjee, S. Kumar and E. Rashid ,A Case Study on Estimation of Software Development Effort" In Proceedings on International Conference on Advanced Computing Technologies(ICACT-2008), Gokaraju Rangaraju Institute of Engg & Technology, Hyderabad, India,p.no.161-164.

[15] Ekbal Rashid, Srikanta Patnaik, Vandana Bhattacherjee "A Survey in the Area of Machine Learning and Its Application for Software Quality Estimation" has been published in ACM SigSoft ISSN 0163-5948, volume 37, number 5, September 2012, http://doi.acm.org/10.1145/2347696.2347709 New York, NY, USA.

[16] Shi Zhong,Taghi M.Khoshgoftaar and Naeem Selvia "Unsupervised Learning for Expert-Based Software Quality Estimation".Proceeding of the Eighth IEEE International Symposium on High Assurance Systems Engineering (HASE'04).

21

A metric based approach for analysis of software development processes in open source environment

Parminder Kaur, Hardeep Singh

Department of Computer Science and Engineering, Guru Nanak Dev University, Amritsar-143005, India

Email address:

parminderkaur@yahoo.com (P. Kaur), hardeep_gndu@rediffmail.com (H. Singh)

Abstract: Open source software (OSS) is a software program whose source code is available to anyone under a license which gives them freedom to run the program, to study, modify and redistribute the copies of original or modified program. Its objective is to encourage the involvement in the form of improvement, modification and distribution of the licensed work. OSS proved itself highly suited, both as a software product and as a development methodology. The main challenge in the open source software development (OSSD) is to collect and extract data. This paper presents various aspects of open source software community, role of different types of users as well as developers. A metric-based approach for analysis of software development processes in open source environment is suggested and validated through a case study by studying the various development processes undertaken by developers for about fifty different open – source software's.

Keywords: Free Software, Freedom, Open Source Software (Oss), Propriety Software, Oss Developer Community, Oss Metrics

1. Introduction

Free software (Stallman, 1983) provides users the freedom to run, copy, distribute, study, change and improve the software. Four essential freedoms are provided to user's i.e.

• The freedom to run any of the programs for any purpose (freedom 0) i.e. the freedom for any kind of person or organization to use it on any kind of computer system, for any kind of purpose, without communicating the developer or any other specific entity..

• The freedom to study how the program works, and how it does computing according to users wish (freedom 1). Access to the source code is a precondition for this.

• The freedom to redistribute copies so user can help their neighbors (freedom 2) i.e. it must include binary or executable forms of the programs as well as source code, for both modified and unmodified versions.

• The freedom to distribute copies of modified versions to others (freedom 3). By doing this, user can give a chance to benefit from his/her changes to whole community.

In order for these freedoms to be real, they must be permanent and irrevocable as long as nothing does wrong. If the developer of the software has the power to revoke the license, or retroactively change its terms, software is not free.

Open source software (Raymond, 1998) is software for which the source code is available to everyone for modification and inspection. This is in contrast with propriety software which cannot be inspected and modified by anyone. In the last ten years, open source software (OSS) has attracted the attention of not only the practitioner, but also the business and the research communities. OSS has proven to produce software of high quality, functionality and wide development. Open Source Definition include the GNU Public License (GPL), the BSD license used with Berkeley Unix derivatives, the X Consortium license for the X Window System, and the Mozilla Public License. Open source software definition includes the following terms listed as:

• Free Redistribution: -Anyone who received the software legally can share all of it with anyone without additional payments.

• Source Code: -The program must include source code, and must allow distribution in source code as well as compiled form. Intermediate forms such as the output of a preprocessor or translator are not allowed. The source code of the software must be distributed as well or be available at reasonable reproduction cost.

• Derived Works:-The modification of the software and the distribution of this derived work must be allowed.

• Integrity of the Author's Source Code:-The distribution of modified source code must be allowed although restrictions to ensure the possibility to distinguish the original source code from the derived work are tolerated, e.g. requirement of different names.

• No Discrimination against Persons or Groups: -The license must not discriminate against any person or group of persons.

• No Discrimination against Fields of Endeavor: -The license must not forbid the usage of the software in specific field of endeavor, e.g. business or genetic research.

• Distribution of License:-The rights attached to the program must apply to all to whom the program is redistributed without the need for execution of an additional license by those parties.

• License must not be specific to a Product:-The rights given by the license must not be different for the original distribution and any other one even when it takes place in a totally different context.

• License must not contaminate other software:- The license must not demand any condition on the software distributed along with the licensed software.

2. Related Work

Open source software is now the demand of era. Literature survey includes various aspects of different researchers. Open source is a term that has recently gained currency as a way to describe the tradition of open standards, shared source code, and collaborative development behind software such as the Linux and FreeBSD operating systems, the Apache Web server, the Perl, Tool Command Language (Tcl), and Python languages, and much of the Internet infrastructure, including Bind (the Berkeley Internet Name Daemon servers that run the Domain Name System), the Sendmail mail server (sendmail.org), and many other programs.

(John, 1998) has viewed that qualitative data analysis (QDA) is a symphony based on three notes: Noticing, Collecting, and Thinking about interesting things. The process has characteristics such as Iterative and Progressive, Recursive. QDA has simple foundation but the process of doing qualitative data analysis is complex. (Katherine and Tony, 2002) has viewed as open source has been most successful in back-end types of applications such as operating systems. They analyzed the projects listed on the www.freshmeat.net developer forum on the basis of two indicators i.e. vitality on the project and the popularity of the project. Vitality has been calculated using the number of announcements about a project and the time since its last release. Popularity is based on the number of people who subscribe to the project.

(Fredrik, 2002) has asked that open source development model is not only producing software but also produces the interacting system of knowing, learning and doing, which organizes the community and its relations with other communities. Users are allowed to download the software

from the Internet and use it without charge and granted the right to study the software's source code, to modify the software, and to distribute modified or unmodified versions to others.

(Jin and Madey, 2004) has told that OSS community as a complex, self-organizing system. Developers are main components in the network. An OSS developer community is composed of a group of loosely-connected contributors. An OSS community can be classified as different roles: active and passive users, peripheral developer, central developer, core developer, project leader. Data is gathered from the 2003 data dump provided by SourceForge.

(Jin Xu et al, 2005) has included users and developers in research paper. Passive users download code and use it for their needs. Active users discover and report bugs, suggest new features. The Peripheral developers irregularly and Central developers regularly fix bugs, add features, submit patches, provide support, write documents and exchange other information. Core developers manage CVS releases and coordinate peripheral developers and central developers. Project leaders guide the vision and direction of a project. Many difficulties exist in collecting, cleaning, screening and interpreting data. (Chris, 2005) has used models for Apache, Mozilla, and Net-Beans to show the relationships between tools, agents, their nonfunctional requirements and functional requirements. The quality assurance (QA) process can be modeled in Mozilla Web browser as a rich hypermedia, Apache release process with flow graph, and Net-Beans requirements and release process, can be modeled formally and reenact. The approaches to modeling software development processes within and across these communities, as well as issues and trade-offs that arise along the way are described.

(David et al, 2006) has suggested that essential characteristics of the software like reliability, maintainability or sustainability cannot be identified by source code inspection alone, but have to include the environment in which it has been created. The requirements are structured into the aspects of various functional, non functional, technical, organizational, legal, economical and political.

(Ismail et al, 2007) has given information about open projects that can be obtained from two main sources, either the source code or the document produced. This is a static source that enables analysis on the quality of the product. Dynamic information is needed to go through the stages of development and the communication between the peers. Various metrics are used to quantify the roles of core developers, release stability are used.

(Henrike et al, 2009) has proved that data collection is time consuming process and requires some effort. To solve this problem, tools are developed for metrics analysis of a large number of software projects. Measurement and data collection is performed in three phases, two automated and one manual phase.

(David, 2011) tells us about the recent analysis of companies contributing code to the Linux kernel. It shows that large companies including Novell, IBM, Intel, Nokia and Texas Instruments are getting serious about engaging in community development. Organisations such as the Linux Mobile (LiMo) Foundation are encouraging their members to work with community projects "upstream", that is, with the community rather than in isolation, to avoid missing out on millions of dollars worth of "unleveraged potential" (PDF link). Sun Microsystems and AOL are prominent examples of companies which went full speed into community development, but were challenged (to say the least) in cultivating a mutually beneficial relationship with community developers.

3. Open Source Software Community

Open source software community (figure 1) can be classified into two groups as: User group and Developer group.

User group further categorizes in Passive users and Active users. Passive users have no contribution in the development of the software projects. They are attracted to OSS mainly due to its high quality and potential of being changed when needed. Active users not only use the system, but also try to understand how the system works by reading the source code. They can suggest new features, discover and report bugs and exchange other useful information by posting messages to forums and mailing lists.

Peripheral Developers contribute occasionally new functionality or features to the existing system. They irregularly fix bugs, provide support, write documents and exchange information. Their period of involvement is short and sporadic. Central Developers are the major development force of OSS systems. They regularly fix bugs, add new features, submit patches, provide support, write documents and exchange information. Core Developers are responsible for guiding and coordinating the development of an OSS project. Core Developers are those people who have been involved with the project for a relative long time and have made significant contributions to the development and evolution of the system. OSS projects in which single Project Leader no longer exists and the Core Developers form a council to take the responsibility of guiding the development, such as the Apache Group and the PostgreSQL core group.

Project Leader is often the person who has initiated the project. He or she is responsible for the vision and overall direction of the project. Bug Fixers fix bugs that either they discover by themselves or are reported by other members. Bug Reporters discover and report bugs. They do not fix the bugs themselves, and may not read source code either. They assume the same role as testers of the traditional software development model. The existence of many Bug Reporters assures the high quality of OSS.

Contributors communicate with each other through online tools and platforms. OSS development process is open involving a large number of developers submitting contributions that may have significant variations in quality. The communication tools are Concurrent Version System CVS), mailing list, bug tracking systems, online discussions forums.

4. Sourceforge.Net: an Open Source Software Community

SourceForge.net is the world's largest Open Source software development web site. On July 2011, the SourceForge repository hosts more than 300,000 projects and has more than 2 million registered users. The aim of SourceForge.net is to enrich the Open Source community by providing a centralized place for Open Source developers to control and manage Open Source software development. To fulfill this mission goal, it offers a variety of services to projects that are hosted, and to the Open Source community. SourceForge.net stores a set of common attributes for all projects. These attributes are divided into two groups, the first contains static information about the project such as the license, and the second contains information such as the number of code changes committed to Concurrent Version System Active users. Passive Users have no direct contribution in the development of the software projects. They are attracted to OSS mainly due to its high quality and the potential of being changed when needed. Active users not only use the system, but also try to understand how the system works by (CVS).

SourceForge.net uses relational databases to store project management activity and statistics (sourceforge.net Research Data available at www.nd.edu). There are over 100 relations (tables) in the data dumps provided to university of Notre Dame. Some of the data have been removed for security and privacy reasons. SourceForge.net cleanses the data of personal information and strips out all OSTG (Open Source Technology Group) specific and site functionality specific information. On a monthly basis, a complete dump of the databases (minus the data dropped for privacy and security reasons) is shared with Notre Dame. The Notre Dame Researchers have built a data warehouse comprised of these monthly dumps, with each stored in a separate schema. Thus, each monthly dump is a snapshot of the status of all the SourceForge.net projects at that point in time. As of March 2007, the data warehouse was almost 500 GBytes in

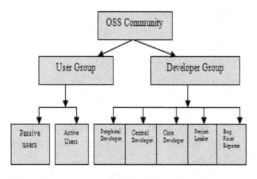

Figure 1. Open source software community [5].

size, and is growing at about 25 GBytes per month. Much of the data is duplicated among the monthly dumps but changes in project activity and structure can be discovered by comparing data from the monthly dumps. To help researchers determine what data is available, an ER-diagram and the definitions of tables and views in the data warehouse are provided. However, SourceForge.net site provide hints as to what types of data might be available in the SourceForge.net data warehouse to support research into the Free/Open Source Software.

A. Types of Data that Can be Extracted from the SourceForge.net Research Data Archive

The following are types of data that have been extracted from the SourceForge.net Research Data Archive:

• Project sizes over time (number of developers as a function of time presented as a frequency distribution)

• Development participation on projects (number of projects individual developers participate on presented as a frequency distribution).

• The extended- community size around each project including project developers plus registered members who participated in any way on a project (discussion forum posting, bug report, patch submission, etc.)

• Date of project creation (at SourceForge.net)

• Date of first software release for a project

• SourceForge.net ranking of projects at various times

• Activity statistics on projects at various times

• Number of projects in various software categories, e.g., games, communications, database, security, etc.

Since all of the archived data is stored in a relational database, data to support F/OSS investigations will be extracted using SQL queries against the data warehouse.

5. Open Source Software Metrics

Metrics are used for measurement, comparison or to track performance or production. Metrics helps to compare the performance of software at various levels. Metrics helps in good decision making or improvements in the project. Metrics should be accurate, timely and actionable. Metrics are derived from the earlier data. These must be understandable, economical and must be useful at the various levels of the development of the project (Pinker S., 2009), (David et al, 2003), (Kaur and Singh, 2011), (Kaur & Kaur, 2012). Metrics used in this research work are:-

A. Total Number of Contributions

A large number of users contribute towards the development of the project but developers appear to become more influential contributors to their open source. Developers play more roles in open source projects. The contributors can contribute either to a single project or multiple projects. This metric is related to the number of contributors for a given project irrespective of their affiliations to other projects.

B. Average Domain Experience of Contributors

Contributors participating in the software development have some expertise and experience in that domain area

contribute to the project. This metric helps in evaluating the average experience of all the contributors taken together and can be represented as

Cumulative Experience of Contributor i.e.

$$E = \sum_{i=1}^{n} e_i$$

[Where e_i is the experience of an individual contributor in that domain.]

Average Experience of Contributors i.e. $E_{avg} = E/N$

[Where N is total number of contributors.]

C. Average Time for a Completion of a version of Project

The average time for a completion of a version of project can be calculated as:

Average Time i.e. Tavg = $T_{total} / N_{version}$

Where T_{total} is total time taken to develop all the versions and $N_{version}$ is the total number of versions generated. Greater average would indicate software development processes resulting from various factors like low number of contributors, their lack in experience or complexity of the project etc.

D. Bugs Track per Version

The detected bugs could be allocated to various development processes like requirement specification, design, coding and testing. This metric helps in measuring the total number of bugs located and repoted per version. Greater the number of bugs detected/tracked more is the inefficiency of various development processes.

E. Patch Accept Ratio

Patches are change sets that can be applied to the software using a specific tool: the patch tool. Patches may introduce new features, fix bugs, translate strings to a different language, or re-structure parts of the software. Every contributor sends a patch to the developer mailing list for the enhancement of the product. Patch tool takes a patch file that contains the details of the modifications and applies them to the original version of some code in order to create a new, updated version.

Patch Accept Ratio i.e. total no of patches accepted /total no of patches sent

A high Patch Accept Ratio indicates high competence of contributors and reverse is true for the less patch ratios.

F. Total Number of Weekly Downloads

Weekly downloads of a particular software can be obtained from sourceforge.net website.

6. Automation of Open-Source Software Metrics

To automate the open-source software metrics, suggested in section VI, a case study deals with 50 open source software's (obtained from www.sourceforge.net) is taken (Annexure 1). A tool named as Software Metric calculation Tool, is developed using Asp.Net Framework with MS-Access as database storage. This study is performed on the basis of following parameters to critically analyze the behavior of open-source software community:

- No. of Contributors
- Average domain experience of Contributors
- Weekly downloads
- Patch submitted
- Patch accepted
- Time to generate first version
- Time to generate last update
- Total number of versions
- Total number of bugs/fixations/updations w.r.t. a particular version
- Weekly downloads

A. Working of Software Metrics Calculation Tool

The working of Software Metrics Calculation tool is shown as below:

- Figure 2 shows that details of software such as project name, weekly downloads, total versions, patch submitted, patch accepted, start date and last update date of the project. Average time and patch accept ratio are calculated automatically by clicking on the calculate button. Information about the new software is added in the database by selecting add new option. Average time is calculated by taking the diff between start date and last update divided by number of versions.

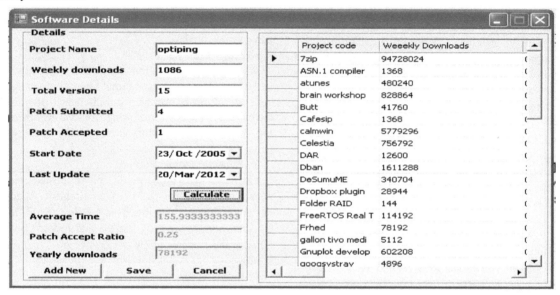

Figure 2. Software Details Form.

- Figure 3 show that user first selects the name of the software and then specify the number of contributors involved in the software.

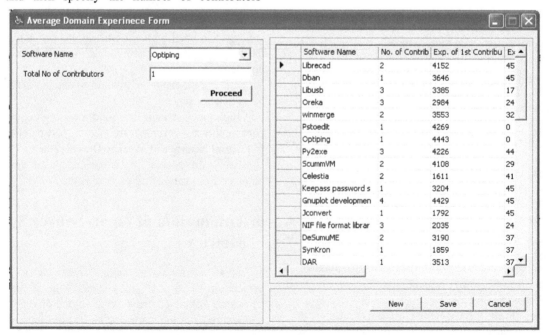

Figure 3. Number of Contributors form

• Figure 4 shows average domain experience, which is calculated in days. If more than one contributor is involved in particular software then experience of each contributor is calculated in number of days and sum is divided by the total number of contributors.

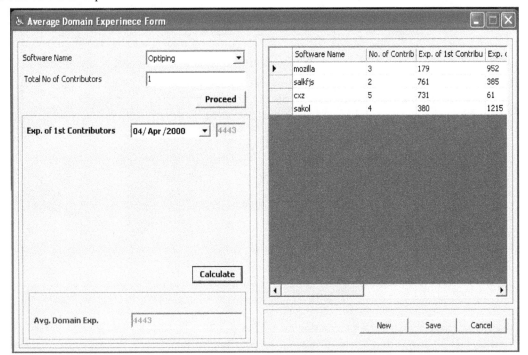

Figure 4. *Average Domain Experience Form*

• Figure 5 represents the way how details of each version are stored in database. These details includes software name, version name, number of bug fixes, number of existing features updated, number of new features added and number of existing features dropped.

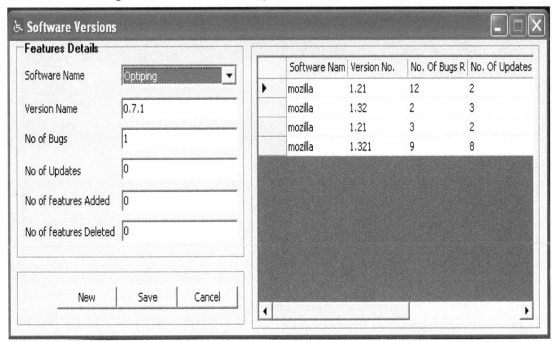

Figure 5. *Versions Details Form*

• Five types of graphs are generated to show the development process of all the versions, total number of bugs fixed, total number of features update, total number of features added and deleted. Figure 6 represents shows development graph of all the softwares.

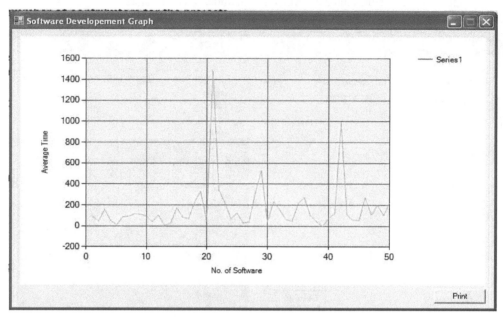

Figure 6.- Development Graph Form

• Around 50 softwares have been taken for validating the proposed set of metrics. Every ach software is evaluated on the basis of total number of bug's fixed, total number of features update, total number of features added and deleted. All details with respect to softwares are manually collected from www.sourceforge.net data dump. A We obtained password is obtained in order to access their data dump. However, the proposed metrics are being calculated automatically by the Software Metric Calculation Tool.

Figures 7, 8, 9, 10 show all these activities simultaneously with respect to software WinMerge (a Windows-based tool for visual difference display and merging, for both files and directories), having weekly downloads numbering 34126, with 72 total number of versions in 2011 having first version on 2000. The total number of patches submitted for this product is 3016, out of this; only 2182 are utilized for generating next versions (Annexure 1).

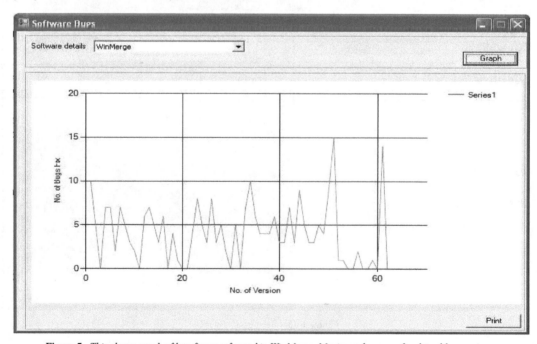

Figure 7. -This shows graph of bug fixes performed in WinMerge. Maximum bugs are fixed in older versions.

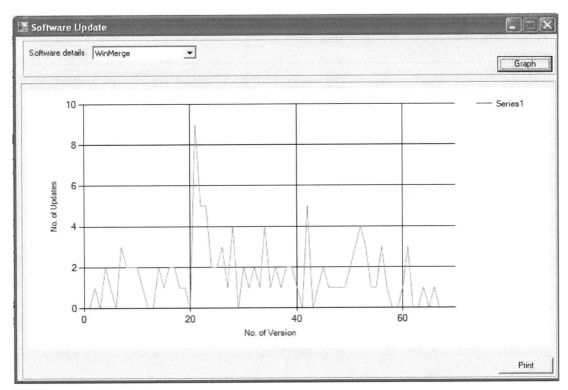

Figure 8.- This figure represents updates performed in WinMerge.

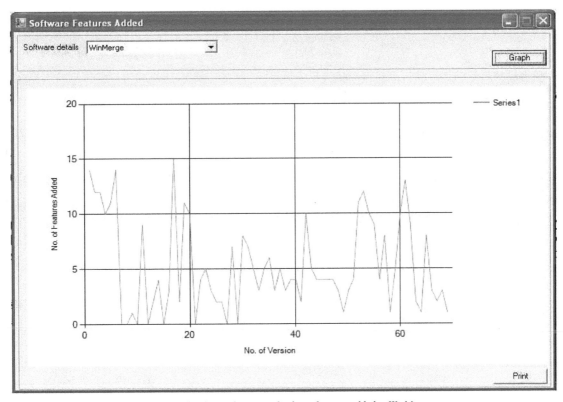

Figure 9.- This figure shows graph of new features added to WinMerge.

7. Conclusions

This paper makes an effort to explore some concepts related to free software, open source software and open source software community. Open source software community is a combination of active users as well as passive users which consists of developers, project leaders, bug fixers & reporters. A great data is available with respect to open source software community through which one can make the comparative analysis between different above said issues and concerns. A metric-based approach is explained to check the evolution of open source software development processes. Future work will include the automation of collection of raw data from various resources.

Annexure - 1

S No.	Project Name	Weekly Downloads	Contributors Name	Staring time in the domain	Patch Submitted	Patch Accepted	Time to generate first versions (Start)	Time till last version complete (last update)	Total number of versions
1	Warkeys	27423	Warkeys	19-2-2006	-	-	20-2-2006	12-1-2012	42(124)
2	Calmwin free antivirus	80268	Alch, gianlivigi tiesi	22-3-2004, 5-6-2000	10	-	25-3-2004	3-4-2012	62
3	Celestia	10511	Ajtribick , chris laurel	5-1-2008, 23-2-2001	7	-	23-2-2001	29-12-2011	4
4	7-zip	1315667	Igor paul	17-8-2000	459	20	10-11-2000	30-6-2011	62
5	Winprint	206	Mieczyslaw nalewaj, przemek czerkas	12-11-2001, 12-4-2004	-	-	12-4-2004	22-5-2012	2(9)
6	Winmerge	34126	Christian list, dean grimm	11-9-2002, 28-8-2003	3016	2182	20-10-2000	14-11-2011	72
7	The ASN.1 compiler	49	Lev walkin	11-11-2000	14	-	6-3-2004	16-6-2011	9(54)
8	T38 modem	149	Jordan kojouharov, vyacheslav frolov	2-11-2005, 27-11-2003	4	1	2-11-2005	5-7-2011	6(19)
9	Out2Gcal	4	Thisita	14-7-2010	-	-	14-7-2010	29-9-2010	7
10	Oreka	268	Bruce kingsland, henrih, Ralph atallah	2-4-2004, 17-10-2005, 11-11-2008	3	-	17-10-2005	18-10-2011	8
11	OptiPNG	1086	Cosmintruta, rctruta	4-4-2000,	4	1	23-10-2005	20-3-2012	15(30)
12	NIF file format library and tools	4606	Alphex, amorilia, pacific morrowind	9-11-2006, 8-9-2005, 6-6-2009	32	7	25-5-2009	20-2-2012	179
13	LMS desktop	4	Gianni ven hoecke, marten, Patrick law werts	23-12-2009, 18-12-2009, 6-5-2010	6	-	5-6-2010	14-10-2011	18
14	Libusb-win32	8279	Stephan meyer, travis robinson, xiaofan chen	26-2-2003, 22-7-2007, 18-2-2006	15	1	5-4-2003	23-1-2012	30
15	Libjpej turbo	958	D.R.commander	13-8-2004	34	1	4-2-2010	10-2-2012	10
16	Lame	23189	Alexen Derliedinge, Gabriel bouvigne, Robert hagemem,takehiro tomingo	16-10-2000, 27-11-1999, 29-11-1999, 28-11-1999	60	14	17-11-1999	28-2-2012	21
17	Keepass password safe	131359	Dominik reichl	28-8-2003	77	62	15-11-2003	14-5-2012	73
18	Jaris FLVPlayer	132	JGM, YLM	27-6-2007, 6-3-2010	1	-	18-5-2008	29-8-2011	11
19	Hylafax	3	Stavan jardine	31-1-2001	-	-	17-2-2006	6-4-2011	20
20	Hava Fun	5	Elfman	21-8-2009	1	-	22-8-2009	28-11-2011	3
21	Grsync	121	Piero clrsoni	3-2-2010	3	1	3-2-2010	13-1-2012	5
22	Graphics magick	757	Bob friesenhaHn	30-12-2000	27	-	7-2-2003	28-4-2012	15(46)

23	Googsystray	68	Jim duchek	11-1-2000	3	1	8-9-2009	6-6-2011	15(24)
24	Gnuplot development	8364	Hons-bernhard broeker, clark gaylord, lars hecking, ethan merritt	20-4-2000, 31-1-2000, 27-4-2000, 2-6-2001	607	344	31-1-2000	12-3-2012	18
25	Gallon tivo media server	71	John kohl, leon nicholls	31-7-2004, 7-8-2003	11	7	11-12-2004	24-3-2011	8
26	Frhed	1086	Kimmo varies	18-10-2002	38	4	10-8-2008	6-6-2011	14(15)
27	Folder RAID	2	Liran	1-7-2010	-	-	31-8-2010	3-12-2011	9
28	Dropbox plugin	402	July ighor	5-11-2009	-	-	5-11-2009	2-10-2011	8
29	DeSmuME	4732	Guillaume duhamel, zeromus	11-9-2003, 18-3-2002	138	46	23-12-2006	26-4-2012	16
30	Dban	22379	Darik horn	10-6-2002	2	2	6-9-2002	29-6-2011	16
31	WCD- change directory for DOS and Unix	6	Erwin waterland	9-9-2001	58	41	9-9-2001	29-2-2012	31(68)
32	libreCad	2576	Ries van twisk, dongxi li	20-1-2001, 10-3-2011	35	2	13-8-2010	24-4-2012	6
33	Vantage	7	Mchansy, raoul van bugen	23-7-2009, 15-5-2011	-	-	27-4-2009	5-9-2011	5
34	Ultradefrag	15580	Dmitri arbhangelski, gearspec, justin dearin, zsolt nagy, Stefan pendl	25-6-2007, 28-12-2008, 8-7-2001, 11-3-2008, 28-4-2009	-	-	25-6-2007	22-4-2012	57(58)
35	Pstoedit	1424	Wolfgang glunz	25-9-2000	2	2			
36	Im4java	158	Bernhard bablok	1-1-2001	-	-	23-1-2009	4-4-2012	11
37	DAR	175	Denis corbin	23-10-2002	30	3	25-10-2002	15-4-2012	47
38	Butt	580	Daniel nothen	20-9-2007	-	-	21-9-2007	14-10-2011	16
39	Open video player	713	AdamGreen Baren, Charles newman, dan sparacice, james mutton, Nicholas brooking, pankaj , tommy petrovic	19-10-2009, 22-10-2008, 2-7-2010, 22-10-2008, 11-11-2008, 24-5-2010, 4-6-2010	3	-	21-8-2008	29-6-2011	23
40	Atunes	6670	Fleax	27-6-2006	42	18	7-3-2006	30-4-2012	49
41	Cafesip	19	Amit chatterjee, becky Mc	16-6-2004, 23-6-2004	-	-	14-5-2005	26-4-2012	16
42	FreeRTOS Real Time Kernel	1586	Richard	4-6-2004	59	2	9-6-2004	14-5-2012	65
43	SynKron	2592	Matus tomlein	4-5-2007	-	-	7-5-2007	25-6-2011	13
44	Py2exe	3479	Jimmy retzlaff, Mark hammOnd, Thomas heller	7-11-2000, 16-2-2000, 3-2-2000	27	5	29-11-2000	3-10-2011	17
45	Kdiff3	3994	Joachim eibl	25-7-2002	13	1	25-7-2002	14-10-2011	11(32)

46	Nbuexplorer	3847	Petrusek	23-8-2007	-	-	2-10-2009	26-5-2012	26(27)
47	Jconvert	636	Eds	10-7-2007	-	-	17-7-2008	8-5-2011	11
48	Brain workshop	11512	Paul hoskison	8-8-2008	1	-	8-8-2008	5-4-2012	12
49	ScummVM	19912	Eugene Sandulenke, Strangerke	5-3-2001, 10-6-2004	1536	1282	5-3-2001	21-2-2012	37
50	iramuteq	123	Pierre	4-1-2010	-	-	4-1-2010	16-1-2012	9

References

[1] Anas Tawileh, Omer Rana, and Steve McIntosh (2008), " A social networking approach to F/OSS quality assessment", In Proceedings of the First international conference on Computer-Mediated Social Networking (ICCMSN'08), Maryam Purvis and Bastin Roy Savarimuthu (Eds.). Springer-Verlag, Berlin, Heidelberg, 157-170. DOI=10.1007/978-3-642-02276-0_16 http://dx.doi.org/10.1007/978-3-642-02276-0_16

[2] C. Jensen and W. Scacchi (2005), "Process Modeling Across the Web Information Infrastructure", Wiley InterScience, available at http://www.ics.uci.edu/~wscacchi/Papers/New/Jensen-Scacchi-SPIP-ProSim04.pdf

[3] Cruz, T.Wieland and A. Ziegler (2006)," Evaluation Criteria for Free/Open Source SoftwareProducts Based on Project Analysis", Wiley InterScience. available athttp://www.idi.ntnu.no/grupper/su/courses/tdt10/curricula2010/P5-1-Cruz06.pdf

[4] David P., Waterman A., Arora S. (2003)," The free/ libre & open source software survey for 2003", STANFORD UNIVERSITY, CALIFORNIA, USA, available at http://www-siepr.stanford.edu/programs/OpenSoftware_David/FLOSS-US-Report.pdf

[5] David Neary, (2011), " Open Source Community Building: A Guide to getting it Right", available at http://www.visionmobile.com/blog/2011/01/open-source-community-building-a-guide-to-getting-it-right/

[6] Fredrik Hallberg (2002), "The use of the open source development model in other than software industries. http://www.opensource-marketing.net/OSD.pdf

[7] H. Barkmann, R. Lincke and W. Lowe (2009), "Quantitative Evaluation of Software Quality Metrics in Open-Source Projects", advanced Information Networking and Applications Workshops. http://www.arisa.se/files/BLL-09.pdf

[8] Ismail Ari (2007), "Quantitative Analysis of Open Source Software Projects", the Handbook of Computer Networks, Volume 2, http://users.soe.ucsc.edu/~ari/ari-quan-OSS.pdf

[9] J. Seidel (1998)," Qualitative Data Analysis", SAGE Publications., available at http://www.quarc.de/fileadmin/downloads/Qualitative%20Data%20Analysis_the%20N-C-T%20Modell.pdf

[10] J Xu and G. Madey (2004)," Exploration of the Open Source Software Community", Available athttp://www.cse.nd.edu/~oss/Papers/naacsos04Xu.pdf

[11] J. Xu, Y. Gao, S. Christley and G. Madey (2005), "A topological analysis of the open source software development community", In proceedings of 38th Hawaii International Conference on Systems Science, Hawaii,http://www.nd.edu/~oss/Papers/7_11_07.PDF

[12] K. Stewart and T. Ammeter (2002), "An exploratory study of factors influencing the level of vitalityand popularity of open source projects", In proceedings of international conference on information systems, available at: http://www.rhsmith.umd.edu/faculty/kstewart/ResearchInfo/StewartAmmeter.pdf

[13] Kaur P. and Singh H. (2011)," Measurement of Processes in Open Source Software Development",in proceedings of Journal , Trends In Information Management, (TRIM) University of Kashmir, Srinagar, ISSN-0973-4163, Volume 7, Issue 2, pp 198-207, available athttp://www.inflibnet.ac.in/ojs/index.php/TRIM/article/viewFile/1254/1135

[14] Kaur M. and Kaur P. (2012), "A Review of an Open Source Software Community", In proceedings of National Conference in Emerging Computer Technologies (CECT 2012), vol. 2, page 107-110.

[15] Nicolas Ducheneaut(2005), "Socialization in an Open Source Software

[16] Community: A Socio-Technical Analysis", Palo Alto Research Center, 3333 Coyote Hill Road, Palo Alto, CA, 94304, USA, available at http://www2.parc.com/csl/members/nicolas/documents/JCSCW-OSS.pdf

[17] Pinker S. (2009),"Software Estimation, Measurement, and Metrics", GSAM Version 3.0, available athttp://www.stsc.hill.af.mil/resources/tech_docs/gsam3/chap13.pdf

[18] Raj Agnihotri, Murali Shanker and Prabakar Kothandaraman, "Theorization of the open source software phenomenon: a complex adaptive system approach", Journal of Management and Marketing Research, available at https://docs.google.com/viewer?a=v&pid=gmail&attid=0.2&thid=1354765351e41826&mt=application/pdf

[19] Stallman, Richard M (2010), "Free Software, Free Society",Selected Essays of Richard M. Stallman, Second Edition. Boston, Massachusetts: GNU Press. ISBN 978-0-9831592-0-9.

[20] Scott Christley, Jin Xu, Yongqin Gao, Greg Madey, (2006), "Public goods theory of the open source development community using agent-based simulation", Computer Science and Engineering, University of Notre Dame., available at https://docs.google.com/viewer?a=v&pid=gmail&attid=0.5&thid=1354765351e41826&mt=application

[21] Vinay Tiwari (2011), "Software Engineering Issues in Development Models of Open Source Software",International Journal of Computer Science and Technology, Vol. 2. http://www.ijcst.com/vol22/1/vinay.pdf

[22] Walt Scacchi (2011)," Understanding the Requirements for Developing Open SourceSoftware Systems", publication with revisions.http://www.ics.uci.edu/~wscacchi/Papers/New/Understanding-OS-Requirements.pdf

22

Optimal performance model investigation in component-based software engineering (CBSE)

Muhammad Osama Khan, Ahmed Mateen, Ahsan Raza Sattar

Department Of Computer Science, University of Agriculture Faisalabad, Pakistan

Email address:

osamagoldpk@hotmail.com (M. O. Khan), ahmedmatin@hotmail.com (A. Mateen)

Abstract: Commercial off-the-shelf (COTS) technologies have emerged over the past decade. COTS technology gained significant popularity by developing the optimal, efficient, economically and quickly software system that mapping business requirement. As a consequence, the need for designing effective strategies for enabling large scale reuse, whilst overcoming the risks involved in the use of a particular technology, still remains. In this situation, the use of "COTS" technology introduces many problematic factors that still have not been fully solved; some of them are the lack of inclusive tools, efficient methods to manage and collect the required information for supporting COTS software selection. Keeping in view all these issues in this research report present an Optimal Performance Model (OPM) for gathering the information that is needed to define COTS market segments in a way that would make software components selection more effective and efficient. Mostly the information we collect possess huge diversity therefore suggest OPM's that will certainly help to cover different aspects and fields of COTS software selection. This design model will base on several software quality standards. Commercial of the shelf software has gained considerable popularity as approach that quickly and economical creates software system that address business requirement. This research work will presents an approach for defining assessment principles for reusable software components.

Keywords: COTS, CBSE, ERP, DBMS, BPR

1. Introduction

An efficient and effective software components selection method is necessary to deliver full Capable to the COTS technology. There are many COTS selection techniques, processes and methodologies that have been articulated. COTS-based systems development requires specific activity like desire component selection, composition and last but not least the most important is component integration. After the successful working of this technique it became more popular as a result of this today a large number of software components are commercially available, components selection a to fulfill the all system requirements which minimize the cost of the system software [21]. In COTS for large system are become common a days. Due to low budget, enhance the system requirement, accelerating rates of COTS improvement defined by software Engineering Institute (SEI). Building cost optimal components is very difficult job. Selecting the best components in cots selection presented many challenges to software engineer to retain in new arena. They should consider many constraints. Two major constraints, first selecting optimal components and then their integrity should be considered [1].In this research, the optimal model for component selection is described. Informally, first choose a set of software components from accessible component set which can satisfy all system requirements for the final product or set of products. To optimize and analyse a set of requirements should assign to each component and should allocate a cost which is the overall cost of selection and integration of that components. Many organizations have claimed for improving the productivity and quality of software development using COTS Selection [28].Therefore many software organizations have introduces COTS technologies in the software industry. A number of COTS components supporting tools have been introduce by software engineers and consultants .The popularity increase of commercial and embeddable software components and software environments following standardization [17]. The quality and standard components more available so more potential reuse candidates. Many developing organizations are spending a large amount of time in COTS selection since the choice of the suitable components has a major effect on the project and final product [17]. We have developed OPM that addresses the selection process, Components software package. OPM has been introduced which supports the selection, search, and evolution of reusable software components and provides specific procedures for defining the development quality standards. If OPM for selection component is not defined then each project finds its own procedure to complete it. This model compares the cost of individual components for cost optimization and analyses the benefits of alternative selection components [28]. Software development organization initiated process for definition of requirements for customer business process in COTS Enterprise Resource Planning (ERP). The software modules are available for commercial vendors that support business processes such as production planning, finance, human resource, accounting and procurement. COTS-ERP integrating the data required for these business processes in a logically single database [7]. COTS ERP systems are based on the principle that the software vendor can map the common business processes more effectively and efficiently than customer organizations. Because ERP software is maintained by the vendor and developing of business processes defined by the vendor. Return on the investment (ROI) of customer and Total cost savings are based on the developing organization adopting the business process [8].Mostly ERP system the required limited customization through changes to configuration settings in the specific module .Configuration setting of the components up to standard then software required less maintenance costs ,if configuration settings is unsupported then software maintenance costs is increase, consequently reducing the overall return on the consumer's investment [13].More and more organizations going toward standardization regarding their process then resulting several organizations like public, state, local government and private are either implementing or planning to implement COTS-ERP systems. COTS -ERP system integrating the required data from these modules in a logically single database [28].

2. Objectives

OPM will satisfy the consistent and relevant system requirement with high quality and reliability for software development.OPM will select and test the candidate components. Component development will lead to the final components that satisfying the requirements with correct

and expected results. The OPM are to select and test the candidate components and check whether they satisfy the system requirement with high reliability and quality.

The system architecture design are to collect the users requirement, identify the system specification, select appropriate system architecture, and determine the implementation details such as platform, programming languages, etc.

3. Materials and Methods

The increased commercial availability of embeddable software components, standardization of basic software environments (such as Microsoft Windows, UNIX), and the explosive popularity of the Internet has resulted in a new situation for reusable software consumers: there are many more accessible reuse candidates. Consequently, many organizations are spending much time in reusable component selection since the choice of the appropriate components has a major impact on the project and resulting product. The component selection process is not defined so each project finds its own approach to it. Here a method has been introduce which supports the search, evolution and selection of reusable software and provides specific techniques for defining the evolution criteria, comparing the cost and benefits of alternatives and consolidating the evolution and selection and benefits of alternatives and consolidating the evolution results in decision making.

Component-Based Software Engineering (CBSE) is concerned with composing, selecting and designing components. As this approach become the more popular of and consequently several commercially available software components grows, selecting group of required components to full fill the   requirements even though minimizing cost is becoming more hard. Optimal component systems selection is not an easy task. It requires not only optimal components selection, although also to take their relationship into account. Selecting component problem described in this research paper. To accomplish this goal, we must to assign each component a set of requirements which satisfies. Each component is assigned a unit cost which is the overall cost of acquirement and integration of that component. Several organizations have supported their reuse with E technologies. Component Based ERP systems have packages which offered by commercial vendors. These packages support main administrative processes such as accounting, procurement, budgeting and human resource management. These integrated System in a single database.

Table 1. Difference between Traditional software development and component based Software development

Traditional Software Development	Custom Development	Component based Software development
Requirements	Creation of system requirements to create a Software system that meets these requirements (the engineers are producers).	Creation of a set of flexible requirements followed by the COTS marketplace exploration for selecting components that best fit these requirements. The engineers are consumers who then integrate the products.
Design	Analyze requirements to produce a depiction of the internal structure and integration of the system that	To integrate the products into a software system that meets the requirements. It implies an iterative

Traditional Software Development	Custom Development	Component based Software development
	will serve the foundation for its construction.	trade-off process of requirements analysis, architecture, COTS availability, prioritization and negotiation.
Construction	Coding the detailed design to implement the system requirements	Some requirement functionalities that were not addressed by any COTS are usually developed in-house. In any case, usually glue code is used to mediate components interactions; as well as bridges or adaptors to smooth over incompatibilities in the component interfaces.
Testing	Integration and evaluation of the product quality by verifying its behavior by a finite set of test cases	Although COTS are tested by the component provider, they should be retested by the user to assure their suitability and their good system integration
Maintenance	Modification to code and associated documentation due to a problem or need for improvement	Due to maintenance effects, COTS-Based systems undergo a technology refresh and renewal cycle that has many implications.

Table 2. Advantages and disadvantages of using COTS software

Advantages	Disadvantages
Immediately available; earlier payback	Licensing, intellectual property procurement delays
Avoids expensive development	Up-front licensing fees
Avoids expensive maintenance	Recurring maintenance fees
Predictable, confirmable license fees and performance	Reliability often unknown or inadequate; scale difficult to change.
Better functionality	Too-better functionality compromises performance and usability.
Repeated upgrades often expect organization's needs	No control over maintenance and upgrades.
Broadly mature and use technologies	Constraints on efficiency and functionality.
Devoted support organization	Dependence on vendor
roadway technology needs	Synchronizing multiple-software vendors.
Hardware /software independent.	Integration not always trivial; incompatibilities among vendors.

Table 3. ERP implementation models

Author(s)	ERP implementation model	Notes
Bancroft et al.(1998)	(1) Focus, (2) Creating As-Is picture, (3) Creating of the To-Be design, (4) Construction and testing, and (5) Actual Implementation	
Kuruppuarachchi et al. (2002)	(1) Initiation, (2) Requirement definition, (3) Acquisition/development, (4) Implementation, and (5) Termination	A model of IT projects
Markus and Tanis (2000)	(1) Project chartering, (2) The project, (3) Shakedown, and (4) Onward and upward	
Mäkipää (2003)	(1) Initiative, (2) Evaluation, (3) Selection, (4) Modification, Business Process Reengineering, and Conversion of Data, (5) Training, (6) Go-Live, (7) Termination, and (8) Exploitation and Development	Three parallel phases in phase number 4.
Parr and Shanks (2000a)	(1) Planning, (2) Project: a. setup, b. reengineer, c. design, d. configuration & testing, e. installation, (3) Enhancement	
Rajagopal (2002)	(1) Initiation, (2) Adoption, (3) Adaptation, (4) Acceptance, (5) Reutilization, and (6) Infusion	Applied from Kwon and Zmud's (1987) model of IT implementation
Ross (1999)	(1) Design, (2) Implementation, (3) Stabilization, (4) Continuous improvement, and (5) Transformation.	
Shields (2001)	Rapid implementation model of three phases and 12 major activities	
Umble et al. (2003)	(1) Review and process to date before implementation, (2) test and Install any new hardware (3) Install the software. (4) Get system training, (5) Training on the conference room pilot, (6) Establish security and necessary permissions, (7) Ensure that all data bridges are sufficiently robust and the data are sufficiently accurate, (8) Document policies and procedures, (9) Improve continually. Bring the entire organization on-line, either in a total cutover or in a phased approach.	
Verville and Halingten (2003)	(1) Planning, (2) Information search, (3) Selection, (4) Evaluations, and (5) Negotiation	Model of the ERP Acquisition Process (MERPAP)

The Critical Success Factors in ERP implementation are described in addition to of the general literature on IT implementation, project management and Business Process Reengineering (BPR). This list was rated by IT managers. The consensus concerning ERP implementation is that multiple factors affect success. They have defined implementation project success as a function of critical success factors (CSFs). ERP implementation research has widely tried to specify the CSFs of ERP implementation projects.

Table 4. *Critical success factors of ERP implementation*

	Critical success factor	Mean	Std. Dev
1	Top management support	4.29	1.16
2	Project team competence	4.20	1.07
3	Interdepartmental cooperation	4.19	1.20
4	Clear goals and objectives	4.15	1.14
5	Careful package selection	3.89	1.06
6	Interdepartmental communication	4.09	1.33
7	Dedicated resources	4.06	1.37
8	Project champion	4.03	1.58
9	Project management	4.13	0.96
10	Vendor support	4.03	1.6
11	Data analysis & conversion	3.83	1.27
12	Management of expectations.	3.81	1.25
13	Use of steering committee	3.79	1.95
14	Minimal customization	3.79	1.16
15	Education in new business processes	3.76	1.18
16	Business Process Reengineering, BPR	3.68	1.26
17	User software training	3.68	1.45
18	Architecture choices	3.44	1.19
19	Use of vendors' tools	3.43	1.34
20	Partnership with vendor	3.39	1.21
21	Change management	3.15	1.57
22	Use of consultants	2.90	1.20

3.1. Optimal Performance Model

We suppose that components are provided with interfaces that explicitly declare the component estimated performance properties. The estimate performance which better fulfills the non-functional and performance-related requirements could be used by the Software Architect. Items in the factor "Project Success" are divided into two groups "Progress" and "Quality" The new factor "Progress" includes questions about project completion on time and within budget, while "Quality" has questions related to system quality and the scope matched with the company's needs. The other variables remained the same as they were in the pilot survey. "Function" is the most important factor for "Quality" of the ERP system. It indicates that selecting the right software and defining the necessary functions should be given the most consideration to enhance the overall quality of the ERP system. "Consultant Support" can also impact on "Quality, but there is no impact expected from "Internal Support".

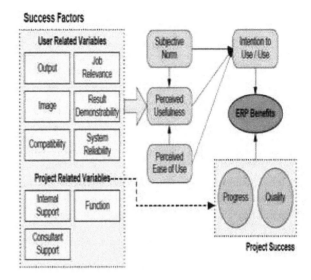

Figure 1. *Optimal Performance Model*

3.2. Survey Questionnaire

This questionnaire (which starts on the following page), gives you an opportunity to tell us your reactions to the SAP-ERP applications you used. The user responses help us to understand different aspects of the ERP system. The results have been used for research purpose only and we will not identify any Organization or individual in any publication.

Please read each statement and indicate how strongly users agree or disagree.

Table 5. *Evaluating Oracle ERP Application*

1	Name (Optional):
2	Current Position:
3	Work Experience with SAP-ERP Applications:
4	Work Experience with other ERP Applications:
5	No of ERP Implementation Project done & Roles:
6	Names of ERP Implementation Organization

The survey tool is planned based on the OPM model, and most relevant parameter in the survey are primarily adapted from the relevant earlier research in the IS contexts. The main survey was conducted to analyse ERP success before proposed model well developed. The main survey to examine whether or not the Data analysis including correlation, factor analysis and reliability test was conducted to adjust survey items and extract factors associated with the success of ERP systems. The new survey instrument which has been used in the main survey and the revised ERP success model after adjustment with the pilot survey are proposed in this chapter. The revised model looks much simpler than the conceptual model.

QUESTIONNAIRE

1 It is easy to learn and understand several transactions involves for completing one business process?

2 It is easy to learn and understand the total number of transactions involves for completing whole Module level business process?

3 Overall, ERP application requires minimum number of transactions to complete business processes?

4 I am satisfied the way transactions and business processes are organized in ERP application?

5 Business processes wise training or reference material for different module is easily available from ERP Vendor or Consultant?

6 It is easy to perform data cleansing & harmonization in ERP application?

7 It is easy to perform data transformation task in ERP application?

8 It is easy to perform testing and data loading in ERP application?

9 It is easy to perform data migration by using API method?

10 Overall, it is easy to learn the process of data migration in this ERP application?

11 Once learned, it is easy to remember data migration process after a period of non-use (at least one or few months)?

12 Service response time on error messages from ERP vendor is too slow?

13 Many peoples handling the same error for service request causes slow responses time?

14 I like using the User interface of ERP application?

15 ERP application has all the functionalities and capabilities that I expect it to have?

16 Overall, I am satisfied with this ERP application?

17 In ERP implementation projects the degree of top management team contributions in support, planning and training, with respect to respondents.

18 ERP software can support its business processes as well as the functionality of the respondent's company.

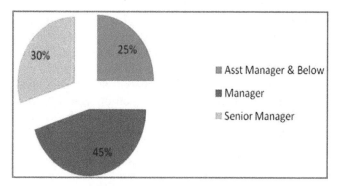

Figure 2. Survey Respondents' Position in their Company

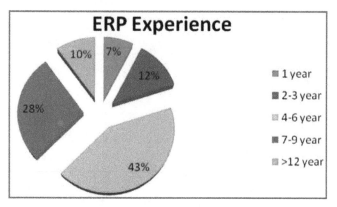

Figure 3. No of year SAP ERP Experience

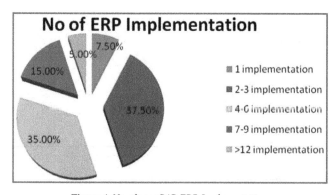

Figure 4. No of year SAP ERP Implementation

4. Results and Discussion

In last four decades information systems have been developed, There are so much research has been conducted to comprehend the develop systems customized to a specific organization. During the last 10 years it however became clear that a different practice had slowly emerged in the area of Enterprise Systems Software. Thus over the years it had become more and more common for software providers to reuse existing code (code developed for prior customer) whenever developing an Information System for a new customer. Thus most Enterprise Software had become pre-developed software targeted at specific lines of businesses instead of tailor-made software for a specific customer. This phenomenon can be observed for different kinds of software e.g. Enterprise Resource Planning (ERP) software, Supply Chain Management (SCM) software, and Project Management (PM). In this thesis I will focus on ERP package software.

The pilot survey was developed by using Google docs and was conducted as a web-based survey. The link to the survey was sent to the contacted individuals so that they can distribute it to other possible participants.

In ERP software consists of number of modules. In the organization, each module deal with a specific functional area e.g. Purchase Inventory, Quality Management , Plant Maintenance , human resource, finance, warehousing, sales or project management, and all the modules in the ERP System are integrated.   ERP have common database. The final product in the Enterprise Package Software is marketed "best practice". Nevertheless, "best practice" does not necessarily mean that only one version of a process is supported by the software. Many functional areas have businesses or different practices experienced. This research originated the conceptual ERP success model based on theories and knowledge gained from several industry practitioners. DeLone and McLean's IS success model was used for recognized success indicators The OPM model adapted the TAM as the Opening point for the arrangement of relationships between factors and indicators. In conclusion, the fundamentals of project management were incorporated into the OPM model for investigated the success of ERP implementation. As a result, for better understanding about the success of ERP systems this OPM model is theoretically sound and can be helpful.

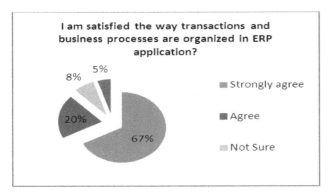

Figure 5. Survey Question

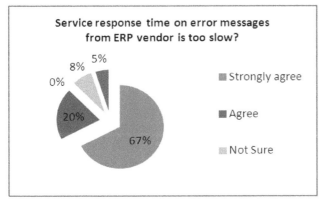

Figure 6. Survey Question

The main research result here is that the new factor proposed from this research, "Function" is the most significant factor to be absolutely linked with "perceived usefulness". Most of the users understand that if the functionality of their ERP system is good enough for business process.

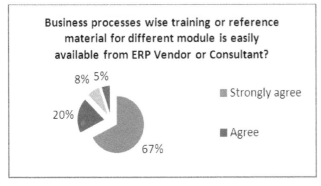

Figure 7. Survey Question

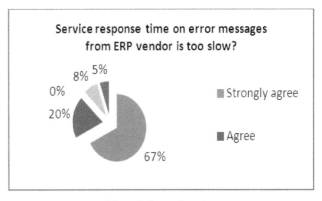

Figure 8. Survey Question

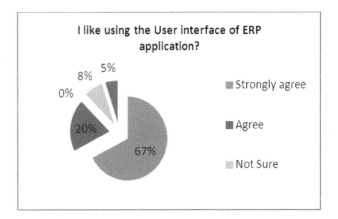

Figure 9. Survey Question

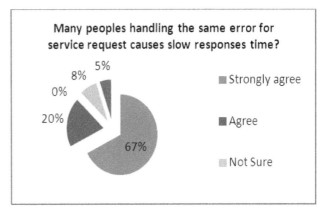

Figure 10. Survey Question

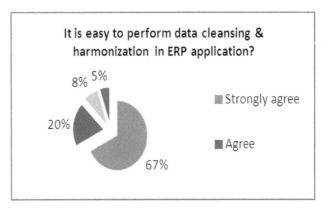

Figure 11. Survey Question

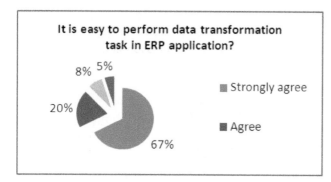

Figure 12. Survey Question

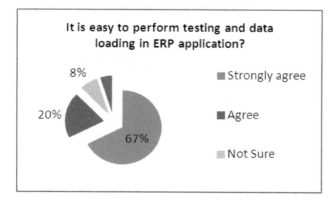

Figure 13. Survey Question

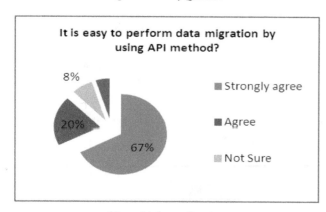

Figure 14. Survey Question

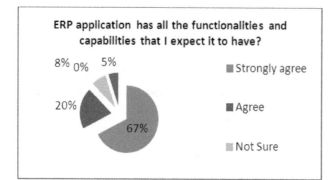

Figure 15. Survey Question

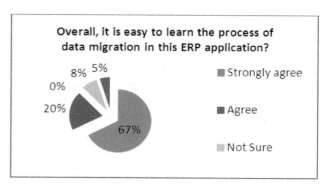

Figure 16. Survey Question

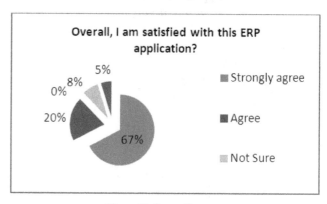

Figure 17. Survey Question

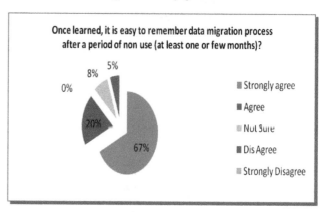

Figure 18. Survey Question

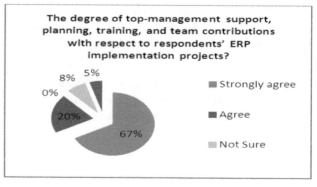

Figure 19. Survey Question

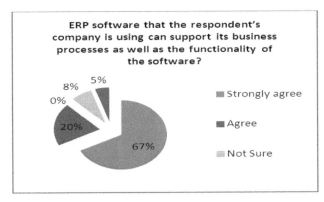

Figure 20. *Survey Question*

The Mostly Users think ERP system is useful. Moreover, how business requirements match the functions of the ERP system. Mainly make the ERP system is more useful. Dissimilar other information traditional systems, necessary functions across the departments in the ERP system needs to integrate within an organization to be fully valuable. This exact feature causes "Perceived Usefulness" have the major impact on "Function" to. It should be renowned that the ERP system must be considered part of business functions and processes sooner than an information system.

It is analyzed that results point to that more use and better quality of ERP systems can add to the benefits of ERP. The two project success indicators (i.e. "Quality and Progress") have a positive impact on success indicator (i.e. "Intention to Use / Use") and on the final dependent variable, "ERP Benefits".

5. Conclusion

In this research discusses relationships between success factors and indicators in more detail, describing the reason behind their relationships. Interpretations of the results about each dependent variable are presented along with its independent variables based on its analysis and other relevant data from the survey. The section discusses why a difference exists in a particular variable, and interprets its meaning with respect to ERP success. In conclusion, the research proposed several suggestions for the accomplishment of ERP systems based on the results of recognizing indicators and the relationships between indicators. These suggestions should allow software engineering have a better understanding of ERP success and help them to abstain failure considering critical factors recognized to successful ERP completion.

Most IT related research in the area of construction business management generally proposes research models without theories. Furthermore, since this kind of research is still comparatively new to construction related research, a lot surveys have been formed without sound theoretical background. They usually recognize the factors which compare the mean values of factors, and rank factors in with their importance showing the higher mean value as the more important factor. This research projects first time

point out the factors affecting ERP success with strong background theories in construction business related research. The OPM adapted three theoretically validated models including D&M IS Success Model and TAM, the fundamentals of project management in ERP implementation. Therefore, the professional contribution of this research project can be found in a deliberate attempt to develop the ERP success model.

There have been few studies attempting to validate empirically the factors affecting both ERP implementation and user adoption. The factors identified in literature were mostly based on the experiences of IT professionals or senior managers involved in ERP implementation projects. For these reasons, this research focused on identifying the factors for the ERP success from both implementation project and user adoption perspectives. Then, identified factors were examined to verify their relationships with success indicators associated with the redefined ERP success, i.e. the success of the project and the success of use. Moreover, the research study proposed recommendations for the ERP success explaining how to approach ERP implementation to avoid failure and what to do more considering the importance of each factor to a given dependent variable based on the findings of the study. These recommendations can give valuable information to engineering firms when they want implementing or upgrading their ERP systems.

References

[1] Aberdour, M. 2007. Achieving Quality in Open Source Software.*IEEE Software*, 24(1): 58–64.

[2] Balbo, G., and G. Serazzi. 1997. Asymptotic Analysis of Multiclass Closed Queueing Networks: Multiple Bottlenecks. *Performance Evaluation*, 30(3): 115-152.

[3] Brownsword, L., T. Oberndorfand C.A. Sledge. 2000. Developing New Processes for COTS-Based Systems. *IEEE Software*, 17(4): 48-55.

[4] Balsamo, S., A. D. Marco, P. Inverardi and M. Simeoni. 2006. Efficient Performance models in Component-Based Software Engineering. *IEEE Computer Society*,38(3): 64-71.

[5] Balsamo, S., A.D. Marco, P. Inverardiand M. Simeoni. 2004. Model-Based Performance Prediction in Software Development.*IEEE Transactions on Software Engineering*,30(5): 295-310.

[6] Becker, S., L. Grunske, R. Mirandola and S. Overhage. 2006. Architecting Systems with Trustworthy Components. *Lecture Notes in Computer Science*, 3938(1): 169-248.

[7] Bertolino, A. and R. Mirandola. 2004. CB-SPE Tool: Putting Component-Based Performance Engineering into Practice. *Component Based Software Engineering*, 3054(1): 233-248.

[8] Becker, S., H. Koziolek and R. Reussner. 2009. The Palladio Component Model for Model-Driven Performance Prediction.*J. Systems and Software*, 82(1): 3–22.

[9]   Chen, S., I. Gorton, A. Liu and Y. Liu. 2002. Performance Prediction of Component-based Applications. *Journal of Systems and Software*, 74(1): 35-43.

[10] Crnkovic, I., M. Chaudron and S. Larsson.2005.Component-based Development Process and Component Lifecycle.*Journal of Computing and Information Technology*, 13(4): 321-327.

[11] Craig. D. C. (2007). Compatibility of Software Components-Modelling and Verification.Ph.D Thesis, Univ., Memorial, Newfoundland.

[12] Denaro, G., A. Polini and W. Emmerich. 2004. Early Performance Testing of Distributed Software Applications.*ACM SIGSOFT Software Engineering Notes*, 29(1):94-103.

[13] Fox, M. R., D. C. Brogan and F. Reynolds. 2004. Approximating component selection, *Winter Simulation Conference*, 25(5): 429-434.

[14] Glenn A., A. Thomas and S. Jajodia. 2004. Commercial-Off-The- Shelf Enterprise Resource Planning Software Implementations in the Public Sector: Practical Approaches for Improving Project Success, *The Journal of Government Financial Management*, 53 (2): 10-15.

[15] Grassi,V., R. Mirandola, and A. Sabetta. 2007. Filling the Gap between Design and Performance/Reliability Models of Component-Based Systems: SA Model-Driven Approach,*J. Systems and Software*, 80(4): 528–558.

[16] Grozev, N. 2011. A comparison of component-based software engineering and model-driven development from the ProCom perspective. M.S thesis.Univ.,Mälardalen,Sweden.

[17] Hofmeister, C., P. Kruchten, R.L. Nord, H. Obbink, A. Ran and P. America. 2007. Generalizing a Model of Software Architecture Design from Five Industrial Approaches, *Journal of Systems and Software*, 80(1):106-126.

[18] Kim, I.Y. and O. Weck. 2005. Adaptive weighted-sum method for bi-objective optimization: Pareto front generation. *Structural and Multidisciplinary Optimization*, 29(2):149-158.

[19] Kontio, j. 1996.A Case Study in Applying a Systematic Method for COTS selection. *IEEE Computer Society*, 32(4):201-209.

[20] Kuz.I., Y. Liu, I.Gorton and GernotHeiser. 2007. CAmkES: A component model for secure microkernel-based embedded systems, *The Journal of Systems and Software*, 80(1): 687-699.

[21] Kaur, A. and K. S. Mann. 2010. Component Selection for Component based Software Engineering. *International Journal of Computer Applications*, 2(1):12-18.

[22] Lau, K. and Z.Wang. 2007. Software Component Models. *IEEE Transaction on Software Engineering*,33(10): 3-8

[23] Madanmohan, T.R. and R. De.2004. Open Source Reuse in Commercial Firms. *IEEE Software*,21(6): 62-69.

[24] Mohamed, A.2007. Decision Support for Selecting COTS Software Products Based on Comprehensive Mismatch Handling. Ph.D. Thesis, univ., Calgary, Alberta.

[25] Mahmood, S. and A. Khan. 2011. An industrial study on the importance of software component documentation: A system integrators perspective. *Information Processing Letters*, 111(12): 583-590.

[26] Navas, J. and J.Babau. 2009. Efficient and Adapted Component-Based Strategies for Embedded Software Device Drivers Development. *IEEE Computer Society*, 2(1): 514-519.

[27] Peslak, A.L R., G.H. Subramanian and G.E. Clayton.2008.The Phases of ERP Software Implementation and Maintenance: A Model for Predicting Preferred ERP Use. Journal of Computer Information Systems, 48(2): 25–33

[28] Rawashdeh, A. and B. Matalkah.2006.A New Software Quality Model for Evaluating COTS Components, 2 (4): 373-381.

[29] Runeson, P. and M. Höst. 2009. Guidelines for conducting and reporting case study research in software engineering. *Empirical Software Engineering*, 14(2): 131-164.

[30] Torchiano, M. and M. Morisio. 2004. Overlooked Aspects of COTS-Based Development. *IEEE Software*, 21(2): 88-93.

[31] Tekumalla,B. 2012. Status of Empirical Research in Component Based Software engineering.M.S thesis, Univ. Gothenburg, Sweden.

[32] Vilpola, I. 2008. Applying User-Centred Design in ERP Implementation Requirements Analysis.Ph.D Thesis,Univ.Technology,Tampere.

[33] Victor, S., C. Becerra andG.Valdes.2010.Empirical Validation of Component-based Software Systems Generation and Evaluation Approaches.*CeliElectronicJournal*,13(1) : 2-9

[34] Wu.X.and M. Woodside. 2004. Performance Modeling from Software Components, ACM/SIGSOFT Software Eng. Notes, 29(1): 290–301.

[35] Wanyama,T. and B.Far. 2008.An Empirical Study to Compare Three Methods for Selecting Cots.Software Components. *International Journal of Computing and ICT Research*, 2(1): 34-41.

[36] Winkelmann, A. 2012. Reference Model Maintenance Based On ERP System Implementations. AIS Transactions on Enterprise Systems 3(1):1-9

23

Application methods of ant colony algorithm

Elnaz Shafigh Fard[1], Khalil Monfaredi[2], Mohammad H. Nadimi[1]

[1]Faculty of Computer Engineering, Najafabad branch, Islamic Azad University, Isfahan, Iran
[2]Engineering Faculty, Department of Electrical and Electronic Engineering, Azarbaijan Shahid Madani University, Tabriz, Iran

Email addresses:
shafighfard@azaruniv.edu (E. S. Fard), khmonfaredi@azaruniv.ac.ir (K. Monfaredi), nadimi@iaun.ac.ir (M. H. Nadimi)

Abstract: As one of the most prestigious and beneficial methods of artificial intelligence, ant colony takes the advantage of communal behavior of ants in nature for solving optimization problems in various fields. However, this useful algorithm requires extensive and repetitious computation, as a result, the processing duration of the present algorithm seems to be one of the most serious challenges about it. In order to solve optimization problems in which duration is very important, this paper attempts to review the previously applied methods and consider the advantages and the disadvantages of each method through highlighting the problems algorithm designers encounter.

Keywords: Ant Colony, Optimization, Process Duration, Artificial Intelligence, Nature

1. Introduction

Nowadays, mathematical and physical methods can easily resolve some issues; on the other hand, their analysis cannot be done via typical methods. Engineers encounter vast complications and alternative solutions in a way that pronouncing a way as the best alternative seems absolutely difficult. Thus, a bunch of new conceptions under the shelter of complementary computation have been proposed for being put into use in optimization process and high speed search. Ant colony is one of the mentioned methods which has been inspired by nature and functions in many fields such as vectoring peddlers, financial issues, management of affairs, designation of axes, etc.(C.Blum,A.Roli,2003). In this algorithm, ants can solve the problems related to optimization by their tendency of mutual collaboration, collusion, and self-renovation. In recent decades parallel applications for the elevation of algorithm performance have been focused. The major problem of these algorithms is that they are time consuming because some calculations are done repeatedly and investigation areas are vast. This can take long hours, even may last for days. Hence, the typical application of such optimized algorithm for most speed functions will be useless. In the following passage, ant colony algorithm and its function will be introduced. The second section will offer some software, hardware, and compound methods together with efficiencies and deficiencies. Possible problems and challenges of designing and applying ant colony have been discussed in the third section and are preceded by the conclusion.

1.1. Ant Colony

Ant colony is one of the most prestigious alternatives of artificial intelligence that was proposed for the first time by Dorrigo and Dicaroin1992. The intelligent element is a being that can perceive environment through sensors and can manipulate environment by operators. While walking, ants usually leave a kind of chemical substance behind themselves called pheromone. The mentioned substance gradually starts evaporating. Shortly after evaporation, ant footsteps remain on the ground. When ants decide on their directions, they usually choose a path containing maximum amount of pheromone or already the way for other ants to pass. In every single phase, each ant builds up a resolution independently and spontaneously based on the distribution probability by using an item which benefits pheromone and heuristic factors as the following formula.

$$pij = \frac{[\tau i,j]^{\alpha}[\eta i,j]^{\beta}}{\sum [\tau i,j]^{\alpha}[\eta i,j]^{\beta}} \qquad \text{Formula 1}$$

After finding a solution for each ant, others begin to update locally and after choosing the best direction, they attempt a universal updating as formula 2 and 3.

$$\tau ijnew = (1-\rho)\, \tau ij(old) + \rho \Delta \tau ij \qquad \text{Formula 2}$$

$$\Delta \tau ij = (n.\, [\![Lnn)]\!]\, (-1) \qquad \text{Formula 3}$$

$$\tau ij^{new}=(1\text{-}\rho)\ \tau ij^{(old)} \qquad \text{Formula 4}$$

Evaporation as formula 4 takes place in all routes because if it does not occur, the result will be divergent and gradually the best routes will lose their quality. The process is repeated until algorithm comes to a conclusion and termination in addition to the offering of the best solution to the applied program.

2. Proposed Methods

In this phase, parallel applications for this algorithm are introduced. They fall under three categories: software, hardware, and compound.

2.1. Software Methods

In the last twenty years, researches have been searching for the techniques to improve traditional method of ant colony and to increase its speed. By categorizing ant colony into groups and sending each group to the processors, the speed application for this beneficial serial algorithm has been optimized (F. Glover, G. Kochenberger, 2003). This application not only improves the speed of algorithm but also presents a new derivation which has positive impact on the results. The major component is usually between the minor particles and grand particles of algorithm application. The most classic suggestion in relation to the parallel method of application such as the applying on multi-processor s, graphic processors, and grade environments are good opportunities for parallel estimations for optimizing the ant colony results and reducing the time of application (Martin, 2011Pedemonte). Various methods have been proposed which can be divided in five groups: 1. Manorial system 2. Cellular 3. Independent run 4. Multi colony 5. Compounds.

2.1.1. Initial Works

In early 1990s, the ideas were focused on the parallel application of ant colony. The first proposal for the application by Dorrigo attempted to develop the quality of algorithm. After Dorrigo, the first application was conducted by minor particle technique (M. Bolondi, M. Bondaza, 1993). An ant was dedicated to a single processor; however, because the deliverance of information should have been done, load of information exchange was a sort of shortcoming and encountered criteria problem. Then, in hierarchical application, several ants were specified to a processor. After the information distribution in hierarchical form, the information exchange was initiated simultaneously. In this case, the problem of criteria is solved but there is still the barrier of exchange (M. Dorigo, G. Di Caro, 1999).

2.1.2. Manorial System

This method is famous for its simplicity and facility of its application. Micro-processors were used as the tenants that undertake the application solutions and local searches have sent the information to landlords for finding the best

ant which proved to be better in speed and quality(E.Talbi, O.Roux, 2001). But in minor particles for the maximum burden, the speed is roughly reduced. The problem has been solved by using shared memories (P.Delisle, M.Gravel, 2005). Of course, the existing landlord in grand particles as a gate can always be raised and it requires more observation.

2.1.3. Cellular Method

Ant colony is located within the pheromone matrix. In this method, each ant is corresponded to a cell and the resolution act of each ant is gradually spread over the entire matrix. This method is not a parallel method. Just an investigation of parallelism has been presented which used distribution memory. That is the best among parallel methods.(M.Pedemonte, H.Cancela, 2010)

2.1.4. Independent Run Method

In this method, several micro-processors focus on a colony and several serial ants run independently in each micro-processor. Different models of it have been proposed for application that the basis for independent run is a colony among many processors in a way that MMAS runs on GPU. Each thread is allocated to an ant and initialing CPU and main algorithm on graphic CPU was conducted on each thread before entering to the critical area that had been blocked so that the former thread finish its task. Specially, in some methods for lack of communication of processors with each other the speed was high. Nevertheless, the existing critical area in this field deserves further study. The model is one of the parallel methods in which several colonies collaborate and their collaboration in a form of ace crone has been illustrated. Most applications have utilized shared intelligence in the platform clustering. Recent studies have aimed to create a balance between ants colony while information transferring. Such an application will be used in greater scale and yield better results in comparison with series. There is something wrong with this algorithm; the expenses of communication cannot be ignored (H.Bai, D.Ouyang, 2009).

2.1.5. Multi colony

This method is one of the parallel methods in which several colonies collaborate. And their collaboration in a form of ace crone has been elaborated in the studies. Most applications have utilized shared intelligence in the platform clustering. Recent studies have aimed to create a balance between ants colony while data transferring. Such an application will be useful in greater scale and will yield better results in comparison with series (R. Michel, M. Middendorf, 1998).

2.1.6. Discussion and Comparison of the Applied Methods

The overview of mentioned applications shows that the methods of grand particles manorial and multi-colony are more reliable. The multi-colony methods have a degree of flexibility which allows them to partake in several parallel cases without wasting their functionality. Due to their flexibility and measurability, they can be conducted in grand particles. This method has the capacity of hardware application. The functionality of the minor and major partition of manorial method stem from the value and frequency the information present in each tenant. Generally, the yielded results indicate that grand partition methods are better than minor ones but when the number of tenants increase, excessive communication will attack landlord and conversions will occur in route. The researchers have suggested the solution of ace crone. The minor scale manorial method was highly proposed so that the application of minor scale method in Graphic processors using shared memory saved in pheromone was proposed. However, the reduction of communication between central processor and GPU must be considered. Parallel cellular method and ace crone have the highest speed and performance.

2.2. Hardware Methods

The problem of this fiscal algorithm will not be solved even if it is installed as software or a powerful microprocessor because the presence of an operator and fetch of hardware will consume time of decoding and executing.

2.2.1. The Hardware Models of Multi colony Algorithm

The hardware methods of multi-colony algorithms the hardware application has high speed in comparison with software. There is no limitation of running the main ant colony algorithm for the flexibility of software but in case of hardware, it is challenging to apply hardware method for the following reasons:

1) For the amount of pheromone and the produced random quantity need to be illustrated in decimal form regarding application limits on logic arrays, there is a problem of designation.

2) Evaporation and heuristic factor that require multiplication are not supportable by most fpga arrays.

3) For choosing the next city based on the distribution probability factor. Total sum of the previously left factors should be estimated and for each pheromone matrix a circuit should be provided. If the number of ns in the problem sours up, there will be the limitations of time and space appearing on the array surface (B. Scheuerman, K. So, M. Guntsch, M. Middendorf and H. Schmeck, 2004). Large decimals and repetitions in addition to divisions, the ant colony should be changed in a way that the result is not influenced by it. Hence, in some algorithms, the heuristic factors in choosing next city are ignored instead of decimals. Definite numbers have been used for powered amounts α andβ are suppositions and shift will function and will be replaced by multiplication. The entire functions resulting in decimals are limited.

2.2.2. Reconfigurable Mesh Method

It is a standard method for models of processors capable of recurrent configurations including processor elements in which they are located in grades of K*N. Every single element has got four parts in order to communicate with its neighbors. Elements utilize their ports for reading and writing. In case several elements initiate writing stimulations, a logical ok is formed among the information. Each element recognizes the position of row and columns containing few registers (R. Vaidyanathan, L. Trahan, 2004). A mesh with two dimensions consisting minor particles is considered for connection organization for applying hardware algorithm of ant colony. The pheromone chart in this N*N is located as figure 1.

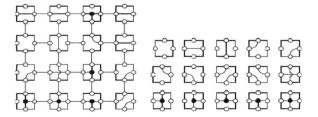

Figure 1. *16 mesh models and communication processor elements*

On the other hand, any processor element knows whether the existing item in the column has been selected or not. Second ant starts selecting his target item followed by first ant considering that there is only one row which makes a distance between them. There are two exceptions in this method that it does not obey the ant colony regulation:

1. Coming to the end of the row and selecting his solution for m-1/2, ant waits till it is checked for the position of solution among the previously selected best solutions then the full update is initiated. While other ant is on the selection route.

2. Instead of using pheromone item directly for selecting the next item, supermom and minimum for speed elevation is used in running algorithm.

In formula 5 t>0, h>l>0 is considered and for each item jεS the very formula is defined.

This algorithm is ideal for elevating the speed of ant colony algorithm application but comparison and pheromone update may be applied several times.

2.2.3. Population Method Based on Field Program Array

In this method, minimum space is allocated to designation and application related to the vivacity of previously conducted researches on the field. It has high speed in comparison with software method. Ants scatter into pheromone chart instead of an n*n matrix which runs repeatedly. A population chart is modeled on the pheromone chart that is about 1-8.This chart includes the population of the best routes gone in the former repetitions. The ants use this newly created chart for direction choice. By an n*k switch, n is the number of the problem items and k the number of the best routes. Each ant is allocated to a row by choosing an item in that row; the ant goes to the next row. This process continues till the number of rows reach to n, and then a new cycle begins. As illustrated in figure 2, this method includes 3 modules. The first module is the population module which is located between the two items of i and j belonging to pheromone factor. That is known as qij. The second module, which is the solution module, is divided into 3 sections: 1. S- array 2.match buffer 3.Selector. The third module is special for evaluation (B.Scheuerman, K. So, M. Guntsch, M. Middendorf and H. Schmeck, 2004).

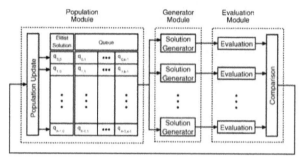

Figure 2. The population based method

Here, the population module bears the responsibility of providing the producer module with an n*k matrix presenting the pheromone amount. Eventually, it places the best solution in zero column and the remaining solutions in population matrix as the first entrance, first exeunt. In figure 3, the overall flow chart for this method has been demonstrated.

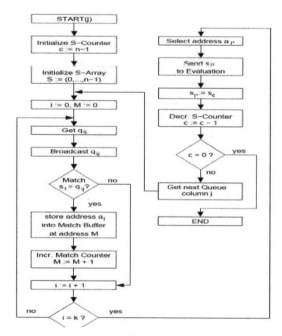

Figure 3. Flowchart of solution

Generally in the flowchart of figure 3, after the passage of each ant from each queue and the comparison of available items in queue i of pheromone matrix with s components, if they were the same, the address for saving in match buffer in case of correspondence of match, the

number production duration will be randomly produced and the item is selected. This continues till all the items of s are selected and a solution is given. S-Array includes all the items of the problem. Every single component of pheromone matrix is compared to s- array and at the end of each queue. The matched items are saved in match buffer even if the saving process occurs several times. The quantity of the matched item M and c=s-l are sent to the selector according to R=c+M∆ is identified between 0 to R for producing random numbers. Selection of an item from a match buffer and one item out of an s- array is previously selected. Selecting an item out of an array, it shifts to right and a flag special to the selected items are disabled. This process goes on till all the s members are selected and the solution to the selection of ants is terminated.

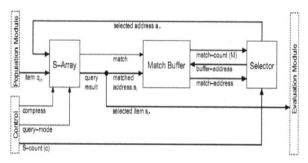

Figure 4. Diagram blocks producing solution.

The route of the next city has been illustrated in figure 5. If r-c causes overflow and r≻c is a collection of match buffer or the previously selected address that has been omitted from match buffer.

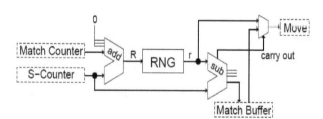

Figure 5. Selector block

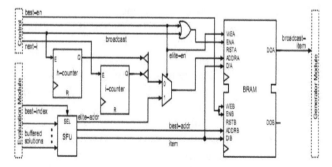

Figure 6. Population module

After all the ants found their solutions, in evaluation module, the best solution is found based on comparison. In BRAM, that pheromone matrix is inside it, via port A the best solution is written in j=o queue. The consideration is that the best solution is not better that the former one when (FIFO) is saved via port B. As is shown in the picture, the two counters of column and queue are sent to the solution module via port A so that a new cycle of solution is started by ants.

As previously mentioned, the size of this matrix is fixed and the oldest solution is deleted from matrix when a new solution is added to it. (In case there is no best solution.) It is noticeable that the pheromone matrix for k times has not been used. The randomly produced quantities will result in the selection of an address including previously selected items that are not in s array. This wastes time. And heuristic factors in selecting the new next city are not interfered.

2.2.4. Duplicators on Field Program Array

The parallel running of hardware application is done with chief purpose of speed elevation. Below are the two types of parallel applications.

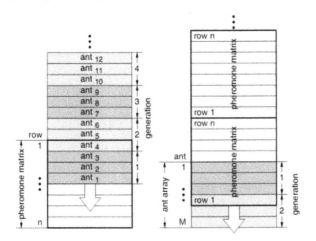

Figure 7. *Parallel method: right is pheromone pipe route, left is the ant route*

In this method pheromone matrix is projected on the array and ants enter linearly into pheromone matrix. Each ant selects an item in each route together with other ants. They intend to select a solution sequentially. However, the ants were not active in series. In these streams, ants are projected on the array stably and pheromone passes the location like a stream. In counter application, the search for algorithm parallel in all phases such as building a solution, evaluation, comparison and upgrading are increased.

Solution setup:

For setting up a solution each ant has to follow these steps:

- ✓ Selection probability calculation: In this method the distribution probability of heuristic items and unselected of pheromones are used instead of calculating the probability of single item.
- ✓ Random number production: A proper number [0: B_i-1] $r_i\varepsilon$ which is the subprime for B_i=max hεs p r_ih, i.e. the maximum amount resulted in the sum of multiplication. O (1) is produced as the random

number.

- ✓ Selection: After producing random quantity for each deselected cell, the statement pr_i, j-1<r_i<$pr_{i,j}$ is calculated. If the mentioned statement in the cell is not compatible, the cell item will be selected and be deleted from s.
- ✓ Evaluation
- ✓ Comparison
- ✓ Pheromone update

2.2.5. Projection of Proposed Method on Fpga

For each cell a circuit is designed in which each ant and the item members of s enters pheromone matrix projected on fpga decadently.

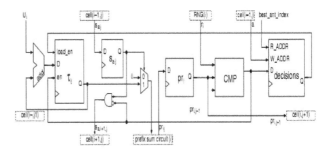

Figure 8. *Cell circuit (i and j)*

As is shown in the figure, if each member of si group is not selected, it is 1. If they have been selected earlier, it is 0. If the amount is 1, it participates in summing the multiplication factor and is compared with random numbers and sum of amount factors resulted from cell. If the case is as mentioned, the cell is zero and it is transferred to the next row in order not to be selected by ant in the next row. For each ant a design maker memory is selected in a form of distribution in fpga, selected items of each ant are saved. The previous ant should wait for the termination of solution selection process of the preceding ant. Then, it should begin to orbit pheromone matrix. This also consumes time and heuristic factor is not interfered in the next city selection. It is theoretically expressed. The third deficiency is because of the distributed memory utilization in cells. Space limitation and problem in items and bit quantity will be encountered (B. Scheuerman, K. So, M. Guntsch, M. Middendorf and H. Schmeck, 2004).

2.2.6. Method Based on CMOS Technology

In this method, the technology of serial transistor cmos has been used (K. Gheysari, A. Khoei, B. Mashroufi, 2011). Certainly, the diverse distance between cities has been influential, as well. The designation consists of five sections. The structure of each cell is illustrated in figure 9. Similar to the previous methods, ants start searching from the initial line of pheromone matrix. Their alternative city declines the amount from one to zero. In the memory set in each cell saves it in 6 bits and transfers to the next row.

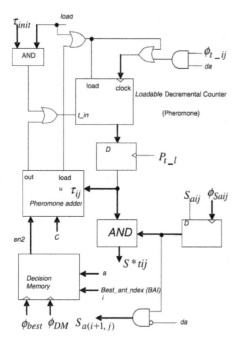

Figure 9. *Internal structure of a cell*

It is obvious which cell has been chosen by which ant. Decision memory, loadable decremented counter, and pheromone adder are considered as the main components of cells.

2. Choosing the next city:

This circuit determines the next city based on pheromone and heuristic amounts present in cells. A cell with high pheromone and heuristic amount will be chosen. As is shown in figure 10, this block includes 4 units: the first unit includes a digital multiplier which multiplies each value. The second unit containing DAC receives an output of multiplier and converts it to analog. For each row, there is a producer of random numbers which is an indirect application of roulette wheel can be seen. For an instance, if $I_{in1} < I_{ri} < I_{in2}$, then, the second node will deserve optional condition.

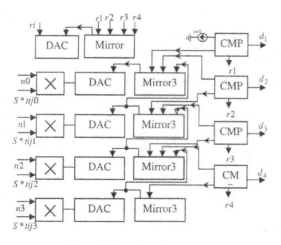

Figure 10. *Next city selection circuit*

The results of additions and multiplications of pheromone in deselected heuristic items are used in choosing the next city. The next city selected by random production of numbers existing in every row of pheromone matrix and by roulette wheel. This method is a function based on the integrated circuits. It has lower consumption of power considering cmos technology and has high speed in comparison with the presented models. However, in this method, each ant has to wait until the preceding process of route choice is finished. This is caused by the present algorithm and the zero-one position of transistors. Then it starts passing pheromone matrix.

2.2.7. Hardware-Software Compound Method

The designation is done on the arrays in a way that C software and hardware arrays have been planned with repartition in Verilog language. The designed framework of algorithm, as shown in figures 11 and 12, is composed of two major sections. Hence, choosing the best route is done by software and is applied in C language on the hidden processors NIOS II. Other algorithm calculations are applied by hardware on array logic which can be reprogrammed. The proposed solution brings a kind of negotiation between hardware speed designation and the flexibility of software planning (S-Anli, M.Hao, C-Wei, Y-Hong, 2012).

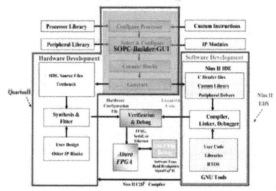

Figure 11. *Software/hardware interaction on array*

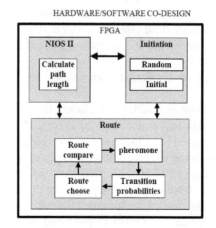

Figure 12. *Ant colony circuit chart*

2.2.8. Hardware Design Based on Deliberate Pheromone Temperation (M. Yoshikawa, H. Terari, 2008)

In this method, the management of ant colony algorithm varieties is important. As the major idea of the method, the variables are focused on the produced pheromone. The pheromone amount is defined according to the three limits; upper, benchmark and lower. According to formulas 2 and 3 for updating pheromone, some decimal calculations should be done.

The calculations for hardware pieces as fpga are not compatible because of their structures. The statement in formula 5 suggested for local update and not using decimals. General update is done like the defined variables in statement 6.

$$\tau(i, j) = \tau + \beta$$

$$\beta = \begin{cases} 8 & if \ 8 < \tau < std \\ 4 & if \ std < \tau < max \\ 0 & if \ 8 = \tau \end{cases} \qquad \text{Formula 5}$$

$$\tau(i, j) = \tau + \varepsilon$$

$$\varepsilon = \begin{cases} 8 & if \ \tau < std \\ 0 & otherwise \end{cases} \qquad \text{Formula 6}$$

2.2.8.1. Search and Node Selection

Like update method, search method is set up in a way that it does not need decimal calculation. The chart information indicate that for pheromone variable 100 distance is dedicated for heuristic factors per 8 block variations. All the application is done on LUT. The quantity of increase, pheromone, heuristic factors, and LUT amount will rise.

Table 1.

$\tau(i,j)$ ＼ $\eta(i,j)$	8	16	24	32	...
0-99	8	16	24	32	...
100-199	8	16	24	32	...
200-299	16	24	32	40	...
300-399	24	32	40	48	...
.	.	.	.		...
.			.		...

2.2.8.2. Design Methodology

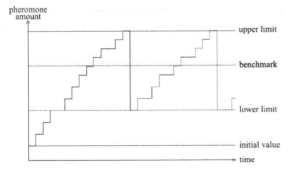

Figure 13. An example of pheromone amount

Every ant makes a different route like the standard algorithm of ant colony. Each search is done parallel to other processes (Figure 13). Several process blocks including management, general update memory composed of composite 6units and processors unit containing processor elements for parallel search have been illustrated in 14.

Selected city unit is constructed of sub-units and float point unit is used for processing decimals in a way that the function quality is the approximation of the real ant colony function (figure 14). The suggested evaluation method with its software equivalence is shown in table 2.

Table 2

	ACO	HAAC
Solution	Opt.	Opt.
Time to 100 tours	.68(s)	0.30(s)
Time to Opt.	6.9(s)	8.3(s)

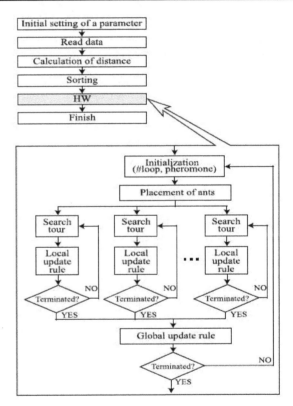

Figure 14. Suggested flowchart

2.2.9. Another Design for ACO Speed Elevation (Masaya Yoshikawa, Hidekazu Terai, 2007)

Ant colony algorithm has some shortcomings:
1. Processing occurs repeatedly and sequentially
2. Pheromone variable value is very little.
3. All the ants should share pheromone variables for transition and update. Due to the repeated processing difficulty, parallel method is perfect. block diagram of this method is shown in figure 16.

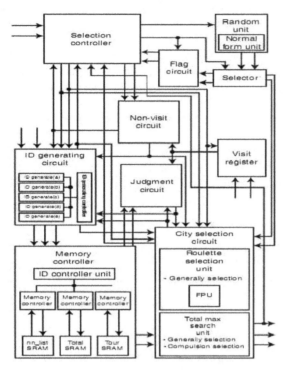

Figure 15. *City Selection Diagram*

Series of ids saved in SRAM memory are used for managing pheromone. They have the similar structure as the below.

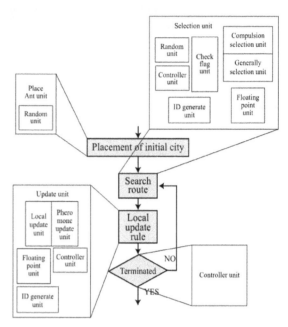

Figure 16. *The relation of processing flow chart with the circuit*

As figure 16, the function of an ant using units is shown in the beginning; each ant selects randomly a node or station. After choosing the next station, each ant for each city drags with 24 bit pheromone from memory and the remaining bits which control selection and deselect of the target city uses it. Immediately after choosing city starts local updating and it does it for all the cities so that one repetition suggests one solution. In chart 3, methods of hardware are compared in a summarized form.

Table 3. *Hardware Methods Compared*

function	Weak point	Strength	Design	Method
Continuous Function in Limited Time	Communication Expenses	Capable of Scaling	A PE System	Mesh
Route Finding	Maximum Comparison- not Capable of Scaling	Limited Space Exploration	FPGA Array	Based on Population
Route Finding	Ant Limitation Caused by Memory of Cells	Pheromone Matrix Exploration- Design Simplicity	FPGA Array	Duplicator
For Noiseless Places	Serial Ant Functioning- not Capable of Scaling – Noise Absorption	Lower Power Limit- Design Simplicity	Combination of Transistor and Comparer	CMOS
Programs Needing Exact Process	Lower Speed Compared to Hardware Type-Expensive	Flexibility-Algorithm Match	Fpga Array and NIOS II Processor	Software- Hardware
Improper Processing	Complex Design	Simple Operations	Combination of fpga and Memory	HAAC
Proper Calculations	Complexity and Difficult Management ID	Fpu usage and Proper Results	Combination of SRAM-FPGA	Hardware Design

3. Challenges and Problems

The reviewed works hardware designs are incomparable with hardware application. Because of the speed running continuous programs they will be deficient. In hardware design we encounter problems. Hardware designation can be divided in two sections: 1. Real designation. 2. Flexible systems.

1. Meaning the approximation of the planned method and the real ant colony is apparent, flexible systems react to

the errors and change, and it is reliable to carry errors.

2. Online radiance: One of the challenges in hardware design is that despite the progress of ant colony algorithm optimization, no satisfying report pertinent to the online radiance is given. Usually, it has been offline; the speed process is very low. This is regarded as the biggest problem in functional programs running by ant colony in industry. If the evaluation of best ants can be collected in the repeated forms and best ants can enter real world, the result of application related to time will be better.

3. Power and Strength: while an error occurs, it is essential to discover the error and resolve it by restarting the program so that no time inconsistency shall happen. But is the error discovering estimated and applied properly? Many reports on discovering error designation of hardware have not been delivered. This is the biggest challenge.

4. Critical Issues: It is important to generalize designation to any environment; whether the designation operates in efficient systems or can optimize every system under possible conditions. The more complex issues in optimization, the more critical issues are generated. In some cases algorithm does not answer properly to these issues. There are 2 possible solutions to these problems:

1. Optimizing hardware designations for speed increasing

2. Optimizing the ant colony algorithm

5. Theoretical Analysis

Theoretical analysis yield a comprehensive function of optimization algorithm but for those who want hardware application it is very proper. A basic theory is that before applying in larger scale, a theory is proposed. Since unlimited time and space is needed is needed for converging algorithm optimization with satisfying results.

4. Conclusion

This paper had investigated time problem in applying the ant colony algorithm. Parallel application of hardware methods together with the advantages and disadvantages were discussed. As a result, the compound method was introduced as the beneficial one according to flexibility and speed. Finally, the changes for hardware designers were pointed out. The investigator hopes that in the future, the hardware flexibility method as a novel and functional method will solve speed challenging problems regarding the application of ant colony algorithm.

References

[1] B. Scheuermann, S. Janson, M. Middendorf, Hardware-oriented ant colony optimization, Journal of Systems Architecture 53 (7) (2007) 386–402.

[2] C. Blum, A. Roli, Metaheuristics in combinatorial optimization: overview and conceptual comparison, ACM Computing Surveys 35 (3) (2003) 268–308

[3] Conference on Parallel Problem Solving from Nature, Lecture Notes in Computer Science 1498 (1998) 692–701

[4] D. Merkle, M. Middendorf, Fast ant colony optimization on runtime reconfigurable processor arrays, Genetic Programming and Evolvable Machines 3 (4) (2002) 345–361

[5] E. Talbi, O. Roux, C. Fonlupt, D. Robillard, Parallel ant colonies for the quadratic assignement problem, Future Generation Computer Systems 17 (4) (2001) 441–449

[6] F. Glover, G. Kochenberger (Eds.), Handbook of Metaheuristics, International Series in Operations Research & Management Science, 57, Springer, 2003.

[7] H. Bai, D. OuYang, X. Li, L. He, H. Yu, Max-min ant system on gpu with cuda, in:Proceedings of the 2009 Fourth International Conference on Innovative Computing,Information and Control, IEEE Computer Society, 2009, pp. 801–804 .

[8] H.Duan ,Yaxiang.Yu , JieZou and Xing Feng .Ant colony optimization-based bio-inspired hardware.

[9] K.Gheysari,A.Khoei,B.Mashoufi High speed ant colony optimization CMOS Chip .

[10] M. Bolondi, M. Bondaza, Parallelizzazione di unalgoritmo per la risoluzione del problema del commessoviaggiatore, Master's thesis, Politecnico di Milano, Italy, 1993

[11] M. Dorigo, G. Di Caro, L. Gambardella, Ant algorithms for discrete optimization, Artificial Life 5 (2) (1999) 137–172

[12] M. Dorigo, Parallel ant system: an experimental study, unpublished manuscript, Cited by [41], 1993

[13] M. Pedemonte, H. Cancela, A cellular ant colony optimisation for the generalized Steiner problem, International Journal of Innovative Computing and Applications 2 (3) (2010) 188–201.

[14] M. Pedemonte, S. Nesmachnow, H.Cancela Survey on parallel ant colony optimization .Applied Soft computing hournal.(2011.)

[15] P. Delisle, M. Gravel, M. Krajecki, C. Gagné, W. Price, Comparing parallelization of an ACO: message passing vs. shared memory, in: Proceedings of the 2nd International Workshop on Hybrid Metaheuristics, Lecture Notes in Computer Science vol. 3636 (2005) 1–11

[16] R. Michel, M. Middendorf, An island model based ant system with lookahead for the shortest supersequence problem, in: Proceedings of the 5th International.

[17] R.Vaidyanathan and J.L.Trahan :Dynamic Reconfiguration :Architectures and Algorithms .Kluwer,(2004)

[18] S.Li,M.Hao Yang ,Chung-Wei WENG,Yi –Hong Chen Ant Colony Optimization design and its FPGA implementation

[19] Yoshikawa ,M and Terai,H 2007 : Architecture for high – speed ant colony optimization .oroceedings of IEEE International Conference on information Reuse and integration ,lasVegas,NV, 1-5 .

[20] Yoshikawa,M and Terai,H 2008:Hardware-oriented ant colony optimization considering intensification and diversification in:Bednorz, W.editor. Advances in greedy algorithms,I-Tech,359-68.

24

The cognitive programming paradigm - the next programming structure

Benjamin Odei Bempong

Information and Communication Technology/Mathematics Department Presbyterian University College, Ghana. Abetifi-Kwahu, Eastern Region

Emailaddress:

benbodei@presbyuniversity.edu.gh / benbodei@yahoo.com (B. Odei Bempong)

Abstract: The development of computer programming started with the development of the switching logic, because, the computer hardware is made up of millions of digital switches. The activation and deactivation of these switches are through codified instructions – (program) which trigger the switches to function. The computer programming languages have gone through a revolution, from the machine code language, through assembly mnemonics to the high level programming languages like FORTRAN, ALGOL, COBOL, LISP, BASIC, ADA and C/C^{++}. It is a fact that, these programming languages are not the exact codes that microprocessors do understand and work with, because through compiler and interpreter programs, these high level programming languages that are easily understood by people are converted to machine code languages for the microprocessor to understand and do the work human knowledge has instructed it to do. The various programming languages stem from the difficulties man has in using one programming language to solve different problems on the computer. Hence, for mathematical and trigonometrically problems, FORTRAN is the best, for business problems, COBOL is the right language, whilst for computer games and designs, BASIC language is the solution. The trend of using individual programming languages to solve specific problems by single processor computers have changed drastically, from single core processors to present day dual and multi-core processors. The main target of engineers and scientists is to reach a stage that the computer can think like the human brain. The human brain contains many cognitive (thinking) modules that work in parallel to produce a unique result. With the presence of multi-core processors, why should computers continue to draw summaries from stored databases, and allow us to sit hours to analyse these results to find solutions to problems? The subject of 'Cognitive Programming Paradigm', analyses the various programming structures and came out that these programming structures are performing similar tasks of processing stored databases and producing summarized information. These summarized information are not final, business managers and Executives have to sit hours to deliberate on what strategic decisions to take. Again, present day computers cannot solve problems holistically, as normally appear to human beings. Hence, there's the need for these programming structures be grouped together to solve human problems holistically, like the human brains processing complex problems holistically. With the presence of multi-core processors, its possible to structure programming such that these programming structures could be run in parallel to solve a specific problem completely, i.e. be able to analyse which programming structure will be suitable for a particular problem solving or be able to store first solution and compare with new solutions of a problem to arrive at a strategic decision than its being done at present. This approach could lift the burden on Managers and Executives in deliberating further on results of a processed business problem.

Keywords: Programming; Structure; Cognitive; Paradigm

1. Introduction

The Computer technology which started with the switching logic and the discovery of binary decimal has gone through an evolution especially in designing artificial language that can talk to electro-digital systems. In process, a number of programming structures have emerged, that dictated the type of electro-digital devices available at the time to be communicated to. There has been a big struggle therefore between Computer Hardware designers, and their counter parts - the software designers. One may ask what are these struggles about? At one time Hardware designers design a system that puts a pressure on Software designers. The Software designers think around it and develop something that challenges the hardware capabilities, thus reducing what earlier the Hardware designers had done. These struggles have made the Computer technology one of the fastest disciplines the world had seen. But is it the end...?. It is the author's believe that with the current breakthrough in technology in terms of dual-core and multi-core processors, high speed processors and the 64-bit word length processors, the challenge has been shifted once again to the Software developers.

2. Types of Programming Structures

In this paper, literature reviews and analysis will be drawn on various programming structures, their importance, advantages and disadvantages, and brought closer to the workings of the human brain, for which these programming paradigms have been prototyped for, but which, it seems, a great omission has been left out, not avertedly, but due to failure of mankind to satisfy both sides of software and hardware developments. In recent times there have been uncountable programming languages whose review would be difficult, however, these programming languages could be grouped under specific programming structures or paradigms that have emerged- structured, procedural, functional, logic, declarative, imperative, abductive logic, metalogic, constraint logic, concurrent logic, inductive logic and Higher-order logic programming. These would be compared with the functions of the human brain to determine if we are getting our programs structures perfect.

2.1. Structured Programming Languages

Structured programming is a programming paradigm aimed on improving the clarity, quality, and development time of a computer program by making extensive use of subroutines, block structures and for and while loops - in contrast to using simple tests and jumps such as the 'goto' statement which could lead to "spaghetti code" which was both difficult to follow and to maintain.

It emerged in the 1960s, particularly from work by Böhm and Jacopini, and a famous letter, "Go To Statement Considered Harmful", from Edsger Dijkstra in 1968 [1] and was bolstered theoretically by the structured program theorem, and practically by the emergence of languages such as AL-GOL with suitably rich control structures. These led to the development of low level structured programming languages. [4]

2.2. Low-level Structure Programming

At a low level, structured programs are often composed of simple, hierarchical program flow structures. These are sequence, selection, and repetition:

"Sequence" refers to an ordered execution of statements.

In "selection" one of a number of statements is executed depending on the state of the program. This is usually ex-

pressed with keywords such as if..then..else..endif, switch, or case.

In "repetition" a statement is executed until the program reaches a certain state, or operations have been applied to every element of a collection. This is usually expressed with keywords such as while, repeat, for or do..until. Often it is recommended that each loop should only have one entry point (and in the original structural programming, also only one exit point, and a few languages enforce this).

A language is described as block-structured when it has a syntax for enclosing structures between bracketed keywords, such as an if-statement bracketed by if..fi as in AL-GOL 68, or a code section bracketed by BEGIN..END, as in PL/I - or the curly braces {...} of C and many later languages.

It is possible to do structured programming in any programming language, though it is preferable to use something like a procedural programming language. Some of the languages initially used for structured programming languages include: ALGOL, Pascal, PL/I and Ada - but most new procedural programming languages since that time have included features to encourage structured programming, and sometimes deliberately left out features that would make unstructured programming easy.

Historically, the structured program theorem provides the theoretical basis of structured programming. It states that three ways of combining programs—sequencing, selection, and iteration—are sufficient to express any computable function. This observation did not originate with the structured programming movement; these structures are sufficient to describe the instruction cycle of a central processing unit, as well as the operation of a Turing machine. Therefore a processor is always executing a "structured program" in this sense, even if the instructions it reads from memory are not part of a structured program. However, authors usually credit the result to a 1966 paper by Böhm and Jacopini, possibly because Dijkstra cited this paper himself. The structured program theorem does not address how to write and analyze a usefully structured program. These issues were addressed during the late 1960s and early 1970s, with major contributions by Dijkstra, Robert W. Floyd, Tony Hoare, and David Gries. [4]

There has been serious debates on structured programming, in which the early users like P. J. Plauger, an early adopter of structured programming, described his reaction to the structured program theorem and said that they have been converted to adopt structured programming but for assembly-language programming it was found difficult to be structured, and neither these were proved by Bohm and Jacopini nor their repeated successes at writing structured code brought them round one day sooner than they were ready to convince themselves that structured programming are different from assembly-language programming.

Donald Knuth accepted the principle that programs must be written with provability in mind, but he disagreed with abolishing the GOTO statement. In his 1974 paper, "Structured Programming with Goto Statements", he gave examples where he believed that a direct jump leads to clearer and more efficient code without sacrificing provability. Knuth proposed a looser structural constraint: It should be possible to draw a program's flow chart with all forward branches on the left, all backward branches on the right, and no branches crossing each other. Structured programming theorists gained a major ally in the 1970s after IBM researcher Harlan Mills applied his interpretation of structured programming theory to the development of an indexing system for the New York Times research file. The project was a great engineering success, and managers at other companies cited it in support of adopting structured programming, although Dijkstra criticized the ways that Mills's interpretation differed from the published work.

As late as 1987 it was still possible to raise the question of structured programming in a computer science journal. Frank Rubin did so in that year with a letter, "'GOTO considered harmful' considered harmful." Numerous objections followed, including a response from Dijkstra that sharply criticized both Rubin and the concessions other writers made when responding to him.

I used to program in Assembly Language using Motorola 68000 at the University, and I can confirm the above difficulties being explained by these writers, that Assembly programming is not and cannot be structured. If one makes a mistake, going back and changing addresses is a hell. In structured programming language like BASIC, one could easily insert a statement between two line statements, and go away, but in an Assembly Language it's not that simple. One has to remember each statement and the number of address bytes each command uses before the correction could be effective. Failure to include remarks in Assembly Language programming comes the difficult for the programmer to remember what the one had done.

The results of these debates came out at the end of the 20th century when nearly all computer scientists were convinced that it is useful to learn and apply the concepts of structured programming. High-level programming languages that originally lacked programming structures, such as FORTRAN, COBOL, and BASIC, now have them. At this point let us look at the various programming structures, starting from Declarative programming:

2.3. Declarative programming

In Comparing programming paradigms, Dr. Rachel Harrison and Mr. Lins Samaraweera described Declarative programming as when one writes a program code in such a way that it describes what one wants to do, and not what one wants to do it. It is left up to the compiler to figure out how. Examples are Structured Query Language(SQL) and Prolog. But even in Prolog, it's only the logical style that look declarative. Prolog is a language that clearly breaks away from the how-type languages, encouraging the programmer to describe situations and problems not the detailed means by which the problems are to be solved. These two programs work with databases and cannot be used to compute business logic. Declarative is 'what of' program-

ming and Imperative is the 'how'. Therefore Declarative programming is a programming paradigm that expresses the logic of a computation without describing its control flow. It is a programming paradigm where problems are described, or conditions on a solution are described, and the computer finds a solution. Often it involves the separation of "facts" from operations on the facts. "Declarative Programming" has also been described as a model of computation that "generalizes the pure functional model". That is, all pure functional programs are declarative programs, and Declarative Programming retains almost all of the advantages of Functional Programming. This is explained in more detail in the book Concepts Techniques And Models Of Computer Programming.

There are subcategories of Declarative Programming that include Logic Programming, Constraint Programming, and Constraint Logic Programming (which, as its name suggests, is a hybrid of the two - see Constraint And Logic Programming). While the above is nice and easy way, it is vague and leads to lots of arguments about whether this or that language is 'declarative' or effectively supports 'Declarative Programming'. Due to the vagueness of the original definition, Declarative Programming is effectively a sliding scale. The following operational characteristics might be used to judge the extent to which a programming model is declarative:

In Declarative Programming, order of statements and expressions should not affect program semantics. For example, they should not affect the termination characteristics and should not affect the observable IO properties, and ideally shouldn't affect performance.

In Declarative Programming, replication of a statement should not affect program semantics. What matters is that some fact or constraint exists, not how many times it is declared or computed. This allows refactoring and abstraction of statements, and is also a basis for many optimizations.

Many languages applying this style attempt to minimize or eliminate side effects by describing what the program should accomplish, rather than describing how to go about accomplishing it. This is in contrast with imperative programming, which requires an explicitly provided algorithm.

Declarative programming often considers programs as theories of a formal logic, and computations as deductions in that logic space. Declarative programming has become of particular interest recently, as it may greatly simplify writing parallel programs.[3]

Common declarative languages include those of regular expressions, logic programming, and functional programming.

2.4. Functional Programming

Functional programming is a programming paradigm that treats computation as the evaluation of mathematical functions and avoids state and mutable data. It emphasizes the application of functions, in contrast to the imperative programming style, which emphasizes changes in state.[1]

Functional programming has its roots in lambda calculus, a formal system developed in the 1930s to investigate function definition, function application, and recursion. Many functional programming languages can be viewed as elaborations on the lambda calculus.[1]

In practice, the difference between a mathematical function and the notion of a "function" used in imperative programming is that imperative functions can have side effects, changing the value of program state. Because of this they lack referential transparency, i.e. the same language expression can result in different values at different times depending on the state of the executing program. Conversely, in functional code, the output value of a function depends only on the arguments that are input to the function, so calling a function f twice with the same value for an argument x will produce the same result f(x) both times. Eliminating side effects can make it much easier to understand and predict the behavior of a program, which is one of the key motivations for the development of functional programming.[1]

Functional programming languages, especially purely functional ones, have largely been emphasized in academia rather than in commercial software development. Programming in a functional style can also be accomplished in languages that aren't specifically designed for functional programming. For example, the imperative Perl programming language has been the subject of a book describing how to apply functional programming concepts.[23]

2.5. Imperative Programming

This is a programming paradigm that describes computation in terms of statements that change a program state. In much the same way that imperative mood in natural languages expresses commands to take action, imperative programs define sequences of commands for the computer to perform.

The term is used in opposition to declarative programming, which expresses what the program should accomplish without prescribing how to do it in terms of sequences of actions to be taken. Functional and logical programming are examples of a more declarative approach.

2.6. Logic Programming

This, in its broadest sense, is the use of mathematical logic for computer programming. In this view of logic programming, which can be traced at least as far back as Alonzo Church[1932], logical inference can be used in programming. This view was further developed by John McCarthy's [1958] advice-taker proposal to use forward chaining under the control of logical propositions. The Planner programming language [1969, 1971] used both forward chaining (invoked by assertions) and backward chaining (invoked by goals).

However, Kowalski [1973] restricted logic programming to backwards chaining in the form:

$$G \text{ if } G_1 \text{ and } \ldots \text{ and } G_n$$

that treats the implications as goal-reduction procedures: to show/solve G, show/solve G1 and ... and Gn.

For example, it treats the implication:

The drive cab is alerted if an alarm signal button is pressed.

as a procedure that from the goal "the drive cab is alerted" generates the sub-goal "an alarm signal button is pressed."

Note that this is consistent with the BHK interpretation of constructive logic, where implication would be interpreted as a solution of problem G given solutions of G1 ... Gn.

The defining feature of logic programming is that sets of formulas can be regarded as programs and proof search can be given a computational meaning. In some approaches the underlying logic is restricted, e.g.,Horn clauses or Hereditary Harrop formulas.

As in the purely declarative case, the programmer is responsible for ensuring the truth of programs. But since automated proof search is generally infeasible, logic programming as commonly understood also relies on the programmer to ensure that inferences are generated efficiently. In many cases, to achieve efficiency, one needs to be aware of and to exploit the problem-solving behavior of the theorem-prover. In this respect, logic programming is comparable to conventional imperative programming; using programs to control the behavior of a program executor. However, unlike conventional imperative programs, which have only a procedural interpretation, logic programs also have a declarative, logical interpretation, which helps to ensure their correctness. Moreover, such programs, being declarative, are at a higher conceptual level than purely imperative programs; and their program executors, being theorem-provers, operate at a higher conceptual level than conventional compilers and interpreters.

Historically, Logic programming in the first and wider sense gave rise to a number of implementations, such as those by Fischer Black (1964), James Slagle (1965) and Cordell Green (1969), which were question-answering systems in the spirit of McCarthy's Advice taker. Foster and Elcock's Absys (1969), on the other hand, was probably the first language to be explicitly developed as an assertional programming language.

Logic programming in the narrower sense can be traced back to debates in the late 1960s and early 1970s about declarative versus procedural representations of knowledge in Artificial Intelligence. Advocates of declarative representations were notably working at Stanford, associated with John McCarthy, Bertram Raphael and Cordell Green, and in Edinburgh, with J. Alan Robinson (an academic visitor from Syracuse University), Pat Hayes, and Robert Kowalski. Advocates of procedural representations were mainly centered at MIT, under the leadership of Marvin Minsky and Seymour Papert.

Although it was based on logic, Planner, developed at

MIT, it was the first language to emerge within this proce-duralist paradigm [Hewitt, 1969]. Planner featured pattern directed invocation of procedural plans from goals (i.e. forward chaining) and from assertions (i.e. backward chaining). The most influential implementation of Planner was the subset of Planner, called Micro-Planner, implemented by Gerry Sussman, Eugene Charniak and Terry Winograd. It was used to implement Winograd's natural-language understanding program SHRDLU, which was a landmark at that time. In order to cope with the very limited memory systems that were available when it was developed, Planner used backtracking control structure so that only one possible computation path had to be stored at a time. From Planner were developed the programming languages QA-4, Popler, Conniver, QLISP, and the concurrent language Ether.

Hayes and Kowalski in Edinburgh tried to reconcile the logic-based declarative approach to knowledge representation with Planner's procedural approach. Hayes (1973) developed an equational language, Golux, in which different procedures could be obtained by altering the behavior of the theorem prover. Kowalski, on the other hand, showed how SL-resolution treats implications as goal-reduction procedures. Kowalski collaborated with Colmerauer in Marseille, who developed these ideas in the design and implementation of the programming language Prolog.

2.7. Abductive Logic Programming

Abductive Logic Programming is an extension of normal Logic Programming that allows some predicates, declared as abducible predicates, to be incompletely defined. Problem solving is achieved by deriving hypotheses expressed in terms of the abducible predicates as solutions of problems to be solved. These problems can be either observations that need to be explained (as in classical abductive reasoning) or goals to be achieved (as in normal logic programming). It has been used to solve problems in Diagnosis, Planning, Natural Language and Machine Learning. It has also been used to interpret Negation as Failure as a form of abductive reasoning.

2.8. Metalogic Programming

Because mathematical logic has a long tradition of distinguishing between object language and metalanguage, logic programming also allows metalevel programming. The simplest metalogic program is the so-called "vanilla" meta-interpreter:

solve(true).

solve((A,B)):- solve(A),solve(B).

solve(A):- clause(A,B),solve(B).

where true represents an empty conjunction, and clause(A,B) means there is an object-level clause of the form A :- B.

Metalogic programming allows object-level and metale-vel representations to be combined, as in natural language. It can also be used to implement any logic that is specified by means of inference rules.

2.9. Constraint Logic Programming

Constraint logic programming is an extension of normal Logic Programming that allows some predicates, declared as constraint predicates, to occur as literals in the body of clauses. These literals are not solved by goal-reduction using program clauses, but are added to a store of constraints, which is required to be consistent with some built-in semantics of the constraint predicates.

Problem solving is achieved by reducing the initial problem to a satisfiable set of constraints. Constraint logic programming has been used to solve problems in such fields as civil engineering, mechanical engineering, digital circuit verification, automated timetabling, air traffic control, and finance. It is closely related to abductive logic programming.

2.10. Concurrent Logic Programming

Keith Clark, Steve Gregory, Vijay Saraswat, Udi Shapiro, Kazunori Ueda, etc. developed a family of Prolog-like concurrent message passing systems using unification of shared variables and data structure streams for messages. Efforts were made to base these systems on mathematical logic, and they were used as the basis of the Japanese Fifth Generation Project (ICOT). However, the Prolog-like concurrent systems were based on message passing and consequently were subject to the same indeterminacy as other concurrent message-passing systems, such as Actors (see Indeterminacy in concurrent computation). Consequently, the ICOT languages were not based on logic in the sense that computational steps could not be logically deduced [Hewitt and Agha, 1988].

Concurrent constraint logic programming combines concurrent logic programming and constraint logic programming, using constraints to control concurrency. A clause can contain a guard, which is a set of constraints that may block the applicability of the clause. When the guards of several clauses are satisfied, concurrent constraint logic programming makes a committed choice to the use of only one.

2.11. Inductive Logic Programming

Inductive logic programming is concerned with generalizing positive and negative examples in the context of background knowledge. Generalizations, as well as the examples and background knowledge, are expressed in logic programming syntax. Recent work in this area, combining logic programming, learning and probability, has given rise to the new field of statistical relational learning and probabilistic inductive logic programming.

2.12. Higher-Order Logic Programming

Several researchers have extended logic programming

with higher-order programming features derived from higher-order logic, such as predicate variables. Such languages include the Prolog extensions HiLog and λProlog.

2.13. Linear Logic Programming

Basing logic programming within linear logic has resulted in the design of logic programming languages that are considerably more expressive than those based on classical logic. Horn clause programs can only represent state change by the change in arguments to predicates. In linear logic programming, one can use the ambient linear logic to support state change. Some early designs of logic programming languages based on linear logic include LO [Andreoli & Pareschi, 1991], Lolli [Hodas & Miller, 1994], ACL [Kobayashi & Yonezawa, 1994], and Forum [Miller, 1996]. Forum provides a goal-directed interpretation of all of linear logic.

2.14. Procedural Programming

Procedural programming can sometimes be used as a synonym for imperative programming (specifying the steps the program must take to reach the desired state), but can also refer (as in this article) to a programming paradigm, derived from structured programming, based upon the concept of the procedure call. Procedures, also known as routines, subroutines, methods, or functions (not to be confused with mathematical functions, but similar to those used in functional programming) simply contain a series of computational steps to be carried out. Any given procedure might be called at any point during a program's execution, including other procedures or itself. In order to understand this procedural programming a comparison will be made with other programming languages.

2.15. Object-Oriented Programming

The Wikipedia, the free encyclopedia defines Object-oriented programming (OOP) as a programming paradigm using "objects" – data structures consisting of data fields and methods together with their interactions – to design applications and computer programs. Programming techniques may include features such as data abstraction, encapsulation, messaging, modularity, polymorphism, and inheritance. Many modern programming languages now support OOP, at least as an option.

Simple, non-OOP programs may be one "long" list of statements (or commands). More complex programs will often group smaller sections of these statements into functions or subroutines each of which might perform a particular task. With designs of this sort, it is common for some of the program's data to be 'global', i.e. accessible from any part of the program. As programs grow in size, allowing any function to modify any piece of data means that bugs can have wide-reaching effects.

In contrast, the object-oriented approach encourages the programmer to place data where it is not directly accessible by the rest of the program. Instead, the data is accessed by calling specially written functions, commonly called methods, which are either bundled in with the data or inherited from "class objects." These act as the intermediaries for retrieving or modifying the data they control. The programming construct that combines data with a set of methods for accessing and managing those data is called an object. The practice of using subroutines to examine or modify certain kinds of data, however, was also quite commonly used in non-OOP modular programming, well before the widespread use of object-oriented programming.

An object-oriented program will usually contain different types of objects, each type corresponding to a particular kind of complex data to be managed or perhaps to a real-world object or concept such as a bank account, a hockey player, or a bulldozer. A program might well contain multiple copies of each type of object, one for each of the real-world objects the program is dealing with. For instance, there could be one bank account object for each real-world account at a particular bank. Each copy of the bank account object would be alike in the methods it offers for manipulating or reading its data, but the data inside each object would differ reflecting the different history of each account.

Objects can be thought of as wrapping their data within a set of functions designed to ensure that the data are used appropriately, and to assist in that use. The object's methods will typically include checks and safeguards that are specific to the types of data the object contains. An object can also offer simple-to-use, standardized methods for performing particular operations on its data, while concealing the specifics of how those tasks are accomplished. In this way alterations can be made to the internal structure or methods of an object without requiring that the rest of the program be modified. This approach can also be used to offer standardized methods across different types of objects. As an example, several different types of objects might offer print methods. Each type of object might implement that print method in a different way, reflecting the different kinds of data each contains, but all the different print methods might be called in the same standardized manner from elsewhere in the program. These features become especially useful when more than one programmer is contributing code to a project or when the goal is to reuse code between projects.

Object-oriented programming has roots that can be traced to the 1960s. As hardware and software became increasingly complex, manageability often became a concern. Researchers studied ways to maintain software quality and developed object-oriented programming in part to address common problems by strongly emphasizing discrete, reusable units of programming logic. The technology focuses on data rather than processes, with programs composed of self-sufficient modules ("classes"), each instance of which ("objects") contains all the information needed to manipulate its own data structure ("members"). This is in contrast to the existing modular programming that had been dominant for many years that focused on the function of a module, rather than specifically the data, but equally provided for code reuse, and self-sufficient reusable units of programming logic, enabling collaboration through the use of linked modules (subroutines). This more conventional approach, which still persists, tends to consider data and behavior separately.

An object-oriented program may thus be viewed as a collection of interacting objects, as opposed to the conventional model, in which a program is seen as a list of tasks (subroutines) to perform. In OOP, each object is capable of receiving messages, processing data, and sending messages to other objects. Each object can be viewed as an independent "machine" with a distinct role or responsibility. The actions (or "methods") on these objects

Object-oriented programming developed as the dominant programming methodology in the early and mid 1990s when programming languages supporting the techniques became widely available. These included Visual FoxPro 3.0,[10][11][12] C++, and Delphi. Its dominance was further enhanced by the rising popularity of graphical user interfaces, which rely heavily upon object-oriented programming techniques. An example of a closely related dynamic GUI library and OOP language can be found in the Cocoa frameworks on Mac OS X, written in Objective-C, an object-oriented, dynamic messaging extension to C based on Smalltalk. OOP toolkits also enhanced the popularity of event-driven programming (although this concept is not limited to OOP). Some feel that association with GUIs (real or perceived) was what propelled OOP into the programming mainstream.

Object-oriented features have been added to many existing languages during that time, including Ada, BASIC, Fortran, Pascal, and others. Adding these features to languages that were not initially designed for them often led to problems with compatibility and maintainability of code.

More recently, a number of languages have emerged that are primarily object-oriented yet compatible with procedural methodology, such as Python and Ruby. Probably the most commercially important recent object-oriented languages are Visual Basic.NET (VB.NET) and C#, both designed for Microsoft's .NET platform, and Java, developed by Sun Microsystems. Both frameworks show the benefit of using OOP by creating an abstraction from implementation in their own way. VB.NET and C# support cross-language inheritance, allowing classes defined in one language to subclass classes defined in the other language. Developers usually compile Java to bytecode, allowing Java to run on any operating system for which a Java virtual machine is available. VB.NET and C# make use of the Strategy pattern to accomplish cross-language inheritance, whereas Java makes use of the Adapter pattern.

3. Comparing Imperative, Procedural, and Declarative programming

Procedural programming is imperative programming in which the program is built from one or more procedures (also known as subroutines or functions). The terms are often used as synonyms, but the use of procedures has a dramatic effect on how imperative programs appear and how they are constructed. Heavily procedural programming, in which state changes are localized to procedures or restricted to explicit arguments and returns from procedures, is known as structured programming. From the 1960s onwards, structured programming and modular programming in general, have been promoted as techniques to improve the maintainability and overall quality of imperative programs. Object-oriented programming extends this approach.

Procedural programming could be considered as a step towards declarative programming. A programmer can often tell, simply by looking at the names, arguments and return types of procedures (and related comments), what a particular procedure is supposed to do - without necessarily looking at the detail of how the procedure achieves its result. At the same time, a complete program is still imperative since it 'fixes' the statements to be executed and their order of execution to a large extent.

Declarative programming is a non-imperative style of programming in which programs describe the desired results of the program, without explicitly listing command or steps that need to be carried out to achieve the results. Functional and logical programming languages are characterized by a declarative programming style.

In a pure functional language, such as Haskell, all functions are without side effects, and state changes are only represented as functions that transform the state. Although pure functional languages are non-imperative, they often provide a facility for describing the effect of a function as a series of steps. Other functional languages, such as Lisp, OCaml and Erlang, support a mixture of procedural and functional programming.

Programs written in logical programming languages, consist of logical statements, and the program executes by searching for proofs of the statements. As in functional programming languages, some logical programming languages such as Prolog, and database query languages such as SQL, while declarative in principle, also support a procedural style of programming.

Many imperative programming languages (such as Fortran, BASIC and C) were abstractions of assembly language.

The hardware implementation of almost all computers is imperative; nearly all computer hardware is designed to execute machine code, which is native to the computer, written in the imperative style. From this low-level perspective, the program state is defined by the contents of memory, and the statements are instructions in the native machine language of the computer. Higher-level imperative languages use variables and more complex statements, but still follow the same paradigm. Recipes and process checklists, while not computer programs, are also familiar concepts that are similar in style to imperative programming; each step is an instruction, and the physical world holds the state. Since the basic ideas of imperative programming are both conceptually familiar and directly embodied in the hardware, most computer languages are in the imperative style.

Assignment statements, in imperative paradigm, perform an operation on information located in memory and store the results in memory for later use. High-level imperative languages, in addition, permit the evaluation of complex expressions, which may consist of a combination of arithmetic operations and function evaluations, and the assignment of the resulting value to memory. Looping statements (such as in while loops, do while loops and for loops) allow a sequence of statements to be executed multiple times. Loops can either execute the statements they contain a predefined number of times, or they can execute them repeatedly until some condition changes. Conditional branching statements allow a sequence of statements to be executed only if some condition is met. Otherwise, the statements are skipped and the execution sequence continues from the statement following them. Unconditional branching statements allow the execution sequence to be transferred to some other part of the program. These include the jump (called "goto" in many languages), switch and the subprogram, or procedure, call (which usually returns to the next statement after the call).

3.1. Prolog

The programming language Prolog was developed in 1972 by Alain Colmerauer. It emerged from a collaboration between Colmerauer in Marseille and Robert Kowalski in Edinburgh. Colmerauer was working on natural language understanding, using logic to represent semantics and using resolution for question-answering. During the summer of 1971, Colmerauer and Kowalski discovered that the clausal form of logic could be used to represent formal grammars and that resolution theorem provers could be used for parsing. They observed that some theorem provers, like hyper-resolution, behave as bottom-up parsers and others, like SL-resolution (1971), behave as top-down parsers.

It was in the following summer of 1972, that Kowalski, again working with Colmerauer, developed the procedural interpretation of implications. This dual declarative/procedural interpretation later became formalised in the Prolog notation

$$H :- B_1, ..., B_n.$$

which can be read (and used) both declaratively and procedurally. It also became clear that such clauses could be restricted to definite clauses or Horn clauses, where H, B1, ..., Bn are all atomic predicate logic formulae, and that SL-resolution could be restricted (and generalised) to LUSH or SLD-resolution. Kowalski's procedural interpretation and LUSH were described in a 1973 memo, published in 1974.

Colmerauer, with Philippe Roussel, used this dual interpretation of clauses as the basis of Prolog, which was implemented in the summer and autumn of 1972. The first Prolog program, also written in 1972 and implemented in Marseille, was a French question-answering system. The use of Prolog as a practical programming language was given great momentum by the development of a compiler by David Warren in Edinburgh in 1977. Experiments demonstrated that Edinburgh Prolog could compete with the processing speed of other symbolic programming languages such as Lisp. Edinburgh Prolog became the *de facto* standard and strongly influenced the definition of ISO standard Prolog.

3.2. Comparison with other Programming Languages

Procedural programming languages are also imperative languages, because they make explicit references to the state of the execution environment. This could be anything from variables (which may correspond to processor registers) to something like the position of the "turtle" in the Logo programming language.

With Object-Oriented Programming, the focus of procedural programming is to break down a programming task into a collection of variables, data structures, and subroutines, whereas in object-oriented programming it is to break down a programming task into data types (classes) that associate behavior (methods) with data (members or attributes). The most important distinction is whereas procedural programming uses procedures to operate on data structures, object-oriented programming bundles the two together so an "object", which is an instance of a class, operates on its "own" data structure. Nomenclature therefore varies between the two, although they have similar semantics:

Procedural	Object-oriented
procedure	method
record	object
module	class
procedure call	message

In comparing Procedural programming with functional programming, the principles of modularity and code reuse in practical functional languages are fundamentally the same as in procedural languages, since they both stem from structured programming. So for example:

Procedures correspond to functions. Both allow the reuse of the same code in various parts of the programs, and at various points of its execution.

By the same token, procedure calls correspond to function application.

Functions and their invocations are modularly separated from each other in the same manner, by the use of function arguments, return values and variable scopes.

The main difference between the styles is that functional programming languages remove or at least deemphasize the imperative elements of procedural programming. The feature set of functional languages is therefore designed to support writing programs as much as possible in terms of pure functions:

Whereas procedural languages model execution of the program as a sequence of imperative commands that may implicitly alter shared state, functional programming languages model execution as the evaluation of complex expressions that only depend on each other in terms of arguments and return values. For this reason, functional programs can have a freer order of code execution, and the languages may offer little control over the order in which various parts of the program are executed. (For example, the arguments to a procedure invocation in Scheme are executed in an arbitrary order.)

Functional programming languages support (and heavily use) first-class functions, anonymous functions and closures.

Functional programming languages tend to rely on tail call optimization and higher-order functions instead of imperative looping constructs.

Many functional languages, however, are in fact impurely functional and offer imperative/procedural constructs that allow the programmer to write programs in procedural style, or in a combination of both styles. It is common for input/output code in functional languages to be written in a procedural style.

There do exist a few esoteric functional languages (like Unlambda) that eschew structured programming precepts for the sake of being difficult to program in (and therefore challenging). These languages are the exception to the common ground between procedural and functional languages.

In logic programming, a program is a set of premises, and computation is performed by attempting to prove candidate theorems. From this point of view, logic programs are declarative, focusing on what the problem is, rather than on how to solve it.

However, the backward reasoning technique, implemented by SLD resolution, used to solve problems in logic programming languages such as Prolog, treats programs as goal-reduction procedures. Thus clauses of the form:

$$H :\!- B_1, \ldots, B_n.$$

have a dual interpretation, both as procedures   to show/solve H, show/solve

B_1 and ... and B_n and as logical implications: B_1 and ... and B_n implies H.

Experienced logic programmers use the procedural interpretation to write programs that are effective and efficient, and they use the declarative interpretation to help ensure that programs are correct.

This article attempts to set out the various similarities and differences between the various programming paradigms, and tend to serve some distinction between programming Languages that help to solve different problems that confront the human nature and those that do not.

3.3. Comparison to Imperative Programming

Functional programming is very different from imperative programming. The most significant differences stem from the fact that functional programming avoids side effects, which are used in imperative programming to implement state and I/O. Pure functional programming disallows side effects completely. Disallowing side effects provides for referential transparency, which makes it easier to verify, optimize, and parallelize programs, and easier to write automated tools to perform those tasks.

Higher-order functions are rarely used in older imperative programming. Where a traditional imperative program might use a loop to traverse a list, a functional program would use a different technique. It would use a higher-order function that takes as arguments a function and a list. The higher-order function would then apply the given function to each element of the given list and then return a new list with the results.

3.4. Criticism on OOP Language

A number of well-known researchers and programmers have analysed the utility of OOP, and have condemned the OOP in many ways. A sampled few of these are made here - Luca Cardelli states that it has bad Engineering properties[30], whilst Richard Stallman said that it is difficult to add OOP to Emacs because its not superior way to program.[31] Potok et al. Stated that there is no significant difference in productivity between OOP and procedural approaches[32]. Christopher J. Date stated that it is difficult to compare OOP to other technologies because of lack of an agreed-upon and rigorous definition of OOP. He and Darwen propose a theoretical foundation on OOP that uses OOP as a kind of customizable type system to support RDBMD. [33], and Alexander Stepanor suggested that OOp provides a mathematically –limited viewpoint and called it "almost as much of a hoax as Artificial Intelligence (AI), but was sorry to be unfair to AI[35] .

3.5. Differences in Programming Terminology

In summary, Imperative programming describes computation in terms of statements that change a program whilst Functional programming treats computation as the evaluation of mathematical functions and avoids state and mutable data. Procedural programming / structured programming specify the steps the program must take to reach the desired state and in Event-driven programming, the flow of the program is determined by events—i.e., sensor outputs or user actions (mouse clicks, key presses) or messages from other programs or threads. Object oriented programming (OOP) uses "objects" – data structures consisting of data fields and methods together with their interactions – to design applications and computer programs. Declarative programming expresses the logic of a computation without describing its control flow whilst in Automata-based programming the program or its part is thought of as a model of a finite state machine or any other formal automata.

None of the main programming paradigms have a precise, globally unanimous definition, let alone an official international standard. Nor is there any agreement on which paradigm constitutes the best approach to developing software. The above suggests that day-in-day out scientists and engineers are endeavouring to imitate something close to solving a problem just like the human brains do.

4. The Human Brains and How it works

According to Professor Jacob Palme of University of Stockholm, every animal you can think of -- mammals, birds, reptiles, fish, amphibians -- has a brain. But the human brain is unique. It gives us the power to think, plan, speak, imagine...etc. It is truly an amazing organ.

The brain performs an incredible number of tasks:

It controls body temperature, blood pressure, heart rate and breathing.

It accepts a flood of information about the world around us from our various senses (seeing, hearing, smelling, tasting, touching, etc).

It handles physical motion when walking, talking, standing or sitting.

It lets one thinks, dream, reason and experience emotions.

All of these tasks are coordinated, controlled and regulated by an organ that is about the size of a small head of cauliflower: your brain.

The brain, spinal cord and peripheral nerves make up a complex, integrated information-processing and control system. The scientific study of the brain and nervous system is called neuroscience or neurobiology.

In his article, Professor Jacob Palme explained that the brain works by activating thought modules called cognitive modules such as the following:

The modules controlling the hands when one rides a bicycle, to stop it crashing by minor left and right turns;

The modules which allows a basket-ball player to accurately send the ball into the basket;

The modules which recognized hunger and says that one needs food;

The modules which cause one to appreciate a beautiful flower, painting or person;

The modules which cause some humans to be jealous of their partners' friends;

The modules which computes the speeds of other vehicles and tells one if one has time to cross before the other car arrives;

The modules which tell one to look both to the right and to the left before crossing a street;

The modules which cause parents to love and take care of their children;

The sex drive modules; and

The fight or flight selection modules.

The above show that there exists several modules that work together to control the human body. However, the modules very important to this article are the those that control the thinking of a person.

4.1. Learned or Inherited

Professor Palme explained that the cognitive modules are learned or inherited, by saying that "Some of these modules are partly based on genetic inheritance, but also the inherited modules can be modified by learning. All one learns, in the childhood, and as an adult, will add new cognitive modules to one's brain. An adult human has millions of cognitive modules. The human species is unique in its capability to develop and modify cognitive modules by learning. Thus, the human species is successful because it is not so much controlled by instinct (genetic modules) and that it can modify or replace genetic modules by learned modules." The analysis drawn from the learned Professor shows that the human brains learns and inherits events in data processing.

4.2. Selecting the Right Cognitive Modules

How, then, does the human brain select the right module to apply to a certain issue? This Professor Palme explained by an analogy with a piano. A piano has a number of strings, one for each tone. If one lets a loudspeaker play a single tone loudly, then the corresponding piano string will begin to vibrate. Other piano strings corresponding to close matches, and to overtones of the played tone, will also start to vibrate, but to a less extent. All the piano strings receive the sound, but only those that match the sound will begin to vibrate. Thus, all piano strings test the sound at the same time.

In a similar way, when meeting a situation, this situation will simultaneously test many cognitive modules in the brain. To test many modules at the same time is known as "parallel processing" and is something which the brain is much better at than computers. But of all tested modules, only those which fit the situation best, are those which are most closely matched with the situation to be managed. The brain then has a selection mechanism, where the cognitive module which is most strongly activated takes over and is used as a model for how to handle the new situation. Examples of this selection mechanism are when one is feeling pain in different parts of the body at the same time, one is only conscious of the strongest of the pains. In the same way, lots of modules may react to one's situation, but only one or two of the strongest will make its way up to the conscious mind.

The human brain contains millions of billions of synaptic connections, in which the cognitive modules are stored. This vast size, and the capability to rapidly find appropriate modules in this large storage, is central to human intelligence.

4.3. Difference Between the Human Brain and Computers

It must be noted that the above description is very different from the way a normal computer functions. Mohammad and Krayem (Scrib Inc.) in defining expert systems described that humans solve problems on the basis of a mixture of factual and heuristic knowledge. Conventional programs are based on factual knowledge, which are indisputable strength of computers. Heuristic knowledge composed of intuition, judgment, and logical inferences. Few computers have this facility of activating and matching millions of cognitive modules and selecting the appropriate one in a new situation. Especially the human capability to recognize cognitive modules which are in some way similar, but not identical, to a new situation, is unique for humans. Computers are good at finding identical situations, but not good at finding similar but not identical situations. This situation could be described of early computers that had single core processors.

In recent advancements in the developments of computer hardware, processor developers have made a break through in the development of multi-core processors. These have led to new developments in software in a form of threads-parts of a program that can execute independently of other parts- that can be executed in parallel mode.

In analyzing the various paradigms, it could be stated that each programming paradigm could solve a specific problem in live or business. However, it could be observed that natural problems and business problems are becoming complex and sophisticated and come with different combinations of solutions which need be coordinated to provide a holistic solution. With the modern computers providing multi-core processing capabilities its more a challenge to combine various programming paradigms to solve natural problems which hitherto had been difficult to be solved on the earlier single processor computers.

Let me sight a typical example of the development of Application software like Microsoft Word. The early word processors that were introduced in the early 1980's like Word Perfect, Word Star, ABC Writer, just to mention a few , had no dictionary nor Spell check. However, current Microsoft word could detect grammar, wrong spellings and even un-required spacing during typing a document, that shows that while one processor is listing the text being typed, another parallel processor will be checking spelling, grammar and spacing, showing that the Application has some level of cognitive aspects in its functions- a group of mental processes that includes attentions, memory, producing and understanding language, solving problems and making decisions. [41]

4.4. Audience

Today's businesses are in the competitive world, with the Top Executives dealing with large corporate data which are difficult to be handled. Businesses have gone out of creating extr ordinary databases, by creating Data Warehousing and using Data Mining tools to shift through volumes of data to discover hidden data attributes, trends and patterns within the Databases. But, these results do not provide holistic solutions to the business community and their Executives, because they have to sit down hours to analyze these trends, patterns and hidden attributes to determine the real

knowledge about the operations. With the breakthrough in the hardware developments, it could be possible for a holistic solution to be obtained through application developments.

5. The Situation Analysis – Programming Perspective

The diagram below Fig. 1 can demonstrate a best approach to current programming perspective.

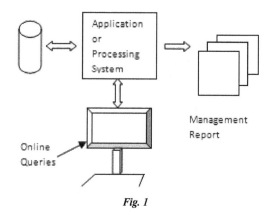

Fig. 1

The current business data processing are based on a number of independent created/ distributed databases which various applications process based on specific objectives to generate management reports. Many a time these reports are produced in hard copies or presented in graphical forms or tables for management to sit at long meetings to analyse the reports for decision making. The quality and accuracy in decision making from such reports may depend on the quality and technical knowhow of the management personnel present and their competence to critically analyse the obtained reports.

This leads to inaccuracies in management decision making resulting in absolute guesses and forecasts for the operations of the company or business, because it's difficult to compare current reports to earlier reports on the operations of the company some years back. Again, if these reports are obtained from different programming languages, analyzing these complex results will be hectic task. To avoid such situation and implement a holistic solution to business problems, the new approach of programming or developing Applications is to lower the risks involved in management making decisions based on guesses and forecasts.

5.1. The Cognitive Programming Paradigm of Next Generation Computing

The term 'cognitive' as borrowed from the functional behaviour of the human brain is used here to describe the next structure of computer programming, that indicates that the new generations of Applications would no longer produce summary information from a gathered database, but the summary information from various programming modules could be analysed and produce a holistic solution that could come from combined solution of all modules to determine trends, patterns and hidden attributes that can logically formulate a final decision making process for scientists, medical Experts, Engineers and chief Executives to help them make right choice decisions. The flow chart Fig.2 depicts this concept.

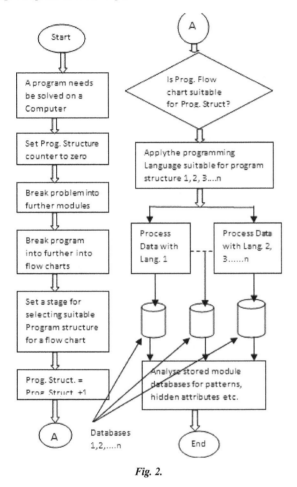

Fig. 2.

5.2. Design Concepts

The design concepts of the cognitive programming paradigm would include but not limited to the following:

computer should be broken into various modules;

Each module is further broken down to flow chart level;

Various programming languages depicting various programming paradigms are stored on computer hard disks;

A comparable analysis is done to select suitable programming language/program structure to a particular flow chart;

Problem modules are processed by suitable programming languages and structures and results are stored in various databases;

Adopt the human brains logic to compare various stored databases to determine trends, patterns, and hidden attributes produced by various programming paradigms logics of the new results with the past stored results to come out with alternative solution before providing final results; and

The final result of the last analysis would produce a definite information that could be the last and best result.

The above block schema depicts the various functional description of the cognitive programming Paradigm concept. With parallel processing and multi-core processors, the various modules' processes can be done in parallel to produce various data to be stored for final analysis to get the final results.

6. Conclusion

The cognitive programming paradigm as the author suggests to be the next programming structure, is to bridge the gap between the human thinking power with computer solutions in which databases are created for programming languages to search for data and analyzed them based on business logics used in designing the application. The other side effects of a problem's solution are not considered and these do not aid in arriving at a holistic solution. For example the human brains solution for a problem depends on the depth of knowledge and experience of the human being, and the problem's solution could combine a number of factors that will provide holistic solution, because the human brain processes a number of issues in parallel on a problem, and provides a holistic solution. Although the right or wrong of the solution depends on a number of factors available to the human being itself. With multi-core processors, programming structures defining different programming languages could be selected to solve various options of a problem in hand, so that analysing the various outputs holistic solution could be obtained.

References

[1]   Edsger Dijkstra, Notes on Structured Programming, pg. 6

[2]   Böhm, C. and Jacopini, G.: Flow diagrams, Turing machines and languages with only two formation rules, CACM 9(5), 1966.

[3]   Michael A. Jackson, Principles of Program Design, Academic Press, London, 1975.

[4]   O.-J. Dahl, E. W. Dijkstra, C. A. R. Hoare Structured Programming, Academic Press, London, 1972 ISBN 0-12-200550-3

[5]   Edsger Dijkstra (March 1968). "Go To Statement Considered Harmful" (PDF). Communications of the ACM 11 (3): 147–148.

[6]   Jacobs, B. (2006-08-27). "Object Oriented Programming Oversold". Archived from the original on 2006-10-15. http://web.archive.org/web/20061015181417/http://www.geocities.com/tablizer/oopbad.htm.

[7]   Shelly, Asaf (2008-08-22). "Flaws of Object Oriented Modeling". Intel® Software Network. http://software.intel.com/en-us/blogs/2008/08/22/flaws-of-object-oriented-modeling/. Retrieved 2010-07-04.

[8]   Yegge, Steve (2006-03-30). "Execution in the Kingdom of

Nouns". steve-yegge.blogspot.com. http://steve-yegge.blogspot.com/2006/03/execution-in-kingdom-of-nouns.html. Retrieved 2010-07-03.

[9] "The Jargon File v4.4.7: "syntactic sugar"". http://www.retrologic.com/jargon/S/syntactic-sugar.html.

[10] "The True Cost of Calls". wordpress.com. 2008-12-30. http://hbfs.wordpress.com/2008/12/30/the-true-cost-of-calls/.

[11]
http://en.wikibooks.org/wiki/X86_Disassembly/Functions_and_Stack_Frames

[12] Roberts, Eric S. (2008). "Art and Science of Java; Chapter 7: Objects and Memory". Stanford University. http://www-cs-faculty.stanford.edu/~eroberts/books/ArtAndScienceOfJava/slides/07-ObjectsAndMemory.ppt.

[13] Roberts, Eric S. (2008). Art and Science of Java. Addison-Wesley. ISBN 978-0321486127. http://www-cs-faculty.stanford.edu/~eroberts/books/ArtAndScienceOfJava/slides/07-ObjectsAndMemory.ppt.

[14] Guy Lewis Steele, Jr. "Debunking the 'Expensive Procedure Call' Myth, or, Procedure Call Implementations Considered Harmful, or, Lambda: The Ultimate GOTO". MIT AI Lab. AI Lab Memo AIM-443. October 1977. [1][2][3]

[15] David Detlefs and Al Dosser and Benjamin Zorn (1994-06). "Memory Allocation Costs in Large C and C++ Programs; Page 532" (PDF). SOFTWARE—PRACTICE AND EXPERIENCE 24 (6): 527–542.)

[16] Krishnan, Murali R. (1999-02). "Heap: Pleasures and pains". microsoft.com. http://msdn.microsoft.com/en-us/library/ms810466%28v=MSDN.10%29.aspx.

[17] http://microallocator.googlecode.com/svn/trunk/MicroAllocator.cpp

[18] Jeffrey Dean, David Grove, and Craig Chambers. Optimization of Object-Oriented Programs Using Static Class Hierarchy Analysis. University of Washington. doi:10.1.1.117.2420. http://citeseerx.ist.psu.edu/viewdoc/download?doi=10.1.1.117.2420&rep=rep1&type=pdf.

[19] Teaching FP to Freshmen, from Harper's blog about teaching introductory computer science.

[20] M.Trofimov, OOOP - The Third "O" Solution: Open OOP. First Class, OMG, 1993, Vol. 3, issue 3, p.14.

[21] 21.Yegge, Steve (2006-03-30). "Execution in the Kingdom of Nouns". steve-yegge.blogspot.com. http://steve-yegge.blogspot.com/2006/03/execution-in-kingdom-of-nouns.html. Retrieved 2010-07-03.

[22] 22. Boronczyk, Timothy (2009-06-11). "What's Wrong with OOP". zaemis.blogspot.com. http://zaemis.blogspot.com/2009/06/whats-wrong-with-oop.html. Retrieved 2010-07-03.

[23] Ambler, Scott (1998-01-01). "A Realistic Look at Object-Oriented Reuse". www.drdobbs.com. http://www.drdobbs.com/184415594. Retrieved 2010-07-04.

[24] Shelly, Asaf (2008-08-22). "Flaws of Object Oriented Modeling". Intel® Software Network. http://software.intel.com/en-us/blogs/2008/08/22/flaws-of-object-oriented-modeling/. Retrieved 2010-07-04.

[25] James, Justin (2007-10-01). "Multithreading is a verb not a noun". techrepublic.com. http://blogs.techrepublic.com.com/programming-and-development/?p=518. Retrieved 2010-07-04.

[26] Shelly, Asaf (2008-08-22). "HOW TO: Multicore Programming (Multiprocessing) Visual C++ Class Design Guidelines, Member Functions". support.microsoft.com. http://support.microsoft.com/?scid=kb%3Ben-us%3B558117. Retrieved 2010-07-04.

[27] Robert Harper (2011-04-17). "Some thoughts on teaching FP". Existential Type Blog. http://existentialtype.wordpress.com/2011/04/17/some-advice-on-teaching-fp/. Retrieved 2011-12-05.

[28] Cardelli, Luca (1996). "Bad Engineering Properties of Object-Oriented Languages". ACM Comput. Surv. (ACM) 28 (4es): 150. doi:10.1145/242224.242415. ISSN 0360-0300. http://lucacardelli.name/Papers/BadPropertiesOfOO.html. Retrieved 2010-04-21.

[29] Stallman, Richard (1995-01-16). "Mode inheritance, cloning, hooks & OOP". Google Groups Discussion. http://groups.google.com/group/comp.emacs.xemacs/browse_thread/thread/d0af257a2837640c/37f251537fafbb03?lnk=st&q=%22Richard+Stallman%22+oop&rnum=5&hl=en#37f251537fafbb03. Retrieved 2008-06-21.

[30] Potok, Thomas; Mladen Vouk, Andy Rindos (1999). "Productivity Analysis of Object-Oriented Software Developed in a Commercial Environment". Software – Practice and Experience 29 (10): 833–847. doi:10.1002/(SICI)1097-024X(199908)29:10<833::AID-SPE258>3.0.CO;2-P. http://www.csm.ornl.gov/~v8q/Homepage/Papers%20Old/spetep-%20printable.pdf. Retrieved 2010-04-21.

[31] C. J. Date, Introduction to Database Systems, 6th-ed., Page 650

[32] C. J. Date, Hugh Darwen. Foundation for Future Database Systems: The Third Manifesto (2nd Edition)

[33] Stepanov, Alexander. "STLport: An Interview with A. Stepanov". http://www.stlport.org/resources/StepanovUSA.html. Retrieved 2010-04-21.

[34] Graham, Paul. "Why ARC isn't especially Object–Oriented.". PaulGraham.com. http://www.paulgraham.com/noop.html. Retrieved 13 November 2009.

[35] Armstrong, Joe. In Coders at Work: Reflections on the Craft of Programming. Peter Seibel, ed. Codersatwork.com, Accessed 13 November 2009.

[36] Mansfield, Richard. "Has OOP Failed?" 2005. Available at 4JS.com, Accessed 13 November 2009.

[37] Mansfield, Richard. "OOP Is Much Better in Theory Than in Practice" 2005. Available at Devx.com Accessed 7 January 2010.

[38] Stevey's Blog Rants

[39] Rich Hickey, JVM Languages Summit 2009 keynote, Are

We There Yet? November 2009.

[40] Teaching FP to Freshmen, from Harper's blog about teaching introductory computer science.

[41] [http://en.wikipedia.org/wiki/cognition].

25

Software reuse facilitated by the underlying requirement specification document: A knowledge-based approach

Oladejo F. Bolanle[1, 2, *]**, Ayetuoma O. Isaac**[1, 2]

[1]Department of Computer Science, University of Ibadan, Ibadan, Nigeria
[2]University of Ibadan, UI, Ibadan, Nigeria

Email address:
fb.oladejo@ui.edu.ng (O. F. Bolanle), ayetuomaisaac@yahoo.com (A. O. Isaac)

Abstract: Reinventing the wheel may not be appropriate in all instances of software development, and so, rather than do this, reuse of software artifacts should be embraced. Reuse offers certain benefits which include reduction in the overall development costs, increased reliability, standards compliance, accelerated development and reduced process risk. However, reusable software artifacts may not be considered useful if they cannot be accessed and understood. In this work, a knowledge based system was designed to capture requirements specification documents as abstract artifacts to be reused. Both explicit and tacit knowledge identification and acquisition- an important step in knowledge base development, was carried out through extraction from customer requirement documents, interviews with domain experts and personal observations. Protege4.1 was used as a tool for developing the Ontology. Web Ontology Language (OWL) was the search mechanism used to search the classified ontology to deduce reusable requirement components based on the underlying production rules for querying and retrieval of artifacts. Knowledge was formalized and result testing was carried out using software requirement specification documents from different domains. Result shows that only requirements with similar object properties called system purpose could really reuse such artifacts. The possibility of accessing more reusable artifacts lies in the update of the repository with more requirement specification documents. Scopes and purposes of previously developed software that would suit a proposed system in the same (or similar) domain would be found and consequently support the reuse of any of the end-products of such previously developed software.

Keywords: Knowledge Based System, Ontology, Reuse, Software, SRSR-Software Requirement Specification Reuse

1. Introduction

The design process in most engineering disciplines is based on reuse of existing systems or components. Mechanical or electrical engineers do not normally specify a design where every component has to be manufactured specially. They base their design on components that have been tried and tested in other systems. These are not just small components such as flanges and valves but include major subsystems such as engines, condensers or turbines. Software reuse "refers to the use of previously developed software resources in new applications by various users such as programmers and systems analysts" [1]. Considering the high cost and much stress involved in producing quality software one would expect that reuse should be a welcome idea to all stakeholders involved in

the process, but research has shown the contrary; reuse has not been broadly applied across all spectrum of the industry.

Reuse-based software engineering is a comparable software engineering strategy where the development process is geared to reusing existing software. The paradigm shift to reuse-based approach in software development is as a result of the demands for reduction in the development and maintenance costs of software, faster delivery and improvement of the quality of software. More and more companies see their software as a valuable asset and are promoting reuse to increase their return on software investments. The tasks of maintaining the large collection of components and allowing the users to easily find out the components they need are critical to reducing the cost of reuse. There is need for effective tools to support cataloguing the components and searching them. To achieve this, we might have to borrow the ideas and techniques from the field of Artificial intelligence (knowledge representation techniques), database management system field, and system science (techniques of building systems with components) [2].

2. Theoretical Background

2.1. Software Development Process and its Phases

Indeed, building computer software is an iterative learning process, and the outcome, something that Baetjer would call "software capital," is an embodiment of knowledge collected, distilled, and organized as the process is conducted [3]. Software development process is a roadmap that provides the framework from which a comprehensive plan for software development can be established. The generic activities carried out in software development process include Software specification- this is where customers and engineers define the software to be produced and the constraints on its operations, software development- software is designed and programmed, software validation- software is checked to ensure it is what the customer actually asked for, software evolution-software is modified to suit changing customer's needs and market requirement. A process model for software engineering- software engineering paradigm is chosen based on the nature of the project and application, the methods and tools to be used, and the controls and deliverables that are required. A number of different process models for software engineering such as waterfall approach, component-based development, concurrent development model, the RAD model, the Prototyping model, Evolutionary software development process models-incremental model and spiral model, have been proposed, each exhibiting strengths and weaknesses[4], but all having a series of generic phases in common, prominent among these phases is a communication link between developers and customers for the purpose of requirement engineering covering feasibility study, requirement elicitation and analysis, requirement specification, validation and management, which goes to show that for a failure-free software product to be produced, a keen attention must be paid to this phase. Understanding what to build is one of the most tedious aspects of software development because sometimes customers do not really know what they want, so capitalizing on previously used abstract artifacts like requirement specification document may open the mind of software customers to more functionalities that could have been overlooked.

In a survey carried out by Standish group in 1994[5], [6] with over 350 companies, asking about the state of their over 8000 software projects, respondents were asked to explain the causes of failed software project. The top factors were reported as: Incomplete requirements-13.1%,

Lack of user involvement-12.4%, Lack of resources-10.6%, Unrealistic expectations-9.9%, Lack of executive support-9.3%, Changing requirements and specifications-8.7%, Lack of planning-8.1%, System no longer needed-7.5%. Notice that some part of the requirements elicitation, definition, and management process is involved in almost all of these causes. Lack of care in understanding, documenting, and managing requirements can lead to myriad of problems: building a system that solves the wrong problem, that does not function as expected, or that is difficult for the users to understand and use [7]. This work focused on the reuse of requirement specification documents that have been used to implement successfully developed and operational software, enabling a developer to choose requirement specification that meet user needs, display well outlined components of requirement specification for ease of understanding and access in order to facilitate timely software development.

2.2. Software Reuse in Software Development Projects

Reuse is the default problem-solving strategy in most human activities, and software development is no exception. Software reuse means reusing the inputs, the processes, and the outputs of previous software development efforts; it is a means toward an end: improving software development productivity and software product quality. Reuse is based on the premise that deducing a solution from the statement of a problem involves more effort (labour, computation etc.) than inducing a solution from that to a similar problem, one for which such efforts have already been expended. While the inherent complexities in software development make it a good candidate for explorations in reuse, it is far from obvious that actual gains will occur. The challenges are structural, organizational, managerial, and technical [8].

With the increasing complexity in software systems, stakeholders in the business of software development need to get acquainted with vast amount of information and knowledge in various areas, likewise the need to store this knowledge for easy access for reuse. The knowledge gathered during the development stage can be a valuable asset for a developer as well as the software company. During the software development process, the management and maintenance of knowledge creation is a necessary thing. Then only that knowledge is integrated to develop the innovative concept from the older one. So the company must store and manage it for reuse [9].

Reusable artifacts can be software components, software requirement analysis manuals, and design models, database schema, objects, code documentation, domain architecture, test scenarios, and plans. The existing software can be from within a software system or other similar software systems or widely in different systems. For example, MS Office 2003 a tool to create and to edit different types of documents, worksheets, presentation slides and databases. They came up with the MS Office 2007 which is the latest version of it (as at 2007). Just like this there are so many examples we can consider as a Software Reuse [10].

Reuse-based software engineering is an approach to development that tries to maximize the reuse of existing software. The software units that are reused may be of radically different sizes. For instance, Application system reuse- the whole of an application system may be reused by incorporating it without change into other systems, Component reuse- components of an application may be reused, Object and function reuse- components that implement a single function may be reused. A complementary form of reuse is concept reuse where, rather than reuse a component, the reused entity is more abstract and is designed to be configured and adapted for a range of situations. Concept reuse can be embodied in approaches such as design patterns, configurable system products and program generators. The reuse process, when concepts are reused, includes an instantiation activity where the abstract concepts are configured for a specific situation. Many techniques have been developed to support software reuse and these techniques exploit the facts that systems in similar application domain are identical and therefore have potential for reuse which is possible at different levels- from simple functions to complete applications [11].

According to Sommerville, (Sommerville, 2008), the followings are the number of ways to support software reuse (i.e. techniques for reuse):

i. Application product lines
ii. Aspect-oriented software development
iii. Configurable vertical applications
iv. Component-based development
v. Component frameworks
vi. COTS integration
vii. Design patterns
viii. Legacy system wrapping
ix. Program generators
x. Program libraries
xi. Service-oriented systems

Seeing that a huge number of techniques for reuse exist, it is therefore pertinent to figure out which is the most appropriate to use for a particular instance of reuse. When planning reuse, key factors one should consider are:

i. The development schedule for the software
ii. The expected software lifetime
iii. The criticality of the software and its non-functional requirements
iv. The background, skills and experience of the development team
v. The application domain and
vi. The platform on which the system will run.

Proponents claim that objects and software components offer a more advanced form of reusability, although it has been tough to objectively measure and define levels of reusability. Reusability implies some explicit management of build, packaging, distribution, installation, configuration, deployment, maintenance, and upgrade issues. If these issues are not considered, software may appear to be reusable from design point of view, but will not be reused in practice.

2.3. Knowledge Engineering Techniques

Knowledge refers to the perception an individual has about a fact or event in certain context [12]. For instance, a medical Doctor practices with the skill he possesses to treat and administer drugs to patients. Such knowledge is known as 'know-how'. Also a procedure manual or recipe for a meal is another instance of knowledge which is regarded as 'know'. There are two main types of knowledge, explicit (objective) and tacit (subjective) knowledge. The various kinds of knowledge are illustrated in figure 1 [13]. Tacit knowledge refers to 'know-how' of an individual while explicit knowledge is the articulated knowledge in form of documents, operation manual, video, etc. Explicit knowledge could be readily transmitted across individuals formally and systematically.

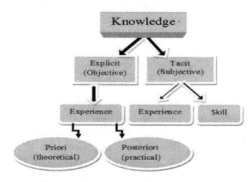

Figure 1. Classification of knowledge [13].

Knowledge Engineering is a branch of AI which analyzes the knowledge of a given domain and transforms it to a computable form for specific purpose. It entails knowledge representation which involves the translation of an informal specification to a formal (computable) one by a knowledge engineer who uses his wealth of background knowledge from reference sources or a domain expert [14]. There are certain guidelines for adequate knowledge representation.

2.3.1. Principles of Knowledge Representation

Certain factors that contribute to adequate representation of knowledge according to Randall in [14], are as follows.

Knowledge representation should serve as a surrogate (substitute/stand-in) for physical objects or events and the relationships amongst them with the aid of symbols and its links to model an external system.

It is a set of ontological commitments that determine various categories of objects of a domain.

It should describe the behavior and interaction amongst domain objects in order to reason about them.

Next is the fact that knowledge representation should be a medium for efficient computation which enables the encoding of represented knowledge in order to facilitate efficient processing with the aid of appropriate computing equipment.

Finally, it should be a medium of human expression in such a way to facilitate the understanding and communication of both knowledge engineer and domain experts.

Knowledge representation is often augmented with reasoning (the process of applying knowledge to arrive at the conclusion) techniques: that is, provision of methods to handle the tracking of transition among system's properties or knowledge and underlying reasons for such transitions. There are two approaches to reasoning techniques, namely, declarative and procedural. The latter is similar to step-wise programming or algorithmic approach while the former requires the use of axioms or logical statements to describe specifications and theorem-proving technique to reason about knowledge [14]. The choice of appropriate techniques for representing and reasoning about domain knowledge actually depends on the nature of requirements for a knowledge-based system.

2.3.2. Development of Knowledge Based Systems

A Knowledge Based System (KBS) is a software application with an explicit, declarative description of knowledge for a certain application [15] (Speel et al, 2001) in Avram. There is no clear separation criterion between a KBS and an information/software system as almost all contain nowadays knowledge elements in them [20] (Schreiber et al, 1999) in [21] Avram. Conventional software applications perform tasks using conventional decision-making logic -- containing little knowledge other than the basic algorithm for solving that specific problem and the necessary boundary conditions. This program knowledge is often embedded as part of the programming code, so that as the knowledge changes, the program has to be changed and then rebuilt. Knowledge-based systems collect the small fragments of human know-how into a knowledge-base which is used to reason through a problem, using the knowledge that is appropriate.

The development process of a KBS is similar to the development of any other software system; phases such as requirements elicitation, system analysis, system design, system development and implementation are common activities. The stages in KBS development are: business modelling, conceptual modelling, knowledge acquisition, knowledge system design and KBS implementation [15] (Speel et al, 2001) in Avram.

A KBS is nowadays developed using knowledge engineering techniques (Studer et al 1998). These are similar to software engineering techniques, but the emphasis is on knowledge rather than on data or information processing. The central theme in knowledge engineering techniques is the conceptual modelling of the system in the analysis and design stages of the development process. Many of the knowledge engineering methodologies developed emphasizes the use of models (Common KADS, MIKE, and Protégé).

In the early stages, knowledge-based systems were built using the knowledge of one or more experts – essentially, a process of knowledge transfer (Studer et al, 1998). Nowadays, a KBS involves "methods and techniques for knowledge acquisition, modelling, representation and use of knowledge" (Schreiber et al, 1999) in Avram

In current practice the transfer of expertise from a domain specialist to a knowledge-based system involves a computer scientist intermediary–or knowledge engineer. The specialist and the engineer discuss the domain in a series of interactions. During each interaction, the engineer gathers some understanding of a portion of the specialist's knowledge, encodes it in the evolving system, discusses the encoding and the results of its application with the specialist, and refines the encoded knowledge. The process is a painstaking one–expensive and tedious. As a result, one of the foremost problems that have been identified for KBSs is the knowledge acquisition bottleneck (Reid, 1985). The shift towards the modelling approach has also enabled knowledge to be re-used in different areas of one domain (Studer et al, 1998). Ontologies and Problem-Solving Methods enable the construction of KBSs from components reusable across domains and tasks.

2.4. Review of Related Works

According to [16] in a paper titled *A Pragmatic Approach to Software Reuse,* published in a Journal of Theoretical and Applied Information Technology, the reliability level of every reusable software artifact (requirement specification document, in this instance), is enhanced by a successful reuse and this success in turn increases the usefulness of such artifact in the reuse repository (such as a knowledge based system), and ultimately, the risk of failure of the resulting software product developed from such artifact is reduced. With the availability of a knowledge based system that serves as a repository for software requirement specification documents, which is a basis for building software adequately reflects the user's need and developer's technical know-how, timeliness in development and cost reduction would be facilitated while validation and verification of software will be enhanced likewise. Higher scheduling accuracy of the various tasks in the software development process is possible due to the reuse of process materials along with a better understanding of the product domain; therefore categorizing requirement specification document in the knowledge base along domain line is worthwhile.

Since the process has been completed before, project managers, having access to previous projects' scheduled and actual hours for production can adjust their current schedule based on previous performance and the amount of reusable artifact in the repository they intend to use. According to Jalender et al., the most substantial but not immediate benefits of reuse is derived from product line approach where a common set of reusable software assets act as a base for subsequent similar software product in a given functional domain. It was posited that the upfront investments required for software reuse are considerable and need to be duly considered prior to attempting a software reuse initiative, repositories of software assets must be created and maintained.

Lethal and Carl (1997) wrote on Automatically Identifying Reusable OO Legacy Code where they are of the view that much object-oriented code has been written without reuse in mind, making identification of useful components difficult. The Patricia system (a tool for object oriented program understanding) automatically identifies these components through understanding comments and identifiers. According to [17], aspects of Object oriented code such as classes, inheritance, and parametric polymorphism underline the need for good, semantically based tools to aid in the understanding, and thus the reuse, of Object oriented code. The paper stated that to determine whether a code component can be reused in a particular domain, or area of application, these semantically based tools must answer two questions: Are the purpose and capabilities of the code component useful in the current domain? Is the quality of the code component sufficient for the needs of the current domain?

Completely understanding what capabilities a class provides involves gathering information from a variety of sources, including the source code, user documentation (such as manuals), and documentation for requirements and design specifications.

In a research work "Towards Principles for the Design of Ontologies Used for Knowledge Sharing", [18] analyzed design requirements for shared ontologies and a proposal for design criteria to guide the development of ontologies for knowledge-sharing purposes. A usage model for ontologies in knowledge sharing was described and some design criteria based on the requirements of this usage model were proposed.

In a paper "Using Ontologies for Knowledge Management: An Information Systems Perspective", [19] surveyed some of the basic concepts that have been used in computer science for the representation of knowledge and summarized some of their advantages and drawbacks. The survey classifies the concepts used for knowledge representation into four broad ontological categories viz: Static ontology which describes static aspects of the world, i.e., what things exist, their attributes and relationships, A Dynamic ontology, which describes the changing aspects of the world in terms of states, state transitions and processes, Intentional ontology, which encompasses the world of things agents believe in, want, prove or disprove, and argue about, and Social ontology which covers social settings, agents, positions, roles, authority, permanent organizational structures or shifting networks of alliances and interdependencies. They advocated a complementary use of concepts and techniques from information science and information systems in knowledge management as a result of the vast, complex and dynamic information environments. The ontology approach from information modeling described in this paper derives its strength from the formalization of some domain of knowledge; however, many domains resist precise formalization. In each domain, there are points at which formalization becomes more of a straightjacket than a liberating force. The challenge therefore is not so much to decide which approach is better, but to develop techniques for the various approaches to work closely together in a seamless way. It was posited that the key to providing useful support for knowledge management lies in how meaning is embedded in information models as defined in ontologies.

3. Research Methodology

3.1. Conceptual Framework for Knowledge Engineering for Reuse

In an attempt to model the knowledge base for the reuse of software requirement specification, the conceptual framework for knowledge Engineering for reuse is first established. This is represented in figure 2, describing how knowledge is represented and computed to produce output for utilization as a solution to an existing problem.

How do we represent what we know? Knowledge is a general term. An answer to the question, "how to represent knowledge", requires an analysis to distinguish between knowledge "how" and knowledge "that". Knowing how to do something, for example, "how to operate a machine" is a Procedural knowledge. Knowing that something is true or false, for instance, "the temperature limit for a machine in operation" is a Declarative Knowledge.

Knowledge and Representation are two distinct entities. They play a central but distinguishable role in intelligent systems. Knowledge is a description of the world. It determines a system's competence by what it knows.

Representation is the way knowledge is encoded. It defines a system's performance in doing something. A good representation enables fast and accurate access to knowledge and understanding of the content. Knowledge representation can be considered at two levels:

a. Knowledge level at which facts are described, and

b. Symbol level at which the representations of the objects, defined in terms of symbols, can be manipulated in the programs.

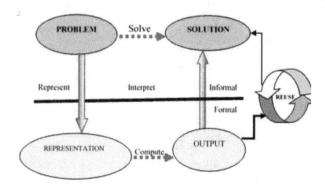

Figure 2. *Knowledge Representation Framework [22] Extended for Reuse*

Different types of knowledge require different kinds of representation and reasoning. The knowledge representation models/mechanisms are often based on: (i) Logic, (ii) Rules, (iii) Frames and (iv) Semantic Network.

Fig. 2 shows a description of framework adapted from [22] for knowledge representation and reuse of such knowledge.

The computer requires a well-defined problem description to process and provide well-defined acceptable solution from a reused component. To collect fragments of knowledge we need first to formulate a description in our spoken language and then represent it in formal language so that computer can understand. This is where ontology comes in into modelling the contents of the knowledge base. The computer can then use an algorithm to compute an answer as illustrated in fig. 2. The steps are:

The informal formalism of the problem takes place first. It is then represented formally in ontology and the knowledge base produces an output upon query. This output can then be represented in an informally described solution that user (software engineers) understands or checks for consistency in line with initial customer's requirements.

It is noteworthy however to state that problem solving requires formal knowledge representation, and conversion of informal knowledge to formal knowledge, as well as conversion of implicit knowledge to explicit knowledge.

3.2. Formalization of Knowledge Engineering Framework for Software Reuse

The Finite Automaton (FA) in fig. 3 is a five tuple $(Q, \Sigma, \delta, So, F)$ describing the process of transmission of software requirement data from one state to another, undergoing refinement and necessary adjustment as required where,

Q is the set of all states in the automaton represented by circles in fig. 3, thus:

$Q = \{S_0, S_1, S_2, S_3, S_4\}$ where:

S_0= Initial customer specification information

S_1= Designer's specification

S_2= Agreed specification (Software Requirement Specification)

S_3 = Formalized knowledge in the knowledge based system

S_4 = Reusable knowledge (for future specifications)

Σ is the string of valid characters that can occur in the input stream. Typically, Σ is the union of the edge labels in fig. 3.

δ: $Q \times \Sigma \rightarrow Q$ is the transition function for the automaton. It depicts the state changes induced by an input character string for each state; δ is represented by the labeled edges that connect states in fig. 3.

$$\{(<S_0, T_1> \rightarrow S_1),$$

$$(<S_1, T_2> \rightarrow S_0),$$

$$(<S_1, T_3> \rightarrow S_2),$$

$$(<S_2, T_4> \rightarrow S_1),$$

$$(<S_2, T_5> \rightarrow S_3),$$

$$(<S_3, T_6> \rightarrow S_2),$$

$$(<S_3, T_7> \rightarrow S_4),$$

$$(<S_4, T_8> \rightarrow S_2)\}$$

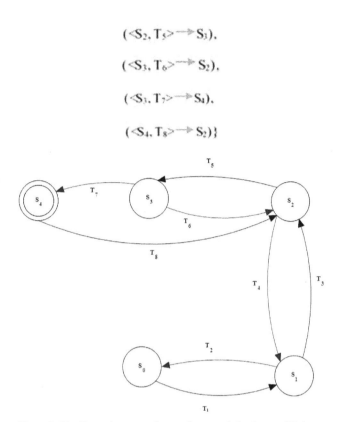

Figure 3. The Finite Automata showing framework for Reuse of Software artifact (requirement engineering

3.3. Knowledge Base Development for Software Requirement Specification for Reuse (SRSR)

The approach to reuse adopted is knowledge-based; a software system with an explicit, declarative description of knowledge for diverse domains. We would expect to find artifacts from which self-contained applications can be constructed based on certain characteristics and the goal (purpose for utilization, driven by requirement specification). The knowledge based system was implemented using protégé 4.1.

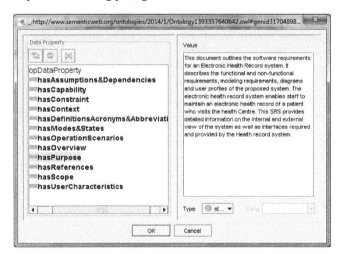

Figure 4. An Existing Health Records System SRS showing its 'PURPOSE'

4. Research Findings and Result

The ontological tool used for the ontological architecture of the knowledge based system is Protégé 4.1. This produces a generalized class of ontology that describes various requirement specification documents for different domains of software. The object properties of the various classes are inherited from the super class called Software Requirement Specification and these properties reflect the content specified by IEEE standard 1233[23]. Fig. 4 shows the screen shot of a requirement specification document retrieved to view its purpose, which reflects the functional and non-functional requirements of the software being developed.

Artifacts stored in this repository possess the attributes shown in table 1, and these make them suitable for reuse.

Table 1. Features of suitability of the artifacts for reuse

Attributes	Comments
Simplicity	Minimum and explicit artifact interfaces which encourage developers to use artifacts, simple and easy to understand artifacts can also be easily modified by developers to suit new applications.
Expressiveness	They are of general utility and of adequate level of abstraction, so they could be used in many different contexts within their domains.
Definite	They are constructed and documented with clarity of purpose, their capabilities and limitations are easily identifiable, interfaces, required resources, external dependencies and operational environments are specified, and all other requirements are explicit and well defined.
Additive	It is possible to seamlessly compose these existing artifacts into new products or other reusable components, without the need for massive software modifications or causing adverse side effects
Easily Changeable	Certain type of problems will require artifacts to be adapted to the new specifications, such changes should be localized to the artifact and require minimum of side effects
Unambiguous	Each requirement is stated in such a way so that it can be interpreted in only one way without ambiguities.
Organized	The requirements and sub-components are well structured in the ontology

5. Conclusion

Software reuse, as appealing as it appears, if it is not carefully implemented, the cost involved in software development using reuse may be much more than that incurred when software is developed from scratch. Therefore, reuse that is facilitated by the knowledge based repository of the underlying the requirement specification documents of previously developed software product is like building a strong foundation for a complex structure, and this gives reliability and assurance of quality. The knowledge based system uses semantic approach to search for reusable requirement components whose product can be partly or entirely utilized for developing a proposed system. With software domain specific repository available, based on the reference architecture and on the requirements we would be able to locate and reuse some domain specific reusable components. This work can be extended to see how the reuse of requirement specification documents alters the conventional software development life cycle.

References

[1]   Y. Kim and E.A. Stohr, "Software Reuse: Survey and Research Directions," Journal of Management Information Systems, 1997.

[2]   R. B. Victor, B. John, G. J. Bok, and H.R. Dieter, "Software Reuse: A framework for Research," Department of Computer Science, University of Maryland, 2002.

[3]   H. Baetjer, Jr., "Software as Capital," IEEE Computer Society Press, 1998, p. 85.

[4]   R. S. Pressman, "Software Engineering. A Practitioner's Approach," 5th ed., McGraw-Hill series in Computer science, 2001.

[5]   Standish Group. The CHAOS Report. Dennis, M.A: The Standish Group, 1994.

[6]   Standish Group. "The Scope of Software Development Project Failures," Dennis, MA: The Standish Group, 1995.

[7]   S.L. Pfleeger and M.A. Joanne, "Software Engineering: Theory and Practice." 4th ed., Pearson Higher Education, 2010.

[8]   M. Hafedh, M. Fatma, and M. Ali, "Reusing Software: Issues and Research Directions," IEEE Transactions on Software Engineering, Vol. 21, No. 6, June 1995.

[9]   G.N.K. Suresh, and S.K. Srivatsa, "Analysis and Measures of Software Reusability." International Journal of Reviews in Computing, 2009.

[10]   P. Nandish, "Software Reuse and/or Software Complexity Management." Networks on Chips, 2008.

[11]   I. Sommerville, "Software Engineering," 8th Edition, (Addison-Wesley Publishers Ltd.,), 2008, pp. 415 - 438.

[12]   B.F Oladejo & A.O. Osofisan, "A Conceptual Framework for Knowledge Integration in the Context of Decision Making Progress," African Journal of Computer & ICT, vol. 4, No. 2. Issue2. Pp.25-32, 2011.

[13]   B. F. Oladejo, V. T. Odumuyiwa, and A. A. David, "Dynamic Capitalization and Visualization Strategy in Collaborative Knowledge Management system for EI process," World Academy of Science, Engineering and Technology pp66, 2010.

[14]   J. F. Sowa, "Knowledge Representation: logical, philosophical, and computational foundations," Brooks Cole Publishing Co., Pacific Grove, CA. 2000.

[15] P. Speel, A. Th. Schreiber, W.V. Joolingen, and G. Beijer, "Conceptual Models for Knowledge-Based Systems." Encyclopedia of Computer Science and Technology, Marcel Dekker Inc., New York, 2001

[16] B. Jalender, A. Govardhan, and P. Premchand, "A Pragmatic Approach to Software Reuse." *A Journal of Theoretical and Applied Information Technology*, 2010.

[17] H.E. Lethal, and G. D. Carl, "Automatically Identifying Reusable OO Legacy Code." *University of Alabama, Huntsville*, 1997.

[18] T.R. Gruber, "Toward Principles for the Design of Ontologies Used for Knowledge Sharing." 1993.

[19] J. Igor, M. John, and Y. Eric, "Using Ontologies for Knowledge Management: An Information Systems Perspective. University of Toronto, Toronto, Ontario, Canada. 1999.

[20] G. Schreiber, H. Akkermans, A. Anjewierden, R. de Hoog, N. Shadbolt, W.V. de Velde, and B. Wielinga, "Knowledge Engineering and Management: The Common KADS Methodology," Massachusetts: MIT Press, 1999.

[21] G. Avram. Empirical Study on Knowledge Based Systems. The Electronic Journal of Information Systems Evaluation, Vol. 8, Iss.1, pp 11-20, available online at www.ejise.com, 2005

[22] D. Poole, "Knowledge Representation Framework," 1998.

[23] IEEE-Std 1233, IEEE Guide for Developing System Requirements Specifications, 1998.

26

Do agile methods increase productivity and quality?

Gabriela Robiolo, Daniel Grane

Informatica, Universidad Austral, Buenos Aires, Argentina

Email address:

grobiolo@austral.edu.ar (G. Robiolo), daniel.grane@gmail.com (D. Grane)

Abstract: The Agile methods popped up in the history of software development methods as a solution to several frequent problems, but what is still not clear is whether they produce a significant improvement in productivity and quality or not, if they are compared to the traditional software development methods. In order to clarify this issue and contribute to a better understanding of these methods, we designed an empirical study in which Agile and traditional methods were compared in an academic context. By applying a traditional method to the development of software products, we managed to obtain a more reproducible result, though we could not obtain evidence of an improvement in quality. On the contrary, by applying an Agile method, we obtained evidence of higher productivity, but with a significant dispersion, an aspect that would be interesting to analyze in future studies.

Keywords: Agile, Rup, Scrum, Productivity, Quality, Extreme Programming

1. Introduction

In the 1990s, new processes and methodologies that deal with software development projects appeared. As they evolved, and because of their particular characteristics, these development methodologies fell into two broad categories: traditional and Agile. On the one hand, traditional methods involve those in which the systems are fully specified, they are predictable and they are built according to meticulous and extensive planning. Besides, these projects are run by a clearly defined head that controls the activities, based on explicit knowledge. The organization where this happens is usually large, bureaucratic, with a high degree of formalization, which makes communication formal too. In addition, the software life cycle of their products may be described as waterfall or spiral, and the testing is most surely performed at the end of the cycle [1].

On the contrary, Agile methods are based on the premise that high quality software -adaptable to different conditions- is developed by small groups, using a design which gets continuous improvement. Besides, constant testing provides a rapid feedback, thus making the early introduction of improvements possible. The management structure of the organization in which Agile methods are used tends to be informally defined; it is based on natural leadership and collaboration. Regardless of the size of the organization, work is divided into small groups, where communication within the teams is informal, the internal organization is flexible and their members are participatory. The life cycle of their products is often evolutionary, which includes requirements management and continuous testing [2].

In fact, the Agile methods popped up in the history of software development methods as a solution to several frequent problems. The principal ideas of this solution are summarized in the Agile manifesto[1], which states: "We are uncovering better ways of developing software by doing it and helping others do it. Through this work we have come to value: individuals and interactions over processes and tools, working software over comprehensive documentation, customer collaboration over contract negotiation and responding to change over following a plan". Their creators consider that the items in bold letter have more value than the others.

The Agile methods [3] have greatly impacted on the manner in which software is developed worldwide, so it is convenient to learn if the Agile methods have actually improved the software development life cycle, principally in aspects such as productivity and quality. Consequently, we would like to answer the following research question: *do the use of Agile methods necessarily lead to improved productivity and quality, if compared to those obtained by traditional methods, or is it that the new methods are just an*

---

[1] http://agilemanifesto.org/

evolution of the traditional ones, without a significant impact on productivity and quality, as observed by Hirsch [4]?

In order to clarify this issue and contribute to a better understanding of these methods by providing more empirical evidence, we designed an empirical experience. This empirical study compared similar applications which were developed by applying either the Rational Unified Process (RUP) , SCRUM or Extreme Programming (XP) in an academic environment. RUP was selected because it is a framework that merges different development methodologies and because due to its characteristics it may be considered a traditional method. SCRUM was chosen because it is popular in the industry [3] and XP because it is the Agile method for which more empirical results have been reported [3].

In the coming sections of this paper a collection of related articles will be commented; the planning, the execution and the results of our empirical experience will be described; such results will be discussed and finally, conclusions will be drawn.

2. Related Work

There has been increasing interest in empirical studies concerning Agile methods for some years [5]. In fact, several empirical studies were conducted in either industrial or academic environments, for which different techniques were employed: formal experiment, survey, case study or post mortem analysis. Lately, the interest to perform objective comparisons has especially increased, principally in aspects such as productivity and quality.

For example, Dyba and Dingsoyr [3] conducted a systematic review of the Agile development methods. Their review points out that three out of the four studies that addressed the comparison of the productivity obtained by Agile and traditional teams found out that using eXtreme Programming (XP) resulted in increased productivity in terms of LOC/h. Also, another study that focused on the use of SCRUM in a very small company [6], which was not included in the previous systematic review, reached, using the same unit of measurement, the same conclusion as regards productivity. However, we may argue that LOC is not an appropriate measure to ensure an unbiased comparison when comparing productivity because experienced programmers have the capacity to summarize in a short statement what novice programmers write in several lines, thus the latter seem to yield a higher production. Nevertheless, we also found out that a later systematic review based on twenty eight very good papers [7] found evidence of the increase in productivity when using the SCRUM method.

Regarding product quality, most studies in Dyba and Dingsoyr's survey [3] reported increased code quality when Agile methods were used. However, none of these studies had an appropriate recruitment strategy to ensure an unbiased comparison, and few quantitative measurements were made, so there seemed to be little scientific support at

that moment to claim such improvement in code quality. In addition, Sfetsos and Stamelos [8] conducted a survey on Agile projects in which internal and external quality -based on the ISO/IEC 9126 standard, which is the same standard used in this article- were evaluated. The survey presented forty six high quality empirical articles, twenty seven of which had been developed in academic contexts. All the articles of the industrial context, but one, described cases in which Test-driven Development was applied, while Test-first Development was used in the academic context. The authors reported an improvement in external quality, measured in terms of the number of defects and successful external testing, but there was not the same evidence for the internal quality of either Test-driven Development or Test-first Development. Regrettably, due to the characteristics of our study, it was not possible for us to show evidence of improvement in external quality and our conclusion on internal quality is similar to theirs.

In addition, some studies have been made on the productivity of geographically distributed development. For example, Sutherland et al. [9] reported that Xebia -a Dutch company- started local projects with teams composed of Dutch and Indian members. After obtaining local hyper-productivity in the performance of a team working with SCRUM in the Netherlands, they moved the Indian members of that team into India. Their work in India, also with SCRUM, was as productive as that in the Netherlands. Based on this experience, Xebia has set a model for high performance, distributed, offshore teams, which have obtained one of the lowest defect rates in the industry. Although their hyper-productive performance was defined in terms of the comparison with only one external project, it was an interesting example of geographically distributed development. Another example of geographically distributed development using SCRUM was reported, but this time, a team of 4 persons did not get a significant productivity improvement, if compared to the previous phase of their project, in which a waterfall process had been applied [10].

Besides, there was a longitudinal industrial study which investigated the effects of SCRUM on software quality -in terms of defects and defect density-, and studied the quality assurance process [11]. The authors reported that they followed a project over a three-year period; they used a plan-driven process to compare the software quality assurance processes and software defects of such project during a 17-month phase, which was then followed by a 20-month phase, during which they used SCRUM to make such comparisons. The results of the study did not show a significant reduction of defect densities or changes of defect profiles after SCRUM was used. Likewise, the same conclusion had already been reached [6] in the context of a very small company. Also, Hashmi and Baik [13] had compared XP to a traditional method which was based on the Spiral model. They did not find a significant difference in the quality measured in Fault Rate (Faults/KLOC).

Moreover, Mirakhorli et al. [14] applied a RDP technique - an XP customization method – to the second version of the Union Catalogue System – a virtual catalogue coordinated by the National Library of Iran-. They reported that higher quality and productivity results may be obtained if XP practices are tailored, considering their project sizes, contexts and capabilities.

Finally, it is interesting to mention that Goldin and Rudahl [15] performed a comparative study (RUP versus XP) in circumstances similar to those in which our empirical experience was conducted. They found out that all the teams understood their assigned processes, but the RUP teams were more successful in applying the method. However, the RUP teams were significantly more likely to say that they would have preferred to use XP rather than their assigned process, which is exactly what was said by the students that participated in our empirical study. Nevertheless, the quantitative measurements focused on software processes did not show clear results in terms of productivity and quality. Another interesting article we should highlight is one which deals with a different approach: the use of a hybrid process which took some characteristics from RUP and others from SCRUM. In this case, the requirements and architectural specifications were written following the RUP method, and the Programming, Testing and Deployment were performed according to the SCRUM method. The authors reported an improvement in productivity when this hybrid method was applied [16].

To conclude, the related work described above shows an increase in productivity and external quality when using Agile methods but, as regards internal quality, there is no evidence of such an improvement, which is similar to what is being reported by our empirical study.

3. Empirical Study

Our empirical study was developed in the context of a design workshop that is part of the curriculum of the Software Engineering degree offered by the School of Engineering of Universidad Austral (Argentina). We followed the recommendations of [17, 18] to develop this empirical experience. Besides, to present this study and its

replications, the guidelines for reporting empirical research in software engineering in [19] were followed as closely as possible.

We will now present the planning of our study, its execution, and the results we obtained, with an explanation of the threats to validity. Finally, there will be a discussion of the results obtained.

3.1. Planning

The planning stage of our empirical study will be presented by defining our goal, explaining how the study was designed and describing the characteristics of its execution.

3.1.1. Goal

The goal of our empirical study was to make an empirical evaluation of how significant the improvement in productivity and quality may be when applying Agile software development methods, if such results are compared to those obtained when using traditional methods.

To clarify this goal, the Goal-Question-metric paradigm was applied [20]. Table 1 shows the results of its application, where the measures used to compare the methods are listed.

It is important to highlight that the ISO/IEC 9126 standard [21] defines Usability in terms of five sub-characteristics: Understandability, Learnability, Operability, Attractiveness, and Usability Compliance. Usability Compliance refers to the capability of the software component to adhere to standards, conventions, style guides and regulations relating to Usability. In our study, these characteristics were evaluated by asking a set of questions of the users.

In order to measure the Maintainability of an application, Parnas [22] introduced the idea of considering the number of affected modules when a change is proposed. Chaumun et al. [1] assessed the changeability of an object-oriented system by computing the impact of the changes made to the classes of the system. We applied the same concept, but in a simpler manner: every class that was modified by a change was counted. The only exception was the addition of a sub-class, as this was considered an extension of the functionality of the class and, due to the advantages of polymorphism, the pre-existing code was not modified.

Table 1. Goal-Question-metric paradigm application.

Questions	Answer	Metric
Which are the most representative Agile methods?	SCRUM and XP are the Agile methods that yield more empirical evidence, which facilitates the comparison of the results [9].	--
Which are the traditional methods?	RUP is a unified method that has all the characteristics of a traditional method.	--
Which are the characteristics and sub-characteristics of quality defined in the ISO/IEC 9126-1 standard that are relevant for the comparison of the selected methods?	Functionality: Accuracy Usability: Understandability, Learnability, Operability and Attractiveness Maintainability: Changeability	Number of Failures reported Degree of usability Number of classes modified when a requirement change is made Degree of understanding of the design
What is productivity in a software development project?	Productivity = Size/Effort	Number of Transactions

Another aspect that may affect the maintenance task is the Degree of understanding of the design (DUD). In our study, this was measured by a set of questions which the developers were asked to answer. In a similar manner, Deligiannis et al [23] included a set of questions in an empirical investigation, as a complement of the maintainability test, which captures the participant's personal opinions regarding the architectural aspects of a system, as well as about the modification tasks.

The main difference between this test and ours is that the participants of their empirical investigation did not develop the product, they only evaluated it.

Productivity was also an important aspect to be considered. As all the projects in our study took the same time to be developed, to compare the productivity of the projects, we only had to consider size. To measure size, the concept Transaction (T) [24] was used, but in this case, it was applied to the final implemented product. Each transaction was identified from the stimulus triggered by the actor into the system, so the functional size was calculated as the number of stimuli in the final product. It is important to note that a T "transaction" has a finer granularity, if it is compared to that of a Function Point (FP) transaction; a FP transaction may be equal to one or more T "transactions". Besides, T has the advantage that it may be applied to game applications.

3.1.2. Design

To measure productivity and quality improvement in software development, we decided to divide our advanced students into seven teams which had to develop a product, using a given developing method in a limited time.

To form the groups, there were two alternatives: either to randomly select members or to form groups of members who had similar capabilities. Although all the students were advanced, their levels of performance were different, so the second strategy was adopted to form balanced groups. To evenly distribute the people into the groups, the following parameters were considered:

(1) Academic performance: the final mark the students had obtained in the prerequisite course was considered.

(2) Experience: number of months they had worked in the industry or in software development labs.

(3) Academic workload: number of courses being attended at that moment and the number of final exams each student still had to sit for.

The developing method - RUP, SCRUM or XP- was randomly assigned to each team.

RUP is the framework which resulted from the unification of different approaches to software development, including the use of UML. It is iterative, incremental, architecture-focused and based on use cases. The process is organized into four phases: initiation, development, construction, transition, and into five processes: requirements capture, analysis, design, implementation and testing. It provides a disciplined approach to defining roles, activities and deliverables. It can be used in large or small organizations, and in formal or informal ones. Besides, it can be used with different management styles because this approach is flexible [25].

On the other hand, SCRUM is an Agile method which is focused on project management. When using this method, software development is performed by a group, during time intervals called "sprints". Each sprint will produce a product increment, which will start with the sprint planning and end with the product increment review. The main roles in SCRUM are: the "SCRUM master", who is the supplier of the process, the "Product Owner", who represents the stakeholders and the business, and the "Team", which is a dynamic and self organized group of about seven people who do the developing task. The Product owner defines the set of requirements that should be implemented, which defines the product "backlog". The Product Owner gives priority to the different requirements and the team determines which of such requirements may be completed during the next sprint, and records this in the sprint backlog. Group members coordinate their work during a daily stand up meeting [26].

Likewise, XP [14] is an Agile method that is defined by a set of rules which characterize it. These rules may be summarized as follows: continuous testing, clearness and quality of codes, common vocabulary, authority to be shared by everybody and at least two people have the understanding necessary to do any task, Test-First Programming is done in pairs.

Table 2 summarizes the main differences between RUP and the Agile methods.

The professor who ran the workshop designed the tasks to be performed by the students. Different tasks were planned for each type of method, RUP or Agile, as presented in Table 3. It is important to note that all the students had to use a Vision Report [12] and a requirements definition, no matter which method they used.

In order to measure the differences between products, we selected the following variables: accuracy, usability, changeability and functionality. Table 4 shows the *variables* involved in the empirical experience and the measure used to measure them. We considered it was necessary to control the following co-factors:

(1) Development environment: all groups worked in similar development environments and used computers with similar specifications.

(2) Time: all the groups worked during the set time.

(3) Level of training: all the students had received similar initial training in each specific topic, and those students who had previous experience in each specific topic were distributed in a balanced way.

(4) Product complexity: the professors controlled the complexity of each product in order to prevent distortions in the developed products. For example, for the game product, a set of complexity rules was defined.

Once the study had been designed, we wrote the following research questions, whose answers would tell us if there are differences in productivity and quality when using RUP and Agile methods:

(1) Is the number of F reported from the application of an Agile method bigger than that obtained when using the RUP method?

(2) Is the DU analyzed for RUP greater than that in Agile?

(3) Is the number of MC resulting from the application of an Agile method bigger than that obtained when using the RUP method?

(4) Is the DUD in RUP team members greater than that in Agile team members?

(5) Is the size, measured in number of T, of a final product developed with an Agile method bigger than that obtained with a RUP method?

Table 2. *Comparison between RUP and the Agile methods.*

Aspect	RUP	Agile Methods
Client	Defines and approves the requirements. Validates the system.	Integrates the development team. Defines priorities.
Strength of the work group	Lies on the process	Lies on the people
Architecture	Architecture centered	Gives importance to code
Requeriments	Use cases	The method to be applied is not explicitly stated, but the method most widely used is User Stories
Documentation	Consists of an adequate selection of artifacts	Included in the code
Testing	Is a discipline	The automated test is essential, it completes the requirements definition
Project management	Is a discipline	The importance of this aspect is not explicitly defined, but results show that when applying the Agile methods, the management control improves
Project size	Small, medium and large	Software release
Team size	Not defined	About 10 people

Table 3. *Tasks to be performed/ artifacts to be developed.*

Method	Task
RUP	Artifacts developed (Vision Report, Use cases, Class Diagram, Sequential Diagrams, External design, Design of test cases) Programming and testing
SCRUM and XP	Artifacts developed (Vision Report, Users Stories) Programming and testing

Table 4. *Variables measured.*

Variables	Measure	Comment
Accuracy	Number of Failures reported (F)	
Usability	Degree of usability (DU)	Number of very low, low, acceptable, high, and very high answers
Changeability	Number of classes modified when a requirement change was made (MC)	The anonymously nested classes implemented in Java were not taken into account
	Degree of understanding of the design (DUD)	Number of clear, confusing and misleading answers
Functional size	Number of Transactions (T)	Number of stimuli dispatched from the actor to the system, measured in the final product

3.2. Execution

Advanced students, who were the *experimental subjects*, were divided into seven groups: 3 used RUP, 1 SCRUM, and 3 XP. These projects were developed in a four-year period; not all of them were done at the same time. Table 5 shows the capabilities of the *experimental subjects*.

The descriptions of the developed products, i.e. the *experimental objects,* are shown in Table 6.

The professors played the role of leaders, owners and clients. The only exception was P3, in which the client role was played by the students. In every product the students played the role of developers. Table 7 shows the roles played.

The projects were developed by the students during an academic year, at the end of which, the students and professors measured the following measures in the context of a final assessment:

(1) CMC: a set of changes to be made to their final product was defined by the professors. Students examined the changes and identified the class that would be affected by these changes.

(2) DUD: the students involved in the empirical experience answered a set of questions. The product characteristics were considered to design such questions.

(3) T: the professors measured the final products.

The measures F and DU were discarded. As regards the first variable, it was found out that the products had been developed up to a level in which no failures had been reported since, prior to delivery, the products had been tested and the errors corrected. The second variable was ruled out because of the limitations imposed to keep the complexity of the products at a comparable level, which obliged the participants to develop products of similar external designs.

Table 8 shows the changes proposed to measure MC and Table 9 shows the questions made to evaluate the DUD of the product.

Table 10 shows the number of weeks set per task. All the products used a Vision Report [12] and a use case description for requirements definition or user stories. P1 and P2 used the same Vision Report and Use Case textual description.

As an example, and in order to highlight the differences between Agile and traditional methods, Fig. 1 shows a comparison of the use of time made by $P2_{SCRUM}$ and $P1_{RUP}$.

3.3. Results

The values obtained when the above mentioned variables were measured are shown in the following sub-sections.

Table 5. Experimental subjects' capability.

Member of group	Final mark obtained in prerequisite course	Work experience (in months)	Number of pending final exams	Courses being attended
P1₁	9.5	3	1	7
P1₂	4	12	5	6
P1₃	9	4	1	7
P2₁	7	5	6	8
P2₂	6.5	0	5	7
P2₃	7.5	5	7	5
P2₄	8.5	12	4	6
P3₁	6.5	0	0	7
P3₂	6	0	1	8
P3₃	4	0	3	7
P3₄	8	0	0	7
P4₁	6	0	5	6
P4₂	7	0	5	7
P4₃	6.5	3	2	7
P5₁	8	12	0	7
P5₂	7	3	1	7
P5₃	7	6	1	9
P5₄	7	0	0	7
P6₁	5	8	9	4
P6₂	4	7	4	6
P6₃	8	7	1	7
P6₄	5	6	1	9
P7₁	7	10	0	8
P7₂	6	18	8	5
P7₃	6	0	4	7
P7₄	8	0	0	7

Table 6. Description of the experimental objects.

Product	Method	Year	Description
P1	RUP	2008	Turn-based strategy game
P2	SCRUM	2008	Turn-based strategy game
P3	XP	2010	Social network
P4	RUP	2010	Social network
P5	XP	2011	3D Social network
P6	RUP	2011	Social network
P7	XP	2011	Social network

Table 7. Roles played

Method	Role	Performer
P1, P4 and P6	Team leader	Professor
P1, P4 and P6	Developers	Students
P1	Client	Professor
P4 and P6	Client	Students
P2	SCRUM master	Professor
P2	Developers	Students
P2	Owner-Client	Professor
P3, P5, P7	Clients	Students
P3, P5, P7	Owner	Professor
P3, P5, P7	Developers	Students

Table 8. Proposed changes.

Project	Proposed Change
P1 and P2	Place more than one troop in a square. Assign multiple improvements to the troops. Create a new special unit that has the ability to build settlements. Incorporate multiple end-game conditions. Insert a stage of buying and selling resources between shifts.
P3	Make the system limit the number of users that can answer a survey, and do not allow the user to modify such limit. Make the system limit the number of users that can answer a survey, but allow the user to modify such limit. Reject the answer given to a survey. Verify that no poll with the same name has been created before. Unsubscribe fake users (SPAM). Vary the condition to accept a survey.
P4	Enable more than one person to own a site. Unsubscribe fake users (SPAM) and cleanse the system of their activities Add a new strategy to recommend sites. Divide the system into regions. Incorporate a contact address book and invite your contacts to contact you. Add a new site from a cell phone, according to current geographical location.
P5	Add an avatar/person to the world (3 avatars/persons). Visit your friend's home when she/he is present. Add a characteristic to an avatar/ person (run). Add a new scenario. Add a new type of message for a sub-set of your friends. Add a new filter.
P6	Show the historical list of messages from your friends. Query messages using several categories. Chat (direct messages). Query tweets sent exactly a year ago. Add the right of admission.
P7	Notify an interest group of the news about a certain type of event. Create an event for a specific family. Add a chat facility. Use the same system to organize a football tournament.

3.3.1. Changeability

Table 11 shows the number of classes affected by the changes outlined in the previous section, in Table 8. The mean was 9 MC for the RUP-developed projects and the mean standard deviation was 1 MC. In the case of Agile methods, the mean was 11.25 MC and the standard deviation was 3.86. The differences between the values obtained for the RUP and Agile methods were not significant, with the exception of P2 -which had been made with SCRUM-, which proved to be the weakest design.

Table 12 shows the responses to the questions listed in Table 6. Responses were classified into clear, confusing and misleading. The P4 group did not respond all the questions because there was not enough time to do so, so the professor selected only some questions to be asked of each of those students.

Table 13 shows the statistical analysis of the responses. The mean of the Agile clear responses was bigger than that of the RUP responses. The standard deviation of the Agile responses was similar to that of the RUP responses in the case of the clear responses, while they were bigger than those of RUP's in the case of the confusing and misleading responses. In any case, these differences did not show a significant difference in the degree of understanding of the designs.

Table 9. *Questions to evaluate the degree of understanding of the product design.*

Project	Questions
P1 and P2	How does the system implement the take over of resources?
	How does the system implement the take over of a source of resources?
	How does the system implement the movement of troops?
	How does the system implement the game over?
	How does the system implement a combination of troops?
	How does the system implement an attack?
	How does the system implement the construction of a troop?
	How does the system implement improvements in a troop?
	How does the system implement the exploration of mysterious places?
	How does the system implement improvements in a settlement?
	How does the system implement the creation of a new game?
	How does the system implement the completion of a game?
	How does the system implement the online upgrade of the game?
	How does the system implement the visualization and rendering of the map?
	How does the system implement the overall control of the game?
	How does the user accept a notification?
	How does the user add a survey?
	How does the system add a user?
	How is a user deleted?
	How is a survey answered?
P3	How is the profile of an owner defined, as opposed to that of a visitor?
	What design pattern was used in the Qnet implementation?
	What is the criterion for listing surveys?
	How does the connection to the database work? What are the layers of the system?
	How did I save the users' tags?
	How is the recommendation of the places made?
	How is a discount added?
P4	Where are the contents uploaded by users stored?
	What would happen to the system if there were thousands of comments about only one place?
	How is a complaint from a place implemented?

Project	Questions
P5	How does the system validate a user input?
	What URL encoding strategies are used?
	How does the system filter search results?
	How does the system manage authentication and authorization?
	How does the system implement the synchronization of the avatar/persons?
	How does the system implement the connection to the database?
	What is the avatar world?
	How does the system implement "the avatars walking in the world"?
	How does the system implement the "bulletin board"?
P6	How does the system implement the connection to the database?
	How does the system implement the synchronization with the cellular phone?
	Describe the API structure.
	How does the system implement the messages update?
	How do the clients migrate to other devices?
	How does the system implement the connection to the database?
P7	How does the system notify of a change in an event?
	How does the system implement the interest groups?
	How does the system implement the algorithm that suggests friends?
	How does the system processes the answers from other users?

Table 10. *Weeks allotted per task.*

Project	Task	Weeks
P1 RUP	Artifacts development (Vision Report, Use cases, Class Diagram, Sequential Diagrams, External design, Design Test)	13
	Programming	19
P2 SCRUM	Artifacts development (Vision Report)	5
	Programming	27
P3 XP	Artifacts development (Vision Report and User stories)	4
	Programming	28
P4 RUP	Artifacts development (Vision Report, Use cases, Class Diagram, Sequential Diagrams, External design, Design Test)	17
	Programming	15
P5 XP	Artifacts development (Vision Report and User stories)	5
	Programming	28
P6 RUP	Artifacts development (Vision Report, Use cases, Class Diagram, Sequential Diagrams, External design, Design Test)	16
	Programming	16
P7 XP	Artifacts development (Vision Report and User stories)	5
	Programming	28

Table 11. *Number of classes affected by the changes.*

Project	Product	MC
P1 RUP	P1	8
P2 SCRUM	P2	17
P3 XP	P3	9
P4 RUP	P4	9
P5 XP	P5	9
P6 RUP	P6	10
P7 XP	P7	10

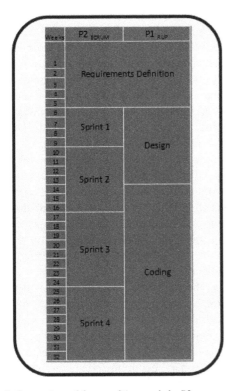

Figure 1. *Comparison of the use of time made by P2_SCRUM and P1_RUP.*

Table 12. *Responses used to determine the degree of understanding of the designs.*

Group	Response		
	clear	confusing	misleading
P1_RUP	35	4	6
P2_SCRUM	28	19	13
P3_XP	39	1	0
P4_RUP	12	5	0
P5_XP	14	5	0
P6_RUP	18	2	0
P7_XP	18	2	0

Table 13. *Statistical analysis of the responses used to determine the degree of understanding of the designs.*

Statistical Analysis	Response		
	clear	confusing	misleading
RUP mean	21.67	3.67	2.00
RUP standard deviation	11.93	1.53	3.46
Agile mean	24.75	6.75	3.25
Agile standard deviation	11.18	8.34	6.50

3.3.2. Functional Size

Table 14 shows the functional size of each product measured in T. The mean functional size was 7 T for the RUP-developed projects, and the standard deviation was 1 T. For the Agile methods, the mean functional size was 30.5 T, and the standard deviation was 17.82 T. These values are significantly bigger than the RUP values.

Tabla 14. *Functional size.*

Project	Product	Measure [T]
P1_RUP	P1	8
P2_SCRUM	P2	10
P3_XP	P3	23
P4_RUP	P4	6
P5_XP	P5	51
P6_RUP	P6	7
P7_XP	P7	38

3.4. Answer to Research Questions

After having analyzed our results, we may answer our research questions:

(1) It was not possible to verify if there was a difference in the F reported by the users of Agile and RUP methods, as none reported any failure.

(2) It was not possible to verify if there was a significant difference in the DU analyzed for RUP when compared to that obtained with Agile methods, as the external designs were similar.

(3) There was not a significant difference in the number of MC obtained when applying an Agile method when compared to that obtained when using the RUP method.

(4) There was not a significant difference between the DUD obtained for RUP and Agile, a result that surprised us because RUP is an architecture-centered method.

(5) The size, measured in number of T, of a final product developed with an Agile method was similar to, or bigger than, that resulting of a RUP product.

3.5. Threats to Validity

Four different types of validity will be discussed: internal, external, construct, and conclusion [18].

(1) Internal. Internal validity concerns the cause-effect relationship, that is, if the measured effect is due to changes caused by the researcher or due to some other unknown cause. In this case, it would mean that any measured difference between the applied methods would not be due to the method.

One of the biggest concerns when designing this study was for the products to be obtained to be comparable, that is, that they should have a similar level of complexity. For the game products (P1 and P2), it was necessary to write a set of specific rules in order to avoid non-comparable developments. For example, the time spent on the graphical interface was limited to that required to achieve the minimum necessary level to understand the product, so the products showed similar graphical interfaces. In the case of P3-P7, for which social networks were developed, the biggest difference was the developing environment, which was controlled by the professor, who led the students to the same level of training in every environment. Besides, the applications may be considered comparable, because both methods were used to develop applications of either one of these two types: game product or social network.

Although the groups were formed in a manner as balanced as possible, it is clear that there are personal factors that are difficult to control. For example, the personal attitude of a person in a certain situation may lead the other members to enhance some of their own personal characteristics, thus resulting in the whole group improving its behavior. Despite this limitation, which is inherent to working with people, the groups had different but comparable behaviors.

(2) External. The external validity of a study describes the possibility to generalize its results. The limited number of projects and measurements does not allow us to generalize our results. However, we think that it was a good experience, which could be replied in academic and industrial software development environments in order to obtain generalized conclusions.

(3) Construct. The construct validity reflects the ability to measure what the researchers are interested in measuring. In this case, the objective was to measure the difference, in terms of productivity and quality, between traditional and Agile methods. It is possible to wonder if the selected variables were suitable to satisfy the purpose of the empirical study. To deal with this limitation, the QGM approach was applied. Also, the measures were selected by giving priority to objectivity and feasibility of measurement, focusing on the internal and external features of the obtained products.

(4) Conclusion. The conclusion validity describes the ability to draw statistically correct conclusions based on measurements. In this experience, the limited available data did not allow us to reach statistically significant conclusions.

4. Discussion

If we want to get an objective idea of the functional size differences between the products developed with the different methods, we have to consider the information we obtained about the weeks spent on programming tasks, which is presented in Table 10, and the characteristics of the persons included in each team, which are described in Table 5. The groups were made up by three or four persons and the best possible combination was sought for, within the restrictions that we had. Also, in these beginner programming teams, we could see that the more people there were on a team, the more coordination problems they had.

The Agile teams began to work in programing tasks no later than in the fifth week, but the RUP teams began to do so between the fifteenth and nineteenth week. So, the Agile groups worked in programming almost twice the time the RUP groups did, but they produced products which had very different functional sizes: from almost similar to that of a RUP product, to three times, or even seven times, bigger than that of a RUP product. We noticed that this increment in productivity was a consequence of the student s' involvement in the planning, estimation and control activities in each sprint. This practice reinforced the commitment and the responsibility of each student and favored the leaders' development, which also contributed to motivate the team.

This shows that Agile groups are usually more productive, but their outcome may have a bigger standard deviation.

One factor that could have produced the dispersion in Agile productivity is pair programming. We believe productivity could be increased by pair programming in XP teams. However, it is important to note that although the premise the students had been given was always to work with pair programming, in fact, they only worked in pairs when the nature of the task justified this type of work. And of course, they did not work in pairs when someone was absent, or delayed, or if for some specific reason, someone worked at home. This type of behavior was also observed by Zazworka et al. [27], so we may conclude that although pair programming is the best option to work, it has to be applied in a flexible manner. Besides, it depends on the persons involved in the task to be done; some people enjoy working in pairs, while others do not.

Moreover, there may be other causes that may explain Agile productivity dispersion. For example, it would be interesting to measure, in order to deeply understand, how motivation may affect the development of a project. In our study, it may have been revealing to learn about the students' and leaders' commitment and motivation, as well as about the leaders' experience in development.

As regards quality, it was not possible to identify significant differences in accuracy, usability and changeability. Actually, the fact that no failures were reported and that the products had similar degrees of usability was a consequence of the conditions we set for the students' products to comply with the academic requisites.

Particularly, it was surprising to see that the Agile methods did not improve changeability, something which is claimed by the developers that use these methods. The reason for this may be that in the context of the ISO/IEC 9126-1 [21] standard, changeability is one of the subcharacteristics of maintainability, not the response given to a client when he/she proposes a requirement change. In fact, we defined the measures MC and DUD to measure the changeability that affects the maintenance phase of a product. So the analysis of the results of such measurement shows there will not be significant differences in the future life of a product, whether a RUP or an Agile method is applied, which is ,in fact, an interesting conclusion.

We may wonder if the selection of the three quality variables was appropriate, as we did not obtain a significant difference when applying the different methods, either RUP or Agile. While planning the empirical study we did not realize that the conditions defined in order to accept the products would not contribute to clarify the differences that the use of these methods would bring about regarding two of the quality characteristics -accuracy and usability-. So, we may suggest not including these two variables in future replications in academic contexts. However, in spite of the fact that the variable changeability was well selected and measured, this sub characteristic is not enough to evaluate the quality an industrial product. Reliability, portability, and efficiency may be key aspects for the marketing of a software product and it would have been interesting to consider them. To conclude, we have not found evidence in an academic context that Agile methods improve quality characteristics, but this conclusion does not necessarily apply to an industrial context.

Finally, to answer the question: do Agile methods increase productivity and quality?, we may say that in the context of our empirical study, they significantly increased productivity, but not quality. In our case, the circumstances that affected productivity were the time allotted to programing tasks, the application of pair programming practices, the planning, estimation and control practices and the leadership growth. On the other hand, quality was not improved by the Agile methods because they do not introduce practices that differ from those of traditional methods; in fact, the quality results were affected by the people involved in each team, the circumstances defined in order to make the products comparable and the limitations of the academic context in which the study was developed.

5. Final Conclusion

This empirical study, conducted in an academic environment, has helped us understand how the selection of a traditional or an Agile software development method may impact on the productivity and quality of a software project. By applying a traditional method, we managed to obtain a more reproducible result, but we could not obtain proof of an improvement in quality. On the other hand, in our study there was evidence about obtaining higher productivity by using Agile methods. However, it would be recommendable to analyze the circumstances that produced the difference in productivity with the Agile methods, focusing our analysis on the motivation and commitment of the developers and leaders, and on the leaders' experience.

In the future, it would be recommendable to replicate this study in an industrial environment, where junior and senior developers may work together, and to evaluate in a longer period of time if Agile methods lead to increased productivity and quality in software development.

Acknowledgments

Our thanks to the Research Fund of Austral University, which made this study possible.

References

[1] M. A. Chaumun, H. Kabaili, R. K. Keller and F. Lustman, A Change Impact Model for Changeability Assessment in Object-Oriented Software Systems, csmr, *Third European Conference on Software Maintenance and Reengineering*, (1999), pp.130.

[2] S. Nerur, R. Mahapatra and G. Mangalaraj, Challenges of migrating to agile methodologies. *Commun. ACM* 48, 5 (May 2005), 72-78. DOI=10.1145/1060710.1060712 http://doi.acm.org/10.1145/1060710.1060712.

[3] T. Dyba and T. Dingsøyr: Empirical Studies of Agile Software Development: A Systematic Review, *Inform. Softw. Technol* (2008).

[4] M. Hirsch, Moving from a plan driven culture to agile development, in *Proceedings of the 27th international Conference on Software Engineering* (ICSE '05) (St. Louis, MO, USA, May 15 - 21, 2005). ACM Press, NY, 38-38.

[5] T. Dingsøyr, S. Nerur, V. Balijepally, N. Brede Moe, A decade of agile methodologies: Towards explaining agile software development, *Journal of Systems and Software*, Volume 85, Issue 6, (June 2012), pp. 1213-1221, ISSN 0164-1212, http://dx.doi.org/10.1016/j.jss.2012.02.033.

[6] E. Caballero, J.A. Calvo-Manzano and T. San Feliu, Introducing Scrum in a Very Small Enterprise: A Productivity and Quality Analysis, *Systems, Software and Service Process Improvement, Communications in Computer and Information Science* Volume 172, (2011), pp. 215-224.

[7] E. S. F. Cardozo, J. B. F. Araújo Neto, A. Barza, A. C. C. França, and F. Q. B. da Silva, SCRUM and productivity in software projects: a systematic literature review, in *Proceedings of the 14th international conference on Evaluation and Assessment in Software Engineering* (EASE'10), Mark Turner and Mahmood Niazi (Eds.), British Computer Society (Swinton, UK, UK, 2010),131-134.

[8] P. Sfetsos and I.Stamelos, Empirical Studies on Quality in Agile Practices: A Systematic Literature Review, Quality of Information and Communications Technology (QUATIC), 2010 Seventh International Conference, (Porto, Sept. 29 2010-Oct. 2 2010),44 – 53.

[9] J. Sutherland, G. Schoonheim, M. Rijk, Fully Distributed Scrum: Replicating Local Productivity and Quality with Offshore Teams, *Hawaii International Conference on System Sciences* (2009), pp. 1-8, 42.

[10] L. Lavazza, S. Morasca, D. Taibi and D. Tosi, Applying SCRUM in an OSS Development Process: An Empirical Evaluation, *Agile Processes in Software Engineering and Extreme Programming, Lecture Notes in Business Information Processing* Volume 48, 2010, pp 147-159.

[11] J. Li, N. B. Moe, and T. Dyba°, Transition from a plan-driven process to Scrum: a longitudinal case study on software quality, in *Proceedings of the 2010 ACM-IEEE International Symposium on Empirical Software Engineering and Measurement* (ESEM '10), ACM Article 13, (New York, NY, USA, 2010), 10 pages.

[12] K. Bittner and I. Spence, *Use Case modeling* (Addison-Wesley, 2003).

[13] S.I. Hashmi, J.Baik, Software Quality Assurance in XP and Spiral - A Comparative Study International, *Conference on Computational Science and its Applications*, (ICCSA 2007), (2007), 367 - 374

[14] M. Mirakhorli, A. Khanipour Rad, F. Shams, M. Pazoki, and A. Mirakhorli, RDP technique: a practice to customize xp, In *Proceedings of the 2008 international workshop on Scrutinizing agile practices or shoot-out at the agile corral* (APOS '08), ACM, (New York, NY, USA, 2008), 23-32.

[15] S.E Goldin and K.T Rudahl, Software process in the classroom: A comparative study, *9th International Symposium on Communications and Information Technology* (ISCIT 2009), (28-30 Sept. 2009), 427 – 431.

[16] W.C. de Souza Carvalho, P.F. Rosa, M. dos Santos Soares and M.A. Teixeira da Cunha Junior, A Comparative Analysis of the Agile and Traditional Software Development Processes Productivity, *Computer Science Society (SCCC), 2011 30th International Conference of the Chilean*, (2011), 74 – 82.

[17] N. Juristo, and A.M. Moreno, *Basics of Software Engineering Experimentation*, Kluwer Academic Publishers, 2001.

[18] C.Wohlin, P.Runeson, M.Höst, M.C.Ohlsson, B. Regnell, and A. Wesslen, *Experimentation in Software Engineering: an Introduction*, Kluwer Academic Publisher (2000).

[19] Jedlitschka, M. Ciolkowoski, D. Pfahl, Reporting Experiments in Software Engineering, *In Guide to Advanced Empirical Software Engineering* (2008).

[20] Basili, G. Caldiera and D. Rombach, *The Goal Question Metrics Approach*, Encyclopedia of Software, Engineering, Wiley, 1994.

[21] ISO/IEC, ISO/IEC 9126-1 Software engineering- Product quality- Part 1: Quality model, 2001.

[22] Parnas, D.L., On the criteria to be used in decomposing systems into modules, *Communications of the ACM.* Volume 15, Issue 12 (December 1972) 1053 – 1058

[23] Deligiannis, M. Shepperd, M. Roumeliotis, and I. Stamelos, An empirical investigation of an object-oriented design heuristic for maintainability. *J. Syst. Softw.* 65, 2 (February 2003), 127-139.

[24] G. Robiolo, C. Badano and R. Orosco, Transactions and Paths: two use case based metrics which improve the early effort estimation, *In Proceedings of 3rd Int. Symp. on Empirical SW Engineering and Measurement* (ESEM 2009) (October S., Lake Buena Vista, Florida, 2009), 15-16.

[25] Jacobson and B. Grady, J. Rumbaugh, *The Unified Software Development Process*, (Addison Wesley, 1999)

[26] K. Schwaber, *Agile Project Management with Scrum.* Microsoft Press (2004).

[27] N. Zazworka, K. Stapel, E. Knauss, F. Shull, V. R. Basili, and K. Schneider. Are developers complying with the process: an XP study, in *Proceedings of the 2010 ACM-IEEE International Symposium on Empirical Software Engineering and Measurement* (ESEM '10). ACM, Article 14 (New York, NY, USA, 2010), 10 pages.

Permissions

All chapters in this book were first published in AJSEA, by Science Publishing Group; hereby published with permission under the Creative Commons Attribution License or equivalent. Every chapter published in this book has been scrutinized by our experts. Their significance has been extensively debated. The topics covered herein carry significant findings which will fuel the growth of the discipline. They may even be implemented as practical applications or may be referred to as a beginning point for another development.

The contributors of this book come from diverse backgrounds, making this book a truly international effort. This book will bring forth new frontiers with its revolutionizing research information and detailed analysis of the nascent developments around the world.

We would like to thank all the contributing authors for lending their expertise to make the book truly unique. They have played a crucial role in the development of this book. Without their invaluable contributions this book wouldn't have been possible. They have made vital efforts to compile up to date information on the varied aspects of this subject to make this book a valuable addition to the collection of many professionals and students.

This book was conceptualized with the vision of imparting up-to-date information and advanced data in this field. To ensure the same, a matchless editorial board was set up. Every individual on the board went through rigorous rounds of assessment to prove their worth. After which they invested a large part of their time researching and compiling the most relevant data for our readers.

The editorial board has been involved in producing this book since its inception. They have spent rigorous hours researching and exploring the diverse topics which have resulted in the successful publishing of this book. They have passed on their knowledge of decades through this book. To expedite this challenging task, the publisher supported the team at every step. A small team of assistant editors was also appointed to further simplify the editing procedure and attain best results for the readers.

Apart from the editorial board, the designing team has also invested a significant amount of their time in understanding the subject and creating the most relevant covers. They scrutinized every image to scout for the most suitable representation of the subject and create an appropriate cover for the book.

The publishing team has been an ardent support to the editorial, designing and production team. Their endless efforts to recruit the best for this project, has resulted in the accomplishment of this book. They are a veteran in the field of academics and their pool of knowledge is as vast as their experience in printing. Their expertise and guidance has proved useful at every step. Their uncompromising quality standards have made this book an exceptional effort. Their encouragement from time to time has been an inspiration for everyone.

The publisher and the editorial board hope that this book will prove to be a valuable piece of knowledge for researchers, students, practitioners and scholars across the globe.

List of Contributors

Hamid Mcheick and Amel Hannech
Computer science department, University of Quebec at Chicoutimi, Chicoutimi (Quebec) Canada

Mehdi Adda
Computer science and Engineering department, University of Quebec at Rimouski, Rimouski (Quebec) wCanadazz

A. Hovakimyan, S. Sargsyan, N. Ispiryan, L. Khachoyan and K. Darbinyan
Department of Programming and Information Technologies, Yerevan State University (YSU), Yerevan, Armenia

Japheth Bunakiye. Richard.
Department of Mathematics/Computer Science, Niger Delta University, Yenagoa, Nigeria

Ogheneovo Edward. Erhieyovwe.
Department of Computer Science, University of Port Harcourt, Port Harcourt, Nigeria

Paul Andre da Fonseca Moreira Coelho and Rui Manuel da Silva Gomes
Escola Superior de Tecnologia e Gestão, Instituto Politécnico de Viana do Castelo, 4900-348, Viana do Castelo, Portugal

Takahiro Hori, Tetsuya Takiguchi and Yasuo Ariki
Graduate School of System Informatics, Kobe University, Japan

Davit Kocharyan
Digital Signal and Image Processing Laboratory Institute for Informatics and Automation Problems of NAS RA, Yerevan, Armenia

Oksana Pomorova and Tetyana Hovorushchenko
Department of System Programming, Khmelnitskiy National University, Khmelnitskiy, Ukraine

Mohammed Basheer Al-Somaidai and Estabrak Bassam Yahya
Dept. of Electrical Engineering, Mosul University, Mosul, Iraq

John Charlery and Chris D. Smith
Dept. of Computer Science, Mathematics & Physics, Faculty of Science and Technology, University of the West Indies, Cave Hill Campus, Bridgetown, Barbados BB11000

Chiu, Kuei-Chen
Institute of Allied Health Sciences, College of Medicine, National Cheng Kung University, Tainan, Taiwan

Basel Magableh
School of Computer Science and Informatics, University College Dublin, Ireland

Butheyna Rawashdeh
Faculty of Computer Science and Information, Ajloun University College, AL-Balqa Applied University, Ajloun, Jordan

Stephen Barrett
School of Computer Science and Statistics, Trinity College, University of Dublin, Ireland

John Charlery and Chris D. Smith
Dept. of Computer Science, Mathematics & Physics, Faculty of Science and Technology, University of the West Indies, Cave Hill Campus, Bridgetown, Barbados BB11000

Zeba Khanam and S. A. M Rizvi
Jamia Millia Islamia, New Delhi

Sonja Pravilovic
Montenegro Business School, "Mediterranean" University, Montenegro

Dipartimento di Informatica, Università degli Studi di Bari "Aldo Moro", Italy

Bassey Echeng Isong
Deptmemt of Computer Science, University of Venda, Thohoyandou, South Africa

Eyaye Bekele
School of Computing, Blekinge Institute of Technology, Karlskrona, Sweden

Houda El Bouhissi, Mimoun Malki and Djamila Berramdane
Dept. of Computer Sciences, EEDIS Laboratory, Sidi-Bel-Abbes University, Algeria

Rafa E. Al-Qutaish
Dept. of Software Engineering & IT, ÉTS, University of Québec,1100 Notre-Dame West, Montreal, Québec, H3C K3, Canada

Güney GORGUN and Ibrahim Halil GUZELBEY
Department of Mechanical Engineering, University of
Gaziantep, Gaziantep, Turkey

Ayman Ahmed AlQudah
Deanship of E-Learning and Distance Learning,
University of Dammam, Ad Dammam, Saudi Arabia

R. A. Khan
Department of IT, Babasaheb Bhimrao Ambedkar
University, Lucknow, India

A. Agrawal
Department of Computer Science, Khwaja Moinuddin
Chishti Urdu, Arabi-Farsi University, Lucknow, India

Ekbal Rashid
Department of CS & E CIT, Tatisilwai,Ranchi, India

Srikanta Patnaik
Department of CS & E SOA University, Bhubaneswar,
Orissa,India

Vandana Bhattacharya
Department of CS & E BIT Mesra, Ranchi, India

Parminder Kaur and Hardeep Singh
Department of Computer Science and Engineering,
Guru Nanak Dev University, Amritsar-143005, India

**Muhammad Osama Khan, Ahmed Mateen and
Ahsan Raza Sattar**
Department Of Computer Science, University of
Agriculture Faisalabad, Pakistan

Elnaz Shafigh Fard and Mohammad H. Nadimi
Faculty of Computer Engineering, Najafabad branch,
Islamic Azad University, Isfahan, Iran

Khalil Monfaredi
Engineering Faculty, Department of Electrical and
Electronic Engineering, Azarbaijan Shahid Madani
University, Tabriz, Iran

Benjamin Odei Bempong
Information and Communication Technology/
Mathematics Department Presbyterian University
College, Ghana. Abetifi-Kwahu, Eastern Region

Oladejo F. Bolanle and Ayetuoma O. Isaac
Department of Computer Science, University of
Ibadan, Ibadan, Nigeria

University of Ibadan, UI, Ibadan, Nigeria

Gabriela Robiolo and Daniel Grane
Informatica, Universidad Austral, Buenos Aires,
Argentina

Index